Distributed Micro/Minicomputer Systems

Structure, Implementation, and Application

Distributed Micro/Minicomputer Systems

Structure, Implementation, and Application

Cay Weitzman

TRW Defense and Space Systems Group

Prentice-Hall, Inc., Englewood Cliffs, New Jersey   07632

Library of Congress Cataloging in Publication Data

WEITZMAN, CAY. (date)
  Distributed micro/minicomputer systems.

  Includes bibliographical references and index.
    1. Electronic data processing—Distributed process-
ing.   2. Microcomputers.   3. Minicomputers.   I. Ti-
tle.
QA76.9.D5W44   001.6′4′04   79-21289
ISBN 0-13-216481-7

Editorial/Production Supervision
and Interior Design by Lynn Frankel
Cover Design by Edsal Enterprise
Manufacturing Buyer: Gordon Osbourne

© 1980 by Prentice-Hall, Inc., Englewood Cliffs, N.J.   07632

All rights reserved. No part of this book
may be reproduced in any form or
by any means without permission in writing
from the publisher.

Printed in the United States of America

10   9   8   7   6   5   4   3   2   1

Prentice-Hall International, Inc., *London*
Prentice-Hall of Australia Pty. Limited, *Sydney*
Prentice-Hall of Canada, Ltd., *Toronto*
Prentice-Hall of India Private Limited, *New Delhi*
Prentice-Hall of Japan, Inc., *Tokyo*
Prentice-Hall of Southeast Asia Pte. Ltd., *Singapore*
Whitehall Books Limited, *Wellington, New Zealand*

Contents

Preface

James Martin, in his book *Principles of Data-Base Management*, calls the 1970s the decade of the data base. It is my firm belief that the 1980s will be the decade of distributed data processing. The continuing decline in processor and memory cost coupled with lower cost communications based on fiber optics, micro-wave transmission, and satellite communications, to use a few examples, will hasten the development and widespread use of distributed systems based on micro- and minicomputer technology.

Many of the ideas and concepts in this book have been influenced by my close involvement as a systems designer at TRW with a large number of multicomputer systems to be used in both commercial and military applications. The intent is to share this knowledge and some of these concepts in a format which can serve both as a college textbook on the topic as well as a general reference source for students and practicing data processing professionals.

It is assumed that the reader has some familiarity with basic building blocks used in distributed micro- and minicomputer systems, such as the micros and minis themselves as well as data communications. It is thus directed to college juniors, seniors, or graduate students while my earlier book, *Minicomputer Systems—Structure, Implementation, and Application*, was written for freshmen and sophomores.

The emphasis is therefore on interconnect structures and related tradeoffs, intercommunications software and multimicro- and minicomputer system hardware unique to such systems, rather than the micro- or minicomputer per se. Insight is also provided into distributed micro- and minicomputer *system* design including a large number of examples of existing experimental and commercial systems. In addition, most problems following each chapter are closely related to actual system design issues.

The intent is to provide useful and proven tools to support the future designer of such systems. Furthermore, a look is taken at some of the most recent technologies believed to greatly impact the future design of distributed micro- and minicomputer systems.

I would like to express my gratitude and appreciation to Frank Stepczyk who helped me plan the scope of this book and largely contributed to Chapters 2, 3, and 6 as well as all my colleagues at TRW whose comments and helpful criticisms have improved the contents of this work; in particular James Huang, Maurice France and Mike Inbar (TRW Research Center) as well as many others.

I also want to extend my thanks to Walter Truszkowski at NASA Goddard Space Flight Center, Dick Sherman and George McClure at Ford Motor Company and Herbert Chang at Bank of America for their support and helpful advice, as well as numerous micro- and minicomputer and communications systems manufacturers such as Digital Equipment Corporation, Data General Corporation, System Engineering Laboratories, General Automation Inc., Modular Computer Systems, Network Systems Corporation and many others.

I also want to thank Sig Hartmann for his unending support and my secretary, Jean Hill, for her infinite patience, without whom this book would not exist. Finally, I want to thank my wife, encore, for her understanding and encouragement, making it all come true.

CAY WEITZMAN

1

Overview

1.1 INTRODUCTION

Multimini- and microcomputer systems presently represent the fastest growing segment of the data processing market, catering to users in the commercial world, the university and research environments, and the military community. Such systems consist of a conglomeration of cooperating, individual minicomputer systems, where each micro- or minicomputer system typically consists of a minicomputer, software, and various types of peripherals. The never ending quest for increased, uninterrupted processing support at lowest possible cost and smallest incremental expansion capability, combined with the demand for enhanced user convenience, are factors influencing the trend toward multimicro- and minicomputer systems. Also, software development and computing operations are becoming more and more expensive, putting further pressure on system designers to increasingly utilize people solely for system functions that computers cannot perform in a cost-effective manner. Mini- and, particularly, microcomputers on the other hand are becoming less and less expensive and are, therefore, increasingly being used for all functions that they can perform effectively. For instance, matters of routine implementation of directions from people, e.g., carrying out plans, are better left to computers. This obviously implies that a large number of computer systems should be spread around to perform repetitive functions. These geographically dispersed micro- or minicomputer systems typically perform functions by spreading the pieces of the function around the total system, also termed the network. Systems may perform in either a load-sharing or a resource-sharing mode or, possibly, in a mixture of the two. Load sharing implies that a system is composed of a

1

number of similar minis, each of which can perform a basic unit of work. If certain minis are busy when a new unit of work comes in, that unit can be assigned to idle minis. Resource sharing implies that a system is composed of a number of dissimilar minis, each of which is functionally specialized and provides resources for the use of other parts of the multimicro- or minicomputer system. The latter may also share unique peripherals connected to different computers in the system.

Also, in a multimicro- or minicomputer environment, the number of complex system components involved in providing user service is larger than for a single computer system, even one having a large number of more elementary devices or components. This large number of micro- or minicomputers may require a greater degree of overall partitioning of tasks to be performed. With a large number of micros or minis, there can be difficulty both in partitioning the task and in controlling the execution of subtasks.

The first move toward distributed processing was prompted by the need for decentralizing computing systems based on a large central processing unit (CPU). This large "host" CPU interfaced peripherals and input-output (I/O) devices via an independent channel or I/O processor. This I/O processor could operate concurrently with the CPU to which it was attached, dedicated to performing I/O related tasks. These channels were, in turn, "front-ended" by hardwired multiplexers to handle a large number of terminals and communications links. The emergence of the minicomputer in the mid-to-late 1960's led to the replacement of the hardwired front-end multiplexer with a programmable, more flexible minicomputer and, somewhat later, the replacement of interfacing "dumb" input-output devices or remote batch terminals with "intelligent" terminals containing a minicomputer. Terminal "intelligence" typically meant that these devices could be reprogrammed to perform various functions or tasks. This trend was accelerated in the early 1970's with the emergence of the microcomputer or "computer-on-a-board." It was now possible to experiment with hierarchical, centrally controlled multiminicomputer systems, where the large central host was replaced with a powerful minicomputer. Mini- and microcomputers have, since then, been interconnected in a large variety of configurations, sometimes colocated in the same room and even in the same rack or chassis. Other multiminicomputer systems are based on minis interconnected via telephone links across the country, using bit-serial lines and standard communication procedure (protocols) and message formats.

The bit-serial interconnect scheme is attractive since it allows the user to interconnect minicomputers made by the different manufacturers and often with different internal architectures without too much concern for the communications impact on the existing system software.

Presently, multiminicomputer systems can usually be developed without much difficulty based on off-the-shelf hardware and software components. In fact, the bewildering assortment of such off-the-shelf components makes it very difficult for the uninitiated to determine which approach is optimal for his or her particular application, whether the user wants to expand the present system or develop a multi-minicomputer system from scratch.

In the past, the minicomputer manufacturers supplied general-purpose systems that required very little configuration mapping. The same manufacturers are now trying to provide turn-key capability for multimicro and mini applications but have met with limited success in the software and systems area. This has put the burden on the user who now may have to perform more of the total system design than he had to in the past.

From a software point of view, however, the new software engineering discipline, which is in the process of revolutionary software development, applies very readily to multiminicomputer systems. Designing software in a structural top-down manner utilizing successive decompositions can usually map one-to-one with the distribution of minis and links in a multiminicomputer system.

The intent of this book is to provide the user with some general guidelines, methodology, and approaches for the design, development, and use of a multimicro- or minicomputer system. Needless to say, due to the proliferation of off-the-shelf micro- and minicomputers ranging from large, 32-bit, multimegaword "midis" to 8- and 16-bit micros, no one solution can be expected to be optimal; considerations must be given to a wide range of needs such as level of performance, system expandability, extensibility, operating environment, ease of use, reliability, availability, maintainability, data confidentiality, and cost, as well as many other nontechnical or quasi-technical factors.

The material in this book is presented in a manner where the reader is introduced to the various multiminicomputer interconnect schemes as well as supporting software and hardware. Several application areas are described and methods are demonstrated whereby the system designer can select and optimize his system configuration based on various hardware and software elements. Optimization techniques presented take into account operational requirements, life-cycle cost, reliability and maintainability, environmental constraints, performance requirements, etc.

Several multimicro- or minicomputer systems used in the process control, banking, scientific processing, and data acquisition environments are described and an overview is presented of key research projects based on both homogeneous and heterogeneous multimini- and microcomputer systems.

An overview is also provided of advanced technology which will probably heavily impact future multimicro- and minicomputer systems. Interconnect technology will range from local, fiber optics loops to satellite links providing bandwidths exceeding those of today's direct memory access channels. Distributed processing nodes will increase in capability based on very large scale integration and various new, low-cost memory technologies and data bases will be geographically distributed using distributed data base management technology. It will also be possible to interconnect multimicro- and minicomputer systems with future systems which differ widely in terms of both hardware and software implementation.

1.2 WHAT IS A MULTIMICRO OR MULTIMINI?

A multimicro or multimini is a system of two or more micros or minis, connected either through shared memory or via high- or low-speed data links. The shared memory may be a multiported main memory, cache memory, or a multiported disc.

The data path may be either a bit-serial or parallel bus connecting I/O ports of two computers or a shared bus to which two or more computers are interconnected in various ways. Data may be broadcasted onto the bus and intercepted by the receiving mini, or, where the communication link is a daisy chain, each connecting mini may pass information on to the next leg of the bus until the intended recipient finally takes the message off the link. Each of these interconnect schemes have their merits, depending on the application.

Multimicro- or minicomputer systems, which employ the shared-memory interconnect approach, have been coined "tightly coupled."* Basically, this means that all the processors in the system can get at all the memories and execute code out of them. Secondly, in tightly coupled systems, I/O and other systems resources (i.e., peripherals) are shared by the processors. Thirdly, the interprocessor communication latency is low due to the potential access time only being limited by the actual memory access time.

"Tightly coupled" and "loosely coupled" systems differ in that a loosely coupled system has disjoint, primary, or main memory address spaces; that is, loosely coupled systems do not share a common primary memory. This means that, at the hardware level, there has to be an explicit communications interface between the micros or minis. A communications interface implies that there is a higher latency of communications between processors than would be the case if they directly shared primary memory.

Furthermore, tightly coupled systems generally require synchronization between cooperating processes, whereas in loosely coupled systems concurrent processes may be performed asynchronously.

Changes in architecture are usually not easily made in tightly or "closely" coupled systems of multiminis. In contrast to a tightly coupled system, shown in Figure 1-1, in a "loosely coupled" multiminicomputer system, each mini stands by itself with its own complement of main storage, as shown in Figure 1-2. Typically, a mini designated the "global" processor with system wide (overall) responsibility is connected to each of the other minis through an I/O interface, where the data is transferred between the computers under program control. The other processors are called *local processors*. All jobs enter the system through the global processor. Often, in case the global processor fails, one of the local processors may assume the function of the global processor. In many cases, the interconnection between minis may be limited to occasional transfer

---

*R. A. McKinnon, "Advanced Function Extended with Tightly-Coupled Multiprocessors," *IBM Systems Journal*, No. 1, pp. 32–59, 1974.

4

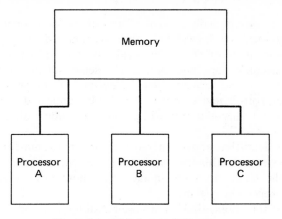

Figure 1-1   Tightly coupled system.

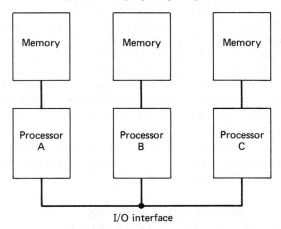

Figure 1-2   Loosely coupled system.

of data files, leaving the minis quite independent, without a global mini in the system. Such systems, are also called *fully distributed*.

1.3   CENTRALIZED VERSUS DISTRIBUTED DATA BASES AND/OR PROCESSING

Multiminicomputer systems generally distribute processing and/or data bases within the system. Distributed processing has been defined by Eckhouse* as "a collection of processing elements, which are interconnected both logically and physically

*Panel discussion on distributed processing, National Computer Conference, Anaheim, Calif., June 1978.

with decentralized, system-wide control of resources for cooperative execution of applications programs." (A logical link or interconnection is a path controlled by software or firmware in contrast to a physical link that consists of a combination of electronic circuits, connectors, and cables. The set of all physical links to a single device or computer is also termed a *logical channel*. Through switching—typically under software control—a device or processor can be connected to one of several physical channels or links.) This definition will generally exclude multiprocessing or closely coupled systems.

Based on the definition above, shared memory, multiminicomputer systems are not distributed systems. In this text, a more "loose" interpretation will, however, be used, including the latter although, in fact, they both fall under the definition of centralized data processing systems.

Depending on the application, data base handling in a multimini system may be assigned to a special-purpose back-end data base management processor that usually can be accessed by all the minis in the system, or the data bases may be distributed throughout the system in such a way that transfer of raw data is to site of the data base and computing updates is performed in a manner that minimizes the load on the communications facility. It is also possible to have either a centrally located data base directory that is frequently updated, to keep files or records locked, or both, to avoid concurrent updates or interference. The three approaches are shown in Figure 1-3. Critical data is usually stored in more than one location, to provide fault tolerance.

The user must, however, generally tailor the data base to his configuration and application.

The multimicro and mini has received its widest acceptance in the process control industry where the computers are interconnected either via a shared bus (Figure 1-4) or based on a hierarchical architecture (Figure 1-5).

1.4 SPECIAL- VERSUS GENERAL-PURPOSE MULTIMINIS—HARDWARE AND SOFTWARE

The "first-generation" multiminicomputer systems typically consisted of two or more standard, off-the-shelf minicomputers, loosely coupled, with a "master" or global mini and several "slave" or local minis, connected to the central master using a bit-serial line, where the local minis "appeared" as teletypes or intelligent terminals, passing data to and from the master based on ASCII code. A limited number of minicomputer manufacturers subsequently developed a common bus with bus adapters, allowing users to interconnect two or more minis via a shared bus. Needless to say, the early users had to develop their own software to support communications over the bus. Eventually, variations were developed to this bus, including devices such as bus switches, bus connectors, bus links, and bus windows. At least one minicomputer manufacturer developed a solid-state multiported, high-speed memory that allowed a user to interconnect up to four minicomputers via the shared memory. All of these schemes depended, of course, on the use of the same type of minicomputer or, as a minimum, a minicomputer from the same family.

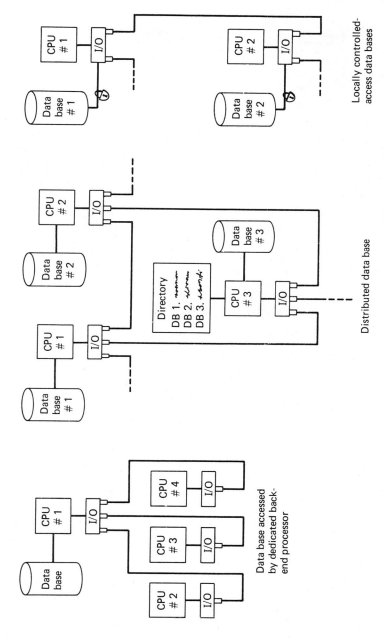

Figure 1-3 Approaches to data base handling in distributed micro- and mini-computer systems.

Locally controlled-access data bases

Distributed data base

Data base accessed by dedicated back-end processor

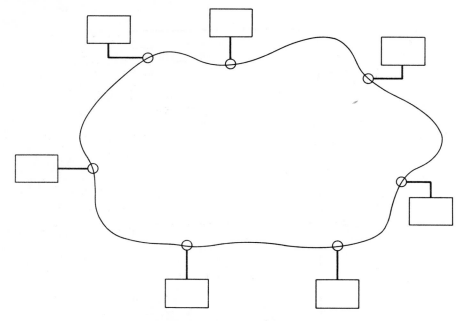

Figure 1-4   Shared bus or loop.

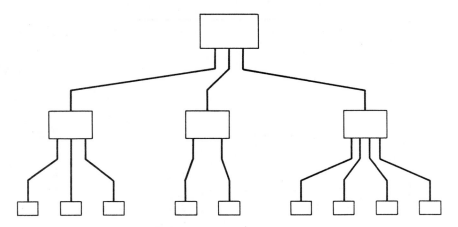

Figure 1-5   Hierarchical structure.

More recently, commercial multiminicomputer systems have emerged that are unique in terms of serving users who requires near 100% availability, where any single failure in the system, regardless of location, has no impact on total system operation. This has typically been achieved through redundancy (i.e., Tandem Computers). This concept is not new and such systems have, for several years, been developed for military and space applications, but at very high cost. Similar efforts have been undertaken by research facilities and several universities, where the multiminis serve as test beds for various research projects.

The commercial multiminicomputer systems are, in most cases, homogeneous, using the same type or family of minis. "Mixed" or heterogeneous multiminicomputer systems are presently being developed by industry, educational institutions, and the Department of Defense, in order to explore task partitioning in both hardware and software and to exploit specialized and unique minicomputer capabilities in emulation, display processing, transaction processing, Fast Fourier Transform (FFT) processing, communications processing, signal processing, etc. Heterogeneous multi-micro- and minicomputer systems have also been created to satisfy needs to share information between systems which, in the past, have been used in dedicated applications but which, at some later point in time, required to be interconnected. One such system, the Ford Motor Company Local Network Architecture, is discussed in Chapter 6. Heterogeneous systems are generally more complex than homogeneous systems due to differences in both computer hardware and software.

1.5 VARIATIONS IN INTERCONNECT—SHARED MEMORY, COMMON BUS, POINT-TO-POINT LINES, AND OTHER APPROACHES

Variations in multimicro- and minicomputer architecture are generally determined by several characteristics such as message rate and size, data paths between micros or minis, and switching elements routing and controlling messages flowing from source (transmitting) micro or mini to destination (receiving) micro or mini. Various interconnect methods are discussed in Chapter 2.

The message may consist of a single character or strings of characters. The character string or message block may be of either fixed or variable length. Also, the message block may contain a header with address information, data on the message length, and information to support error checking. Alternatively, the block may contain purely data-only with control information sent over a parallel and physically separate path. Issues related to message formats and data link control are treated in more detail in Chapter 3. (Data Link Control Protocols are also described in Appendix.)

The data paths between two or more minis in a multimicro or mini system may be either dedicated to information transmission between any two micros or minis or shared between several micros or minis, with access from more than two points (see Fig. 1-6). This path may consist of a multiported memory (shared by two or more minis), a twisted pair of wires, radio or satellite links, common-carrier data transmission facilities, coaxial cable, or a fiber optics bus. Various data paths are discussed in more detail in Chapter 7.

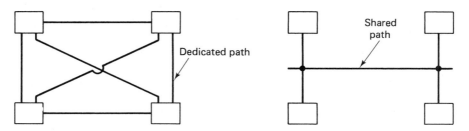

Figure 1-6   Dedicated and shared path structures.

1.6   WHY MULTIMICROS AND MULTIMINIS?

Multimicro- and minicomputer systems are being, and will be, used in a large number of applications such as control of electric power generation, distribution, and consumption; nuclear power processing facilities' safeguarding and control; health-care delivery in hospitals and medical centers; climate control, security, waste disposal, and fire protection in large buildings; urban and intercity mass transportation; manufacturing; agricultural production, processing, distribution, and marketing; and energy and other nature-resource exploration and use. Several multimicro- and minicomputer applications are described in Chapter 6.

Why are multimicro- and minicomputer systems useful in all these applications? The reasons are several: They usually make it easier for the user to access the system, they generally provide increased performance through resource sharing, and they often increase the availability of a system. A network of micros or minis can quite often duplicate the capability of one large expensive system at lower total cost. Multimicro- and minicomputer systems can provide adaptability and rapid reconfiguration with the system functioning at different times as a very large and complex problem solver or as a network of smaller machines each dedicated to a unique task, or as something in between. They can usually also provide increased reliability since the total system can continue to operate despite individual micro- or minicomputer failures, albeit with reduced capabilities, provided that some of the links between the micros or minis remain intact. Also, since redundancy can be achieved at a lower cost using processors distributed over a larger area, the survivability of the system, particularly in military applications, can be increased.

Furthermore, a distributed micro- and minicomputer system can provide increased, distributed processing power and responsiveness because it can be closely tailored to the application. Additional micros or minis can be provided as needed, to ensure proper response time.

Multimicro- and minicomputer systems can also be designed to be cost effective when applied to a wide variety of applications, where the number of computers can be determined by the distributed processing requirements. A properly designed distributed micro- or minicomputer system threatened by overload can be incrementally expanded by simply adding more micros or minis.

The disadvantages may or may not outweigh the advantages, depending on the system-unique requirements. On the minus side, the designer may be faced with increased software complexity. Applications software may be more costly to develop for a distributed than for a centralized system. In contrast to a single central processor-based system with only one executive, a distributed system typically requires each micro or mini to contain its own, individual executive that must be capable of communicating with all the other executives in the total system. This, in turn, will require that each invididual executive provides a task-handling capability where tasks resident in various processors can communicate with each other, and, in case of local software (or hardware) errors, diagnostic capabilities exist to localize "bugs." This is not to say that diagnostic or error checking software is not needed or used in large centralized, single processor systems; however, the diagnostic software development for a distributed system is usually more difficult (and costly).

A distributed micro- or minicomputer system, by definition, is also more dependent on communications technology, particularly where the computers are widely dispersed and the peak traffic demands between the computers are high.

Finally, the design and development of a unique distributed micro- or minicomputer system may require expertise both in the hardware and software areas that is not readily available. This, in turn, depends to some degree on how much of the system elements are available off-the-shelf. (Chapters 3 and 4 provide some insight into what elements are available from micro- and minicomputer vendors.)

The answer to "why multimicros or minis?" is, therefore, obviously dependent on how and where the multimicro- or minicomputer system will be used. The pros and cons are summarized in Figure 1-7.

Advantages of Multimicros and Minis	*Disadvantages of Multimicros and Minis*
• Increased reliability • Increased survivability • Increased distributed processing power • Increased responsiveness • Increased modularity • System expandability in smaller increments	• Increased software complexity • More difficult system test and failure diagnosis • More dependence on communications technology • Unique expertise needed during design and development phase

Figure 1-7   Advantages and disadvantages of multimicros and minis.

1.7 ARE MULTIMINIS FINANCIALLY ATTRACTIVE?

Is one large computer "equivalent" to two medium-sized computers, four midicomputers (large minicomputers), eight minis, or 16 micros, and what does the word *equivalent* mean?

A widely used approach to comparing computers is to postulate a set of throughput needs or "requirements" for a central processing unit and its associated peripherals. A ratio is then taken of the performance or workload capacity versus cost (i.e., capacity, per $100,000 or some other dollar figures, being either a combination of monthly maintenance and monthly rental or purchase cost including amortization). Throughput is often thought of as the amount of processing (work) that can be performed in a given time period. This could be number of instructions performed per second, number of programs processed in an hour, number of data base accesses performed per minute, or some other quantifiable (and possibly measurable) quantity. Workload capacity is often a composite of various performance characteristics related to both the central processing unit, I/O channels, and peripherals. More sophisticated models exist which take into account relative cost effectiveness of product lines in a given situation which varies in terms of growth or utilization over a predetermined number of years.*

The selection process is somewhat simpler where the system is designed to perform a dedicated task rather than being used in a multiuser environment where the types or kinds of usage vary from one hour to the next or from one user to another.

Traditionally, large computers have generally been used in a multiuser environment either in a batch or real-time mode (or both), whereas minicomputers serve the single user in a dedicated environment. However, the use of multiminicomputers has tended to change this traditional utilization pattern. In fact, multiminicomputer systems present an economically more viable alternative due to their inherent decentralization (geographic distribution) combined with the single-mini specialization, whereby the highly sophisticated and, also, large-overhead operating system software used by the large computers can be reduced or eliminated. The relative ratios of operating system software to application software for the two types of systems are illustrated in Figure 1-8.

Figure 1-9 illustrates the difference in geographic distribution of a large computer system versus a distributed multiminicomputer system.

The other financially attractive feature of a multiminicomputer system is the distribution of real-time operations closer to the user, with less reliance on a centralized facility. Intelligence can thereby be added on a more flexible basis and in smaller cost increments.

An additional "bonus" is, of course, the reduced life-cycle cost since minis, in general, do not incur the high software and hardware maintenance and support costs associated with large central computing facilities.

Also, as already pointed out, existing multiminicomputer systems can be incrementally expanded at lower cost, compared to the single processor, centralized systems, which usually (when reaching their performance limits) are replaced by a totally new system.

The wider acceptance of multiminicomputers will entice manufacturers to develop more sophisticated hardware and software building blocks for multiminicomputer systems.

*Philip Ein-Dor, "A Dynamic Approach to Selecting Computers," *Datamation* pp. 103–8, June 1977.

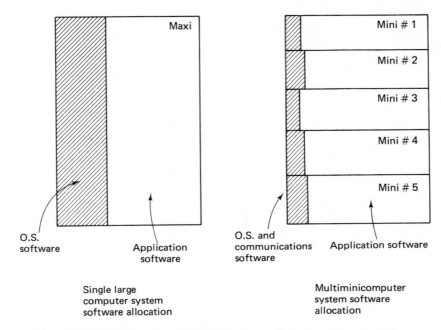

Figure 1-8 Relative ratios of operating system software to application software for large central system and distributed multiminicomputer system.

The question of cost ratios between large computers and minis must consequently be viewed from a procurement, operational, and maintenance cost point of view.

The procurement cost is generally related to the complexity and size of the system and the difficulty in "making the total system play." The risk factor often shifts from mainly a software-oriented problem to a combination hardware- and software-related problem when the choice is made to go with a multiminicomputer system rather than a large, central host. Typically, the mix of cost elements differs between the two types of approaches.

The price range of microprocessors to large computers, in the late 1970's, is summarized in Figure 1-10.

The range within each category is, to a large extent, a function of added main memory cost. It is quite obvious from this comparison chart that quite a few minis can be used before the hardware cost will equal that of a large computer.

Computer software costs are, however, more labor sensitive than hardware costs. In spite of the development of higher level languages and structured programming tools, software development cost has been steadily increasing over the last decade.

The question, therefore, arises: Will increased software development costs for a distributed multimicro- or minicomputer system cancel out the cost savings of not using a central large computing facility?

As a rule, productivity (production per person) in software engineering varies

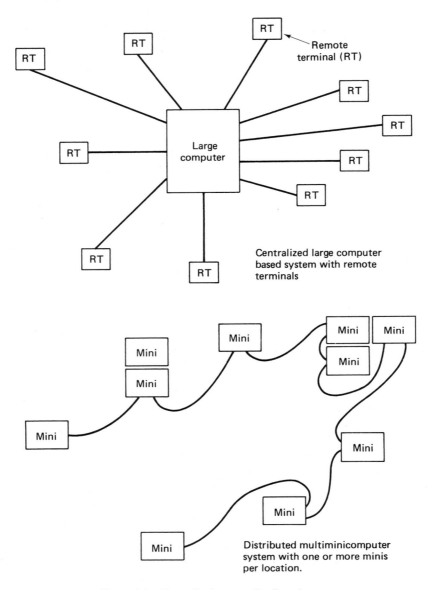

Figure 1-9 Centralized versus distributed systems.

inversely with the size of a project work force (the larger the work force, the less productive is the individual programmer), due principally to the increasing overhead required to communicate information accurately and reliably concerning the system under development. Large cost savings can, therefore, be achieved using separate, distributed minis and, hence, less manpower for the individual minicomputer system.

Processor	Word Size (bits)	Purchase price ($)
Micro	8–16	500– 5,000
Mini	16	1,000– 30,000
Midi	32	50,000– 200,000
Large (maxi)	32–60	300,000–1,000,000

Figure 1-10 Hardware cost ranges. (Included in this price is a limited to a large amount of peripherals.)

It can also be questioned, since labor costs are beginning to assume primacy in the operational phase of system life cycles, how large, if any, are the potential operational cost savings of a multiminicomputer system vis-à-vis a large central computer.

Attacking personnel costs head on means that a system usually has to be oriented not only to technical requirements but also to the requirements of the people who have to use and maintain the system. A system should provide the man-machine interfaces and capabilities each user needs to be productive on the system.

A multiminicomputer system, based on optimal architecture, can generally be tailored to user requirements in a more flexible manner than a monolithic, central facility. The optimal architecture is, of course, achieved primarily due to the fact that a higher degree of tailoring can be made for each particular application.

Before cost tradeoffs can be made, comparing procurement, operational, and maintenance cost for a set of alternative systems, a host of performance tradeoffs must be performed and a variety of questions must be answered, such as

- What are the most attractive topologies?
- What performance will be required by each mini as well as the total system?
- What are the relative importances of availability, fault tolerance, fail-soft capability, new software design, protocols, interconnect schemes?
- What types or kinds of links should be used (i.e., bit-serial two-wire, coax, parallel lines, fiber optics links, microwave, digital radio, satellite, etc.)?
- What off-the-shelf hardware and software should be used?
- What are the relative difficulties of integrating and testing a multimini?
- What are the technical risks?

Information in this book is given with the intent to provide the reader with tools to derive answers (hopefully) to most of the questions above.

1.8 STANDARDS APPLICABLE TO MULTIMICRO- AND MINICOMPUTER SYSTEMS

Most standards available to the multimicro- and minicomputer system designer are in one form or another, related to device interconnections. These standards generally apply to interfacing peripherals or communications equipment to minis or to interconnect two or more minis. Standards also exist for line or link protocols where one minicomputer "talks" to another mini (see Appendix). These standards are of great value, particularly in multimicro- and minicomputer systems where a larger number of interfaces generally exist than in a single computer system. Standards provide both internal and external system compatibility, valuable both during design and system test as well as when the system is expanded.

The RS-232C standard is used widely primarily to interconnect communications interfaces in minis to modems, where bit-serial communication takes place. The first new standard, the RS-423, supersedes part of the old, RS-232C standard and covers unbalanced-voltage, digital-interface circuits.

The second new standard, RS-422, applies to technology not covered in the old standard: balanced-voltage interface circuits for high-speed binary-data exchange. Appreciable improvement can thus be achieved in noise immunity and cross talk, resulting in lower error rates and greater error-free range.

The major advantage of the RS-422 and RS-423 integrated circuit compatible standards over the RS-232C standard lies in the fact that the latter was formulated during the era of individual components. Today, if a piece of equipment, with integrated circuits, is plugged into an RS-232C, 25-volt interface, some of the IC's may burn up because they often are not designed to withstand such relatively high voltages.

The RS-232C interface standard is also widely used to interconnect low-speed peripherals such as serial printers, cassette tape units, and CRT displays to minis. In contrast to the RS-232C standard, originally intended for low-speed computer-to-modem interfacing, the military standard (MIL-STD-1553A) has been developed for bit-serial communication between subsystems that may consist of micro- or minicomputers. In fact, the MIL-STD-1553A data bus standard is used in the F-15 fighter aircraft Global Positioning System (GPS). Here sensors, activators, displays, receivers, antennas, the inertial navigation system, and the air data computer are interconnected via a 1-Mbps, multiplexed data bus.

Two parallel-bus standards are presently also available; CAMAC* and the IEEE STD-488-1975. CAMAC was originally developed in Great Britain in the mid-1960's and has subsequently been approved internationally, by both the European Standard of Nuclear Electronics (ESONE) Committee and the National Bureau of Standards (NBS) in the United States.

CAMAC consists of a mechanical, a logical, and an electrical standard. The main component is the definition of a "Dataway" for exchange of information between connected devices. The mechanical implementation consists of a "Crate" with carefully defined dimensions.

Since CAMAC was originally intended for systems servicing nuclear facilities, particle accelerators, and the like, however, where these extremely hostile environments required special electronic design approaches as well as extensive individual module shielding, the data processing industry has generally not adopted this standard.

In the United States, the Hewlett-Packard Co. has come up with its own standard

---

*Dale Horelick and R. S. Larsen, "CAMAC: A Modular Standard," *IEEE Spectrum*, pp. 50–55, April 1976.

interface for use in calculator and minicomputer control of a wide range of bench-type electronic measuring instruments. The system has some similarities to CAMAC, but only to a point. This HP standard, called HP-IB, has been adopted by the Institute of Electrical and Electronic Engineers (IEEE) and is called the STD-488-1975. The STD-488 has also been approved by the American National Standards Institute (ANSI).

In addition to the described interface standards above, also summarized in Figure 1-11, a wide variety of data communications protocols exists, some of them standard-

---

EIA RS-232C. Interface between data terminal equipment and data communication equipment employing serial binary data interchange. Specifies electrical signal characteristics, connector pin assignments, functional interchange circuit description for serial binary data interchange, two primary channels, and two secondary backup channels, one in each direction.
Maximum distance modem-to-computer, 50 ft.

IEEE Standard 488–1975. Digital interface for programmable instrumentation. The Hewlett-Packard "ASCII-Bus" system for use with groups of up to 15 instruments or computers, with a combined cable length between units of less than 67 ft (20 m). Provides an 8-bit data highway at up to 1 byte/μsec.

CAMAC
IEEE Standard 583–1975 Modular Instrumentation and digital interface system standard for basic crate and dataway specifications.

IEEE Standard 595–1975. Serial Data Transmission System Standard extending IEEE STD 583 to provide a bit or byte serial highway between up to 62 crates.

IEEE Standard 596–1976. Parallel Data Transmission System Standard extending IEEE Standard 583 to provide a 24-bit duplex, parallel, data highway between up to seven crates, called the "Branch Highway."

MIL-STD-1553A. Multiplexed bus standard for bit-serial transmission using a central bus controller. Word size is 16 bits plus one parity bit. Devices are transformer coupled to bus. Maximum bus length is 300 ft for 1-Mbps data rate.

Figure 1-11 Summary of the more commonly used standards applicable to multimicro- and minicomputer interfacing.

ized by the American National Standards Institute (ANSI),* International Organization for Standardization (ISO), and International Consultative Committee for Telephones and Telegraphs (CCITT). These standard protocols are used to control data moving among computers and their peripherals.

The use of a particular data communications protocol and interface standard is determined by the application and should be viewed in context of the overall design. Some of the link and message formats and related issues are discussed in more detail in Chapter 3.

*An American National Standard; IEEE, Standard Digital Interface for Programmable Instrumentation, April 4, 1975; IEEE, 245 East 47th Street, New York, N.Y. 10017.

These standards above are closely related to interconnect structures discussed in Chapter 2 and form the basis for the lowest interconnect protocol level (the hardware or "plug-connect" level) described in Chapter 3.

PROBLEMS

1-1 A simplistic method for assessing relative processing speed for real-time applications is based on the use of instruction mixes.

Determine throughput rates in kilo-instructions-per-second (KIPS) for six minicomputers assuming their instruction times are as follows:

Instruction	Instruction Times for Minis (in μsec)					
	Modcomp IV	PDP-11/45	DG Eclipse	SEL 32	I-7/32	I-8/32
Arithmetic (Floating Point)						
ADD-Single Precision (SP)	9.2	4.4	3.1	2.25	20.0	2.3
ADD-Double Precision (DP)	14.6	5.8	3.1	2.85	20.0	3.5
MULTIPLY-SP	6.9	6.4	4.9	3.90	33.0	3.0
MULTIPLY-DP	13.0	10.2	8.1	6.90	33.0	4.5
DIVIDE-SP	11.0	7.4	6.1	6.75	55.0	5.4
Control						
LOAD (R-X)	1.60	1.85	1.0	1.20	3.5	1.30
STORE (R-X)	1.60	1.85	0.95	1.20	3.4	2.0
BRANCH	1.52	0.90	0.65	0.60	2.5	0.4
Logical						
COMPARE (Reg. with Mem.)	2.40	4.0	1.90	1.20	6.0	1.80
SHIFT (16 bits)	3.44	3.15	3.80	3.60	6.75	1.30
AND/OR (Mem. and Reg.)	2.16	4.35	0.60	1.20	3.5	1.30
I/O Control						
PROGRAM I/O TRANSFER	1.60	1.85	2.40	0.60	4.25	4.0

Use the following instruction mix:

ADD(SP); 12.6%, ADD(DP); 1.4%, MULTIPLY(SP); 10.8%, MULTIPLY-(DP); 1.20%, DIVIDE(SP); 2%, LOAD(R-X); 30%, STORE(R-X) 20%, BRANCH; 10%, COMPARE(Register with Memory); 2%, SHIFT(16 bits); 7%, AND/OR; 1%, PGM. I/O TRANSFER; 2%.

For the remainder, assume a miscellaneous instruction that is the average of all instruction times.

1-2 Select two contemporary microcomputers and repeat the analysis above using the same mix ratios. Discuss difficulties using this procedure.

1-3 Benchmark runs have been performed using the six minis listed in Problem 1-1 based on programs typical for a real-time environment in which these machines would be used. The results of these runs were as follows:

	Benchmark Results (*in msec*)		
Mini	*Mix 1*	*Mix 2*	*Mix 3*
Modcomp IV	80	100	130
DEC PDP-11/45	78	33	50
Data General Eclipse	40	13	20
SEL 32	36	11	14
Interdata 7/32	309	90	1060
Interdata 8/32	66	18	420

Compare parametrically throughput rates based on the instruction mix used for the same minis in Problem 1-1 with the benchmark results above. Explain the most obvious discrepancies or anomalies. What criteria should be applied to selecting one of the candidates above? How would you relate the results of this analysis to computer cost effectiveness?

1-4   Three commonly used mixes are summarized below. Select two contemporary mini-computers and compare their theoretical throughput capacity based on each of these mixes.

System Mix	*Gibson*	*Real-Time*	*Message Processing*
Fixed (single precision)			
Add/subtract	6.1%	16.0%	5.0%
Multiply	0.6	5.0	0.5
Divide	0.2	2.0	0.5
Logical			
Compare	3.8	12.0	1.0
Shift (6 bits)	4.4	5.0	3.0
And/or	1.6	4.0	15.0
Control			
Load/store	31.2	33.0	47.0
Conditional branch	16.6	10.0	14.0
Increment and store index	18.0	4.0	3.0
Move register to register			
no memory reference	5.3	5.0	5.8
I/O Control			
Programmed I/O transfer		2.0	0.0
Initialize buffered I/O		1.0	0.1
Interrupt response and			
store 4 registers	12.2	1.0	0.1

A shortcoming of the Gibson mix is the I/O instructions, which do not exist on the PDP-11. In addition, the INCREMENT AND STORE index-type instructions are not represented in the PDP-11, as these operations are usually done automatically by the addressing logic through the autoincrement and autodecrement options. However, separate accounting for the time used by the autoincrement and decrement can be made by breaking out PDP-11 equivalent instructions. In case of the selected minis, if necessary, make adjustments similar to the ones relating to the PDP-11 instruction set.

(For further study of the technique above, the reader is referred to Jack Corsiglia, "Matching Computers to the Job—First Step Towards Selection," *Data Processing Magazine*, December 1970; Louis Wolin, "Procedure Evaluates Computers for Scientific Applications," *Computer Design*, November 1976.)

1-5 It has been claimed* that in comparing distributed micro- or minicomputer systems with large computer systems, cost savings ranging from 40: 1 to 3.6: 1 and, quantitatively, up to $250,000 per month (the New York Off-Track Betting System) have been achieved.

In order to partly substantiate this claim, perform a gross estimate of hardware cost ratios between minis and a single, large computer with 2 million bytes of memory using the instruction mix from Problem 1-1. Assume 20% overhead for message processing and main memory size between minis in the distributed system, and exclude the cost of peripherals and interconnect facilities. Select a contemporary large main frame (i.e., IBM, CDC, Univac, Honeywell, Amdahl, or equivalent). The throughput capacities of the distributed minicomputer system (less 20%) and the large single processor should be approximately equal. Information used should be based on readily available, current sales literature (i.e., programmer's reference manuals and computer vendor price lists).

1-6 Elaborate in more detail on potential problems that are unique to distributed micro- and minicomputer systems (i.e., testing, time lags, control of dispersed data, security, interprocessor communications overhead, response time, etc.).

1-7 What general reliability techniques would/would not be applicable to distributed micro- or minicomputer systems (i.e., error checking, hardware redundancy, diagnostics, file protection, etc.)?

1-8 List positive and negative factors in response time and throughput for distributed micro- and minicomputer systems (i.e., parallel activities, CPU overhead, distributed data file overhead, etc.), and compare these with a single, large, central computer solution.

1-9 What man-machine interfaces (control panels, teletypewriters, display terminals, etc.) would be unique to a distributed system?

1-10 What approach should be taken in selecting the appropriate standards for a distributed system?

---

*Burt Liebowitz, "Distributed Processing," *International Computing*, Bethesda, Md., 1977.

2 Multiminicomputer Architecture

2.1 INTERCONNECT TECHNOLOGIES

In Chapter 1, six basic multiminicomputer architectures were described, including tightly and loosely coupled systems.

To a significant degree, distinctions between these systems can be related to the level of geographic dispersion; a shared memory-based multiminicomputer system is usually contained in one or two adjacent racks, whereas a bus or loop-based system may be distributed within a single structure. A hierarchical system can be dispersed between several plants or buildings, whereas a packet or circuit-switched system may have one or more minicomputers located on the West Coast of the United States and others on the East Coast, or even in Europe.

Each topology has thus certain attributes that affect its suitability for a particular application. These attributes are related to cost, reliability, responsiveness, speed, throughput capacity, ease of development, modularity, reconfigurability, logical complexity, and (as mentioned above) physical dispersability.

The cost of a distributed system is usually evaluated in terms of nonrecurring, developmental cost (software and/or hardware) and, in case of a large micro- or minicomputer system, recurring hardware cost.

Recurring cost includes the cost of additional computers and peripherals as well as communications equipment, be it modems, adapters, cabling, switches, etc. The major nonrecurring cost differential between dedicated single-computer systems and multimicro- or minicomputer systems is the cost of communications/interconnect hardware and software. However, much software and hardware for distributed processing is presently available off-the-shelf from various computer manufacturers.

In summary, the total development cost of a multiminicomputer system is divided among the cost of the minis, mini interfaces, communication links including switches and buffers (where needed), and the communications software.

Cost can also be evaluated in terms of incremental expansion of a multiminicomputer system. For instance, in a star-type configuration where a centralized switch provides a path between all the minis when the switch is fully utilized, the addition of one or more minis to the system may be impossible without replacing the switch with a larger one.

Multiminicomputer system reliability can be measured in terms of mean-time-between-failures, fault tolerance, graceful degradation, mean-time-to-repair, and failure reconfiguration time. Mean-time-between-failure is typically measured in hours and can be related to component reliability and level of redundancy. Graceful degradation is usually applications related. For instance, in a point-of-sale application where several cash register terminals are linked to a central concentrator, the failure of one register means, at worst, that sales personnel will have to use one of the operational cash registers until the failed unit has been either replaced or repaired. On the other hand, in a system where a single failure completely halts total system operation, no graceful degradation exists. Graceful degradation is particularly important in tactical weapons systems that require a so-called "bullet hole" design; minicomputers are dispersed and interconnected in a manner that minimizes the effect of failures on the total system.

Mean-time-to-repair can be minimized with built-in redundancy, built-in real-time, self-check and diagnostics; and the use of on-site highly trained maintenance people, coupled with an extensive spare parts inventory.

Failure reconfiguration generally requires redundant paths and/or minis that can be activated, as soon as a failure occurs and is detected.

Speed, responsiveness, and throughput capacity of a multiminicomputer system are all interrelated. These parameters are related to overall architecture. Increased processing speed and/or throughput capacity in terms of the interconnect structure will usually result in improved responsiveness.

Speed can be improved by proper balance between processing and communications. The selection of micro- or minicomputers, including type of main memory and peripherals, will usually influence speed. So will the selection or design of operating systems and communications protocols. Total system speed can also be improved based on task partitioning and allocation in a computer network.

Inadequate link bandwidths or nonoptimal task prioritization may result in build-up of queues and related message delays causing degradation in system response. This is also true for high message rates not anticipated during the system design phase.

System designs based on high internal and/or external message flow may cause saturation if heavy reliance is made of shared resources such as central switches, shared buses, or loop-based architectures.

Saturation may also occur if the chosen architecture is based on communications links exhibiting high error rates, thereby requiring a large number of retransmissions.

Degradation or even saturation can result from poor software design due to overly large communications software overhead that may unnecessarily tie up available system resources in unproductive work.

The proper choice of architecture, including the interconnect structure, processors, and software, will therefore greatly influence the speed, throughput capacity, and responsiveness of a distributed system.

The ease or difficulty of development can often be estimated during the conceptual design phase. The selection of an unproved approach may later in the design process force the design team to change direction and start all over with a new design approach.

Modularity can be assessed in terms of the incremental cost of adding a mini to the system and the ability to make incremental changes in system capability by reconfiguring the system. Reconfiguration of a star-based system may be fairly simple compared to reconfiguring a shared memory system.

The logical complexity of a multiminicomputer system is a function of nature and a number of decisions that must be made to effect communications within the total system. The control may be implemented in either the source or destination minis or in the switching entity. The major impact of logical complexity is on software cost that is often difficult to quantify.

The following sections provide detailed descriptions of the six major interconnect technologies. In Chapter 5, these technologies are evaluated in terms of the attributes above.

2.2 SHARED MEMORY

In this class of systems, the principal means of interaction between mini- and microprocessors is provided by common memory. Though normally the connection is by primary memory, additional interaction can occur through secondary memory (e.g., disk). This class of systems has in the past been referred to as multiprocessor systems. The definition of a "true" multiprocessor, as defined by Enslow,* is

1. A multiprocessor contains two or more processors of approximately comparable capabilities.
2. All processors share access to common memory.
3. All processors share access to input-output (I/O) channels, control units, and peripheral devices.
4. The entire system is controlled by a single operating system.

The definition above applies to tightly or closely coupled, shared memory systems where all program execution occurs in the common memory. Current examples are all large machine configurations such as the Univac 1110, IBM 370/168MP, and Honeywell 6180. Most multiminicomputer shared memory systems today do not conform to the definition of a "true" multiprocessor. Each minicomputer usually has its own private memory with its own executive software. Shared memory is used for sharing

*Philip Enslow, *Multiprocessors and Parallel Processing*, John Wiley & Sons, New York, 1974.

data between the processors and not for program execution. The basic organization of a shared memory, shared I/O system is shown in Figure 2-1.

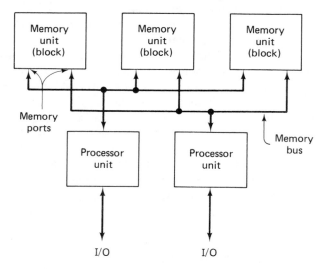

Figure 2-1   Basic organization of a shared memory multiminicomputer system.

Shared memory minicomputer systems are normally found in dedicated real-time applications such as signal and image processing and communication systems. These systems have stringent data transfer performance requirements and usually must achieve a high level of availability.

Shared memory, I/O systems are characterized by the following general types of physical and logical interconnection schemes:

- Time-shared common bus
- Crossbar switch   } Physical
- Multibus/multiport memory
- Virtual   } Logical
- Mailbox

In this section, each of the types above of shared memory organizations will be described. Following this, a comparison of these organizations will be presented with a discussion of additional hardware considerations necessary for shared memory systems. Finally, a general analytical model for computing the performance of various shared memory system organizations is described.

2.2.1   Time Shared/Common Bus, Shared Memory

The simplest interconnection system for multiple processors is a common communication path connecting all the functional units as shown in Figure 2-2.

Since the common bus is a shared resource, a means must be provided to resolve

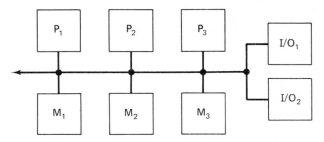

Figure 2-2   Time-shared common bus, shared memory system.

contention using such schemes as fixed priorities; first-in, first-out (FIFO) queues; and daisy chaining.

The most serious limitations of this organization are its reliability and the interference between processors requesting the bus. Since there is only one path for all transfers, the total overall transfer rate within the system is limited by the bandwidth and speed of this single path. For this reason, private memory and private I/O are highly advantageous. The failure of the common path can cause complete system failure.

An example of this type of system utilizing multiple minicomputers is the SL-10 Data Switch* for the Bell Canada Datapac network. The Datapac network is a call-based store-and-forward packet switching network. The hardware configuration of the SL-10 network processor is shown in Figure 2-3.

A number of processors are interconnected via a common bus. The common bus provides arbitration logic to serialize simultaneous requests by a number of separate processors. Processors cannot access addresses on another processor's private bus. An individual processor's bus is used to interconnect a central processor, some private memory, a bus switch interface, and a number of I/O interfaces.

The common or shared environment of the common bus consists of memory arbitration logic, some shared memory, shared I/O, and a bus switch interface. It also contains a special "concurrency box" referred to as a List Controller. This unit provides a synchronization capability by means of semaphores and queue operators.† There are three functional groups of processors used in the system: Trunk Processor, Line Processor, and Control Processor. The Trunk Processor, which is a microprogrammed intelligent Direct Memory Access (DMA) device, is used to interconnect the nodes of the network. Trunk modules each interface a single high-speed trunk or line (e.g., 56 Kbps). The Line Processor and Control Processors are 16-bit minicomputers. Each Line Processor can handle up to 62 subscriber lines. Control modules can be added to the system without software reconfiguration.

The bus switch interface logic provides write protection. Addresses in common memory are divided into 32-word blocks, and each of these blocks may be hardware protected or unprotected. The concurrency box on the common bus can link these

---

*Designed by Bell-Northern Research and manufactured by Northern Telecom Ltd.
†Semaphores and queue operators are explained in Chapter 3.

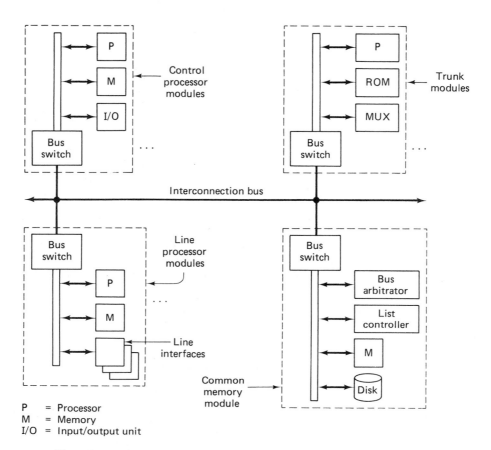

P   = Processor
M   = Memory
I/O = Input/output unit

Figure 2-3 Bell Canada DATAPAC SL-10 switch multiprocessor (From: "A Message-Switched Operating System for A Multiprocessor," C. J. Bedard, F. Mellor, W. J. Older, Computer Software & Applications Conference, Nov. 1977).

blocks onto any of 128 queues. The SL-10 concurrency box is implemented with a special microprocessor whose function is to make synchronization operations invisible and to provide the necessary arbitration.

2.2.2 Crossbar Switch Shared Memory

If we were to increase the number of buses in the previous organization to the point where there is a separate path available for each memory unit and I/O unit, we would have a crossbar switch-based multiminicomputer system. The interconnection is called a *crossbar matrix* and is shown in Figure 2-4.

In an $N \times N$ crossbar switch, there are N active elements (processors and I/O units) and M passive memory elements (M). Functional units in such a system need

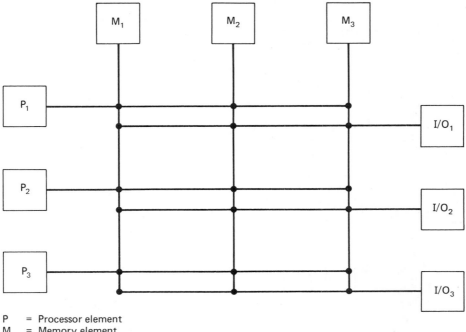

P   = Processor element
M   = Memory element
I/O = Input/output controller

Figure 2-4   A crossbar switch-based multiminicomputer system.

minimal bus interface logic since they perform neither conflict resolution nor recognition of data intended for them. These functions are done by the switch matrix that necessarily is complex, costly to control, and physically large. One line in the crossbar carries address, data, and control bus signals that might correspond to as many as 32 to 64 wires. The complexity grows exponentially as N and M become large. A major advantage of the crossbar switch is its ability to support simultaneous transfers between all processors and memory units. The logic for switching and arbitration of all transfer requests must be included in the switch. An example of this type of system, using multiple minicomputers, is the C.mmp system. It is based on a 16×16 crossbar interconnect scheme where the processor units are various models of the Digital Equipment Corporation PDP-11 Family (some are PDP-11/20's and others are PDP-11/40's). The memory modules each contain 1 million words. The basic configuration is shown in Figure 2-5 and provides an upper limit of 16 memory modules and 16 processors. Initially, 9 processors and 2.2 megabytes of memory were implemented. This was later expanded to 16 processors.

Each processor has associated with it a block of dedicated private memory. This block is used to support the dedicated memory locations used for PDP-11 interrupts and traps.

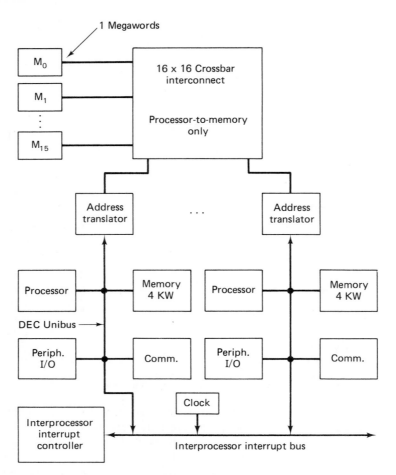

Figure 2-5 A 16×16 crossbar interconnect scheme (based on the Carnegie-Mellon C.mmp).

Another feature of C.mmp is a separate unit functioning as the address translator for all accesses to the shared memory, since the address space of the main memory greatly exceeds that of the PDP-11 itself. In this system, each I/O device is associated with a single processor and cannot be shared. Original plans for C.mmp called for an I/O switch in addition to the processor-memory switch, but no switch was ever built. The UNIBUS on the PDP-11 is also used to access a special bus that supports the synchronization of interprocessor communication. This interprocessor communications facility allows any processor to start and stop any subset of the processor as well as post an interrupt at one of three priority levels for any of the processors in the configuration. The clock on the interprocessor bus provides a master time base for the whole system. The C.mmp system comes closely to any multiple minicomputer system meeting the definition of a "true" multiprocessor. The C.mmp incurs a minimum of 250 nsec delay in the switch, for each shared memory access. Compared with MOS memory access time of 250 nsec, the switch delay impacts significantly overall memory access time. This system is also a "virtual shared memory" system. Such systems are described in more detail in Subsection 2.2.4.

2.2.3 Multibus/Multiport Shared Memory

In a multiport memory system, the control, switching, and priority arbitration logic, rather than being distributed throughout the crossbar switch matrix, is concentrated at the interface to the memory units.

Multiported systems, such as the one depicted in Figure 2-6, employ multiple dedicated buses connecting processors with memories and shared I/O units.

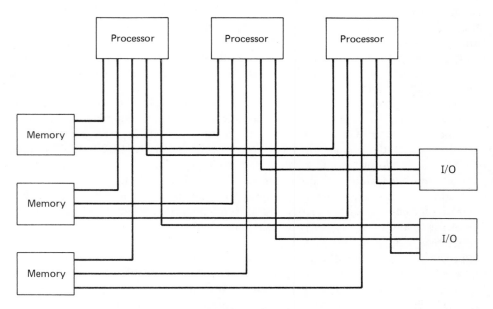

Figure 2-6 Multiported memory system.

Each of the latter two passive elements (memories and I/O units) is said to have multiple ports, one for each connection to a processor.

Contention logic must be built into each passive element to arbitrate between processors competing for the resource. A method often utilized to resolve memory access conflicts is to assign fixed priorities to each memory port.

Because of their high throughout capability, multibus/multiport memory systems are used quite commonly. The flexibility is somewhat limited if one wished to allow more processors access to the memory than originally planned for (such as having three processors accessing a two-ported memory).

Many of the multiport schemes, as well as other interconnection schemes, can also be represented by logical interconnection. There are two major forms of this interconnection utilizing shared memory. The first is to incorporate shared memory into a virtual memory environment. Virtual memory, developed to provide addressing capability to a larger memory space given that there are more active computing elements, incorporates a virtual address space beyond the size of any processor's real memory and requires address translator hardware and various segmentation techniques. The second form of logical interconnection is to utilize shared memory in a "mailbox" fashion where the primary use of the common memory is as a message center and where each CPU can leave messages for other CPU's and pick up messages intended for it. These two schemes are described in the following sections.

2.2.4 Virtual Shared Memory

An example of a virtual shared memory minicomputer system is PLURIBUS* developed by Bolt Beranek and Newman. This system makes use of a number (typically from 6 to 14) of Lockheed SUE minicomputers to obtain its processing power. Each processor has a 4K-word local memory as well as access through a bus coupler to a larger shared memory (32K–1024K words). All processors are identical and equal and can access all memory.

The SUE processor has a single bus for accessing both memory and I/O. A separate module, the Arbiter, controls bus access and resolves conflicts. It is possible to connect up to four SUE processors to a single bus. This will, however, greatly reduce the efficiency of the system on a per-processor basis. In the PLURIBUS system, therefore, only two processors are connected to a single bus. Using a four-processor, dual bus approach, almost no processor performance is lost. Communication between a module on one bus and a module on another bus is handled by means of a Bus Coupler that consists of two cards and an interconnecting cable. One use of a Bus Coupler is to allow a processor to access shared memory. In this case, one card of the Bus Coupler is plugged into a shared memory bus and the other card is plugged into the processor's bus. When the processor makes a memory request in the address range that the Bus Coupler recognizes, it sends a request down the cable to the memory bus.

The memory bus arbiter then is responsible for granting access to this request just as if it came from a processor directly connected to the bus. From the viewpoint of the requesting processor, the memory reference appears no different from a request to a memory on the same bus except possibly for an additional delay due to the Bus Coupler. In addition to permitting accesses to other buses, the Bus Coupler also does address mapping. It contains four registers that the processor can load with bits to be used for the high-order part of a memory address. The processors have 16 address bits and can thus address 64K bytes. The Bus Coupler registers provide a means for forming 20-bit addresses and thus for reaching 1024K bytes of memory. A diagram of a prototype PLURIBUS system is shown in Figure 2-7. As shown, this system contains

*F. E. Hearts, S. M. Ornstein, W. R. Crowther, and W. B. Barker, "A New Minicomputer/Multiprocessor for the ARPA Network," National Computer Conference, 1973.

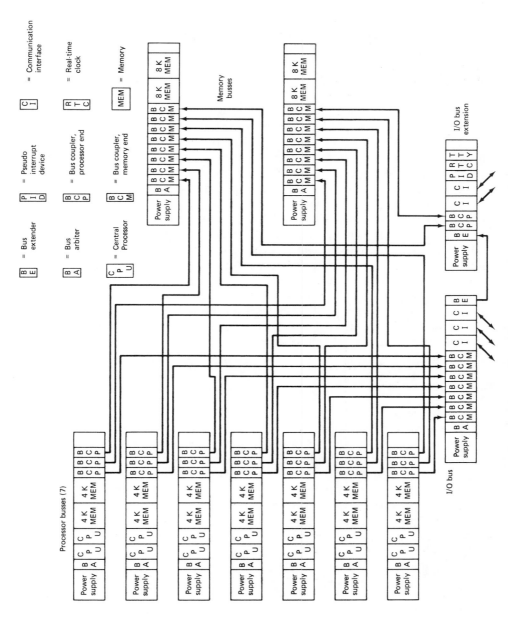

Figure 2-7 The PLURIBUS system. (From: "A New Minicomputer/Multiprocessor for the ARPA Network," F. E. Heart, S. M. Ornstein, W. R. Crowther, and W. B. Barker, AFIPS Conference Proceedings, 42, National Computer Conference, 1973).

14 processors with 23 Bus Couplers, 7 processor buses, 2 memory buses, and an extended I/O bus.

Task scheduling is handled by means of a special hardware device called a *Pseudo Interrupt Device* (PID). The PID maintains a list of pending tasks (entered by processors of I/O devices). When a processor is ready for a new task, it reads the PID that returns to the processor the identification of the highest priority pending task. Thus, task scheduling is done by means of a passive hardware queue, avoiding the problem of routing interrupts to the proper processor.

A more sophisticated shared memory, virtual environment, is the Cm*[*] system developed at Carnegie Mellon University. In the Cm* system, DEC LSI-11 micro-computers are grouped into clusters and share two levels of address mapping controllers. Each processor has its own private memory that is also the shared memory for the system. A simple three-cluster Cm* system is shown in Figure 2-8.

The primary unit in the Cm*, as shown in Figure 2-8, is the computer module. It consists of a processor, memory, and peripherals interfaced to a local memory bus and a local switch (SLocal). This switch connects the processor, its local memory bus, and the Map Bus. The Map Bus provides communication between up to 14 computer modules within a cluster and is centrally controlled by the Kmap, a high-performance microprogrammed processor. Each Kmap interfaces up to two intercluster buses by means of which it communicates with the other clusters in the system.

The memory local to each processor is also accessible as shared memory by all other processors in the network. Thus, each processor "sees" the same shared 28-bit virtual address space, but the switch delay is not uniform across the address space. The virtual address space is subdivided into up to 2^{16} segments with a maximum size of 4096 bytes.

2.2.5 Mailbox Shared Memory

Measurements indicate that when the number of processing elements exceed three, severe contention problems will arise in cases where each CPU must access common memory for a substantial fraction of its cycles. Hence, where a common memory is used, reference to it by individual CPU(s) should be minimized. Local memory is, therefore, highly desirable. The common memory then acts as a message center. This scheme works well when the memory access characteristics of the application are well known, as in dedicated real-time systems.

This scheme is more advantagous than the virtual environment since there is no extra overhead in address translation associated with each memory reference. Some examples of systems utilizing shared memory in this fashion are described below.

The MIDISS[†] system developed for the Navy consists of a multiprocessor telemetry ground station. It contains a microprocessor-controlled data pre-processor

R. J. Swan, S. H. Fuller, and D. P. Siewiorek, "Cm—A Modular Multi-microprocessor," National Computer Conference Proceedings, 1977.

†D. L. Feinberg, "MIDISS: A Unique Multiprocessor Telemetry Ground Station," International Telemetering Conference, Los Angeles, Calif., 1976.

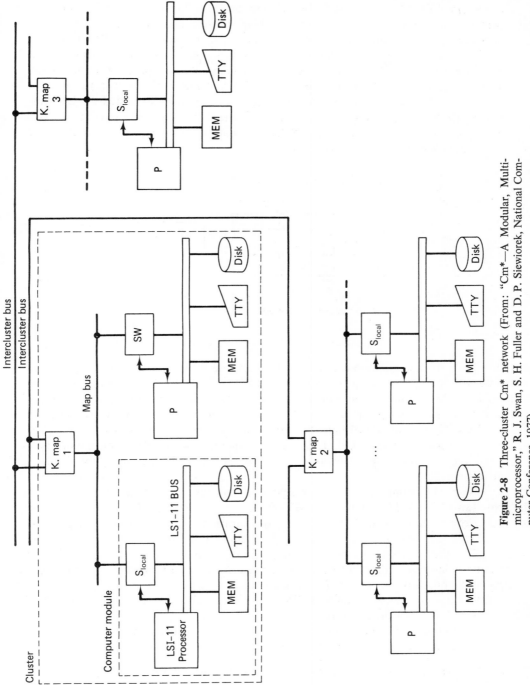

Figure 2-8 Three-cluster Cm*—network (From: "Cm*—A Modular, Multi-microprocessor," R. J. Swan, S. H. Fuller and D. P. Siewiorek, National Computer Conference, 1977).

33

called SPACEPIPE. The SPACEPIPE decommutates multiple satellite down-links and performs data compression and alarm checking. These data are passed to a PDP-11/40 host computer through a shared memory. The primary function of SPACEPIPE is, at all times, to maintain the most current value for each channel in memory. The SPACEPIPE consists of two microcomputers connected into a pipeline configuration. The configuration is shown in Figure 2-9. The first microprocessor in the pipeline performs preliminary data verification. Selected data may be extracted for buffering directly to the host PDP-11/40 minicomputer, while other data are passed to the second microprocessor, which completes the decommutation and compression of the data. These data are also passed to the host.

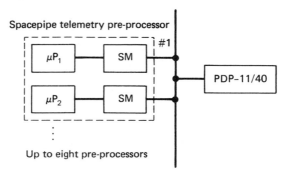

Figure 2-9   SPACEPIPE configuration.

The primary communication path between the SPACEPIPE and the host computer is implemented using two dual-ported PDP-11 UNIBUS compatible memories, each one dedicated to a microprocessor. Data are deposited by each microprocessor into its assigned dual-ported memory, where it can be accessed asynchronously by the PDP-11/40. Low-speed control information is also communicated between the microprocessors and the PDP 11/40, using the shared memory (SM). When immediate attention is required, each microprocessor in SPACEPIPE can interrupt the host processor.

A second example of the use of shared memory is found in the microcomputer-based small PACUIT switch on the M3200 network developed by Computer Transmission Corporation. Figure 2-10 shows the configuration of the switch that is responsible for data concentration, error control, and switching for remote nodes on the network.

The first microprocessor performs scanning and frame construction, and the second microprocessor handles automatic retransmission of requests. The first microprocessor builds blocks of data in the shared memory while the second microprocessor controls the movement of data blocks to the processor that implements the SDLC protocol.* The first processor is given priority to the shared memory.

An example of a dual-ported secondary memory system where the memory is a disk is briefly described. As shown in Figure 2-11, Tandem Corporation's basic

*For description of data link control protocols, see Chapter 3 and Appendix.

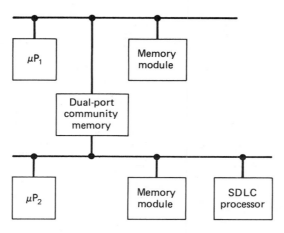

Figure 2-10   PACUIT switch configuration.

Tandem 16 multiprocessor* consists of two processor modules connected to one or more dual-port device controllers.

The controller handles the data transfer between the I/O devices and memory. In the event of a failure of a processor module or I/O path, the second processor takes control automatically to ensure that the system, at any given time, will accept commands from a processor. Additionally, processor modules are connected by a dual bus called the *Dynabus*.

2.2.6   Additional Hardware Considerations

Two additional hardware considerations are (1) the control of shared memory and (2) the use of cache memory.

Currently, the control of shared memory is accomplished both by hardware serialization and an interrupt scheme.

In a uniprocessor mode, a CPU is neither aware of nor affected by other CPU's. Controlled access to critical system areas and data can be accomplished by software locks, priority levels, and disabling interrupts. This results in a serialization of access to share data. This same serialization must also be provided when many processors are accessing a shared resource such as memory. The serialization will guarantee that critical regions in main storage are not modified in an undetected fashion by another CPU. Interlocks will prevent a CPU from observing or modifying a storage location being worked on by special instructions issued by the other CPU. The most common instruction found in current multiprocessor systems that accomplishes this is the TEST AND SET instruction. To ensure interlocks, the memory must be capable of a read-modify-write cycle before permitting further accesses (see also Section 5.7.1, Interprogram Communications).

*The basic purpose of the Tandem system is to provide the user with fault tolerance. Any single failure in the system will have no impact whatsoever on total system performance.

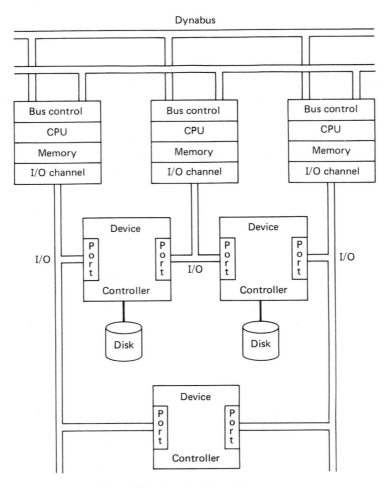

Figure 2-11   Tandem-16 multiprocessor.

Additional control schemes have been used, but only on large multiprocessor systems. The interested reader is referred to the discussion of the IBM Advanced Function Extended hardware for the IBM 158 MP system.*

Interrupts are used in shared memory systems to notify the second processor of memory synchronization. If an interrupt scheme was not used, all processors would have to poll the shared memory, thereby degrading system performance. Shared memory multimini systems, therefore, include dedicated interrupt lines.

External device interrupts are handled by the processor to which the I/O device is

*R. A. McKinnon, "Advanced Function Extended with Tightly-Coupled Multiprocessing," *IBM Systems Journal*, **13**, No. 1, 1974.

connected. In most of the current multimini/micro systems, the I/O devices are private to the individual processors.

The use of a cache memory has been proposed to reduce access conflicts in a multimini multiprocessor system. A cache is a fast buffer memory between the processor and the main memory. It is used for storing frequently used data and/or instructions. Typically, the cache memory contains the contents of the most recently addressed main memory location and the contents of a limited number of contiguous memory locations. It can rarely be predicted which specific data items will be used next by a software program, but a small collection of data items can be stored in the cache memory with a high probability that the next access will come from that collection. (Two independent effects make data caching effective. These are the reuse of data since a data item that just has been accessed by the CPU is likely to be accessed again. The second effect is sequential access. A data item is more likely to be accessed if the item logically preceding it has just been accessed.)

In a multiprocessor system, the total throughput depends critically on the degree of memory interference. By reducing the number of accesses to shared memory, the interference is reduced. Actual measurements have shown the hit ratio to be around 90%; that is, the data will be found in the cache memory 90% of the time, eliminating the need for the processor to access the main memory.

A multimini cache system involves multiple caches. There is one major problem regarding the validity of data in a system with multiple caches when more than one copy of the data may exist. The problem arises when data are subject to modification by one or more of the sharing processors. Unless all the caches are updated simultaneously, which is extremely cumbersome and costly to achieve, stale copies of the data may exist in some caches. There is the need for additional hardware in a multimini cache-based system to distinguish between shared data and private data in the cache itself.

2.2.7 Comparison of Shared Memory Systems

A number of factors can be considered in comparing the previously basic organizations or evaluating their use in specific applications. The most important are cost, reliability, growth potential, system throughput, and transfer capacity.

Time-Shared Bus:

1. Lowest overall system cost for hardware.
2. Least complex (the interconnection bus may be totally passive).
3. Very easy to modify the hardware system configuration physically by adding or removing functional units.
4. Overall system capability limited by bus data transfer rate.
5. Failure of bus results in catastrophic system failure.
6. Expansion of system by the addition of functional units may degrade overall system performance.

7. Maximum system efficiency (based on simultaneous use of all available resources) is lowest of all the basic interconnection schemes.
8. This organization is usually appropriate for smaller systems only.

Crossbar:

1. The Crossbar is the most complex interconnection system.
2. Functional units are the simplest and least expensive since control and switching logic is contained in the switch (the interfaces to the switch are simple and usually require no bus couplers).
3. Potential exists for high total transfer rate.
4. Maximum system efficiency may be achieved.
5. The reliability of the switch and, therefore, the system can be improved through segmentation and/or redundancy within the crossbar switch.

Multiported Memory:

1. This approach requires the most expensive memory units since most of the control and switching circuitry is included in the memory unit.
2. Very high total transfer rates in the overall system may be achieved.
3. Size and configuration options are determined (limited) by number and types of memory ports available; design decision must be made early in design process and system is difficult to modify.
4. A large number of cables and connectors are required.

When the multiport/bus shared memory organization is used, one can treat shared memory as part of the virtual environment. The advantages are as follows:

1. Ideal for low-speed applications (access speed to memory is not critical).
2. Applications with large storage requirements that do not need the software complexity of overlay logic.
3. Memory can be hardware protected in segmented blocks.
4. Virtual memory permits utilization of local memory in inactive processors.

Disadvantages of using shared memory when part of virtual memory are as follows:

1. Memory management policy (e.g., allocation) is fixed (hardwired).
2. If the mailbox or message scheme is based on shared memory, then it is fixed in the virtual memory hardware.
3. Additional overhead for virtual memory addresses is required.

2.2.8 Performance

The effective performance of a shared memory multiple processor system is determined to a large extent by the degree to which processors interfere with each other. Interference occurs whenever the number of processor requests to the shared memory exceeds the number of allowed simultaneous access, thereby imposing a delay. Interference occurs whenever more than one processor accesses the same memory element. An analytical means of computing the interference above for symmetric processors accessing multiported memories is now given. This approach developed by Richard Eckhouse* can be used to handle cache-based multimini systems and extended to handle loosely coupled systems where each processor has a large bank of private memory in addition to the shared memory.

This analysis assumes that all the processors access the shared memory uniformly (with the same memory request distribution) and that the system is based on the DEC PDP-11 architecture with a central bus. The representative model is based on the following logical utilization factors.

r_1 = fraction of P_c time requesting cache memory

r_2 = fraction of average memory time requesting backing (main) memory

r_3 = fraction of backing store (main memory) time that locks memory access and where P_c = processor

The relationship between the computer elements, including processor, memory and bus is thus:

$$\underbrace{P_c - M_{\text{cache}}}_{r_1}\underbrace{-S_{\text{bus}}}_{r_2}\underbrace{-S_{\text{mem.}}}_{r_3}{}_{\text{port}} - M_p$$

where M_{cache} is cache memory, S_{bus} is the DEC UNIBUS, $S_{\text{mem.port}}$ is one of main memory ports and M_p is main memory.

The product of logical utilization factors is

$$r = r_1 r_2 r_3 \qquad (2\text{-}1)$$

For each P_c cycle, the probability of a particular memory being selected is $1/M$ where M = number of parallel memory banks. Therefore, the probability that the memory is locked is r'/M where r' = actual utilization (fraction of time) of memory by processor including interference and the probability that the memory is unlocked is $1 - r'/M$.

For NP_c's, the probability that the memory is unlocked becomes

$$\left(1 - \frac{r'}{M}\right)^N \qquad (2\text{-}2)$$

where N = number of P_c's and the probability that memory is locked or busy due to NP_c's is

$$1 - \left(1 - \frac{r'}{M}\right)^N \qquad (2\text{-}3)$$

*R. H. Eckhouse, and D. Nelson, "Closely Coupled Multiprocessor Systems," 14th Annual Southeastern Regional ACM Conference, April 1976.

For $N = M = 1$, the memory utilization (fraction of processor time that memory is locked) is $r' = r$. Therefore, the rate of memory cycles (throughput) normalized to that of a single processor-single memory system is

$$\left(\frac{1}{r}\right)\left[1 - \left(1 - \frac{r'}{M}\right)^{N}\right] \tag{2-4}$$

and the total system throughput ratio of all M's is

$$T = \left(\frac{M}{r}\right)\left[1 - \left(1 - \frac{r'}{M}\right)^{N}\right] \tag{2-5}$$

where $T =$ throughput ratio of system (units of one P_c).

By approximating $r' = r$ in Eq. (2-5), a relatively simple closed form expression is obtained that has been compared to more accurate forms (described below) to within 10% (see Figure 2-12). What follows is a derivation relating actual utilizations, r', to logical utilizations, r, as a function of T and N, thereby obtaining an accurate equation for T.

Letting t and t_m be the average processor cycle time (mean time between references of a single P_c) and memory locked time, respectively, and t_e be the average incremental time spent waiting for locked memory, then r and r' can be expressed as

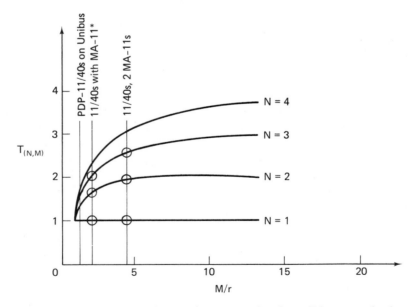

Figure 2-12 System throughput ratio versus ratio of parallel memory banks versus processors. Solutions shown are based on Eq. (2-5) where $r' \sim r = 0.45$ has been assumed. (The regions have been plotted to an accuracy of 10%.)

$$r = \frac{t_m}{t}; \qquad r' = \frac{t_m + t_e}{t + t_e} \tag{2-6}$$

which results in

$$t_e = \frac{(r' - r)t}{1 - r'} \tag{2-7}$$

By our definitions, T/N is the ratio of the instruction rates of a processor with and without contention. The instruction rate without contention is clearly $1/t$, and the instruction rate with contention is $1/(t + t_e)$, so that

$$\frac{T}{N} = \frac{t}{t + t_e} \tag{2-8}$$

Using the expression above for t_e, we find

$$\frac{T}{N} = \frac{1 - r'}{1 - r} \tag{2-9}$$

giving

$$r' = 1 - \frac{T}{N}(1 - r) \tag{2-10}$$

Substituting this into Eq. (2-5) and rearranging terms, we obtain an Nth-order polynomial equation that can be solved for the system throughput ratio, T.

$$T - \frac{M}{r}\left(1 - \left\{1 - \frac{1}{M}\left[1 - \frac{T}{N}(1 - r)\right]\right\}^N\right) = 0 \tag{2-11}$$

Determining r. The effective utilization factor represents the fraction of processor cycle time that is spent in a contended (nonparallel) memory cycle. The numeric value for r can be obtained by multiplying the invididual utilization factors of components that are accessed serially in time. Accordingly, we have defined r_1, r_2, and r_3 as the fraction of time that (1) processor spends accessing memory, (2) fraction of time that the memory system spends accessing backing memory, and (3) fraction of time that backing store is locked during a cycle, respectively. What follows is a brief analysis of each factor.

Determining r_1. Measurements have been made to determine the fraction of time the processor accesses memory on PDP-11/40's by measuring the average bus cycle (1.8 μsec) and the average amount of time that the processor is not accessing memory (0.6 μsec), giving

$$r_1 = \frac{1.8}{0.6 + 1.8} = 0.75$$

This says that on average the 11/40 spends about 75% of its time accessing memory.

Determining r_2. The fraction of time the memory system spends accessing backing store is estimated by assuming a cache configuration that requires a full memory cycle on Writes (10% of all requests) and a partial memory cycle on Reads not found in the cache (13% of the remaining 90% of all requests). We obtain an average cycle time of

$$t_{ave} = 0.90(0.87t_{cache} + 0.13t_{mread}) + 0.10t_{mwrite} \quad \text{(assuming 300-nsec cache)}$$

For $t_{cache} = 300$, $t_{mread} = 600$ and $t_{mwrite} = 1100$ nsec

$$t_{ave} = 0.783 \times 300 \text{ (cache)} + 0.117 \times 600 \text{ (reads)} + 0.10 \times 1100 \text{ (writes)}$$
$$= 415 \text{ nsec}$$

If we assume that the write portion of the read-to-core requests are completely overlapped with subsequent cache hits (so that the processor does not wait), then the fraction of memory time that requires the UNIBUS is

$$r_2 = \frac{0.117 \times 1100 + 0.10 \times 1100}{415} = 0.6$$

Determining r_3. The fraction of time that backing store is locked has been obtained from measurements performed on a two-processor 11/40 system having a single memory bank indicating an effective throughput ratio of 1.7 for compute bound jobs. Using the previously derived expression, we find that the value of $r = 0.45$ corresponds to the observed value of $T = 1.7$. Now, since the 11/40 is noncached, $r_2 = 1$, and we obtain the value of r_3 (for the DEC MA11*) to be $r_3 = r/r_1 = 0.45/0.75 = 0.6$.

Analysis of Eq. (2-11). Equation (2-11) has been numerically solved for the system throughput ratio, T, for several configurations listed in Table 2-1.

Table 2-1 Throughput ratio, T, for several configurations

Configuration	r	T
Two 11/40's:		
1 UNIBUS as memory switch	0.75	1.3
1 MA11 memory control as switch	0.75 × 0.6	1.72
2 MA11's, interleaved	0.75 × 0.6	1.88
Three 11/40's:		
2 MA11's, interleaved	0.75 × 0.6	2.63
4 MA11's, interleaved	0.75 × 0.6	2.84

*For a description of the DEC MA11, see Section 4.2.

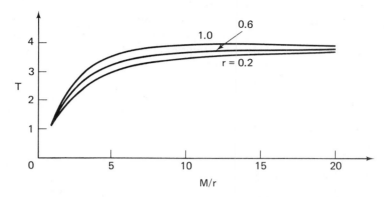

Figure 2-13 System throughput versus number of memory banks for four processors ($N = 4$) [curves shown are solutions to Eq. (2-12)].

Comparisons of Eq. (2-5) and (2-11) have shown that, to first approximation, T is a function of the ratio M/r, rather independent of specific values of M and r. Consequently, for simplicity, T is plotted as a function of M/r for several values of N, using a constant value of $r = 0.45$. Figure 2-13 shows the relatively small dependence on r, where T as a function of M/r has been plotted for several values of r using a constant value of $N = 4$.

The performance data show that when two processors are connected to the same multiport memory, and both processors are accessing that memory, then a program executes about 27% slower due to the second processor's interference. The performance data also show that multiprocessing is an effective way to increase the performance range for system designs having high values of M/r.

If cache was used in the system, r_2 would be 0.6 rather than 1. Hence, r would decrease and M/r would increase, resulting in improved performance.

If each minicomputer had its own private memory in addition to the shared memory, then this model could be extended by assuming that the private memory would function as a cache memory without the extra memory cycle on writes. The hit ratio would, therefore, increase. This would further reduce r_2 and thus r and would increase M/r to ensure even better performance.

2.3 SHARED BUS

Bus or shared path structures are those in which the connected minicomputers communicate over a common channel and employ the technique of continually addressing each addressee or receiving computer. In bus systems, many messages can coexist, but all carry unique addresses that permit any one to be distinguished from all others. The bus in a typical bus-based multiminicomputer system is time-shared, allowing attached minis to transmit information in short duration, high-speed bursts. Bus-based multiminicomputer systems are widely used in aerospace-, industrial-, and laboratory-automation applications. Most bus-based systems are local with all minis located in the same or adjacent racks, in the same room, building, or (at the most) building complex. The bus itself may be nothing more than one or more twisted pair of wires, or a multiwire, coaxial, or fiber optics cable. It could also consist of two or more parallel wires such as the CAMAC or IEEE-488 standard buses described in Chapter 1. Most tightly coupled systems use parallel buses, whereas loosely coupled systems are generally implemented with a serial bus. (Multiple buses may also be interconnected. The bus window provides a path for transmitting messages between different bus systems.) Each of the links above, whether parallel or serial, has its unique advantages and disadvantages, which are described in Chapter 5.

The control of the bus may be either centralized or decentralized. In centralized control, the hardware used for passing bus control from one device to another is largely concentrated in one location. All messages are first transmitted to a shared switch that retransmits the messages over the same bus to the proper destination (mini). The centralized control can be within one of the minicomputers connected to the bus or it can be performed by a dedicated bus controller. The dedicated bus controller may operate in a polling mode, polling each of the minis connected to the bus, in an interrupt mode where each incoming message is stored and forwarded, depending on its priority, or in a centrally assigned environment where each mini may request one or more time slots for message transmission.

In a decentralized control environment, bus control logic is largely distributed throughout all the minis connected to the bus. This latter approach, based on a global bus, is the most commonly used technique. Most common variations to the global bus are the frequency division multiplexed (FDM) bus, where each receiver and transmitter associated with a mini has a dedicated frequency slot; the time division multiplexed (TDM) bus, where each transmitter and receiver has one or more dedicated time slots; and the multiple access (MA) bus, which operates in a contention mode using collision control software algorithms.

Bus system performance is determined by bus bandwidth, number of minicomputers connected to the bus, bus access control, bus protocol, timing and other tolerances introduced by the design approach taken, and the average and peak bus-user traffic rates.

Each of the bus structures above will be discussed in greater detail in this section, starting with centrally controlled multiminicomputer bus systems.

2.3.1 Centrally Controlled, Polled Bus

In a polled bus system, minicomputers connected to the bus transmit only when interrogated by the bus controller. If there is no message for transmission when a mini is polled, automatic response logic in the mini will transmit a status message to inform the bus controller that the polled mini is operational. The capacity required by a polled bus is equal to the sum of the capacities needed to transmit the data from one of the minis to one or more other minis on the bus, plus the capacity needed to perform the controller-to-minicomputer interchanges of polling messages. The time required for the latter function depends on the physical length of the bus because of the propagation delay involved. (This delay is approximately 1.5 nsec/ft). In most cases, the propagation delay is minor compared to the processing delay involved in the polling interchange.

The bandwidth requirements of a polled-bus system are determined as follows:

$$t_s = t_p + \frac{\bar{b}}{C}*$$ (2-12)

where t_s = total time required to service a transmitting mini

t_p = time required to issue a poll

b = random variable equal to the number of bits in a message, including overhead

$\bar{b}$ = mean value of b

C = bus capacity

The variables above are related in the following diagram:

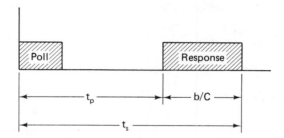

In the equation above, t_p includes the processing time required by the mini and all propagation delays. The term b/C is the time required to transfer b bits at a rate of C bits per second. If the polled mini does not have a message ready, then b is very small (a standard control message indicating that it has nothing to report). If the mini does have a message, b is equal to the total number of bits in the message; t_s is the total duration of the polling cycle and generally a random variable that depends on the number of bits in the transmitting mini's message.

The average time required to service a single mini on the bus can be estimated from the relationship above provided that the variance of b is much less than $\bar{b}$. For large variations in message length b, the mean value of b may be significantly larger (or smaller) than the average message length.

Each minicomputer attached to the bus issues an average of a messages per second. For M number of minis in the system, the total system demand is aM messages per second and the average time interval between message arrivals is $1/aM$

*L. W. Hill, H. Willensky, and R. C. Labonte, "Modular C^3 Architecture—Digital Communications Interconnect Alternatives Study," The Mitre Corporation, Bedford, Mass., October 1976.

seconds. Therefore, to avoid unstable queues, the mean service time ($\bar{t}_s$) must be less than or equal to the mean interarrival time, or

$$\bar{t}_s = t_p + \frac{\bar{b}}{C} \leq \frac{1}{aM} \tag{2-13}$$

Solving for C,

$$C \geq \frac{aM\bar{b}}{1 - aMt_p} \tag{2-14}$$

When $C \geq aM\bar{b}/(1 - aMt_p)$, the queue length at each mini is zero. This follows naturally from the fact the each mini will be polled on the order of every $1/a$ seconds and will have a message available every $1/a$ seconds.

This is illustrated by an example: A multiminicomputer system using 16 minis is interconnected by a 1-Mbit per second, bit serial bus where each mini on the bus transmits an average of 20 messages per second. A central bus controller requires 20 μsec to issue a poll. This includes worst case delay on the bus. The mean message length is 1000 bits, which includes the message header and error checking code. Using Eq. (2-14), the mean time required to service a transmitting mini is thus

$$\bar{t}_s = 20 \ \mu\text{sec} + \frac{1000 \text{ bits}}{1 \text{ Mbps}}$$

$$= 1.02 \text{ msec}$$

Also, the mean interarrival time is

$$\frac{1}{aM} = \frac{1}{(20 \text{ messages per sec}) \times 16} = 3.125 \text{ msec per message}$$

It is obvious that messages can be serviced three times faster than the rate at which they arrive.

The polling scheme described above has been called "roll-call polling." Another technique of polling called "hub polling" is based on the central controller inviting the mini farthermost away on the bus to send a message. If the mini polled first is not ready with a message, it will pass the request to the second mini and so on (see Figure 2-14). This technique is efficient when the minis on the bus are generally inactive and the bus is very long.

Whenever a mini replies with an information message, the controller forwards it and then resumes the polling sequence by inviting the next mini to proceed until the mini closest to the controller is polled, whereupon the cycle is repeated by starting all over again, with the farthermost mini. In this way, an active mini near the beginning of the bus is prevented from monopolizing the attention of the central bus controller. This type of polling is used in telemetry systems, for example, where a long bus is used to collect data and a large number of microprocessors are connected to measuring instruments along the length of the bus.

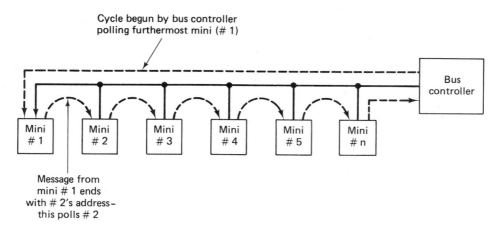

Figure 2-14 Hub polling bus configuration.

The throughput of a polled bus can be increased by eliminating overhead needed for control message transfers. This can be accomplished by adding separate control lines to the system. A second alternative is to have control information transmitted on a frequency different from data information. The latter approach will, however, complicate the system, requiring modulators, demodulators, and bit synchronizers at each input-output port.

The advantage of having separate control lines for polling is that time required between data transmission by different minis connected to the bus is no longer a function of system size and tends to be a much smaller quantity. This overhead is needed only for a guard period to prevent overlap between messages from different subscribers. The disadvantage is obviously the additional lines needed to connect each mini to the controller. Regardless of how control is handled, only one message at the time can be transmitted on the bus.

2.3.2 Interrupt Driven, Centrally Controlled Bus

The interrupt driven system is identical to the polled bus system that is using separate control lines. Rather than using these control lines for successively polling each minicomputer, the bus controller receives random requests from minicomputers ready to transmit data and queues them. This type of protocol is preferable to a polling system only when a small percentage of minis on the bus want to transmit during an interval, because the overhead associated with polling minis that do not have messages ready for transmission is eliminated. Conversely, if the load is fairly constant, polling is a better choice. Essentially, an interrupt driven central controller-based bus system is a contention system as far as getting access to the bus. The request messages or interrupts are short, however, thereby reducing the contention problem to contention between seldomly occurring interrupts. Thus in an interrupt driven, central controller system, Request to Send (RTS) messages are sent spontaneously by minis to the central controller that queues the requests and sends acknowledgement to the requesting minis. If no acknowledgement is received after a random wait, a mini will automatically retransmit a request. When the bus is available, the central controller will inform the requesting mini that it can use the bus. At the end of the message transfer, the bus is allocated to another mini.

For randomly arriving RTS messages, with large time delays between these requests, the probability of two or more requests interfering with each other is

$$P_c = 1 - e^{-2MaT} \tag{2-15}$$

where M = number of minis on the bus
a = message arrival rate in messages per second
m = number of bits in the request message
T = duration of a request in seconds where $T = m/C_r$ and C_r = capacity allocated to requests.

When requests are repeated, the effective arrival rate will exceed a. Based on Poisson statistics* the conflict probability therefore becomes

$$P_c = 1 - e^{-2AT} \tag{2-16}$$

where A is the effective arrival rate of requests per T-second interval and defined as

$$A = Ma + AP_c \tag{2-17}$$

Substituting Eq. (2-16) into (2-17),

$$A = Ma + A(1 - e^{-2AT}) \tag{2-18}$$

The throughput of the system can be defined as

$$MaT = ATe^{-2AT} \tag{2-19}$$

To maximize the effective throughput, MaT is differentiated with respect to AT and the result is set equal to zero.

$$\frac{d(MAT)}{dAT} = e^{-2AT} - 2ATe^{-2AT} = 0 \tag{2-20}$$

$$1 - 2AT = 0 \tag{2-21}$$

$$AT = \frac{1}{2} \tag{2-22}$$

Computer Communication Networks, edited by Norman Abramson and Franklin F. Kuo, Prentice-Hall, Inc., Englewood Cliffs, N.J., 1973, Chapter 14, "The Aloha System," Norman Abramson.

Substituting this value for AT into the expression for MaT yields

$$(MaT)_{\max} = \frac{1}{2e} \qquad (2\text{-}23)$$

$$M_{\max} = \frac{1}{2eaT} \qquad (2\text{-}24)$$

Since $T = m/C_r$,

$$M_{\max} = \frac{C_r}{2eam} \qquad (2\text{-}25)$$

These equations provide a method of determining the maximum number of minis that can be on the bus for a given bandwidth for interrupt requests before the requests begin to develop a serious contention problem. It should be noted that the equations above are based on a *separate channel* for bus service requests to the central bus controller. In general, when estimating total service time, the request contention issue is neglected and the access time to the bus controller is lumped together with processing and bus propagation delay times.

The queue delay can be determined by the arrival and service rates. The total service time t_I includes t_s (lumped access time, switching time, etc.) plus the time to transmit the data or $\bar{b}/C$, where C is bus capacity in bits per second. Thus

$$t_I = t_s + \frac{\bar{b}}{C} \qquad (2\text{-}26)$$

This equation is in the same form as the equivalent equation for a polled bus system [Eq. (2-13)].

A measure of throughput for this system is f, where

$$f = at_I \qquad (2\text{-}27)$$

If $f > 1$, then the messages will arrive faster than they can be serviced and unstable queues develop.

For $f \leq 1$, however, the queue will remain finite. f is the ratio of the mean service time to the mean interarrival time of messages.

The probability of a queue of length n is thus

$$P_q = f^{n-1} (1 - f) \qquad (2\text{-}28)$$

and the average delay $\bar{D}$ is

$$\bar{D} = \sum_{n=0}^{\infty} (nt_I)P_q \qquad (2\text{-}29)$$

The model above will provide answers to the probability of any specific delay. Since

t_I depends on the system capacity, this provides a method of finding the probability that a mini will experience a specific delay for a given bus capacity.

The analysis of delays and throughput is complicated for systems where minis attached to the bus are given differing levels of priority in accessing it. It is also possible to assign various priority levels for messages from the same mini. The priority level must be decoded by the central controller before inserting the service request in the proper position in the queue.

In a multiminicomputer system with 16 minis connected to an interrupt driven, central controller bus, as shown in Figure 2-15, the average message arrival rate per mini is 20 messages per second.

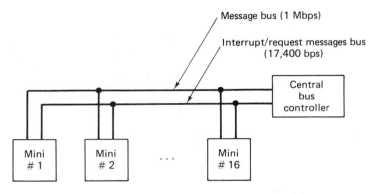

Figure 2-15 Interrupt driven centrally controlled bus.

For a maximized effective throughput of interrupt requests to the bus controller, the duration of a request is

$$T = \frac{1}{2eMa} = \frac{1}{2e \times 16 \times 20 \text{ messages per sec}} = 0.574 \text{ msec per message}$$

For 10-bit requests messages, the capacity that must be allocated to requests is

$$C_r = \frac{m}{T} = \frac{10 \text{ bits}}{0.574 \text{ msec}} = 17,400 \text{ bits per second}$$

In a 1-Mbps bus system where the average message length is 1000 bits, the total service time per mini, based on Eq. (2-26), is

$$t_I = t_s + \frac{1000 \text{ bits}}{1 \text{ Mbps}} = t_s + 1 \text{ msec}$$

Assuming $t_s \ll 1$ msec,

$$t_I \approx 1 \text{ msec}$$

Using Eq. (2-27),

$$f = (20 \text{ messages per sec})(1 \text{ msec per message}) = 0.02$$

f is thus significantly less than 1 and messages can be serviced in time.

2.3.3 Centrally Controlled, Slotted Bus

The centrally controlled slotted MITRIX bus shown in Figure 2-16 consists of a cable distribution system of two one-way cables interconnecting computer terminals in six buildings at MITRE's Bedford Headquarters. Time is divided into intervals called *slots*, and the slots are combined into larger intervals called *frames*. Terminals are connected in parallel between inbound and outbound cables via a Bus Interface Unit (BIU). The transmitting terminal transmits a message in assigned time slots on the inbound cable. This message is received by a Digital Bus Repeater (DBR) and retransmitted on the outbound cable. The receiving terminal's BIU detects the address on data content and routes the message to the receiving terminal.

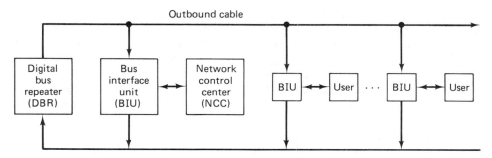

Figure 2-16 MITRIX bus structure.

A Network Control Center (NCC) assigns slots uniquely to terminals. This assignment consists of a starting slot and 2^N evenly spaced slots within a frame (N integral). The time slots recurring within frame periods and allocated by the NCC to individual BIU's are based on service specified by the user. A single frame lasts 2.56 sec, and there are 8192 slots per frame. Each data slot contains a single 256-bit message, which includes an address and 192 bits of data. Assigning one or more slots per frame to an individual BIU for data transmission yields the 75×2^N bus service rate. These relationships set the system transmission rate at 819,200 bps.

Assignments are made at 2^N slots per frame as shown in Table 2-2, varying according to the desired data rate.

Service requests are made in slots dedicated for that purpose, in a contention mode, similar to message requests in the Interrupt Driven Central Controller Bus System described in Subsection 2.3.2. The slot assignment granted by the NCC is unique for each terminal so no slots are shared and slot assignment only changes on a log on-log off basis.

Table 2-2 MITRIX service rates

N	Slots Per Frame (2^N)	Service Rate (75×2^N)
0	1	75 bps
1	2	150
2	4	300
3	8	600
4	16	1,200
5	32	2,400
6	64	4,800
7	128	9,600
8	256	19,200
9	512	38,400
10	1,024	76,800
11	2,048	153,600
12	4,096	307,200

Permanent or slowly changing slot assignments are not well matched to the requirements of bursty users, i.e., a high data rate channel required for a short time. The more bursty the traffic on the bus, the less efficient will be the capacity utilization. The effect is to require a much greater transmission rate on the bus. Since each BIU must operate at the total bus rate and the BIU is the most replicated and, consequently, cost sensitive component in MITRIX, this drives up the total bus cost.

The general terminal and computer traffic in business and scientific environments exhibits, however, bursty traffic statistics.

A system combining the features of the Centrally Controlled, Slotted Bus and a slotted contention system has also been developed by the MITRE Corporation. This prototype system is called the Dual-Mode Slotted TDMA Digital Bus. It provides optimized bandwidth utilization for users with high duty cycle and/or synchronous data and low duty cycle asynchronous data. High duty cycle users and/or synchronous users are assigned dedicated slots as in MITRIX. Low duty cycle users are assigned a common set of contention slots, as shown in Figure 2-17.

In the MITRE-developed prototype system shown in Figure 2-18, the transmission rate is 7.373 Mbps and there are 16,384 slots per 0.8533-sec frame. Each slot contains 384 bits: 128 header bits and 256 data bits. The nominal contention slot (also called ALOHA slot based on the packet switched, ALOHA radio network) assignment is every 30-sec slot or 512 slots per frame.

In case of message collision in these contention slots, the retransmission control strategy has been implemented as follows. The repeater (see Figure 2-18) detects empty slots in the contention subbus on the inbound cable. It sends slot detection indication directly to the Network Control Center (NCC). The NCC uses this to determine the fraction of collisions in a window and finds the new retransmission probability by using an algorithm based on number of users having suffered collisions. This is determined by parameters such as probability of a message arrival from a user not

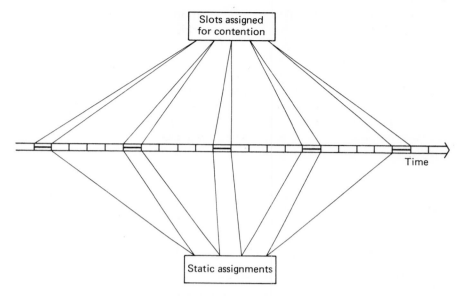

Figure 2-17   Dual mode slotted TDMA slot structure.

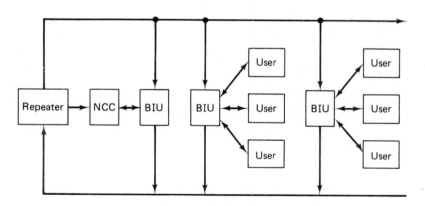

Figure 2-18   Dual mode bus.

currently in the queued state, the probability of retransmission in a slot, the total number of users, slots in a window that are empty, and the duration of a window with a certain number and length of slots.

This retransmission probability is broadcast by NCC to all BIU's, replacing the value from the previous window. When the BIU is in the queued state, it compares the retransmission probability with an internally generated pseudorandom number. If the pseudorandom number is less than the retransmission probability, the BIU broadcasts in the next contention slot. If it is greater than or equal to this probability, it does not attempt to broadcast in the next contention slot. The pseudorandom number is generated by inverting and using the low-order bits of an internal clock.*

2.3.4 Global FDM Bus

Global Frequency Division Multiplexed (FDM) systems typically use a shared coaxial cable where messages are frequency modulated and sent directly from the transmitting mini onto the bus. The modulated carrier is subsequently demodulated by the receiving mini's modem, as shown in Figure 2-19.

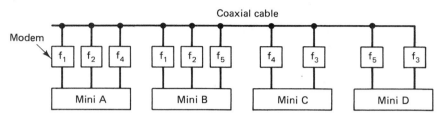

Figure 2-19 Global FDM bus.

The data are transmitted over the cable at discrete radio frequencies (RF's) at a broadband frequency range of 5 to 300 MHz. The RF range is broken into forward and reverse channels. Typically, frequencies below 116 MHz are used for reverse channels and frequencies above 159 MHz for forward channels. Frequencies between 116 and 159 MHz are not used to provide adequate separation of forward and reverse channels. Using a 60-KHz channel width, for example, the forward range of RF's can be divided into 2350 separate channels and the reverse range into 1850 channels.

As shown in Figure 2-19 the forward transmitter of Mini A is tuned to frequency f_1 and the receiving mini's (B) receiver is tuned to the same frequency. This FDM scheme has been implemented by Interactive Systems, Inc., for an in-plant information network.

It is clear that multidropping, using this scheme, is not feasible. Only one channel per mini can communicate with the corresponding channel on another mini and we have, in effect, a bus system analogous to a point-to-point connected multiminicomputer network with all its inherent inflexibilities. In practical applications based on a coaxial cable, a multidrop scheme may be implemented, where several mini's transmitters/receivers are tuned to the same forward and reverse channels. All minis on the coaxial bus are then polled for data, and data are sent to a central controller in a manner previously described. Multidrop, coaxial cable-based systems may also be used based on multiple access techniques.

*Norman B. Meisner, Joshua Segal, and Malcolm Y. Tanigawa, "Dual Mode Slotted TDMA Digital Bus," Fifth Data Communications Symposium, September 1977.

2.3.5 Global TDM Bus

A time division multiplexed (TDM) multiminicomputer bus may be based on either a serial or parallel data bus. The key elements of such a system are the control approach to multiplexing and synchronization and to the line design. The bus control logic in a global bus system is largely distributed through the minis connected to the bus. The decentralization of control increases the reliability (but also complexity) of a bus-based system, since a single failure in a single controlling processor (based on the centralized approach) would disable the entire network of minis.

A synchronous TDM bus is usually characterized by the existence of fixed, equal width time slots that are either generated or synchronized by a central timing mechanism. The bus timing may be generated globally or both locally and globally.

A globally timed bus contains a central oscillator that broadcasts clock signals to all minicomputers attached to the bus. Depending on logical structure and physical layout of the bus, clock skew may become a serious problem. This can be somewhat alleviated by distributing a globally generated frame signal that synchronizes a local clock in each mini. The local clocks may drive counters that are decoded to identify the time slots assigned to each device. A synchronization pulse occurs every time the count cycle (i.e., frame) restarts.

Skew can still exist if a separate frame synchronization (sync) line is used but can be avoided by carrying frame sync with the data. The sync signal then must be separable from data by a coding scheme. If the sync signal is not coded as a special binary sequence, it could be confused with normal data and may require complex decoders.

Time slots may be assigned to the transmitting and receiving minis on either dedicated or nondedicated basis. A mix of both dedicated and nondedicated slots may be used. A bus system with nondedicated time slots will, however, require some form of centralized control. In such a system all requests for time slots on the bus must be received by a bus management program resident in one of the minis on the bus. By examining its tables, this program will determine if an available slot exists and whether or not the requestor may get the slot. Appropriate table entries are updated and a control message is sent to the requesting mini. In fact, file transfers and the assignment of processors to perform required tasks can be handled by similar table driven programs. This approach is analogous to the interrupt driven, central-controller bus system.

The dedicated time slot bus requires, in addition to slot synchronization, slot count to permit each mini to use its preassigned slots and not to interfere with another mini's communication.

Thus usable capacity of the approach above depends on the number of minis to which capacity is allocated, the capacity allocation to each mini, and the required overhead for bus control and monitoring. The capacity required is thus independent of the actual traffic statistics. This differs from the other approaches since capacity is determined strictly by the number of minis and their burst transmission rates.

The response time provided by this approach is determined by the interval between slots assigned to the lowest data-rate mini on the bus.

The relationship between message length, frame size, slot size, number of minis on the bus, and system capacity is clarified by the following numerical example. Let us assume that each of 20 minicomputers on a bus is allocated an equal number of time slots and that each slot contains 256 data bits and 64 overhead bits. Furthermore, let us assume that the average message length (b) is 1000 bits and the arrival rate (a) is two messages per second. Assuming a 0.4-sec frame period, this translates to

$$0.4 \times \bar{b} \times a = 0.4 \times 1000 \times 2 = 800 \text{ bits}$$

This means that the average mini on the bus must transfer 800 bits of data in each frame. A slot is $256 + 64 = 320$ bits long but contains only 256 data bits. So, a total of $800/256 = 3.13$ slots per frame are required to transfer 800 bits. Since the total number of slots in a frame must be an integer power of two, however, the slot assignment becomes 4 slots per frame. For 20 minis, the number of slots per frame must exceed $20 \times 4 = 80$.

These results can be used to determine the response time and system capacity. Assuming slots in assignments are evenly spaced in the frame and, since each mini has 4 slots per frame, the interval between a minicomputer's slots per frame is $0.4/4 = 0.1$ sec. If the message arrivals are uniformly distributed, this gives a mini on the bus a $0.1/2 = 0.05$-sec average access time.

If a shorter time is required, the mini can be given a larger assignment. This results in a tradeoff between access time and bandwidth utilization.

If there is a requirement that the average access time be on the order of 0.01 sec, each mini must have an assignment of 20 slots. Using the same number of minis (20) the new value for the number of slots required to transfer data is 400. The total number of slots per frame would thus be 512.

The system capacity is found by dividing the total number of bits per frame by the frame period. Since there are 80 slots per frame each containing 320 bits, the number of bits per frame is 25,600. With a frame period of 0.4 sec, the capacity is 102.4 Kbps. Recall that only 80% of this can be used for data and that an even smaller fraction is actually used for data transfer.

2.3.6 Global Multiple Access Bus

One of the most well-known experimental, global multiple access bus systems is the Ethernet developed by Xerox Corporation.* The Ethernet consist of some 100 nodes connected to a one-kilometer long coaxial cable. Coordination of access to the bus for data transmission is distributed among the contending transmitting stations using controlled statistical arbitration. Ethernet uses a branching two-way 3-Mbps bus as shown in Figure 2-20. Coaxial bus segments are interconnected via bidirectional transceivers and bus repeaters. A message in the form of a packet is broadcasted onto the bus. The packet heard by all stations on the coaxial bus segments is copied by the

---

*Robert M. Metcalfe and David R. Boggs, "Ethernet: Distributed Packet Switching for Local Computer Networks," *Communications of the ACM*, 19 No. 7, July 1976.

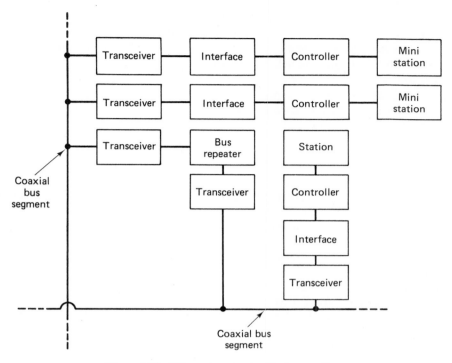

Figure 2-20 Ethernet segment with three stations.

receiving node based on the packet's address. Transmission initiated at a node is deferred by a message transmission that may already be in progress. A transmission is aborted and rescheduled by its source station if interference with other packets is detected. If no interference exists, the packet will run to completion. To avoid repeated collisions, Ethernet controllers in colliding stations each retransmit at random intervals. To keep bus utilization near optimum with changing network load, a packet's retransmission intervals are adjusted as a function of collision history.

Global multiple access bus systems can be either unslotted or slotted. In an unslotted bus, users may transmit at any time, whereas in the latter type of bus users are constrained to transmit in slots or predetermined time intervals. It is apparent that, in a slotted bus, "collisions" will occur only if two or more packets arrive at the receiver during the same slot interval. Since there can be no overlap of packets from adjacent intervals, the capacity of this scheme is exactly twice that of an unslotted multiple access bus. Although a slotted system provides a substantial improvement in allowable throughput over an unslotted system, however, the former is more complex; all transmitting computers must be synchronized to the receiver.

The Ethernet is a slotted bus system where the slot is the maximum time between a node on the bus starting a transmission and detecting a collision, or one end-to-end round-trip delay. An Ethernet controller begins transmission of each new packet with a mean transmission interval of one slot. Each time a transmission attempt ends in collision, the controller delays for an interval of random length with a mean twice that of the previous interval, defers to any passing packet, and then attempts retransmission. Since nodes on the bus defer to passing packets before starting transmission, the slots are synchronized by the tail of preceding acquisition interval. When a slot contains only one attempted transmission, then the bus has been acquired for the duration of a packet, the contention interval ends, and transmission interval begins.

In a slotted contention system

$$A = \left(1 - \frac{1}{Q}\right)^{(Q-1)} \tag{2-30}$$

where A = probability that exactly one station attempts a transmission in a slot and acquires the bus

Q = number of stations queued to transmit a packet

The efficiency of the bus or the fraction of time the bus is carrying good packets is determined as follows.

The time on the Ethernet is divided between transmission intervals and contention intervals. A packet transmission takes P/C seconds where P is the number of bits in an Ethernet packet and C is the peak capacity in bits per second carried on the bus. The mean time to acquisition is $W \cdot T$ where W is the mean number of slots of waiting in a contention interval before a successful acquisition of the bus by a station's transmission and $W = (1 - A)/A$.

The efficiency E of the bus system is thus

$$E = \frac{P/C}{(P/C) + WT} \tag{2-31}$$

where P = bits in a packet

C = bus peak capacity in bits per second

T = slot time or number of seconds it takes to detect a collision after starting a transmission

The efficiency of the Ethernet where $C = 3$ Mbps and $T = 16$ μsec is computed based on 48-bit, 512-bit, 1024-bit, and 4096-bit packets and 1 to 256 nodes in the contention state, as shown in Table 2-3.

Even when transmitting without source-detected interference, a packet on the Ethernet may still not reach its destination without error. The transmitting station has no way of determining whether the message has been received correctly.

Ethernet does not provide a built-in message acknowledgement check scheme such as that available in ring networks. A modification to the Ethernet has therefore been proposed* where a message packet is used to notify the transmitting station that

---

*Mario Tohoro and Kiichiro Tamura, "Acknowledging Ethernet," *Fall CompCon*, September 1977.

Table 2-3 Ethernet efficiency (From "Ethernet: Distributed Packet Switching for Local Networks," Robert M. Metcalfe and David R. Boggs, *Communications of the ACM*, Vol. 19, No. 7, July 1976.)

P Q	4096	1024	512	48
1	1.0000	1.0000	1.0000	1.0000
2	0.9884	0.9552	0.9143	0.5000
3	0.9857	0.9447	0.8951	0.4444
4	0.9842	0.9396	0.8862	0.4219
5	0.9834	0.9367	0.8810	0.4096
10	0.9818	0.9310	0.8709	0.3874
32	0.9807	0.9272	0.8642	0.3737
64	0.9805	0.9263	0.8627	0.3708
128	0.9804	0.9259	0.8620	0.3693
256	0.9803	0.9257	0.8616	0.3686

a message has been acknowledged. Three alternate methods to packet acknowledgement have been explored;

1. Provide a cable for acknowledgement in addition to the cable used for data transmission.
2. Transmit data and acknowledge packet using the same cable but at different frequencies by frequency domain multiplexing.
3. Give priority to an acknowledged packet transmission rather than a data packet transmission.

Methods 1 and 2 require two sets of transmitters and receivers. This causes an increase in cost and a decrease in reliability. Besides, method 1 doubles the cost of cables and method 2 causes substantial reduction in transmission capacity. The third approach is therefore the most attractive. This latter scheme has been proposed by members of the engineering faculty of Keio University in Japan and has been called "Acknowledging Ethernet."

2.3.7 Shared Bus Reliability

The reliability of a shared bus is a function of the number of shared components between minis or micros attached to the bus. The most reliable shared bus systems, from a total systems point of view, are based on passive, fully distributed buses where no repeaters are used to amplify the signals on the bus. This does, of course, limit the physical length of the bus and the number of minis that may be attached to the bus. Systems where each node acts as a bus repeater are obviously less reliable than systems using bus repeaters. The reliability is reduced further depending on the width of a bus. A single, coaxial bus is more reliable than a bus using two or more twisted-wire pairs.

Equally important is the way in which minis are coupled to the bus. A failed direct-current (DC) coupling may result in all signals on the bus being attenuated to a point where the signals (bit pulses) can no longer be distinguished from noise. The bus coupling for MIL-STD-1553A is, therefore, based on the use of transformers to DC-isolate all devices connected to the bus (see Chapter 4). The use of a fully distributed global bus increases the complexity of each node thereby reducing its reliability (and increasing its cost).

A centrally controlled bus provides a compromise solution, where the bus-arbitration logic is contained in the bus controller. The most reliable of the centrally controlled bus systems is based on polling. This approach is, however, also the least efficient in terms of bandwidth utilization, when the traffic is bursty.

The least reliable of the centrally controlled approaches is the slotted bus, which requires two buses as well as bus repeaters. It is, however, also the most efficient in terms of bandwidth utilization for bursty traffic.

Most of the previously described systems are either experimental or custom built for specific applications, using serial buses. The largest number of multiminicomputer, shared bus systems in commercial and industrial use are, however, based on parallel bus technology (i.e., Minicomputer Manufacturers' off-the-shelf buses such as the Data General MCA and systems based on the CAMAC and IEEE-488 bus standards). Detailed hardware descriptions of these buses as well as other off-the-shelf systems are provided in Chapter 4.

2.4 LOOP TECHNOLOGY

A loop multiminicomputer system consists of a high-speed, unidirectional, digital communication channel (e.g., twisted-wire pair or a fiber optics link) which is arranged as a closed loop or ring. Nodes such as mini-or microcomputers, terminals, or peripherals can be attached to the loop channel by a hardware device known as a *loop* or *ring interface.*

To send a message from one node to any other, the message is entered on the ring. It will then travel around the ring until it either reaches the node addressed or returns to the transmitting node. In some systems, the originating node removes the message, whereas in others the destination node removes it. In the former case, the originating node can compare the original, transmitted message with the same message when it returns, having circulated around the loop, thereby also performing an error check on it. A bit is usually set in a predetermined bit position in the message by the destination node, to signal the transmitting node of message receipt. In the latter case, the destination node usually performs the error checking on the message. This approach obviously also reduces the traffic load on the loop.

A loop configuration is very attractive in a multimicro- or minicomputer system for the following reasons:

1. The problem of message routing in the system disappears, since there is only one path for the message to follow in reaching its destination. A transmitter

need not know the location of its receiver. Also, broadcast message transmission is very easy to achieve since every node can pick up the message.

2. Connections can be established very quickly and easily, which is of importance for traffic with short message duration. Several multimicro- and minicomputer systems are based on data traffic of intermittent inquiry-response nature and messages are generally quite short. This is true in credit-card verification, electronic fund transfer, goods ordering, and information retrieval applications.

3. Data transmission is usually digital, eliminating the need for modems and thus data conversion.

4. There is a low initial capital investment in loop configurations with the cost proportional to the number of users or interfaces.

5. A loop configuration provides a very high throughput because (a) the nodal loop interfaces and not the processors are used to relay the messages and (b) more than one message can be in transit at a time.

6. Loops provide for easy implementation of distributed switching mechanisms without the need for any sophisticated common control because each loop interface can provide its own bus arbitration and synchronization.

The major disadvantage of a loop is reliability. It is very vulnerable to failures of the interfaces because of its serial organization.

In a loop system, message transmission takes place in the form of addressed blocks of data called *frames* or *slots*. The local loop interface forms a frame, giving the address of the destination interface, and transmits the frame onto the loop. Each loop interface downstream of the transmitter receives this frame, checks it destination address, and immediately retransmits it back onto the loop if the proper destination for the frame has not been reached. When a receiving loop interface recognizes its own address as the destination of an incoming frame, it removes the frame from the loop and delivers the message to the local attached minicomputer. The general organization of a loop is shown in Figure 2-21.

Digital transmission on the ring is time division multiplexed. The channel capacity of the ring is multiplexed into a series of time slots. Loop technology will be presented in the following three sections. The first section presents an overview of three major loop types. Several examples are given of each type. The second section discusses performance properties of the various loop types. Finally, the third section discusses various techniques to improve reliability of loops.

2.4.1 Types of Loops

Loop technology categorization is based on type of message-transmission mechanism employed. Three main types will be considered: the Newhall-type, Pierce-type, and Delay Insertion type. In Newhall-type loops, a control token or character is passed around the loop in a round-robin fashion, from loop interface to loop interface. Only the interface currently in possession of a token is allowed to transmit messages of

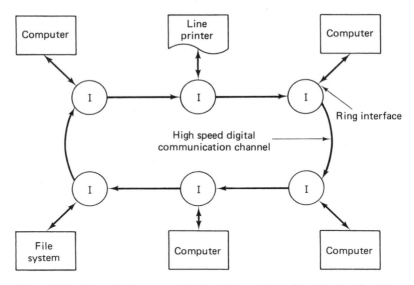

Figure 2-21   General loop organization (From: "Interface Design for Distributed Control Loop Networks," Young Oh and Ming T. Liu, National Telemetering Conference, Los Angeles, 1977).

arbitrary length onto the loop; the other interfaces are allowed only to receive during this time (see Figure 2-22).

When a transmission is completed, the control token is passed to the next node downstream, thus allowing the node to transmit. Based on this scheme, an interface will never experience interference during the transmission of a message, since only one transmitter can be active at any one time. When an interface is ready to transmit a message, however, it must always wait for the control token to be passed to it, even if the portion of the loop channel it needs is free and unused by the current transmitter. A Newhall loop therefore does not allow concurrent use of the loop channel by two or more transmitter interfaces even though they could possibly use distinct nonoverlapping portions of the loop. However, a Newhall loop does provide for variable length message transmission.

There are in fact two possible schemes for passing control in a Newhall loop. The first scheme is based on messages in the queue of the selected interface being transmitted onto the loop before the token is passed. The second scheme allows control to be passed only after a message has been output on the loop, regardless of whether other messages are ready in the queue. Use of the first scheme results in longer mean and maximum queue lengths but shorter total message transmission times.

The first Newhall-type loop was constructed by Farmer and Newhall in 1969. The prime example of a Newhall loop is the Distributed Computer System (DCS) loop constructed by David Farber at the University of California, Irvine, in 1972. It is shown in Figure 2-22 and consists of three Lockheed SUE and two Varian 620/i minicomputers connected to a data ring, operating at a 2.3-Mbps data rate.

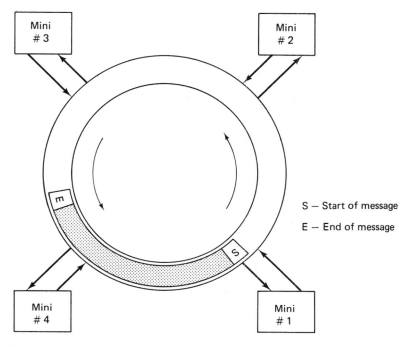

Figure 2-22 Message flow in the loop (From: "A Loop Network for Simultaneous Transmission of Variable-Length Messages," Cecil C. Reames and Ming T. Liu, Second Annual Symposium on Computer Architecture, January 1975).

The key to successful loop operation lies in the design of the loop or ring interface (RI). The original RI on the DCS system consisted of 140 integrated circuit chips. This made for a very expensive interface. The ring interface has subsequently been rebuilt utilizing two custom LSI chips, a power supply, and several line drivers.

On the DCS system messages are addressed to processes rather than locations. Information is included in the logical message format passed by a node computer to its interface. The logical message consists of the data fields used by a process to send a message. Each ring interface has a list of process name specifications stored in an associative memory. These names represent the processes in the attached host. (An associative memory, in addition to being a storage device, has the attributes that the memory words are addressable by content and the memory has a parallel-search capability.) When the ring interface is instructed by the attached host to transmit a message, the RI will add a connector field before the logical message, to ensure synchronization to the start of the message. Match and Accept bits are added after the message data field and both bits are initialized to zero. As the message passes each RI on the ring, the RI compares the message address against a table of process names. If a name matches, the RI will copy the message. The receiving RI sets a ONE into the Accept bit if successfully copied or sets a ONE in the Match bit if the copy fails. The

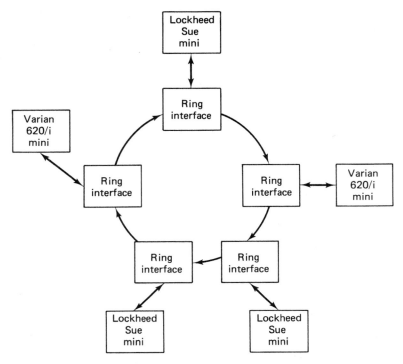

Figure 2-23 UC Irvine DCS loop (From: "The System Architecture of the Distributed Computer System—The Communications System," David J. Farber and Kenneth C. Larson, Symposium on Computer-Communications Networks and Teletraffic, Polytechnic Institute of Brooklyn, April 4-6, 1972).

copy may fail because the attached host has not activated the RI for input or there are errors in the data. The transmitting RI will record the setting of these bits in the returning message. The four possible outcomes are shown in Table 2-4.

The two synchronization patterns used are the Connector and Token patterns. The Token is continuously circulated around the ring when the ring is idle. When an RI wishes to transmit, it waits for the Token to arrive. As the Token passes the RI that wishes to transmit, the RI changes the Token into a Connector. Following the Connector the rest of the message is output with a Token at the end.

If two adjacent RI's transmit, a message train of two packaged messages followed by a Token will pass out of the second RI, as shown in Figure 2-24.

When a ring interface outputs a message, it remembers to delete it as it returns around the ring. Input/Output First-In First-Out (FIFO) buffers are used to buffer the data. They would normally be connected by a Direct Memory Access (DMA) channel to the host. Buffers allow more efficient connection of slow speed devices, such as terminals, to the ring interface.

In the Pierce-type loop, communication space on the loop is divided into an

Table 2-4 Match and accept bits in DCS

Match Bit	Accept Bit	Meaning
0	0	The message was addressed to a process that does not exist; no RI recognized the message.
0	1	The message was successfully transmitted to one or more processes; at least one RI recognized and copied the message.
1	0	No process received the message; however, at least one RI recognized the address in the message.
1	1	The message was addressed to processes in at least two hosts (a special mask field allows this). At least one RI was able to copy the message, and at least one RI was unable to copy the message.

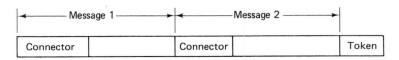

Message train

Figure 2-24 Message train format on DCS (From: "On The Design of Local Network Interfaces," Paul V. Mockapetris, Michael R. Lyle, and David J. Farber, IFIP Congress Proceedings, B. Gilchrist, editor, IFIP, North Holland Publishing Company, 1977).

integer number of fixed-size slots into which message packets can be stored (see Figure 2-25). It might be thought of as a circular track, with box cars end to end, where some may be full and others are empty. The control of a Pierce-type loop is centralized.

Each slot contains a bit that indicates whether it is filled (with a packet) or empty. Thus, all a transmitter needs to do is to divide each message into packets, to wait for empty slots to pass by, and when this occurs, to fill them with packets.

Since slots are of fixed size, user messages are blocked into fixed-size packets, prior to being multiplexed onto the line. It is possible to utilize various multiplexing techniques such as Demand Multiplexing (DM) or Synchronous Time Division Multiplexing (STDM). In STDM each device is assigned a packet slot that recurs periodically, depending on the speed of the ring channel. Addressing information is not needed. When DM is used, packets are multiplexed on the line asynchronously, into unoccupied packet slots. Several simulation studies have shown that DM is clearly

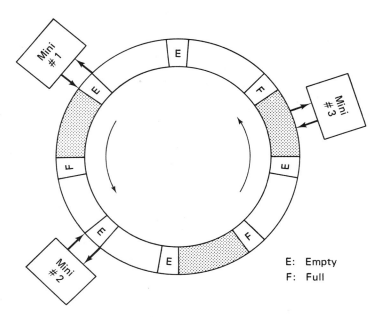

Figure 2-25 Pierce-type loop (From: "Interface Design for Distributed Control Loop Networks," Young Oh and Ming T. Liu, National Telemetering Conference, Los Angeles, 1977).

superior to STDM.* This superiority is more pronounced for light loading, where multiplexing time is the largest contributor to delay. Pierce-type loop networks using Demand Multiplexing are the most common. The first loop of this type was constructed by J. R. Pierce at the Bell Laboratories in 1971 utilizing two Honeywell DDP-516 minicomputers and the Bell Systems T1 carrier system. (T1 is a 1.544-Mbps carrier link.)

This early design scheme used a control machine called "A" Station that served to close the loop, selectively repeating message transmissions around the loop and providing clocking and synchronizing information for all messages on the loop. Other interfaces, called "B" Stations, utilized the clock and synchronizing information provided by the A Station to write fixed-length message blocks onto and read message blocks from the transmission loop. There were many B-type boxes but only one A-type box. Two general message types were provided: Private and Common. The Common message was used to broadcast the same message to a number of stations on the loop. The A Station disposed of undeliverable messages resulting from messages being addressed to busy or nonexistent stations.

*Lynn, P. West, "Loop-Transmission Control Structures," IEEE Transactions on Communications, June 1972; and J. F. Hayes, "Modeling an Experimental Computer Communication Network," Datacom 73, Third Data Communications Symposium, Nov. 1973.

An example of the Pierce-type loop is a system constructed by the Acoustics Research Department in Bell Labs. It consists of four Honeywell DDP-516 minis and a signal processor (CSP-30) from Computer Signal Processors, Inc. As shown in Figure 2-26, the loop contains one A Control Station and five B Stations. Data are entered into and taken from the system in fixed-size blocks of 26 words. Each data block starts with a unique synchronization word and a three-word header that contains source and destination addresses as well as control information (e.g., status of the message block such as whether the block is vacant or full).

The B Stations provide access ports to the data loop system. The Interface (I)

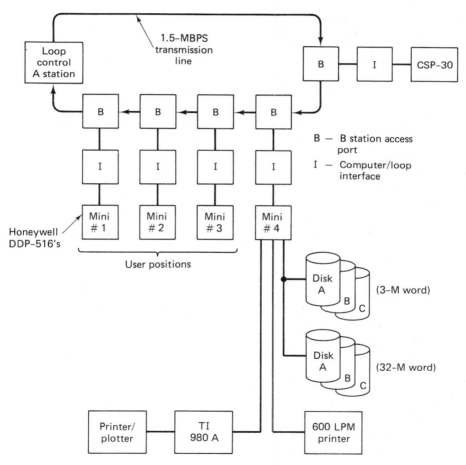

Figure 2-26 The Bell Laboratories Acoustic Research Department Pierce-type loop system.

to the user machines (those providing speech processing algorithms and data) provide the following features:

1. Automatic segmentation of a single message (data transmission) into blocks of data, headed by a destination address and control information.
2. Automatic reformatting of a message from a number of loop blocks, removing address and control information.
3. The options of receiving through more than one data channel, automatic error checking, and time-out on nonreceipt of a message.

Another Pierce-type loop system is Spidernet implemented by Fraser at Bell Laboratories. Spidernet is an experimental packet-switched data communications system that multiplexes 64 full-duplex channels, each with a maximum data rate of 500 Kbps, onto a single T1-line-type loop. The minicomputers and a central switching computer (GTE TEMPO 1) are on the loop. All messages are first routed to the switching computer and then redirected to the appropriate destination processor based on a data table in the Tempo computer.

The third loop category is the Delay Insertion-type. Various performance studies have shown that its overall performance is superior to those of the previously described two loop types. This technique was simultaneously developed by E. R. Hafner for telephone switching purposes and by researchers at Ohio State University for the Distributed Loop Computer Network (DLCN) system. The major difference between the two is that variable rather than fixed messages are used in the DLCN scheme. The general operation of Delay Insertion-type loops is described utilizing the loop communication system developed by Hafner. Hafner refers to this scheme as "loop extension strategy." Each ring interface has a complete set of control capabilities. The diagram shown in Figure 2-27 illustrates the basic principle of ring interface operation.

The Receiving Shift Register (RSR) is permanently connected to the incoming line and performs both receiving and removing messages from the loop. There is a second shift register (TSR) for transmitting, i.e., preparing message blocks for insertion in the loop from the node processor. Sending and receiving are controlled by a three-position switch (SW) that connects the output of the TSR, the RSR, or the incoming loop line to the outgoing loop line.

The sequence of events is as follows: When a message is to be transmitted, the switch, initially in Position 1, opens the loop for a well-defined time interval. Since the flow of incoming message blocks cannot be interrupted without loss of information, bits arriving in the RSR are temporarily buffered. Immediately after a message inserted by the node has left the TSR (which must have a buffer of equal length as the RSR), the switch goes to Position 3 and the output is "delayed" by one message length (see Figure 2-27). The interface has not been interconnected to the loop, which is active as opposed to passive, if the switch were to remain in Position 1.

The process of transmitting a block can be initiated only from the passive state. A second message cannot be transmitted until the interface has been switched into a

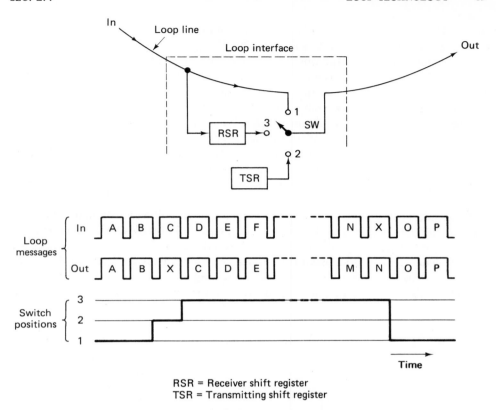

RSR = Receiver shift register
TSR = Transmitting shift register

Figure 2-27 Loop interface operation for the distributed loop computer network (DLCN) (From: "A Digital Loop Communication System," E. R. Mafner, Z. Nenadal and M. Tschanz, IEEE Transactions on Communications, June 1974).

passive state (i.e., the node has been disconnected from the loop). This is accomplished by changing the switch position from 3 to 1, which prevents the block in the RSR from circulating in the loop. Each node on the loop removes its own messages that have circled the loop. (Message X in Figure 2-27 is removed before the switch is returned from Position 3 to Position 1.)

A central monitoring station is used in this loop system that checks for blocks with bad addresses and provides clocking and synchronization for the entire loop.

An example of a system organized in the form of a ring that uses the equivalent of the Delay-Insertion-Message-Transmission-Scheme is the modification by Case Western Reserve University to the serial CAMAC system. CAMAC is a line-sharing system first proposed by the European standards organization for nuclear instrumentation. As originally specified, the CAMAC system was a parallel bus consisting of 86 lines running from instrument to instrument and to a computer. The serial version, which is more common today, consists of as many as 62 data acquisition devices called "Crates" connected via a closed loop communication data highway, as shown in Figure 2-28 (see also Chapter 1 and Section 4.3).

Transmission around the ring is performed in groups of 8 bits or bytes. The ring transmits 8 bits synchronously and messages (a sequence of bytes) asynchronously. The line acts as a shift register in that each Crate controller receives bytes at its input terminals and returns bytes from it output terminals.

Serial CAMAC line-sharing messages circulate unidirectionally around the ring-like communication line to and from the computer and the Crates. Case Western Reserve University has added the ability to interface microprocessors to the CAMAC system, in addition to Crates, to support a distributed microcomputer data acquisition system. The overall structure of the distributed CAMAC system is shown in Figure 2-29.

The microcomputers, as well as the minicomputer, will issue command messages that include both source and destination addresses. A 12-bit Toshiba microcomputer was used in the prototype for the CAMAC serial bus controller. The messages are variable length. Each node examines a message as it passes through, to determine whether or not it is addressed to that node. Messages are separated by one or more null bytes. A message can only be inserted on the ring by a node between other

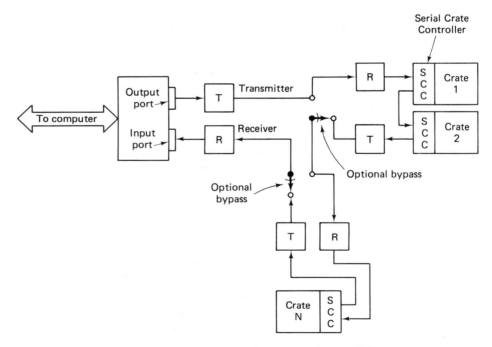

Figure 2-28 Serial version of the CAMAC system (From: "Microcomputers for Data Acquisition," C. W. Rose and J. D. Schoeffler, Instrumentation Technology, Sept. 1974).

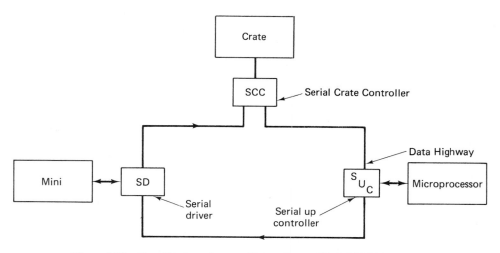

Figure 2-29   Case Western Reserve University modified CAMAC system.

messages, which means that a node could replace a sequence of null bytes by a message or, alternatively, increase the length of the ring by switching in a buffer containing the message. In the former case, the node would have to delay many bytes in order to determine that the sequence of null bytes was long enough to be replaced by the designated message. This is undesirable, so the second solution was adopted. The message is placed in a buffer, and the buffer switches into the ring after a null byte passes through the node. As a new message shifts out of the buffer and into the ring, the following message shifts into the buffer and then out on the ring (see also Figure 2-27). This process of inserting a message into a ring is typical of the delay-insertion technique.

In order for a node to transmit a second message, it must recover the buffer. For example, anytime the buffer is filled with null characters, it may be switched out and the ring returned to its original length. This type of message transmission tends to even out the utilization of the line by different computers and devices since when a device or processor inserts its message into the ring, its message buffer is switched into the ring and it is unable to insert another message until it recovers the buffer. If the ring is heavily utilized, the probability of a long sequence of null bytes is low and hence other devices and processors are given an opportunity to insert their messages. On the other hand, the delay introduced by forcing a computer to wait until it recovers its full buffer could be intolerable.

A modified strategy has therefore been introduced called the Shrinking Buffer Policy. Based on this approach, the buffer is allowed to shrink one byte at a time. Whenever two null bytes in succession are detected, one null byte is removed from the buffer. Thus, a buffer with 15 characters can be retrieved by detecting a number of null character sequences rather than one null sequence of length 15. Research at Case Western Reserve has been focused on using the Intel 3000 microprocessors arranged in a pipeline fashion to implement a bus controller with 24-bit wide read/write data paths.

The bus controller will handle the address decoding, function decoding, and data removal from or placement onto the CAMAC bus.

2.4.2 Loop Performance

Several research groups have performed analyses of multimini/microcomputer distributed loop systems. One such group at Ohio State University has addressed the relative performance difference among the Newhall loop, the Pierce loop, and the Delay Insertion technique on the Distributed Loop Computer Network (DLCN). Simulation models have been used in this performance study. The general model consisted of six nodes. Messages produced at each node were uniformly addressed among the other five nodes, message traffic was entirely symmetric, and random message data lengths were based on an exponential Poisson distribution with a mean of 50 characters. Simulation and analytical studies have shown that the optimum packet size in a Pierce loop is 36 characters for the type of traffic above. The results of the simulation study showed that for low channel utilization the performance of the Newhall loop closely approaches that of the DLCN delay insertion loop.* As the traffic level increases, however, the comparative attractiveness of the Newhall loop soon diminishes. If all message queues are empty, the control token in the Newhall loop (assuming no propagation delay on the communication channel itself, and 2 units of delay for each interface) will circulate around the loop once every 12 time units. When the traffic load increases, the control token is increasingly delayed and takes longer to make a complete circuit. Even if only one transmitter interfacing the loop is active at all times, the mean line utilization can only be about 50%. (On the average, messages travel only halfway around the loop before being received.)

At low levels of line utilization the Pierce loop approach is less attractive than either the Delay Insertion (DLCN) loop or the Newhall loop. The reason for this is that a message always has a mean wait time of half a packet interval (one-half of 36 characters is 18 character time units) and must then be transmitted in several packets, with a mean of 2.36 packets per message. These results agree with the results of various analytical studies on loops. At higher traffic levels the performance of the Pierce loop is better than that of the Newhall loop since the packet mechanism allows for two or more concurrently active transmitters. A Delay Insertion Loop is more efficient than either of the other two types since it does not require a message to be divided into packets and does not have to wait for a control token or an empty packet to arrive.

The Pierce loop exhibits optimal performance characteristics if the message is the same size as the packet. This does not generally occur in a realistic multiminicomputer system environment.

For Pierce and Newhall loops, the average transmission time on a loop is inde-

---

*H. Jafari, J. Spragnis, and T. Lewis, "A New Modular Loop Architecture for Distributed Computer Systems," *Trends and Applications*: *1978 Distributed Processing*, IEEE Symposium, National Bureau of Standards, Gaithersburg, Md., May 18, 1978.

pendent of traffic load. In the delay insertion loop, the mean transmission time increases significantly with higher traffic loads. The Delay Insertion message transmission technique is superior where queuing delays for messages entering the loop are short.

Pierce-type loops have a natural priority structure that has a heavy influence on the performance, as seen by the various sources. There may be a large variance between average delays experienced by different ring interfaces, depending on the traffic rates and patterns. For example, let 1, 2, 3, . . . be the order of ring interfaces on the loop corresponding to the direction of bit flow, and assume that RI 1 has a high input rate, as shown in Figure 2-30. In this case RI 1 will capture many of the empty slots, resulting in a high ring utilization as seen by RI 2 and consequently a high average delay. The "ring domination" problem can be resolved by priority protocol controls resulting in a lower maximum throughput.

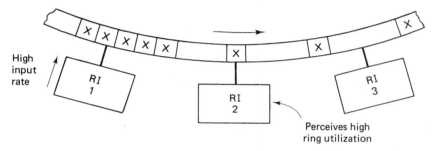

Figure 2-30   Illustration of Pierce-type loop "ring domination" problem.

2.4.3 Loop Reliability

The major drawback of a loop configuration is its vulnerability to errors and lack of fault tolerance due to single-point failures. Transmission errors can affect the proper functioning of loop organization in the following way: A distortion of the receiver address will either result in a packet being delivered to the wrong destination or, if a mutilated address is not being "handled" by the system, a "lost packet" will keep circulating around the loop. Several message-transmission schemes for loop-based systems use a central monitor to check the loop and remove packets that have circled the loop more than once without being received by any of the nodes. Schemes exist where each interface acts as a loop monitor.

Loop interface failures can cause either a loss of access to the loop or a breakdown in loop operation because of the serial nature of a loop. Farmer and Newhall have shown that a loop interface can be constructed as two electrically independent devices: a very simple primary section that is line-powered and transformer-coupled to the interface and a locally powered secondary device. The secondary device contains a relay circuit, which, in case of failure, short-circuits the device and allows the primary device to continue functioning thereby maintaining loop operation. A total bypass of the entire interface can also be provided, allowing the secondary device to be switched out of the loop for repairs. In the DCS loop system, the number of components in the ring interface forwarding section have been minimized to improve the reliability of the loop. If the ring interface loses power, a relay will automatically disconnect the secondary device from the ring interface.

As additional protection, opto-isolators may be used to decouple the ring interface from the ring. Bailey Meter offers a multiplexing system called the C-link that communicates serial data over a 1.544-Mbps shielded, twisted-pair cable. All data are transmitted in a ring structure. The interface between the communication ring and the module assemblies provides electrical isolation such that an electrical failure inside a module does not propagate along the link.

The reliability of loop networks can be increased by providing a standby loop that parallels the main loop. There are two ways in which a standby loop can be used in multiminicomputer system design. The first approach is based on the Bypass technique and is shown in Figure 2-31.

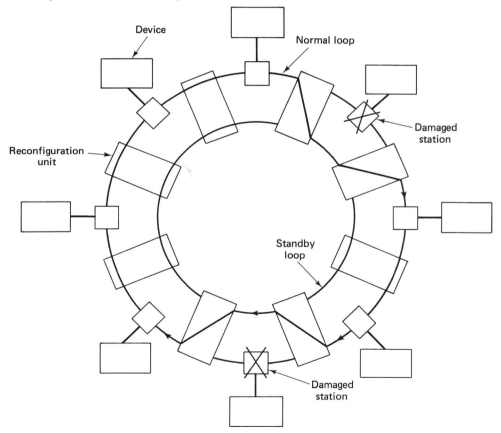

Figure 2-31 Bypass technique for loop systems (From: "An Addressable Ring Conveyor," Kenneth Dean Holberger, Department of Computer Science, University of Illinois at Urbana-Champaign, Urbana, Ill., January 1976).

In loops using the Bypass technique, traffic can be routed around any number of malfunctioning interfaces, thereby maintaining the connectivity of the loop. The major shortcoming of this technique is the effect of a failure on a reconfiguration unit.

The second technique is based on the isolation or Self-Heal connection, as shown in Figure 2-32.

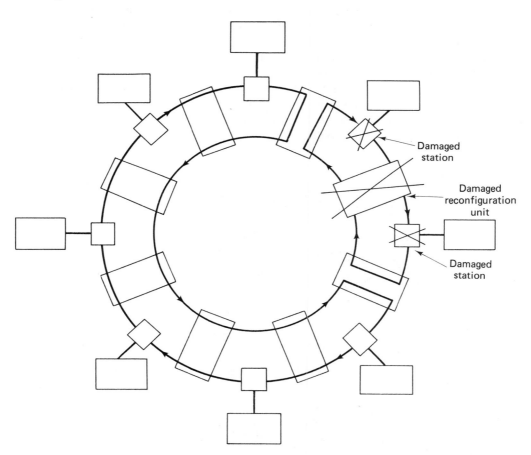

Figure 2-32 Self-heal technique for loop systems (From: "An Addressable Ring Conveyor," Kenneth Dean Holberger, Department of Computer Science, University of Illinois at Urbana-Champaign, Urbana, Ill., January 1976).

It is based on a bidirectional, double-loop structure. By using the Self-Heal technique, complete connectivity can be maintained when any number of adjacent terminals or reconfiguration units fail. When two nonadjacent nodes or reconfiguration units fail, the sections of the loop on either side of the failure are isolated. The Self-Heal method is highly reliable where a limited number of devices are attached to the loop.

Cutler-Hammer* has introduced a multiplex system called Directrol, which uses a cable containing a pair of twisted wires to transmit serial digital data at up to 190 Kbits per second. Reconfiguration is possible with this system using two redundant communication loops, as shown in Figure 2-33.

Should there be a break in both lines, the system will be reconfigured using the Self-Heal technique. Cutler-Hammer has incorporated a microprocessor in the communications station to aid in fault detection. Another technique for achieving reliability in a loop system is to use hierarchical multiloop systems. An example of a two-stage network is the Collins C-System† shown in Figure 2-34; a three-stage net as proposed by Pierce is shown in Figure 2-35.

The two-stage loop consists of first-level loops to which devices are attached. The first-level loops themselves are connected to a single second-level loop. In the three-stage loop proposed by Pierce,‡ the loops are connected by special interfaces called C boxes that transfer blocks from one loop to another. These C boxes also super-

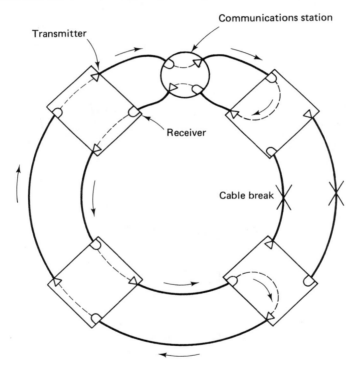

Figure 2-33 System reconfiguration after cable break in Directrol system (Cutler Hammer, Inc.).

---

*Directrol Multiplexer, Cutler Hammer, Inc. Logic Device & Systems Division, Milwaukee, Wis. 53201.

†C-System Basic Description, CPN 523-0699448-73J, Collins Radio Company, Dec. 1972.

‡J. R. Pierce, "Network for Block Switching of Data," *Bell System Tech. J.*, July/August 1972.

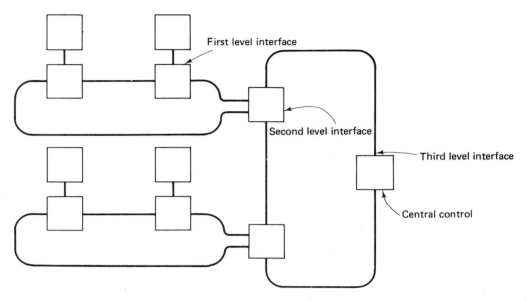

Figure 2-34   Two-stage network (Collins C-System).

vise the routing of messages through a maze of loops to their ultimate destination.

It has been shown analytically by Zafiropulo of IBM that substantial improvements in reliability can be achieved by modifying a simple loop network into an optimum two-stage network. In general, the reliability improvement obtained by increasing the number of stages beyond three does not warrant the added network complexity or cost.

Hafner* has developed a new loop configuration called a Braid that provides a substantial increase in loop availability compared to a double loop, without increase in cost or complexity. In Figure 2-36, (a) shows a double loop; (b) and (c) show braided structures.

In all these structures, the outer circular path is the main path containing the device access points, the inner paths, and bypasses that can be used for bridging the main path between two interface switches. The double loop and the braids are based on identical switch configurations, i.e., two inputs and two outputs, independent of the number of parallel paths. The complexity of the switch is therefore the same as it selects one of the two inputs—according to priority—and connects it to both outputs. The main advantage of the Braided Loop lies in the fact that a switching point, including its four connections, may be destroyed or removed without causing system breakdown. Multiple-switch failures will disrupt the loop shown in Figure 2-36(c) only if three neighboring switches fail.

*E. Hafner, "Enhancing the Availability of a Loop System by Meshing," 1976 International Zurich Seminar on Digital Communications.

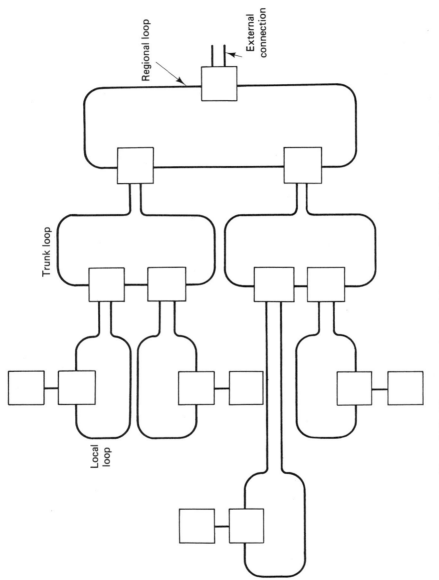

Figure 2-35 Three-stage net proposal by Pierce (From: "Reliability Optimization in Multiloop Communication Networks," Pitro Zafiropulo, IEEE Transactions on Communications, Vol. COM-21, No. 8, August 1973).

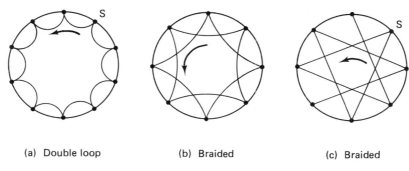

(a) Double loop   (b) Braided   (c) Braided

Figure 2-36   Loop structures.

It has been estimated that the simple forms of a Braid has 50% higher line requirement than a double loop, but the line cost of a single loop is only a fraction of the cost of electronics.

The loop techniques above are compared in Table 2-5.

Table 2-5   Comparison of loop techniques

Loop-type Characteristics	Electrical Isolation in Ring	Standby Loop		Two-stage	Three-stage	
		Bypass	Self-heal	Loop	Loop	Braid
Degree of reliability	Low	Medium	High	High	High	High
Cost	Low	Medium	Medium	High	High	Medium
Implementation complexity	Low	Medium	Medium	High	High	Medium

2.5 STAR TECHNOLOGY

In a multiminicomputer system based on a star configuration, one minicomputer forms the center, acting as the system control (master), with separate lines to all other minicomputers (slaves), as shown in Figure 2-37. Typically, when Minicomputer A wants to send a message to Minicomputer B, a Request to Send (RTS) message is sent to the Switch S (or the master), which, in turn, will establish a path to B upon receiving a Ready to Receive (RTR) message from B. If Minicomputer C wants to send a message to B while transmission is in progress between A and B, C must wait until the S to B link becomes available. However, typically, C can transmit a message to D while the A to B transmission is in progress.

Many star technology-based systems operate in a mode quite similar to a two-level hierarchical system, where the central switch may serve a dual function, both as

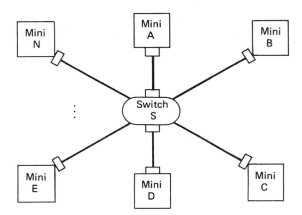

Figure 2-37   Typical star-technology-based multiminicomputer system.

a message switch and as a general-purpose data processing facility.* (Obviously, star configurations can be expanded into hierarchies, where one slave minicomputer can be a master minicomputer for a different star.)

An example of a star configuration is the Network-Oriented Data Acquisition System (NODAS) designed for a medical, multilaboratory environment at the University of Texas Health Science Center. This system is utilizing a large DECsystem-10 time-sharing system as its master and small no peripheral PDP-11 processors as satellites. To the DECsystem-10 host, the remote slaves appear to be nothing more than intelligent interactive terminals. Thus, as many slave processors can be supported as regular DECsystem-10 terminals. The interface between the remotes and the central host is over a "hard-wired" 20-mA current loop-serial, asynchronous line operating at 9600 bits per second. The normal distance from remote processor to host is from 700 to 1000 ft. Programs for the satellite minis or micros are developed in the host in a normal time-sharing manner, and load modules are also treated on the central host and sent down-line to be loaded into the remote satellite.

The more common approach is, however, to limit the functions of the central element to message switching and diagnostic operations.

A star configuration is, in some respects, similar to an interrupt driven, centrally controlled bus system. In either approach, the distributed minis send messages via the central controller that performs command queuing of prioritized messages. The bandwidth requirements are, however, less stringent since simultaneous transmissions can be supported by the system. Furthermore, reliability problems are also less severe since a bus failure between any of the minis and the switch will only disable the mini connected to the failed link.

The central switch function is more complex in a star configuration than in a

*Shelley I. Saffer, David J. Mishelevich, Shirley J. Fox, and Victor B. Summerour, "NODAS—The network-oriented data acquisition system for the medical environment," Proceedings, National Computer Conference, 1977.

bus-based system since the controller has to control a larger number of message paths concurrently.

At least one star configuration is available as an off-shelf multiminicomputer system. This system, called the Digital Data Distribution Network, has been developed by Data General and is described in more detail in Chapter 4.

The capacity required in a central switch depends on the processing time required per message and the message rate throughput. The processing time per message is, to some degree, dependent on the number of minicomputers in the system and upon the message length. The time required for the central switch to process a single message is designated as t_s. Hence, t_s is the time required to transfer a message from input buffer to output buffer. Assuming a message switching computer is used that has an average instruction cycle of 2 μsec (which is a conservative estimate) and 100 instructions have to be processed for each message (which is also a conservative number), $t_s = 200$ μsec.

The total throughput time is the sum of three elements:

- Input buffering time while the message awaits processing
- Processing time t_s
- Output buffering time

Queuing time in the input buffer is typically on the order of milliseconds. Output buffering time is equal to the time required for a multiplexer to cycle to the appropriate receive address and output the message. For a multiplexer operating at typical computer channel rates, this time is usually much less than a second for 1000-bit messages.

2.6 HIERARCHICAL CONFIGURATION TECHNOLOGY

A hierarchical configuration, as its name implies, consists of a tree structure of minis. In general, the capability of the processor increases as the top of the pyramid is reached. This is often, due to practical rather than theoretical reasons. Similar to a corporate organizational structure, the capabilitites at the base are generally applications-dependent, with a special-purpose capability, dedicated to performing well-defined, specialized tasks, whereas the top of the organization has a more general-purpose capability, controlling and coordinating the entire system. In a hierarchical system, the processors at the base of the pyramid are often microprocessors or small minicomputers with a limited number of peripherals, whereas the top of the pyramid may contain a midicomputer or even a large central processor with minicomputer front-end processors. In such a system, processing functions are usually distributed, as shown in Figure 2-38. The tedious repetitive functions and algorithms, such as data collection and reduction, are handled at the lowest levels, whereas data processing, command execution (control), and summary processing are performed at the top. Typically, shared data bases are also stored at the top rather than distributed throughout the system.

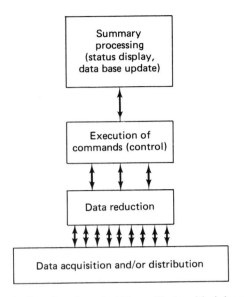

Figure 2-38 Task allocations in typical hierarchical multiminicomputer system.

Information is passed vertically between the various levels in the hierarchy. This information may consist of programs, data, or commands, or a combination of the above.

A typical hierarchical multiminicomputer system is shown in Figure 2-39. This system consists of three levels: Level 0 may be a microprocessor or hardwired unit connected to transducers that convert analog voltage temperature, pressure, fluid flow, wind velocity, contact closure indications, or other types of information into computer-readable 8- or 16-bit word information. Level 0 may also perform threshold detection, unit checking, or other comparative functions. Any changes, out-of-limit values,

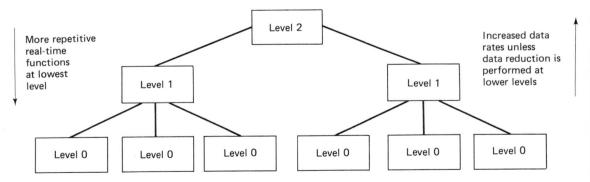

Figure 2-39 Three-level hierarchical system.

or discrepancies may subsequently be stored, whereas "no-change"-type information is discarded. Level 0 may also periodically store information for diagnostic or status verification purposes. In many hierarchical systems, the only functions performed at Level 0 are signal conditioning, conversion, and buffering.

The Level 0 processors are thus highly specialized, performing dedicated, well-defined tasks and shipping data collected in the field to the Level 1 computer(s) instead of storing it locally. Certain Level 0 standard peripherals can be justified for field use. For example, a high-speed reader and punch may be useful for entering programs and obtaining results, should the Level 1 computer become unavailable. Such peripherals would also allow diagnostic programs to be run in the field. In many applications, Level 0 minis can fulfill their duties with modest CPU specifications. Most low-level computers must provide quick response to external events; however, deciding upon what values to retain for processing does not usually require mathematical complexity.

The intelligence of a Level 1 mini will usually be much greater than that of Level 0 minis or micros. The specific duties of this level can be extremely varied. At a minimum, they would include transmitting previously prepared programs and/or commands to the Level 0 minis and receiving transmitted data and storing it on mass storage devices. Level 1 minis may, in addition, perform on-line analyses of data and program development. In addition to its communications functions, the Level 1 mini may support batch processing, on-line interpretive languages, and other background services. Level 1 may operate in a polling mode requesting change values from Level 0, or it may act as a transparent switch with all polling performed by the mini or minis on the next level (Level 2). Level 1 may also operate as a buffer, storing all change values and interrupt Level 2 only when changes are detected and stored.

In a simple, two-level hierarchy, Level 0 may be polled by Level 1 on a round-robin basis and requested to transfer data up to Level 1 when changes occur, or Level 0 may interrupt Level 1 on a contention basis and transmit change values.

It is obvious that the transfer of significant amounts of data across more than one level can rapidly become prohibitive in terms of communications overhead. Typically, the communications processing capacity increases when the top of the pyramid is reached.

With several intermediate processors (several levels), the turnaround or response time of a hierarchical system can be relatively long.

2.6.1 Reliability Aspects

There are at least two major aspects to reliability in a hierarchical structure; if a failure occurs in the processor located on top of the pyramid, total system control is lost. Secondly, if any of the interconnecting links fail, all processors in levels below the failing link are disconnected from the rest of the system. These two problems can be minimized through redundancy. Such redundancy is quite expensive, however, since it will double all communications paths as well as the number of processors at the top (see Figure 2-40).

It is also possible to use a discrepancy processor between primary and alternate

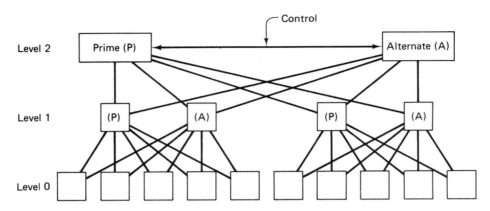

Figure 2-40   Redundant hierarchy with prime/alternate (backup) minis.

processors at each level. The discrepancy processor monitors the prime computer for failure and switches in the alternate computer if a failure is detected. The cost of alternate or redundant processor(s) is high, since typically the processor on top of the pyramid is the largest and most complex in the total system. (Because of its size and complexity, it is also the least reliable.)

Consequently, the addition of redundancy will greatly increase the complexity of the system as well as software overhead. A system doubling of hardware will thus not necessarily increase the reliability of the system by the same ratio.

Whether redundancy is used or not, hierarchical multiminicomputer systems should be designed to operate in a degraded mode. The loss of a single mini should result in the absolute minimum amount of information being lost and should not cause the entire system to cease functioning. To ensure operation in a degraded mode, the following design features should be incorporated:

1. When a Level 0 minicomputer fails, all its process outputs should be frozen and transfer should automatically be made to backup control (either analog or manual).
2. Each mini should be able to store for a reasonable period of time information destined for another computer. The information could be transmitted when the target computer becomes operational again.
3. No mini should depend on information arriving from another mini. Crucial programs should always exist at the site where they are needed. Mathematical results should be replacements for old results (calibrations for example) and old results should continue to be used until new ones become available.
4. By appropriate means, human operators and supervisors should be informed when multimini computer system trouble occurs and be directed to the source of trouble.

2.6.2 Multiminicomputer Communications

The communication scheme in a hierarchical multiminicomputer system is usually based on dedicated point-to-point links between various levels. File transfers between minis are typically based on the transfer of data packets. These packets may be of either fixed or variable length. Usually the packet header describes the contents of the packet, its destination and any other relevant information. Each packet includes a check sum or error correcting code. Before the next transmission can occur, the receiving mini verifies the check sum and issues appropriate acknowledgement. The link itself is either bit-serial or parallel, and the transfer of packets is asynchronous. Because Level 0 minis usually control ongoing processes, control must be maintained during the periods that communication is occurring with Level 1. An executive program must therefore remain active in memory while a new program is under transmission. Similarly, old data, such as calibration data, must remain in memory until new data have been completely received. Depending on the transmission rate and the amount of information to be transferred, the total time could take several seconds or more. Some means of buffering must thus be provided for the incoming information, without overwriting the executing program. This buffering can be performed with extra memory or a disk unit.

Level 1 minis are subject to more demanding requirements. These minis must be able to handle data communications with possibly a very large number of Level 0 minis. The system can be designed based on a polling scheme where the Level 1 mini polls sequentially each of the Level 0 minis. The access time for any of the Level 0 minis is determined by the number of Level 0 minis since the system must cycle through all transmitting minis in a predetermined sequence.

Alternatively, Level 0 minis could access the level above in an interrupt mode. In this approach, because of the possible simultaneous reception and transmission of messages with many Level 0 minis, possible loss of information may occur. One solution would be to ignore certain lines and await the subsequent retransmission or to compromise somewhat on the communications flexibility. A better solution would be to employ serial line controllers that have access to the minis' Direct Memory Access (DMA) channel(s), to minimize communications processing in the mini. If many Level 0 minis are being supported, considerable buffer space may be required at Level 1. Each level 0 mini being supported must have a buffer area assigned to it equal in size to the longest possible message size from that mini. Additionally, since it is assumed that simultaneous bidirectional communications are possible an acknowledgement and a message from a Level 0 mini could arrive very close together in time. Therefore another smaller buffer is required for the acknowledgement. Since the Level 1 computer has direct control of output messages, buffer space for such messages can be more modest. It is possible for the operating system to pool an output buffer area among all Level 0 minis, each section within the area being assigned dynamically, as required.

2.6.3 Hierarchical Multiminicomputer System Performance

The performance capability of a hierarchical multiminicomputer system can be defined both in terms of *impulse response* and *steady-state service*. Impulse response, or settling time, in this case, is defined as the amount of time that observable activity occurs in the hierarchical multiminicomputer system once a set of jobs has been introduced from the various level computers. For practical purposes, impulse response is defined as a single value, not a time continuum. For example, should a single Level 0 mini introduce a job that requires some action on Level 1, and the last returned message occurs 10 sec after initiation, one would say that the impulse response for the work load is 10 sec.

A situation could exist where a number of Level 0 minis must perform a control action simultaneously, but these minis must be informed of the action by Level 1. Level 1 would decide upon the required action only after receiving necessary data from the involved Level 0 minis. Clearly, the time interval between when Level 0 first started to send data to Level 1 and when the control action could be taken is the impulse response defined above.

The second measure of hierarchical multiminicomputer performance will be referred to as the system's steady-state service. This service is a measure of how well the computive demands of the multimini's jobs are being satisfied. The service will be obtained when all active minis introduce their jobs on a regular, periodic basis. The service S is defined as follows:

$$S = \frac{\text{ideal turn-around time for first job} + \text{ideal turn-around time for second job} + \cdots + \text{ideal turn-around time for } n\text{th job}}{\text{actual turn-around time for first job} + \text{actual turn-around time for second job} + \cdots + \text{actual turn-around time for } n\text{th job}} \qquad (2\text{-}32)$$

From this definition, the service S can vary between 0 and 1.0.

The ideal turnaround time for each job is obtained by examining the appropriate job parameters that accompany the jobs:

1. Execution time.
2. Number of input and output messages per job.
3. Communications delay per byte or packet.
4. Number of bytes or packets per message.

The difference between actual and ideal turnaround times depends on *variations* in interrupt processing times, message arrival rates, I/O interference, and job execution times.

When only one job at a time is active in the multiminicomputer system, its total execution time can be accurately predicted. The time to receive, execute, and output messages are all known. When jobs overlap in time, it becomes more difficult to predict the length of time a particular job remains active. This difficulty is due to the following factors:

1. If another job is already in the execution stage, a job that has just arrived at the Level 1 or 2 mini will have to enter a wait queue. Execution of that job cannot begin until all jobs ahead of it have been executed (jobs requiring no execution are passed directly to the output task not necessitating any queuing).
2. A job execution on Level 1 is slowed down by coincident interprocessor communications.
3. If a job is being transmitted from a Level 1 mini to any other mini (Level 0 or 2), other jobs destined for that same mini must wait until the current job has been completely transmitted.
4. The transmission and reception of messages can be slowed down if communication is occurring simultaneously with many minis. This slowdown increases continually with increased interference, until saturation is reached. Saturation is thus reached if jobs continue to be introduced into the system at a rate faster than they can be retired.

Impulse response and steady-state service are illustrated by the following example: Shown in Figure 2-41 is an integrated production-control, factory-feedback application. The Level 2, or host processor, handles long-range scheduling for the entire factory, operating mainly in a batch mode. Production scheduling, which uses a large data base, determines what will be built and when and how the factory equipment will be used.

Each Level 1 minicomputer is assigned control for one or more of the factory's production lines. The Level 1 mini's local data base contains schedule and status information for that line or lines. Each Level 1 mini passes operational commands down to the process controllers, as needed, and receives periodic process status information in return. The Level 1 minis regularly inform the Host on Level 2 of production status, and the Host informs the appropriate mini on the level below it of any production schedule changes.

The Level 0 process controllers provide the real-time interface with the factory devices converting analog-to-digital signals and vice versa, sampling operational parameters, such as temperature, flow, speed, rotation, and pressure, turning on or off switches, checking alarms, and monitoring status indicators.

Functionally each of the process control Level 0 minis multiplex all input and output signals between themselves and the production line equipment, and transmit the information to the Level 1 minicomputer, as shown in Figure 2-41.

In a worst case condition, eight production line status messages must be received and processed by the Level 1 Mini A before a command can be issued to the Level 0

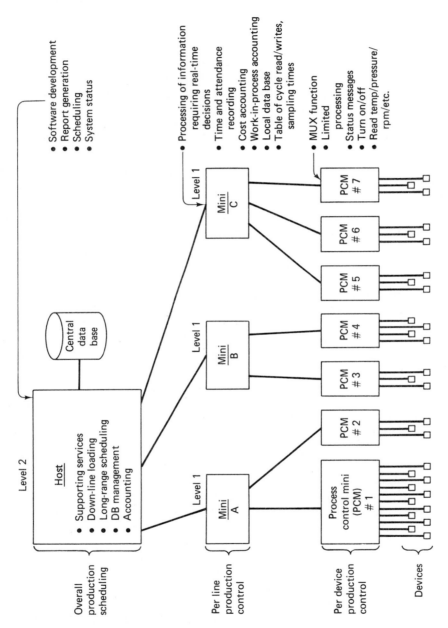

Figure 2-41 Production-control system.

88

Process Control Minis 1 and 2 (Figure 2-41). Each status message contains five normalized parameter values that in turn are formatted into a 16-bit word. The communications links between the Level 0 and Level 1 minis consist of 1200-bps bit-serial lines, and the communications mode is asynchronous. The average message interrupt processing time in Mini A is 100 μsec. The average instruction time for processing the input messages and generating the appropriate command is 2.5 μsec per instruction. Two disc accesses are needed to store the messages and access the command list stored on the disc. It is assumed that each input word requires an average of 100 instructions for appropriate processing, and the average disk access time is 70 msec. One word is needed for control commands to the Level 0 minis. The impulse response time is thus obtained as follows:

$$t_{in} = \left[(2) \times \left(10 \, \frac{bits}{word} \right) \times \left(5 \, \frac{words}{message} \right) \times \left(\frac{1 \, message}{1200 \, bps} \right) \times (8 \, values) \right]$$

$$+ \, (8 \times 100 \, \mu sec \text{ interrupt processing})$$

$$= \left(\frac{800}{1200} \, sec \right) + \left(400 \, \mu sec \right) = 667 \text{ msec} + 0.8 \text{ msec} = 668 \text{ msec}$$

$$t_{processing} = \left(\frac{2.5 \, \mu sec}{word} \right) \times \left(\frac{5 \, words}{message} \right) \times \left(\frac{100 \, instr.}{word} \right) \times (8 \, values)$$

$$+ \, (2 \times 70 \text{ msec disk access time})$$

$$= 10 \text{ msec} + 140 \text{ msec}$$

$$= 150 \text{ msec}$$

$$t_{out} = \frac{(8+2)(2) \, bits}{word} \times \frac{1}{1200 \, bps} \times 2 \text{ minis}$$

$$= 3.3 \text{ msec}$$

Hence,

$$T_{impulse \, response} = t_{in} + t_{proc} + t_{out} = 668 \text{ msec} + 150 \text{ msec} + 3.3 \text{ msec}$$

$$= 821 \text{ msec} \tag{2-33}$$

It is clear that the impulse response time can be vastly improved by increasing transmission data rates and reducing the disc access time using a faster access disc. The least costly improvement is typically to increase the line bit rates. In this example, increased processing speed and fewer instructions have limited impact on improving the impulse response time.

The steady-state service can be determined from actual job turnaround measurements. The following example will illustrate the relationship between the key parameters.

Four major jobs are run on the Level 1 mini, and the actual job turnaround times have been measured as follows:

Job 1—400 msec
Job 2—500 msec
Job 3—550 msec
Job 4—400 msec

The ideal turnaround times are determined as follows:

	No. of I/O Messages/Job	Comm. Delay/Job (sec)	No. Words/Message	Execution* Time (msec)
Job 1	80	$\dfrac{200}{1200}(80) = 13.5$	10	300
Job 2	120	$\dfrac{400}{1200}(120) = 40$	20	340
Job 3	200	$\dfrac{500}{1200}(200) = 83.3$	25	405
Job 4	20	$\dfrac{1680}{1200}(20) = 28$	84	322

*Average of four disc accesses per job at 70 msec each and 25 μsec average processing time per word have been assumed.

Hence, the steady-state service is

$$S = \frac{300 \text{ msec} + 340 \text{ msec} + 405 \text{ msec} + 322 \text{ msec}}{400 \text{ msec} + 500 \text{ msec} + 550 \text{ msec} + 400 \text{ msec}} = 0.74$$

The larger measured values for job turnaround include interrupt processing, variations in message arrival rates, and various other delays difficult to determine theoretically, such as compiler efficiency, true average instruction time, and variations in disc access time. In addition, the poor granularity of measured job turnaround times (to nearest 50 msec) indicates that accuracy could only be provided to a level permitted by the internal clock rate in the computer that was used to obtain the measurements.

2.7 POINT-TO-POINT PARTIALLY OR FULLY INTERCONNECTED SYSTEMS

A point-to-point interconnected multiminicomputer system consists of two or more minicomputers connected by bit-serial lines. The interconnect complexity of such a system grows rapidly with the numbers of minis being connected to the system. In many such systems, however, all minis are not necessarily connected to every other mini, as shown in Figure 2-42 for a six-minicomputer system. This configuration con-

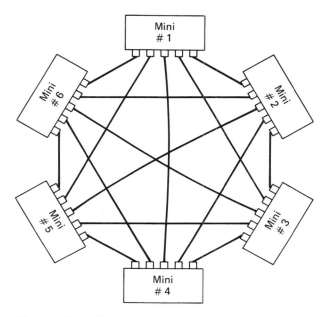

Figure 2-42   Fully interconnected, six-minicomputer system.

tains 15 links. A single link failure will have a very limited effect on the system. Based on this approach, however, the interconnection of a large number of minis over long distance would make a system very expensive. Also, each new mini added to the system would require an additional interface to all the previously existing minis or a total of $N(N-1)/2$ links as well as $N-1$ interface controllers in each mini being added (N being the total number of minis in the system). It is therefore more common for point-to-point interconnected systems to use a partial interconnect scheme based on circuit, message, or packet switching. In circuit-switched systems, a connection between a transmitting or "calling" mini and a receiving or "called" mini is established on demand for exclusive use of a common-carrier circuit until the connection is released in a fashion identical to that of a voice telephone call. The dominant current application of the point-to-point interconnection is, however, to use geographically dispersed minicomputer networks. In such systems the paths are usually also supplied by a common carrier and the switching is done by processors dedicated to that function.

In large distributed networks of minicomputers (and terminals that may contain intelligence), several geographically distributed store-and-forward communications processors are connected together either partially or fully with dedicated transmission links, to form a communication subnet as shown in Figure 2-43. The subnet acts as a common-user service to minicomputers (and terminals). In order to communicate, minis must first access a store-and-forward communications processor, which is also a mini.

Messages are then sent through the subnet by the communications processors.

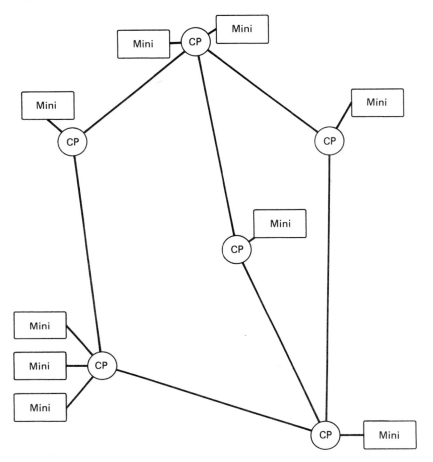

Figure 2-43 Distributed point-to-point interconnected multiminicomputer system using a subnet of store-and-forward communications processors (CP).

Networks of this type are normally classified according to their use of message or packet switching for transmission switching within the subnet.

In message switching systems, messages are sent in their entirety along a predetermined, fixed transmission path from source to destination mini, through the subnet. At each communications processor along the path, the message is first stored, typically on disk, and then forwarded to the next communications processor when the required transmission channel is available. This approach has the following inherent disadvantages:

- Communications processors are expensive.
- Long message delays can be incurred depending on the level of traffic.
- Network resources are utilized inefficiently.
- Limited flexibility is available to adjust to fluctuations in network conditions.

Packet switching is an alternative that is presently gaining widespread popularity as an alternative to message switching. Packet switching was first introduced with the development of the now famous ARPANET, which has been followed by numerous other systems such as Telenet, Graphnet, Packet Communications Inc., and Autodin II.

Packet switching differs from message switching in that a message is divided into frames or packets before it is transmitted and is reassembled when it reaches its destination, as shown in Figure 2-44. The primary advantages of packet switching are that packets can be stored in the main memory of the communications processor, and if the latter is busy, they can be sent over alternate paths to their destination. These features reduce substantially both the message delay time and the communications processor cost.

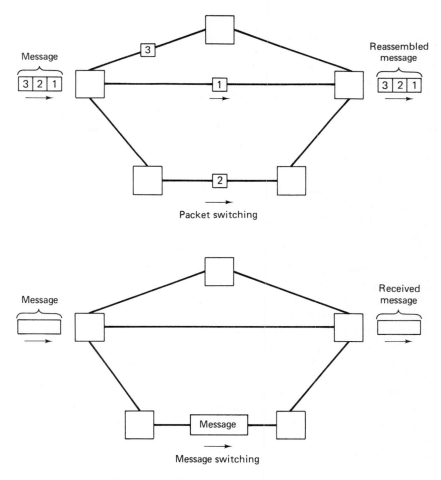

Figure 2-44 Packet versus message switching.

Many of the packet switching's desirable characteristics result from the use of adaptive routing. This is where the transmission path between any two points in the network is not chosen in advance but is dynamically chosen based on network conditions at the time of transmission. With this ability to allocate its resources based upon current conditions, the network is able to overcome the adverse effects of temporary channel or communications device overload or failed subnet components.

To transmit a message, the transmitting mini precedes the message text with a terminal address and sends it to its associated communications processor. This communications processor then dynamically determines the best transmission path, or route, provides error control, and notifies the source of message receipt.

When a message is ready for transmission, the originating communications processor divides the message into one or more packets (typically approximately 1000 bits each) where each packet carries the appropriate header information. Each packet is then transmitted and makes its way independently through the network to the receiving minicomputer communications processor, where the packets are reassembled into the original message and then sent to the intended mini. The communications processor and associated mini or minis are usually colocated in the same room or facility and interfaced via a 16-bit parallel data path.

The basic difference between circuit- and message- or packet-switched systems is that, in the former case, as a rule, no "intermediate" network buffers exist. Circuit switching resembles closely the fully interconnected system shown in Figure 2-42. Rather than using dedicated, hard-wired interconnections between all computers, however, each one can "dial" any of the other computers in the network. This will increase throughput delay due to the inherent time required to establish a dial-up connection but will save on the number of links and ports in each computer. In most cases, however, circuit switching provides a fast method of moving data between two computers, particularly for large message blocks.

A packet-switched, distributed multiminicomputer system is simpler to implement when it is required that data be passed randomly through a network with many nodes—that is, where the desired paths through the net are not predictable. Thus, it is advantageous over other approaches, such as message switching, only if there is a vary large amount of traffic among a large number of widespread users. The major advantages of a communications processor are that the connecting minis are freed from communications tasks and the communications processor software cost can be amortized over several identical minicomputer systems. Also, the ability of a packet-switched system to provide a standard network access protocol (see also Chapter 3) is a major area where packet switching possesses a clear advantage over circuit switching. (However, for many years, this advantage is likely to be largely a conceptual one since the implementation implications for users are significant.) Nevertheless, where only a few minicomputers need to be interconnected point to point over long distances, a simple bit-serial dedicated or circuit-switched (dial-up) communications interface with modems and voice-grade lines may be the most economical solution.

PROBLEMS

2-1 Solve Eq. (2-11) for the system throughput ratio for the following two configurations:
(a) Four PDP-11/40's with 2 MA-11's interleaved.
(b) Four PDP-11/40's with 4 MA-11's interleaved.
How are throughput ratios and utilization factors affected by the change from two to three PDP-11/40's and three to four PDP-11/40's?

2-2 Using roll-call polling for a distributed system, a number of microcomputers are to be interconnected by a 1-Mbps bit-serial bus and where each micro transmits an average of 10 messages per second. Each message size is 2000 bits. A central bus controller is used that requires 30 μsec to issue a poll.

What is the maximum number of microcomputers that can be attached to the bus?

If a hub polling scheme were to be used, and assuming each micro requires 10 μsec to pass a request to an adjacent micro, what would the maximum growth of the system be?

2-3 Derive the maximum theoretical throughput ($1/2e$) for an unslotted, global multiple access bus system (Pure Aloha) that has a large number of identical users. Repeat this for a slotted contention system.

What percentage improvement in maximum throughput can theoretically be achieved by selecting a slotted Aloha scheme instead of a pure Aloha scheme?

2-4 Several approaches to loop topologies exist; Pierce uses a fixed-size slot that includes an empty/full flag. The loop always contains an integral number of slots, and the micros or minis on the loop wishing to transmit wait for an available slot sharing the line equally. The Newhall approach has been called the complement of the Pierce loop. Explain why.

2-5 Fiber optics has been called the ideal communications medium for loop-type systems due to its inherent wide bandwidth (200 Mbps or above). Why is the DLCN approach unattractive for loop systems based on fiber optics?

2-6 A drawback of all TDM-based loop systems that divide a single high-speed channel into short, fixed-length slots is the requirement for a loop controller or synchronizer to generate and monitor frame marking from which all nodes locate their assigned slot. The frame marking may be eliminated by substituting channel identification by label in place of channel identification by position. This technique has been called Labeled Slot Multiplexing (LSM).

What solutions do you propose for an LSM system in terms of the control of propagation of a newly structured slot, message addressing, and removal?

Show a proposed message or packet format, addressing technique, error control, and message protocol alternative for a LSM loop system.

2-7 In the example of turnaround time determination for steady-state service (Subsection 2.6.3) communications delays per job range from 13.5 to 83.3 sec. What effect will this have on steady-state service?

2-8 An electronics manufacturing company uses Hewlett Packard HP 3000, HP 1000, and HP 2026 minicomputer-based systems, as shown below, to coordinate their activities on the factory floor.

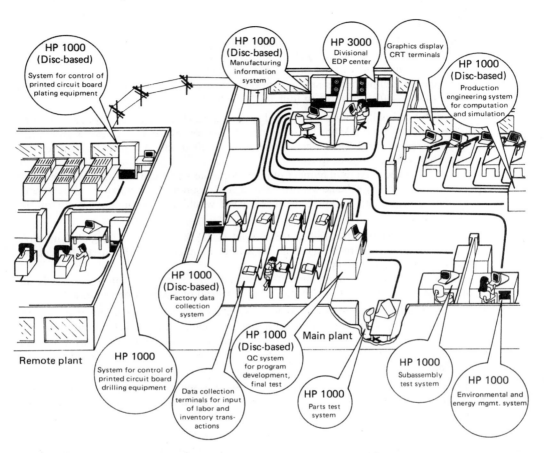

Courtesy, Hewlett Packard Corp., Palo Alto, Calif.

The major components include a factory data collection system with multiple data collection terminals to monitor labor equipment utilization, production status, and inventory transactions. A quality control "subnetwork" comprised of three systems is used for parts, subassembly, and finished-product testing. Also, a disc-based manufacturing information system (HP 1000) is linked via telephone lines to systems that control automated manufacturing operations in an adjacent plant. In addition, two HP 1000 systems are used for environmental and energy management, and computation and simulation are supported by graphic display CRT terminals. Finally, a manufacturing information system is used that summarizes key production data and transmits it to a divisional data processing center.

The manufacturing information system performs six major jobs, each associated with six of the systems interfaced via synchronous, 9600-bps bit-serial links. Each job is based on the receipt/transmission of 10 messages, and the messages contain the following number of words:

	Words per Message
● PC board drilling and plating status.	10
● Factory data collection of labor and inventory transactions.	10
● Quality control data from parts and subassembly test.	30
● Environmental and energy management.	10
● Computation and simulation.	60
● Divisional EDP center.	20

Determine whether the Manufacturing Information System is processor or I/O bound assuming error-free transmission and 1.5-disc accesses per job. The average disc access time is 30 msec. State additional assumptions. For a 0.5-sec measured job turnaround time, what is the steady-state service of the Manufacturing Information System mini?

3

Multimicro- and
Minicomputer Software

.3.1 INTRODUCTION

Chapter 2 introduced various interconnect structures including comparisons of
features such as throughput, reliability, and implementation complexity from a systems
point of view. This chapter will explore these same fundamental structures (tightly
and loosely coupled multimicro- and minicomputer systems) from a software stand-
point: What additional software is needed beyond that required for a single processor
system; how complex a software structure is required, and how much of it is available
off-the-shelf? (Chapter 4 will attempt to answer the same questions from a hardware
point of view.)

A single processor is controlled by an operating system that consists of two types
of software:

1. Control programs
2. Processing programs

Control programs typically manage the use of system resources, provide easier access
to and more efficient use of the physical resources (the user interface), and perform
data management.

Control programs usually contain a scheduler (also called Supervisor or Executive) that allocates CPU resources to tasks (processes), activates, suspends, and
destroys tasks; performs memory management, input and output control, control of
and storage and movement of files among storage media; and provides protection,
access control, and security for information. In real-time environments, the scheduler
also controls interrupt handlers associated with both internally and externally generated interrupts.

Processing programs include application and support software where the latter contains text editors, language translators (assemblers and compilers), file management utilities, diagnostic software, etc. Support software generally comes contained in the operating system package and is maintained by the minicomputer manufacturer.

An operating system is consequently a collection of programs that organizes a central processor and peripheral devices into a working entity for the development and execution of applications programs.

Operating systems on microcomputers are generally not widely used since, in the majority of applications, micros are dedicated to performing a single task or, at the most, three to four tasks.

Operating systems have, as a rule, very limited portability. Conversion or reprogramming of an operating system designed for one type of computer to fit another type of computer is at best a costly and time-consuming problem and should not be attempted.

The relationship among users, the operating system, and the hardware is shown in Figure 3-1.

Multimicro- and minicomputer system software differs from single processor system software in both the control and processing software areas. Often, control programs must not only manage resources in the local micro or mini but also in other interconnected computers. The degree or level of management "responsibility" depends to a large extent on the total system architecture. In a hierarchical structure or a centrally controlled bus or loop system, the computers are, as a rule, organized into a master and slave (subordinate) structure. The information flow is controlled by a central switch or computer(s) located at higher level(s) in the hierarchy. The control is consequently centralized. In a global bus, star, or point-to-point structured system, however, the control is often fully distributed and each of the micros or minis in the system is logically equal to all the others (master-to-master relationship).

The control function, whether centralized or distributed, must assure that software controlled processes performed by the various computers in the system do not interfere with each other in a harmful manner whereby one program may cause another program to crash either at system start-up or during system operation. Time-dependent race conditions must be avoided as well as situations where system deadlock may occur (deadlock is discussed in Subsection 5.7.2).

The synchronization of processes/processors has been discussed from a hardware point of view in Chapter 2 as, for example, the slotted bus, various contention protocols such as the one used on Ethernet (Subsection 2.3.6), or the token protocol on the DCS ring (Subsection 2.4.1). This chapter will explore software approaches to synchronization, such as the use of Semaphores and the Monitor Concept of Concurrent Pascal.

A second dimension of control is related to coupling. A tightly coupled system requires a control structure and control mechanisms quite different from a loosely coupled system. The former, which usually shares system resources (i.e., memory) to a higher degree, requires various mechanisms to resolve conflicts and contention.

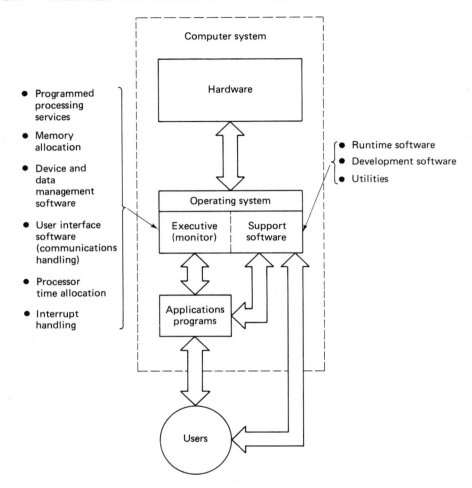

Figure 3-1   Relationship among users, the operating system and the hardware.

Loosely coupled systems that, by definition, do not share memory (limited amount of shared data with less frequent updates), require a message communications capability between the computers.

The third element, often unique to distributed systems, is task handling and partitioning. Depending on application requirements, the operating system may have to provide an environment that supports resource sharing where the system resources consist of heterogeneous micro- and/or minicomputers, each with some unique capabilities in terms of files, processing capability, or peripherals. Tasks would therefore have to be assigned to unique processing elements, optimizing, for instance, system response. On the other hand, the system design may dictate the use of a large number of identical or similar micros or minis where tasks are assigned to whatever processor is available at any given point in time in the total system. Both of these approaches require intertask communications and remote task control capability.

Task partitioning and centralized versus distributed control are discussed in more detail in Chapter 5.

Finally, distributed micro- and minicomputer software must be able to provide features such as diagnostics and recovery procedures beyond those of a single processor-based system. Such software often becomes a sizable part of the total system software.

In case one of the micros or minis in a system either stops or starts generating faulty messages, other processors must detect this and take appropriate action, such as working around the failed element and reporting the failure to a system operator thereby allowing him or her to reconfigure the system.

Various software approaches for improving system reliability consist of internal self-checks by processors such as checksumming of critical tables, keeping redundant files that are updated by independent processors and backed up by audit trails of all transactions stored on disc or magnetic tape, and the switching of communications lines from a failed to a fully operational micro or mini.

For two-processor configurations operating in critical real-time environments, the "dead man's grip" approach is used for fast, automatic fail-over where one processor prevents a clock or timer in the second processor from timing out by interrupting and resetting it at fixed intervals. A failure to provide an interrupt is interpreted as a processor failure by the second processor, which will automatically take over by disconnecting the current processor.

Error detection can also be provided by message-handling software that is above and beyond that used in a single, stand-alone processor facility.

One of the most critical system control functions of a multimicro- or minicomputer system is thus to provide coherent communication between the system objects such as the input-output devices, programs or processes, data files, and terminals residing at the different processor nodes. The term *interprocess communication* will be used to refer to the function above. Processes or tasks represent activities that are themselves purely sequential but can be executed concurrently and asynchronously with other tasks in a system. Each process has its own private data structures and can be independently scheduled for execution on a single processor. Objects such as I/O devices, data files, or terminals can be controlled by software processes that "represent" the object to the communication environment. Thus object-to-object communication is accomplished, in practice, by process-to-process communication. In addition to interprocess communication, system (network) resource control, remote file, or record transfer, the operating system must provide the capability to down-line load programs and provide across-the-system program development support capability and overall system security.

The added dimension of interprocess communications is illustrated in Figure 3-2

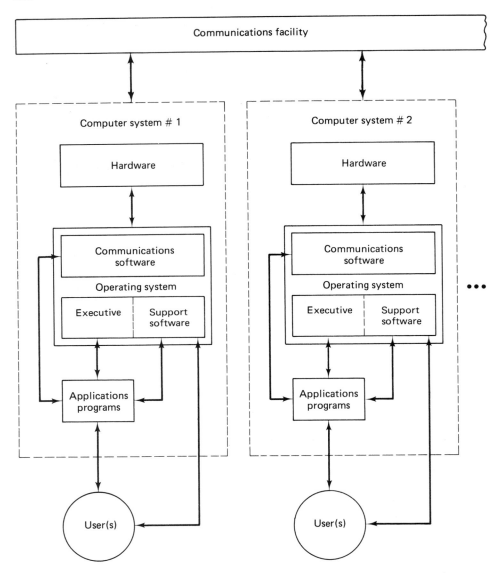

Figure 3-2 Relationship between users, the operating system, the hardware, and other computer systems and users in a distributed systems environment.

where two or more computers are interconnected via a communications facility, be it a bus, loop, shared memory, or point-to-point data link.

Micro- and minicomputer interprocess communications software is, to a large extent, based on the use of protocols.

A general protocol model can be visualized as at least two processes communicating over a logical link or channel, as shown below:

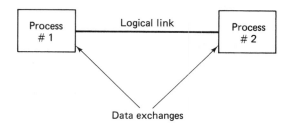

By extension, one can also refer to a protocol for certain classes of commonly used functions such as file transfer, terminal access, and remote job entry. A protocol is, in that case, a set of rules describing how these functions are carried out. In other words, it is equivalent to the functional specifications of a distributed system being able to perform specific tasks. Based on this definition, a protocol can be viewed as the command language of a particular distributed system, such as a file transfer protocol being the command language of a distributed file system.

The following sections provide descriptions of software architectures and software implementation approaches for both tightly coupled shared memory and loosely coupled message communication systems, including a brief overview of various operating system design approaches.

3.2 SHARED MEMORY COMMUNICATION SOFTWARE

Unlike message communication, which is a highly controlled form of communication requiring a protocol and explicit cooperation between processes, direct shared memory communication is not explicitly controlled and requires the use of a global shared memory. (For various shared memory system descriptions, see Section 2.2.) The processes in this case read and write the data directly in the shared memory. Whereas in message communication, the sender may have to wait for an acknowledgement from the receiver process before or after the message is sent, no such acknowledgement is needed in direct shared memory communication as the message "remains" in shared memory space. Processes may read/write the data when necessary.

The two forms of communication, message versus direct shared memory, may be described by the following analogies: Complicated message communication typically resembles the operation of postal service, in sending and receiving mail. Considerations such as special delivery, mail pickup, and transportation cause this facility to be highly general purpose in nature but also quite complicated. A simpler form of message communication can be achieved using a shared mailbox scheme (see Figure 3-3). An example of this is the data processing facility where users submit their data processing jobs and receive their computer output. Many installations have boxes

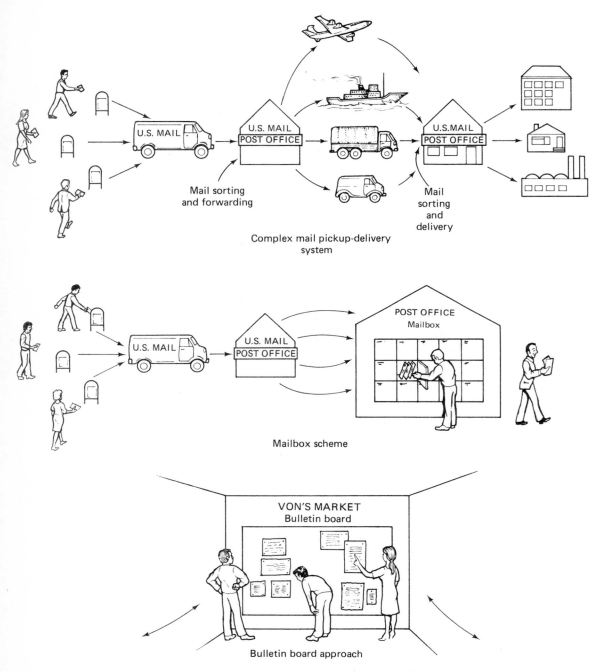

Mail sorting
and forwarding

Mail
sorting
and
delivery

Complex mail pickup-delivery
system

Mailbox scheme

VON'S MARKET
Bulletin board

Bulletin board approach

Figure 3-3 Message communications analogies.

categorized by the first letter of the last name for the user to find his computer output. As often can be seen, especially in university environments, users are "busy waiting" for the operator to put their output listings in their box. In this case, there is no explicit acknowledgement of "message" delivery but an implied one in that the user removes the completed output job from his box.

The direct shared memory scheme can also be compared to a bulletin board, sometimes found in a grocery store or supermarket where users post information such as ads for merchandise or help wanted notices. The bulletin board acts as a central repository for existing information that can be read or updated by anyone. Normally, however, physical transfer of information does not occur as in the mailbox scheme. In the bulletin board example, the information is shared among "users."

The following major differences exist between the two communication methods:

1. Direct shared memory communication is much faster than message communication.

2. In message communication, the message or a pointer to the message must be passed from one process explicitly to another process. Although multimini-computer systems exist that are based on general message broadcast capability (see Chapter 2), they are not as common as the "normal" form of message communication. Depending on the complexity of communication requirements, issues such as buffer allocation, acknowledgements schemes, routing, flow control, and error control may have to be considered. In direct shared memory communication, the data remains in shared memory, and processes access it there.

3. Direct shared memory communication can only be used in the presence of actual shared memory. Message communication can be implemented, however, using a large variety of processor interconnect schemes, even shared memory (see Subsection 2.2.5; mailboxes).

Direct shared memory communication does not necessarily require a global shared memory between all processors. Only those processors which contain processes which must share the same data need a connection to a shared memory block which contains this data. Depending on the application, a tree structure of shared memory boxes may have to be configured, for example, as shown in Figure 3-4.

The major problem in direct shared memory schemes is how to ensure the integrity of shared data. This can be accomplished by synchronizing the accesses to the global, shared data.

Three techniques for ensuring correct synchronization when reading or writing shared data are described. Each of these techniques can be used in a multimini/micro processor environment that contains shared memory.

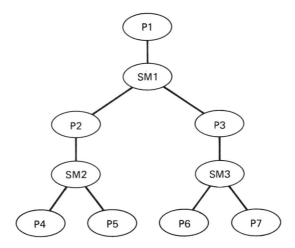

Figure 3-4 Shared memory "boxes" configured into a tree structure where P=process and SM=shared memory.

3.2.1 Process Synchronization by Semaphores

Dijkstra* introduced the semaphore concept for synchronizing processor in a multiprogramming environment. A semaphore S is an integer variable initialized to some value. Associated with the semaphore is a queue that can hold the names of processes. Two operations are defined in the semaphore: Wait(S) and Signal(S). [Dijkstra has called these P(S) and V(S), respectively.] If a process P executes Wait(S), then the value of S is decremented. If this new value is negative, the name of P is placed on the queue associated with the semaphore, and P is blocked from executing. If, on the other hand, S is nonnegative, P is allowed to continue. If a process P executes Signal(S), then the value of S is incremented. If the new value of S is less than or equal to zero, then the name of one process is removed from the queue, and this process is allowed to resume execution.

Semaphores provide a means to suspend the execution of a process until certain conditions are satisfied. If processes perform semaphore operations in conjunction with their accesses to shared, global variables, necessary synchronization in the system can be achieved. For example, a semaphore with initial value 1 can be used to maintain mutual exclusion of processes accessing a shared variable. A process that is updating the data base in an airline reservation system, for instance, must have exclusive control of the data base so that the data base will remain in a consistent state (unchanged) during each transaction.

If several processes wish to access the data base without changing the data base's state, these accesses can proceed concurrently. Furthermore, if a process wants to

*E. W. Dijkstra, "Cooperating Sequential Processes," Mathematics Department, Technological University, Eindhoven, The Netherlands, 1965. (See also Alan C. Shaw, "The Logical Design of Operating Systems," Prentice-Hall, Inc., Englewood Cliffs, N.J., 1974, pp. 65–68.)

read only one word in the data base, there is no danger of finding the data base in an inconsistent state; hence this access can proceed even while other processes are updating the data base. To find out how many seats are available on an airline flight, a process would simply execute the statement:

$$n: = \text{available (flight)}$$

The Carnegie Mellon C.mmp and Cm* multiprocessors systems discussed in Section 2.2 implement semaphore types of locks. In the case of the Cm* system, the synchronization is handled by the Kmap (refer to Chapter 2). The Kmap maintains a private lock on each segment. The hardware provides micro-coded operations to lock and unlock these integer valued locks. The indivisible DecrWord operation decrements the integer lock value in the case that value preceding the decrement is greater than zero. The indivisible InerWord operation increments an integer value by one. Both operations require about 40 μsec. The operations are indivisible thereby preventing two or more processors from testing the lock simultaneously and then each setting it whereby they would gain access to the shared data at the same time.

3.2.2 Process Synchronization by Monitors

The monitor construct that defines a shared data structure is found in the Concurrent Pascal programming language.* Monitors were developed to allow a more structured format for concurrent programs than is possible with semaphores. Unlike semaphore programs, all information about a set of shared resources and how they are used is contained in a single area of the program, "the Declaration of a Monitor." The Declaration of a Monitor includes a number of procedures that define operations on shared resources. These procedures are available to all processes in the system. When a process wishes to access a shared resource, such as a global (network-wide) variable or a shared hardware resource, it must do so by executing one of the procedures of the corresponding monitor. It should be emphasized that a monitor does not itself cause any action in the system. Instead, it is merely a collection of procedures that can be executed by the processes in the system.

Monitors are implemented in such a way that the execution of the procedures of a particular monitor are mutually exclusive. Hence, a process retains exclusive control of the resources of a monitor while executing one of the monitor's procedures, until it surrenders its control. A process can surrender its control of the monitor in one of several ways. First, it can complete the execution of the monitor procedure, at which time some other process can begin execution of one of the monitor's procedures. This form of control passing is sufficient to implement mutual exclusion of processes. For example, the airline reservation system discussed above utilizes only this form of control passing. Other forms of control passing are provided by condition variables along with the operations Delay and Continue. A condition variable has

---

*Per Brinch Hansen, "The Programming Language Concurrent Pascal," *IEEE Transactions on Software Engineering*, **SE-1**, No. 2, June 1975.

no visible value, although it does have an initially empty queue associated with it. When a process executes the statement Delay (Cond) in the body of a monitor procedure, the process name is placed on the queue for Cond, the process is blocked from further execution, and control of the monitor is released. When a process executes the statement Continue (Cond), this process is temporarily blocked (unless the queue for Cond is empty), and one of the processes on the queue for Cond is resumed. Once this reawakened process is completed, the process that executed the Continue (Cond) statement is resumed. The monitor-process interaction is illustrated in Figure 3-5.

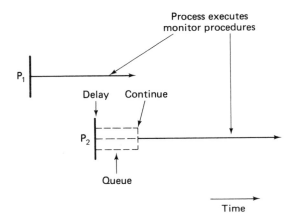

Figure 3-5 Pictorial representation of the Delay/Continue Monitor control of two processes, P_1 and P_2.

A monitor can thus either delay a calling process in a queue or continue a process waiting in a queue. Control is thereby provided for the order in which competing processes use shared physical resources. In short, a monitor can synchronize concurrent processes and transmit data among them that is a necessary requirement in a shared memory multiprocessor environment.

The monitor construct provides more modularity than semaphores, which, in turn, yields more understandable programs. The ways in which a resource may be accessed are contained in a single section of the system specification rather than in the programs for each process (or the common data structures). This modularity also makes the system easier to modify.

3.2.3 Process Synchronization by Monitors without Mutual Exclusion

In a realistic airline reservation system environment, an agent would obviously want to know more about a flight than the number of seats available. Hence, processing an "info" request would require reading several words of memory. If the data base is altered in the middle of these reads, the information returned to the agent may contain inconsistencies. To program a sophisticated shared memory, multiprocessor-based reservation system, the types of transactions would have to be divided into two classes: (1) those which only read the data base (the Readers) and (2) those which alter the data base (the Writers). A number of Readers can proceed concurrently, but a Writer must have exclusive control of the data base. Programs which solve the Readers-Writers problem have used both semaphores and monitor schemes which involve mutual exclusion: All other processes are denied access to the data item while one process is modifying it. Mutual exclusion requires that a Writer wait until all current read operations are completed. This may be undesirable if the Writer has higher priority than the Readers; however, exclusion in a multiprocessor system could cause considerable overhead. A scheme used for the Readers/Writers problem in the case of a single Writer is based on allowing processes to read and write at any time. After reading, a process checks to see if it might have obtained an incorrect value, in which case it repeats the operation. The algorithm can be used if either it is undesirable to make the Writer wait for a Reader to finish reading or the probability of having to repeat a read is small enough so that it does not pay to incur the overhead of a solution employing mutual exclusion. Of course, it allows the possibility of a Reader looping forever if writing is done often enough.

This algorithm maintains two version numbers for the data: V1 and V2. The writer increments V1 before writing the data item and increments V2 after writing. The reader reads V2 before reading the data item and V1 after reading it. If it finds them equal, then it knows that it read a single version of the data.

It is assumed that V1 and V2 are common variables and that initially V1 = V2. The algorithms for reading and writing are given below. There may be any number of readers, each executing its own copy of the reader's algorithm. The writing algorithm may only be executed by one writer at a time.

```
        Monitor
        Writer:
            V1 := V1 + 1
            (write)
            V2 := V1
        Reader:
            Repeat
                Temp := V2
                (read)
            UNTIL V1 = temp
```

If reading is an extensive operation, then the Reader's temp: = V2 statement should be changed to

$$\text{repeat Temp:} = V2 \text{ until } V1 = \text{temp}$$

This keeps a Reader from performing a read operation if the Writer has already begun writing.

3.2.4 Implementation Approaches

The major software issues in implementing shared memory micro- or minicomputer systems are consequently related to memory access and access synchronization using either semaphores or monitors. In implementing semaphores or monitors for such systems, a basic "indivisable" operation is needed that can test and set a shared memory location without being interrupted. In addition, a method of signaling one processor from another is needed to implement the semaphore construct. This is typically implemented using an interrupt line.

Indivisable operations on the PDP-11 are implemented utilizing the UNIBUS Modify-Write memory cycles. Read-Modify-Write instructions maintain control of the memory between read and write phases to allow a modification of the memory cell by that process. No other process can use the memory until that instruction is completed.

Figure 3-6 depicts an efficient implementation of the P, V synchronization primitives on certain PDP-11's (not the 11/60 or 11/70) where the semaphore is initialized to −2 in 2's complement (the P and V primitives are explained in Subsection 3.2.1).

P	ASR	SEMAPHORE	TEST AND SET SEMAPHORE
	BCS	P	LOOP IF ALREADY SET
V	ASL	SEMAPHORE	RESET SEMAPHORE

Figure 3-6 An implementation of P, V in the PDP-11.

The implementation in Figure 3-6 is a form of "busy waiting." The continuous testing of the semaphore causes extra requests for memory. The extra memory traffic can cause congestion and deny memory cycles to nonwaiting processes. Thus, it is desirable to put processes "to sleep" if they are not successful in their first attempt to gain access to a resource. Sleeping processes do not consume any system resources (other than the overhead involved in making them dormant/active). Some form of queuing is also necessary to ensure that no process is permanently blocked.

When two processes use the same resources in a multimicro- or miniprocessor system and process synchronization occurs through shared memory, an "Exchange Register with Memory" instruction is used for nonbusy semaphore communication. When P1 wants to use a shared resource, it places its identity in a register and executes an Exchange instruction. If the new value in the register is zero, then the resource is available for use. If it is nonzero, then some other process is using the resource, and the requesting process puts itself to sleep (turns off its run flipflop or awaits an interrupt). When the process finishes with the resource, it awakens the process identified by the semaphore variable (unless it is itself). Figure 3-7 depicts an implementation of P, V using the Exchange instruction.

Some means of notifying other processes of memory access status is required. One mechanism, used on the C.mmp multiminicomputer system (16 PDP-11 minicomputers communicating with 16 memory units through a crosspoint switch, see

110

```
P :   Move myidentity to R
      Exchange R,S
      If R ≠ 0 then wait
V :   Clear R
      Exchange R,S
      If R ≠ myidentity then awake process identified by R
```

Figure 3-7 Implementation of P, V using the Exchange instruction.

Subsection 2.2.2), is to provide an interrupt register addressable by all processors. Writing a one into i bit causes an interrupt in Processor i.

The Exchange instruction mechanism breaks down when more than two processes need to utilize a resource. An alternative scheme, employed on the C.mmp, uses the interrupt register and two semaphores. Processes test the primary semaphore in the normal manner. If it is nonzero, they OR a bit corresponding to their processor number into a word (called Processes Pending) in memory. When the process wants to give up the resource by performing a V, it places the "processes pending" word in the interrupt register and clears the primary semaphore. Processes reawakened by the interrupt attempt to perform a P on a secondary semaphore recording their identity if they lose. The process that wins then performs a P on the primary semaphore. In this manner the semaphores are only tested when the resource is known to be free.

For high-speed operation, the sequence of operations above can be implemented in hardware or microcode. Likewise, instead of generating an interrupt and suffering the associated delay, the interrupt register can be replaced by a register formed by processor run flipflops. If the random process for selecting the next task by interrupting all sleeping tasks or processes is undesirable, logic can be added to the interrupt register to select only one processor to be interrupted [on a strict priority basis, using a first-in, first-out (FIFO) queue, on a round-robin basis, etc.]. It may be necessary however, to ensure that no process is permanently blocked.

In order to show the implementation of the Monitor construct in a multiprocessing environment, a design based on the Monitor construct scheme in Concurrent Pascal is described.

In the preceding discussion of monitors, a condition variable within the monitor for handling interprocess synchronization was discussed. Using the Concurrent Pascal monitor, interprocess synchronization is achieved through the delay-queue construct described in Subsection 3.2.2 by which a monitor procedure can delay its calling process or continue another process that is waiting in a delay queue.

A run-time Kernel* is needed, however, to manage the concurrent processes and provide the monitor support above.

---

*The run-time environment of the Concurrent Pascal compiler is a kernel of 4K words. This is the only program written in machine language. The kernel is a body of functions which directly interfaces with hardware and which contains the control/coordination interface from software to hardware, from hardware to software and between software modules. The kernel multiplexes its host processor among concurrent processes and gives them exclusive access to monitors. The kernel is also a basic set of

In a multiprocessor configuration, monitor code can be either executed out of shared memory or replicated in each processor's private, local memory. The separate representations can even be implemented differently (for example, microcoded) in different processors provided they execute the procedures as required by their respective processes. Monitor code can be duplicated in different processors because the run-time kernel permits only one version to execute at any given time. Only one copy of a monitor's variable data structure can exist, however, and it must be located in shared memory to be accessible by the different processors. Each physical processor must contain a run-time kernel. Collectively, these kernels will create a virtual machine that supports an integral distributed processing system.

A basic flow chart of four key kernel routines developed by Price is used to show how the kernel implements the monitor construct (Figure 3-8). Illustrated are mechanisms for entering and exiting a monitor and for a implementing the "delay" and "continue" operators. These routines are executed in behalf of the using program when requesting the services of the kernel.

Contention problems, where more than one kernel tries to access a common kernel structure, are resolved using a hardware Read-Modify-Write function (Test and Set instruction) whereupon the data structures are manipulated in place in the shared memory. The logic for manipulating the data (i.e., the monitor's program code) is located along with the data. (The Test and Set instruction is employed to lock a data structure before a kernel accesses it.) When a kernel finds a structure busy, it "spins" on the "lock," testing it until it becomes free. Locking is depicted in Figure 3-8 by boxes with titles.

Processor time consumed while spinning on a lock is data contention overhead and will degrade total system performance if the frequency of accessing a given structure is high among the processors. Probability of contention can be minimized by dedicating a separate lock for each monitor and for each process dispatch chain in the system. Upon exiting a process from a monitor, the kernel interrogates the monitor's busy chain and makes a waiting process (if any) ready for executing the monitor.

Process dispatching is distributed (except for the control structures in shared memory) because any processor's kernel can set processes ready for execution on other processors in the system. As illustrated in Figure 3-8, this can happen when a process waiting on a monitor busy chain is activated and when a process waiting in a delay queue is continued.

An interprocessor interrupt facility enables a kernel in one processor to signal the kernel in another processor when setting one of its processes ready for execution. All idle processors can thus be alerted when readying a shared process. The interrupt need not convey any information except to cause the recipient kernel to cycle through its Dispatch routine. The interrupt facility is not an absolute requirement, however. When in idle mode with no work to perform, the kernel could continually cycle

---

primitive operations and processes from which the remainder of the operating system is constituted. It is sometimes also called the "nucleus." For more on kernel structures, see Per Brinch Hansen, "*The Architecture of Concurrent Programs*," Prentice-Hall, Inc., Englewood Cliffs, N.J., 1977.

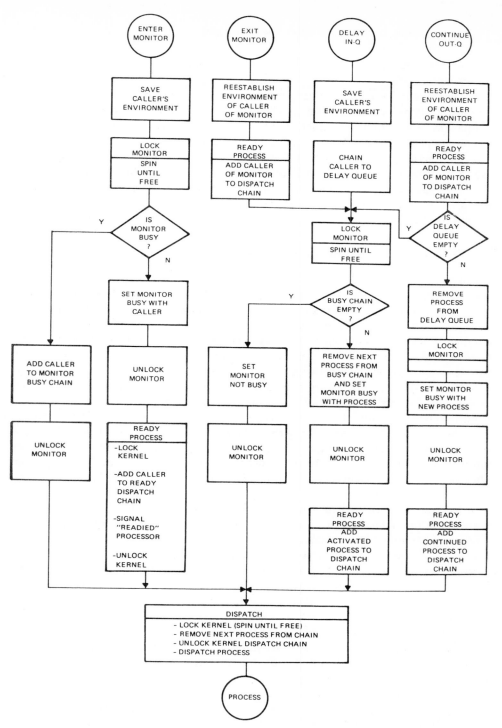

Figure 3-8 Kernel procedures to support monitors (From: "Multiprocessing Made Easy," Ronald J. Price, AFIPS Conference Proceedings, **47**, 1978; National Computer Conference, Anaheim, Calif. 1978).

through its dispatch chains instead of going into a wait state (or perhaps periodically on a clock interval).

The Concurrent Pascal Kernel/Monitor concept has also been proposed for loosely coupled systems and, as shown in Chapter 6, successfully implemented. (Loosely coupled systems require, however, additional supporting features mainly in the area of communications discussed in the following sections.)

The methods described above for implementing direct shared memory systems are, by no means, unique. Alternate kernel designs are possible and consideration should be given to both system requirements and hardware constraints (for more on the latter, see Chapter 4). The use of the monitor construct is also discussed in Subsection 5.7.1 and Section 6.5.

3.3 MESSAGE COMMUNICATION SOFTWARE

The most common form of interprocess communication in a distributed software system is by means of message-type protocols. This approach is valid for both large resource-sharing networks of micro- or minicomputers connected by asynchronous lines and less complex systems consisting of as few as two micro- or minicomputers interconnected via a high bandwidth bus link, in a dedicated real-time control application. Most multimicro- and minicomputer system communication capabilities fall somewhere between these two extremes.

Message-type protocols are commonly structured into quasi-independent levels or functional layers. Ideally, each level is using lower level properties through a well-defined interface, without any knowledge of their inner workings. This approach provides various advantages, among them the capability to replace a layer with a new one without changing interfaces, thereby providing system extensibility. Also, the internals of each protocol level are transparent to the protocol levels above them. Only the high-level system services are visible to users and applications programmers.

As shown in Figure 3-9, the protocol control structure can be visualized as an inverted pyramid because, in general, there are more protocols at the higher levels than at the lower levels. For example, Level 4 may consist of several protocols for separately handling files, terminals, and remote jobs. Level 3 contains the end-to-end logical connections between processes including message routing, flow control, and message accountability. At Levels 1 and 2 are the physical and logical connections between adjacent micros or minis. Here, mechanical, electrical, and data protocol interface specifications enable bit strings to be transferred reliably from one computer to another over a single link.

The applicability of one or more of these protocols, whether Level 2, 3, or 4, is to a great extent dependent on the particular interconnect scheme used. This is particularly true of the Level 3 and 4 protocols that generally are uniquely written for a particular minicomputer or family of minis. They often fall under the name of a total network software package such as DECnet written for the DEC PDP-11 family of minis, Maxnet for Modular Computer Systems minis, or HP-DSN for Hewlett-Packard's minis, to name a few.

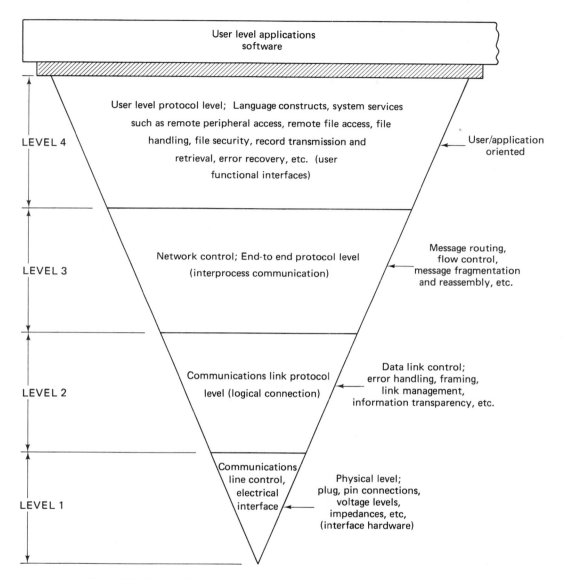

Figure 3-9 Protocol levels are usually implemented as a series of software and hardware layers. Improvements can be made in any layer without affecting layers above or below.

The following subsections will explore the various message communication protocol layers, in terms of features and constraints starting with Level 2. Level 1, the hardware "plug" level, has been omitted since it is assumed that the reader is familiar with the commonly used commercial RS-232C and/or the military Mil-Std-188 standards for interfacing bit-serial links. (Some of the commonly used commercial electrical and mechanical interface standards, such as RS-232C, RS-422, and RS-423 are summarized in Chapter 1.)

3.3.1 The Data Link Control Layer

The data link control layer contains the "grammar" or set of rules whereby data can be transferred reliably over a single communications link between two computers or a computer and a computer terminal. To implement data link control in a multimicro- or minicomputer system, it is necessary to recognize the structure of the system or network and the simultaneous levels of communication that may be occurring within it.

The structure of the network usually determines the complexity of the data link control. Figures 3-10 through 3-12 illustrate three progressively more demanding multimicro- or minicomputer systems. The centralized, star configuration of Figure 3-10 contains a central hub or processor serving several multiple users that may be minicomputers or terminals containing one or more microprocessors. In a terminal-based configuration, each terminal, typically, provides relatively simple functions of data and control input and displays output to a human user. These terminals may provide local intelligence (programmable under software control), graphics capability, or local storage using cassette tapes or floppy disks, or they may include other features to streamline the user's interaction with the central, host computer.

The configuration shown in Figure 3-11 usually imposes a heavier demand on the data link by interconnecting two minicomputers via a dedicated or switched line. The data link control should provide for communications between two computer

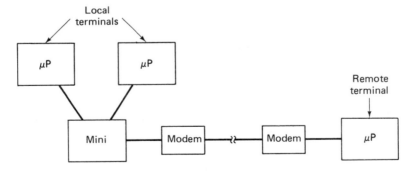

Figure 3-10 Terminal-oriented, centralized configuration (star).

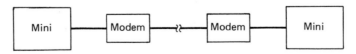

Figure 3-11 Computer-to-computer configuration.

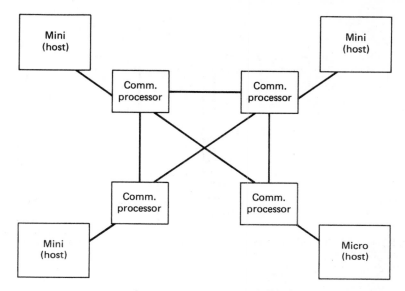

Figure 3-12 Multimini/micro-computer network using communications processors.

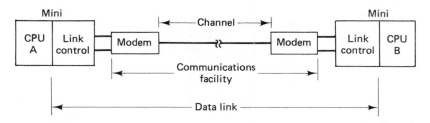

Figure 3-13 Point-to-point interconnect structure for two minicomputers, A and B.

operating systems as well as users, to allow resource sharing, communication of programs and data files, and scheduling coordination. Such a structure, shown in Figure 3-13, is also termed *point to point*.

Additional complexity arises in multiple-connected networks of micros and/or minis, as shown in Figure 3-11. In this particular example, the communications processing is handled by dedicated communications processors to relieve the host computers of detailed link management tasks. Two typical interconnect structures, bus-oriented and loop-based, both with centralized control, are shown in Figures 3-14 and 3-15.

The eight major functions usually performed by data link control protocols include the following.

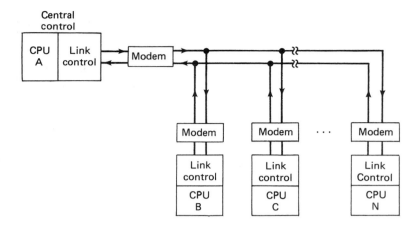

Figure 3-14 Bus-oriented multiminicomputer system with a central controller (CPU A).

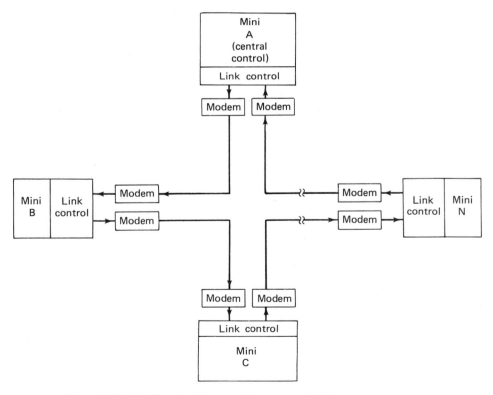

Figure 3-15 Unidirectional loop or ring-type multiminicomputer system.

- Data transfer control
- Error checking and recovery
- Information coding
- Information transparency
- Optimization of line utilization
- Maintenance of synchronization
- Communications facility transparency
- Bootstrap capability

This section details these functions and summarizes various data link control requirements independent of the interconnect structure.

Data transfer control. The major functions performed by data link control protocols include error-handling, information coding, providing information transparency, link optimization, maintenance of synchronization, providing communications facility transparency to users, and down-line loading/bootstrap capability.

Messages are typically framed by a header or control field and trailer or error checking field as shown in Figure 3-16. The framing of the message block provides the location of the start and finish of a message by identifying groups of bits that act as message delimiters.

Once framed, the message blocks require link management. This function controls transmission and reception on the link by, among other things, directing transmission, deciding who may transmit, identifying sender and receiver, and establishing and terminating a logical link* connection between two computers in the system (one or both computers may be microprocessors controlling intelligent terminals).

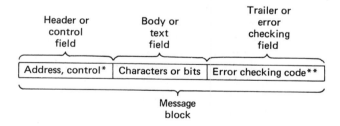

* May also contain synchronization bits (characters), flag(s), and/or error checking code.

** May also contain flag bits.

Figure 3-16 General message block format.

*A logical link is a discrete conversation path between two cooperating processes.

The following five types of control information are, as a rule, contained in most data link control protocols:

1. *Field delimiters*, e.g., special characters such as SOH (start of header), STX (start of text), and ETX (end of text). Fields may also be delimited by position within the message block.
2. *Addressing*—provides source and destination of the block.
3. *Sequence control*—prevents the loss or duplication of message blocks.
4. *Control flags*—indicates whether block contains data or supervisory message, whether first, intermediate, or last block, etc.
5. *Acknowledgement information*—handshaking response to indicate good or bad reception, request a wait before further transmissions, etc.

This information is also part of the error recovery procedures. Each of the seven major data link control functions are discussed in more detail below.

Error checking and recovery. Error checking protocols provide detection of errors produced by communication link: noise, faulty hardware, and other sources. Error checking is normally accomplished by detecting inconsistencies within redundant data. Redundant bits may be supplied within a character (e.g., one or more parity bits added to a character), or they may be generated by a coding algorithm and appended to the message block. The latter code is called a *block* or *frame check code* and is normally found in the trailer (see Figure 3-16).

Primary types of error checking codes found in data link control protocols are

1. VRC (Vertical Redundancy Check)—checks parity by character.
2. LRC (Longitudinal Redundancy Check)—checks parity at end of message.
3. CRC (Cyclic Redundancy Check)—checks message by dividing the message bits by a polynomial and appending the remainder to the message block. Upon receipt, the message plus CRC bits are divided by the same polynomial; if a nonzero remainder occurs, an error is present. A popular version is "CRC-16," which uses a polynomial of the form $x^{16} + x^{15} + x^2 + 1$.

Error recovery is the reaction to an error condition that is prescribed by the rules of a specific protocol. Two types of error recovery are normally followed:

1. Positive or negative acknowledgement (ACK or NAK) with request for retransmission: The common term for this procedure is ARQ (Automatic request for repeat), and common usage shows two types, stop-and-wait ARQ and continuous ARQ. Stop-and-wait ARQ requires the sender to wait until acknowledgement is received for the current block before another block can be sent, with a resulting waste of some of the link capacity, as shown in Figure 3-17. In continuous ARQ, the sender continues to send blocks while simultaneously listening to a return channel. If an erroneous block is flagged

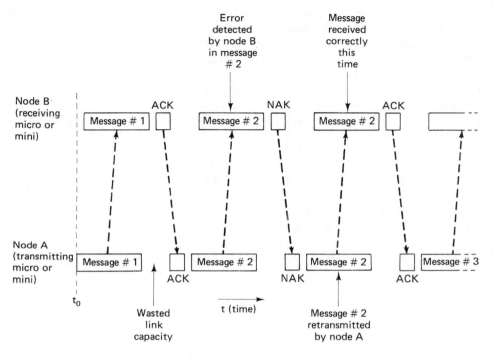

Figure 3-17   Stop-and-wait ARQ procedure between nodes A and B.

on the return channel, the sender retransmits this block at the next opportunity and then resumes normal transmission.

This method also wastes bandwidth since all messages received after the erroneous ones are also retransmitted (also called continuous ARQ with pullback). Continuous ARQ is also used in a mode where only the incorrectly received block is retransmitted (sometimes called Selective Repeat ARQ).

2. Forward error correction: In this technique, the receiving station discovers and corrects the errors by using special decoding of redundant bit structures imbedded in the data. Forward error correction cannot give as much protection as ARQ without adding unacceptably high overhead to the message and is normally not used unless ARQ is infeasible. (Overhead is defined as any part of a message block that is not data, e.g., control codes, error codes, and delimiters.)

Information coding.   The type of code structure used by the data link control protocol that requires that data and control information be represented by members of a predefined character set is called a *character-oriented* protocol. The character set is divided into two parts, data and control. A control character is not allowed inside the data field unless precautions are taken. Types of character codes that may be used in character-oriented protocols include ASCII (7 bits + parity bit), EBCDIC (8 bits), Baudot (5 bits), 4-of-8 code (8 bits), BCD (4 bits), and Transcode (6 bits).

A second major type of protocol is the bit-oriented protocol, a more recent development in digital communications. No special character code is required, since control information is placed positionally within the message and may be quantized to the individual bit level. There is only one special character, called a *frame flag*, that cannot be duplicated within a frame.

Information transparency.   In many cases, it may be desirable to transmit arbitrary characters or bit patterns in the text of a message without allowing them to be accidentally interpreted by the protocol as link control information. The realization of this goal is called *information transparency*. There are three basic techniques that depend on the type of protocol used.

For character-oriented protocols, two techniques in use are character stuffing and data field count (Figures 3-18, 3-19, 3-20). Character stuffing is the insertion of

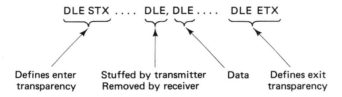

Figure 3-18   Character stuffing for achieving transparency (used in IBM's BSC).

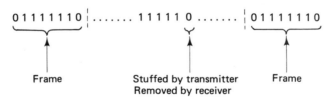

Figure 3-19   Bit stuffing for achieving transparency (used in HDLC, ADCCP, SDLC, etc.).

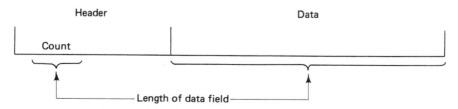

Figure 3-20   "Count" for achieving transparency (used in DEC's DDCMP).

a special control character, such as DLE (Data Link Escape), immediately before the control character that is to be ignored. Upon message receipt, the line control software strips away the inserted character and delivers the original text to its destination. An alternative to character stuffing is to supply a count in the message header that defines the number of characters in the text. The receiving terminal ignores any accidental control characters occurring within the counted field.

The bit-oriented protocols share a common technique called *bit stuffing*. The frame flag is a unique character defined as 01111110 (zero, six ones, zero). A sequence of six consecutive ones is prevented within the message by inserting (stuffing) a zero bit after any consecutive run of five ones. The extra zero bit is removed at the receiving terminal to reconstruct the original message. Information transparency is desirable for handling pure binary data and machine language computer programs, making it possible to down-load computers remotely and to share data files and programs.

Optimization of line utilization. The characteristics of a protocol involved with line or link utilization are as follows:

1. Direction utilization. Communication links may be designed to operate in simplex, half-duplex, or full-duplex modes. Simplex is defined as a one-way communication mode between two stations. Half-duplex allows two-way communications on an alternating basis. Full-duplex permits simultaneous two-way communications, allowing potentially higher throughput and response time than half-duplex. A given protocol may accommodate only one mode, or it may allow two or more directional modes, depending on its capabilities.
2. Control overhead. Control and error checking bits and messages, although necessary for link management, add nothing to the information content of the message and are considered overhead. Overhead contributes directly to the degree of efficiency of line utilization.
3. Acknowledgement handling. Message acknowledgements are another form of control overhead that impact throughput and response time. For example, continuous ARQ with acknowlegements imbedded in the return message blocks is more efficient than stop-and-wait ARQ with separate ACK messages.
4. Number of stations. The number of stations a protocol can accommodate simultaneously on a line, e.g., point to point, multipoint, or switched, affects its applicability.

Maintenance of synchronization. The protocol usually provides a unique sequence of bits or special synchronization characters at the start and end of a message block to allow message framing. Also, the line protocol generally cooperates with the signaling and data clock extraction circuitry in providing a message that is amenable to bit synchronization.

Communications facility transparency.   This characteristic of a protocol concerns the type of communications path that can be accommodated. The basic facility types include serial asynchronous, serial synchronous, and parallel. The physical realization of each type may be dedicated hard-wire, leased, or dial-up lines, and communication satellite or other RF links. The more effective protocols can handle a diversity of facility types with no basic changes in format and procedure.

Providing bootstrap capability.   Finally, a data link control protocol should include the capability for bootstrapping. Bootstrapping provides a means for minicomputers in a multiminicomputer system to set remotely the initial states and control modes for other minis in the system through down-link loading rather than having a human operator perform this function locally, either from the front panel of a mini or using a peripheral device such as a card or paper tape reader or a disc. Most of the commonly used data link control protocols are summarized and compared in Appendix. The trend is to incorporate these protocols into hardware. A summary is therefore also included of some hardware devices that perform the data link control protocol functions.

In selecting the most effective line protocol for a multimicro- or minicomputer system, it is necessary to consider the requirements imposed on the protocol by the communications facilities and the desired application of these facilities.

Data link control protocol selection.   The use of certain types of communications facilities may by their nature influence the protocol implementation. For example, in distributed systems where satellite communications are used, inherently long propagation delays exist (e.g., $\frac{1}{4}$ sec). In such systems, a greater need exists for numbering message blocks than would be necessary for purely terrestrial systems. This need for greater numbering capability, along with a two-way, simultaneous control capability, would be required for efficient use of the network. Typical application requirements are described below:

Conversational applications.   Conversational applications are typified by relatively balanced traffic from and to an operator-oriented terminal. The traffic is composed of messages of fairly short length with operator participation on a record-by-record basis. Each exchange of records represents a completed unit that is considered by the system to be functionally independent from other such exchanges.

Since the amount of information used for data link control can become a significant percentage of the total traffic, optimization of data link control overhead is an important requirement. Relatively fast response time is also a requirement, but consistency of response time is even more significant in order to maintain user satisfaction. Since the operator may become involved in procedures for recovering from system-detected errors, automatic error recovery is less of a requirement than for some other applications, such as batch applications. Whether recovery is mostly automatic or mostly reliant on the operator will depend on tradeoffs between hardware and software costs versus operator convenience and human factors considerations.

Inquiry applications.   Inquiry applications are typified by relatively short input messages and relatively long output messages; thus, there is a traffic imbalance. It would not be unusual for this input-to-output traffic ratio to reach one to four or even larger imbalances. The requirements imposed on data link control by inquiry applications are much the same as for conversational applications; however, an advantage can be obtained if a second inquiry can be accepted while the response to the first inquiry is being outputted. This implies using a particular form of duplex transmission, i.e., receiving input from one micro- or minicomputer or display terminal on a multipoint link while simultaneously sending output to another node in the network. Such a form of duplex operation has been termed *multipoint*. Involvement by the operator in recovery procedures from system-detected errors can be expected.

Batch applications.   Batch applications (e.g., terminal-to-processor remote job entry) are typified by relatively large quantities of input and/or output data per job. Because of this, it is less important that the number of data link control characters used for control (resulting in overhead) be at an absolute minimum since they represent a smaller percentage of the total traffic. Further, the effects of turnaround delays are less significant than they are for short length messages (blocks); thus, half-duplex facilities are usually employed. Batch applications are usually expected to operate without direct operator participation on a record or transmission block basis. Thus, the requirement for automatic detection of and recovery from errors is greater than in applications that are more closely attended by an operator. It should be noted, however, that multimicro- and minicomputer systems are less often used in a batch mode.

Processor-to-processor applications.   In processor-to-processor applications, the traffic, in many cases, is relatively balanced; however, the traffic pattern may be highly variable and dependent on the division of function between the processors for the particular job being performed. The effects of data link control overhead tend to be less significant than in most of the other cases mentioned, but there is a high requirement for recovery from system-detected errors to be fully automatic and for operator intervention to be held to an absolute minimum.

3.3.2   The End-to-End Interprocess Communication Layer

Several of the interconnect schemes described in Chapter 2 consist of "netted" micro- or minicomputers where messages from one computer to another have to be forwarded by one or more intermediaries. Examples of such systems are the hierarchical networks where messages may have to be forwarded through several hierarchical levels of minis, loop-based systems where a message may have to be passed around the loop from one computer to its neighbor until it reaches its intended destination or packet-switched networks where messages, broken into packets, are switched via several intermediate node processors or network switches to reach their destination host. The Level 3 protocols define formatting and control procedures for end-to-end connections in such distributed systems. These procedures include message routing, as well as message accountability from an originating computer to a destination computer.

When more than one user or process wants to access a computer at the same time, several logical links may appear to operate simultaneously over a single physical communications link. The primary function of Level 3, therefore, is also to perform all the bookkeeping required to allow many users, each with one or more logical links, to share a physical link. The logical separation of data might be compared to a telephone company providing many private communications links over a single circuit. The end-to-end interprocess communication layer is, therefore, also termed the *logical link control layer* [in contrast to the physical (real) or data link control layer].

Several end-to-end transmission layer strategies are in common use, such as circuit, message, and packet switching.

Circuit switching implies the establishment of dedicated channels, or physical circuits, in support of communications. These circuits are set up prior to commencement of the transmission of a message.

In the circuit-switched case, communicating parties are connected via real circuits. A real circuit is set up during a "selection phase" and released during a "clear phase," after the transmission of data has been completed. The selection phase may be a significant part of the total transmission period.

Circuit switching is more efficient than packet switching when long messages, such as large files, are continually being transmitted between two computers in a system. Normally, this transmission strategy is implemented at the data link control level. The star topology (see Section 2.5) can be viewed as a special case of a circuit-switched system.

The end-to-end interprocess communications layer does, in some cases, contain two sublayers: the transport layer and the transmission layer. The distinction between these two sublayers is often quite fuzzy, and a duplication of functions exists between the two.

The major purpose for having these two sublayers is to separate the independent feature of a particular technology base such as packet switching from end-to-end controls themselves. The transport layer generally provides a transport service to functional- or applications-oriented protocols located in the top layer (Level 4). The transmission layer is closely coupled to the particular technology used for interconnecting micros and/or minis, be it point-to-point links, a global bus, private (telephone) lines, or circuit-, message-, or packet-switched systems. The transmission layer may, in fact, encompass the data link control layer as is normally the case for circuit-switched systems.

The transmission layer is of particular significance in packet-switched systems. As previously discussed, packet switching is a message switching technique in which the messages are broken into fixed-length packets and routed individually through network "switches" to host minis. The switches may be dedicated computers or other host minis. A packet is defined as a group of binary digits including data and call control signals (e.g., address) that is switched as a composite whole. Each addressed packet occupies a transmission channel for the duration of the transmission of the packet only.

The channel is then available for use by packets being transferred between other computers or processes. Thus, channels between packet switches are shared between many processes or users on a demand basis. To a user, a packet switching can be regarded basically as the acceptance and delivery of packets. For the host mini, a simple protocol is also required for the immediate link with the network to deal with local flow and error control and with those control signals that are outside the stream of data packets.

The two most well-known modes of operation for packet switching systems are based on the use of datagrams and virtual circuits.

A datagram is a packet that flows through the network without prior announcement or call setup. In the virtual circuit mode, transmission of information is preceded by a selection phase in which the setup of a virtual circuit is completed and followed by a clear phase in which the virtual circuit is cleared. (The virtual circuit mode is defined in the X.25 recommended standard by CCITT.) Current packet networks are based on either the datagram or virtual circuit forms of packet switching.

The datagram packet transmission strategy does not usually include end-to-end network controls in it. Packet switching is of most benefit when a large number of processes exchange infrequent short messages. In this case, it is not economical to maintain or establish a data path for each message such as would be the case in circuit switching.

Forms of packet switching are also found in some of the ring or loop systems discussed in Chapter 2, such as the DCS system and the Pierce loop. In these cases, the routing logic is very simple.

The Institute for Information Processing (IFIP) internetwork end-to-end transport protocol* is exclusively proposed for end-to-end control. Although the CCITT X.25 packet-switched protocol does include some end-to-end requirements, these are, in some respects, ill-defined or incomplete. For example, X.25 does not specify the establishment of multiple, simultaneous, virtual circuits between two nodes. The reason for this is that X.25 service was intended to support terminal-to-terminal or terminal-to-computer transmission rather than transmission relative to an interprocess communication facility.

The IFIP internetwork transport protocol will, however, make up for the deficiencies in X.25 and interface with lower level protocols.

The primary functions of this standard are related to multiplexing/demultiplexing, opening and closing of connections, message fragmentation and reassembly, data transfer, and error control.

---

*V. Cerf, A. McKenzie, R. Scantlebury, and H. Zimmermann, "Proposal for an Internetwork End-to-End Transport Protocol," International Federation for Information Processing Working Group 6.1, Computer Network Protocols Symposium, University of Liege, Belgium, Feb. 1978.

The IFIP end-to-end protocol functions are used to provide an overview of major elements included in an end-to-end protocol, such as multiplexing and demultiplexing of messages, opening and closing of connections between processes (local and remote), message fragmentation and reassembly, data transfer, error control, and message flow and routing control. Both DECnet and ARPANET are used to illustrate some implementation approaches to Level 3 end-to-end protocol structures.

Multiplexing/demultiplexing. As several tasks or user processes in a given host or minicomputer network node may request the services of an intermediate node or "transport station" that is capable of forwarding messages to a receiving minicomputer-based node, the problem of multiplexing and demultiplexing must be resolved.

The notion of a transport station is based on the need for an interprocess communications facility that is itself distributed and may be represented as two distributed processes whose cooperation is governed by the transport layer protocol. Other names used to describe this facility are "transmission control program" and "network control program."

The transport station must be able to support several sessions and it is, of course, on the virtual link of each session that error and flow control must be enforced. The multiplexing/demultiplexing functions are inherent in some of the other transport protocol functions, described in the following paragraphs.

Opening and closing of connections. Protocols for opening and closing of connections between tasks (virtual links) are required in order to avoid having to maintain perpetually the state of all possible conversations in a network. Furthermore, in the case of a host crash, the protocol must be reinitialized to allow reliable communication to proceed from the time of failure. Also, processes or tasks may wish to make themselves available for communication at some times and to refuse communications at other times.

When a process or task wants to establish a connection with another process, it sends a request block to its local transport station. The request block contains mainly one of three kinds of operation codes and parameters.

1. Parameters related to the addresses of processes involved and the identification of the request connection.
2. Parameters related to the level and characteristics of the service to ensure during the data transfer phase.
3. Parameters that are of no concern for the transport station level but have to be transmitted to the remote process.

After the processing of the request block, the transport station will send a message to the other transport station involved in the requested connection. If the remote process has indicated its willingness to be involved in a connection (by a request block), the remote transport station sends to it a response block which contains the information which will enable the called process to accept or reject the connection by another request block sent to its transport station. This transport station will return a message to the other transport station that, at the end of this exchange, will be able to confirm or reject the opening of the connection.

The brief scenario above, which is not the only one possible, puts into evidence the interaction between a process and its local transport station (through exchange of request blocks and response blocks) and the interaction between two transport stations (through exchange of messages). For the closing of a connection, the same kind of exchange has to be considered.

Fragmentation and reassembly.   The unit of information presented to the transport functions from a user process is the message. For communication purposes, it may be more cost effective to break that message into smaller information units called *fragments*. These fragments must be reassembled at the destination. In cases where the transmission layer strategy is based on packet switching, the fragment is called a *packet*.

Data transfer.   Opening and closing a connection is concerned with achieving specific effects by the transfer of self-contained commands. In contrast, data transfer is concerned with the transfer of a sequence of fragments across the network, and each fragment must be related to the overall sequence.

A noticeable difference in handling fragments at the receiver end derives from the sequence of arrivals. When the sending order is normally maintained by the communication medium, any fragment can be identified by its order of arrival. Since errors may occur, fragments carry a sequence number, and any fragment arriving out of sequence is an indication of an error.

On the other hand, when fragments may normally arrive out of sequence, they should not be rejected, except if the occurrence is practically negligible. Thus, some buffering is needed to hold temporarily early fragments waiting for logical predecessors. Fragments must be labeled so that identification can take place. This identification usually occurs by including a header preceding the text or the descriptor of the fragment proper.

Error control.   To provide reliable communications, some form of error control is needed. Messages may be lost due to (1) hardware interface or transmission path failure, (2) software failure, and (3) congestion. At the end-to-end network protocol level, error control functions may exist either in the transmission layer or transport layer, or in both. There is no simple criterion to help determine at which level or layer error control would be most effective. Error control overhead in transmission, processing, or buffering depends on the many variants in acknowledgement schemes. Also, error and traffic patterns, user constraints, and system characteristics are major factors bearing on error control effectiveness.

A simple scheme for error control found at the data link protocol level is based on the use of check sums. The sender calculates a check sum and attaches it to the message. The receiver also calculates a check sum and compares it with the check sum transmitted with the message. If a discrepancy is found, an error has occurred.

For additional information, the sender must have some way of knowing that a message arrived at its destination correctly or incorrectly. A simple way to provide this knowledge is to have the receiver acknowledge each correctly received message. The sender can then assume that if no acknowledgement is received by the end of a time-out period, then the message either was afflicted with errors or was undelivered. In this case, the sender retransmits the message. Note that the acknowledgement must also be check summed since it is transmitted via the same media as the message and therefore is subject to errors in the same way.

One of the deficiencies of the IFIP Internetwork Transport Protocol is the fact that it fails when the finite time for message delivery and the variability of that time are considered. If the delivery time in one instance is approximately equal to the time-out period, then the sender can decide to retransmit just as the receiver decides to send the acknowledgement (of the first copy). These then pass each other in the communications network. The result is that the receiver accepts two copies of the same message and the sender gets an extra acknowledgement. Furthermore, either one of the acknowledgements could be afflicted with errors, thereby also prohibiting the sender from detecting the problem. Some means of identifying a message would, therefore, have to be added to the protocol; for convenience, numbers could be used. Thus, if the sender attaches a sequence number to each message, the receiver can check to be sure it has not previously accepted a copy of the same message. If a maximum sequence number, n, were to be used, the sequence numbers could be used cyclically; that is, after sequence number n is used, the sequence would be restarted at zero.

Flow control.   Flow control is the set of mechanisms whereby a flow of data can be maintained within limits compatible with the amount of available resources. Most practical problems encountered with flow control involve insufficient throughput rather than flooding a system with messages. When the latter occurs, it is usually traceable to a design flaw or an erratic component. The primary function of flow control is, therefore, to keep the data moving smoothly.

Resources required to carry a flow of data can be categorized in two classes:

1. Basic: buffers, transmission bandwidth, processor time, etc.
2. Incidental: name space, table entries, logical channels, etc.

Basic resources are always required in store-and-forward communications. Incidental resources are usually required, but they are primarily implementation-dependent.

Flow control schemes are complex constructions and include combinations of several interacting functions working at one or several layers in a system architecture. The more well-known flow control schemes or throttling tools are based on methods such as Stop and Go, Credit, Rate, Delay, or Class Indicator. These, as well as some incidental schemes, are described below.

Stop and go. A source is controlled by signals of a binary nature. Either it can send traffic without limit or it can be barred from transmitting. This technique is used in most data link control procedures, such as BSC or HDLC (see Appendix). It is also the principle of handshaking signals in electrical interfaces. A stop or go signal takes effect immediately, or at the earliest opportunity after a transmission currently in progress.

The receiver has to take into account the transit delay necessary to carry stop/go signals to the sender. On terrestrial links, this delay is negligible with regard to the transmission time of a message of tens or thousands of bits. Satellite links may introduce delays equivalent to the transmission time of several consecutive messages. Thus, when a receiver sends a stop, a certain amount of traffic may continue to arrive for a while. This amount of traffic is composed of outstanding messages at the time the stop signal is sent by the receiver, plus additional messages sent while the stop signal is carried to the sender. One can easily understand that long and variable transit delays make this tool completely ineffectual, since the amount of outstanding traffic may vary within large limits.

Credit. The sender cannot transmit unless it has received from the receiver an indication about the amount of traffic that can be accepted. This quantifying scheme protects completely the receiver from an excess of arrivals.

The amount of acceptable traffic may be indicated in terms of bits, characters, messages, sequence of messages, message numbers, etc. An extreme case is an infinite credit, which puts the sender in a freewheeling mode.

Polling may be viewed as a particular case of a credit scheme, since a poll message conveys the right to send just one sequence of messages. Error control schemes are often used as a rudimentary form of credit flow control. Indeed, acknowledgements usually carry two meanings: good reception and a credit to send one or more additional messages. This does not mean that error and flow control are the same thing. It only means that, in certain implementations, error and flow control signals may be condensed in the same messages.

Furthermore, a credit scheme requires certain safeguards. For example, should a credit be given forever and possibly not used? What if a credit gets lost or duplicated?

Rate. The sender transmits traffic at a predetermined rate, which may have been evaluated with regard to resources required. Rates may be adjusted dynamically when the resource supply is changing.

A typical application of that scheme is the feeding of output peripherals, working at a well-known speed. Devices such as character printer terminals are usually unable to control senders. The only way they can operate properly is to be fed characters at their own pace.

Time slot allocation schemes are a variety of rate controlling mechanisms. They have been used extensively for CPU sharing and transmission line servicing by a communication controller. Loop-based systems, as described in Chapter 2, commonly use slotting methods.

Delay. In any organization, increased delay is a way of throttling, if not discouraging, user demands. Indeed, the useful lifetime of information is limited. When transmit delays increase, some sources give up, as service degradation becomes intolerable. This is typical of on-line applications, where tolerance is related to human behavior. With automated users, tolerance is usually determined by the setting of a timer or by a threshold in the number of unsuccessful attempts.

An extreme case of increase delay is discarded traffic, which is tantamount to infinite delay. In other cases, senders do not give up; they just keep sending. This may have adverse effects depending on transmission protocols.

A conventional message switching system equipped with secondary storage may be considered as an infinite sink and can introduce long transit delays. In this case, increased delays have no immediate effect, as senders are usually not aware of the received traffic. Thus, other mechanisms are necessary to prevent input traffic from using up all available storage when some destination gets blocked.

More often, senders and receivers are coupled via an end-to-end protocol requiring some form or receiver acknowledgement, which limits the amount of outstanding traffic. In this case, increased delay has an immediate effect in throttling senders, because they have to wait for receiver acknowledgement before they can proceed.

Delay may result from the saturation of a shared resource (processor, line, buffer pool, etc.) or from a deliberate decision in traffic management, such as low priorities or diversion onto longer routes.

Using delay as a throttling tool is often difficult to implement successfully. Indeed, outstanding traffic must be stored and somehow managed for a longer time. Thus, more resources are required to carry the same amount of traffic while degrading the service. The system may enter an unstable domain where more and more resources are consumed with less and less delivered traffic. A good analogy is traffic jams in busy city intersections.

Class. Traffic is offered with a class indicator. When enough resources are available, all offered traffic is accepted and carried. Otherwise, some classes are restricted depending on criteria that appear to strike an acceptable balance between conflicting user demands. Restriction may be in the form of longer delay, limited input rate or credit, and limited number of destinations, or a class may even be denied service entirely.

In other words, a class scheme is just a level of traffic segregation, leading to the application of some specific throttling policy, which may be selected dynamically. In a sense, it is a preliminary level of service selection. For example, in some military networks used for command and control, messages are segregated into precedence levels where time-critical, high-priority messages preempt the transmission of routine information. (These systems have been called "precedence networks.")

Flow control based on incidental throttling tools. As the qualifier *incidental* implies, there may be an almost unlimited number of mechanisms that may induce throttling as a side effect. Some examples of such mechanisms are provided, such as "name space," use of table entries, initialization, traffic overhead, and response time.

In some systems, names must be obtained to designate sender and receiver before they can exchange useful traffic. If names are not sharable among several pairs of correspondents, and if they are in limited supply, traffic will necessarily be kept under some limit. This is the case when a sender or receiver may not use more than a certain number of "logical channels" to communicate with other correspondents.

Another example of traffic throttling due to a restricted name space is a cyclic message-numbering scheme. Since message numbers are reused and are usually essential for error control, traffic must be stopped when unacknowledged messages take up all available names.

A third example is based on table entries. Any Store and Forward communication system uses internal tables to keep track of the resources being managed. In some systems, there may be a table of active transactions. In others, each "virtual circuit" occupies table entries in a number of network nodes. Since the number of ongoing calls is not necessarily predictable, there may be traffic limitations due to a lack of available table space. A similar blocking effect can be observed in telephone systems, where connection devices are equivalent to table entries.

In some systems, traffic may not be carried between two correspondents until after they have set up a logical connection, or a virtual circuit. The delay taken by this initialization, compounded with the resources used, puts some limitation on the rate of interactions.

Another throttling effect may be the result of overhead traffic and response time. Control information exchanged between components of a communication system uses up a certain amount of resources. It takes the form of additional messages or additional control fields in message headers. Wrapping and unwrapping data over and again through layers of protocols is a customary cause of creeping overhead and bandwidth limitation.

Also, since traffic is almost always controlled by a number of superimposed protocols, making up a layered structure, each layer must somehow submit requests to and wait for answers from an adjacent layer. As each layer shares its resources among several concurrent requests, queuing time associated with transit delays introduces some time lag between consecutive requests. As a result, traffic throughput between correspondents may be lower than what available resources would allow.

In summary, end-to-end flow control is the set of mechanisms whereby an endpoint receiver maintains the sender traffic within limits compatible with the amount of resources available at the receiver end. Hence, end-to-end flow control is not concerned with problems of resource availability that may arise within intermediate subsystems interposed between sender and receiver such as may be reflected in the transmission layer strategies. Typically, intermediate subsystems are shared between a number of sender-receiver pairs such as a telephone line or a packet subnetwork. Flow control in an intermediate subsystem is referred to as Congestion Control. It is a set of mechanisms that maintain input traffic within limits compatible with the amount of resources available to the subsystem. If the software for a multiminicomputer system must handle a particular transmission layer strategy such as packet switching, then the major flow control issues will reside in Congestion Control.

End-to-end flow control, as described above, is a mixture of two distinct concepts. The first concept is a flow control protocol, i.e., a set of conventions followed by both sender and receiver to exchange control information pertaining to the flow of data; for example, stop and go signals, credits, rates, and priorities. The second concept is the resource management scheme that is highly dependent on the local environment. The resources could include buffers and links.

Some typical requirements for flow control are

1. Specified throughput determined by the slower end point, for steady data flows.
2. Maximum throughput when the subsystem limits traffic.
3. Minimum delay for bursty traffic.
4. Guaranteed delay and throughput for real-time traffic.

In case 1, end-to-end flow control has an effect only when the receiver is the bottleneck, e.g., an output peripheral. A specified throughput is obtained when the receiver never has to wait for traffic. In other words, there are always one or several messages queuing for the receiver. Since the sender must keep copies of transmitted messages until it has an acknowledgement, there is no advantage in building long queues in front of the receiver; the smaller, the better. Ideally, it would be sufficient that a new message arrive just at the time the receiver would go idle. In the absence of variations in transmit delay, this would require perfect synchronization between sender and receiver. This is impractical, and transmit delays do vary. Therefore, it is necessary to provide for some queuing on the receiver side, in order to damp out the variations in transit delay and sender output rate.

A credit scheme is quite appropriate to that sort of flow control requirement, as it allows periodic sender wake up for a certain amount of traffic. In addition, an indication of the desirable rate may help the sender schedule its output process.

In case 2, the approach is based on providing message traffic up to the subsystem acceptance limit. End-to-end flow control has no effect for dealing with pathological conditions arising within the subsystem, which needs mechanisms to protect itself and throttle senders.

In case 3, average throughput may be highly variable but normally below acceptable thresholds. The emphasis is on low transit delay. End-to-end flow control is only effective to curb long bursts, which would appear as case 1. In normal conditions, low delay depends on the characteristics of the subsystem.

Case 4 may involve bursty or steady traffic. It appears as a combination of the requirements of cases 1 and 2. So far, experience is lacking to assess properly the implication of end-to-end protocols on subsystem characteristics.

In conclusion, end-to-end flow control is an appropriate and little constraining tool for cases 1, 2, and 3 as long as the subsystem helps when its characteristics introduce some limitation. The various flow control mechanisms are summarized in Figure 3-21.

Method	Approach	Typical Applicability
Stop and Go	Binary, Possible Buffer Overflow Is Function of Link Delay	Point-to-point Systems
Credit	Number of Transmitted Messages Must Be Predetermined	Message and Packet Switched Systems Hierarchical Systems
Rate	Flow Is Dynamically Adjustable	Point-to-point Systems
Delay	Flow Control Through Receiver Acknowledgement	Loop, Point-to-point, Packet- or Message-switched, Hierarchical Systems
Class Indicator	Messages Must Be Prioritized	Most Interconnect Structures
Logical Channel Restriction	Control of Allocatable Bandwidth or Channel Usage Period	Point-to-point, Meassage- and Packet-switched Systems
Table Entry	Number of Transmitted Messages Controlled by Size of Message Table	—Same—
Miscellaneous System Delays	Throttling-based System Becoming Saturated —Usually Difficult to Predict or Control	Most Interconnect Structures

Figure 3-21 Flow control methods in systems where flow is *not* controlled by a unique hardware implementation approach, such as a slotted loop or bus.

Routing control. Routing Control is a set of mechanisms that prevent network resources from being underutilized while other equivalent resources are overtaxed. Routing functions may reside in either the transport or transmission layer. If the transmission layer strategy is packet switching implemented with an independent packet subnet subsystem, the routing control function would be included at this level. When this is not the case, routing control must be addressed at the end-to-end network control level. A fundamental step in designing a routing algorithm is, therefore the choice of the control regime to be used in the operation of the algorithm. The following are four types of control regimes:

1. Nonadaptive is a fixed algorithm that makes no real attempt to adjust to changing network conditions; no routing information is exchanged by the nodes, and no observations or measurements are made at individual nodes.
2. Centralized adaptive algorithms utilize a central authority or network Supervi-

sor that dictates the routing decisions to the individual nodes in response to network changes. This type of routing is reflected in the TYMNET network.

3. Isolated adaptive algorithms operating independently with each node making exclusive use of local data to adapt to changing conditions.

4. Distributed adaptive algorithms utilizing internode cooperation and the exchange of information to arrive at routing decisions.

The DECnet network services end-to-end transport protocol is used to illustrate a typical implementation scheme for flow control, message segmentation and reassembly, and message routing. Routing is also described for the ARPANET packet switching environment that is significantly different from that of DECnet.

Key DECnet network services end-to-end transport protocol features. The DECnet Network Services Protocol (NSP) permits two cooperating tasks, each on a different node in a network of PDP-11 minicomputers to communicate with each other in terms of exchanging messages and data, as shown in Figure 3-22. In addition, NSP provides the following capabilities or functions:

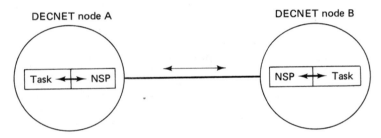

Figure 3-22 Two cooperating tasks at Nodes A and B, respectively, communicate with each other through DECnet NSP.

1. Functions to the dialog level:
   - Establishment of a task as an active network process capable of communicating with other processes in the network.
   - Creation of a logical link or conversation path with another task.
   - Acceptance or rejection of logical link connection from a remote task.
   - Transmission and receipt of data over a logical link.
   - Disconnection of a logical link connection or termination of a task's network activity.
   - Sending of interrupt messages to other tasks.
2. Functions for operation of link:
   - Multiplexing of logical links into physical links.
   - Control of traffic over logical links.
   - Segmentation of messages.
3. Functions for network supervision:

- Detection of node and link failures.
- Maintenance of routing paths.
4. Functions for network maintenance:
- Maintenance of error logs.

NSP provides the following services on logical links:

1. It guarantees delivery of data to the receiving process or notification if delivery is impossible.
2. It guarantees that message sequencing will be maintained over the logical link. It provides a mechanism to help prevent network buffer deadlocks* by providing a flow control mechanism on each logical link.

The guarantee of message delivery and proper sequencing are accomplished via message numbering with acknowledgment. Nonacknowledged messages are detected by time-out and recovery is by retransmission. Flow control is provided by a message request scheme. A message is never sent by NSP (even though the user has requested a transmission) unless the communicating process at the other end has issued a corresponding receive request. Multiplexing NSP logical link messages is accomplished by including unique, logical link identifying information with each data message. In addition, multiple NSP messages may be blocked into a single DDCMP† (or equivalent) transmission block.

The purpose of traffic control is merely to minimize buffer occupancy throughout the network by assuring that the receiving device has a buffer available to store the message. To assure efficiency, a link-status message (when used for traffic control) does not have to request one message at a time but instead can request a number of messages in the request-count field. Another field acknowledges messages received earlier.

In multinode networks, the receiver waits a prescribed period of time for a response after sending a link-status message. If nothing arrives, the received repeats its link-status message.

Messages can be of up to 8K bytes in length. NSP will divide the message into smaller "segments" that are sent over the communication line one by one. The segment length is preassigned at system generation time and is typically between 128 and 512 bytes, depending on line characteristics. Message acknowledgement and retransmission are performed only after all the segments comprising a message have been reassembled at the destination node.

In addition, a node can send a message indicating the maximum segment size that it can receive, thus allowing small end nodes to use just small segment sizes.

Receipt of a defective message causes the return of an error message. There are three categories of errors. The error message indicates the appropriate category and

---

*Distributed system deadlock is discussed in greater detail in Chapter 5.
†See Appendix for description of DDCMP.

then lists the specific type of error. Appended to the error message is all the erroneous message or else its header. The categories of error conditions and specific error types are

- Message flag error—routing or segmentation is not supported or message count is erroneous.
- Message routing error—destination nodes do not exist, path is out of service, message queues are full, routing header is invalid, or sequential delivery is impossible.
- Errors in other parts of the message—control message type is not supported, numbering is in error, request count is negative, address is invalid, type of connection specified in the message is not supported, or interrupts are too long.

DECnet's NSP handles message routing in the following manner: When the routing header of each segment enters a node, it is examined by NSP to determine whether or not the node is the final destination. If not, NSP executes a routing algorithm, which associates the destination address with a physical link to the next node along the route, one step closer to the final destination. A properly designed group of algorithms provides for the packets to move over reasonable direct routes, avoiding bottlenecks in the system. For reasons of efficiency, a routing header is not used when the source and destination nodes are directly connected via a physical link.

The routing algorithms range in complexity from simple table lookups to calculations for finding the optimum path for each packet. Therefore, the difficulty lies in deciding which node to send a packet to. The other aspects of routing—receiving a message, checking the header, and sending the message on to another node—are rather straightforward. The specific routing technique used is decided by the user, and it is in no way inherent in the NSP design.

The simplest form of routing is done where there is only a single physical path to a destination node, as in simple hierarchies. In such a case, the routing information may be stored in a table that relates the destination address to the physical link. Backup paths also can be listed in case the usual path is busy or out of service. The routing table is usually entered along with the other system software and changed by a programmer or operator when the need arises.

For networks that are prone to change, an optional message type, the routing message, permits the routing tables to be automatically updated from a single neighboring node. Other routing algorithms may require additional message types for proper network updating. Good network management requires that routing messages be promptly exchanged between neighboring nodes whenever there is a change.

When the traffic between two nodes exceeds the capacity of the lines between them, several paths may be taken simultaneously. Multiple logical paths can be implemented with NSP by assigning multiple addresses to nodes and different routing paths for each address. Also, multiple physical links can be developed with DDCMP, using a single NSP logical group address.

Routing messages from node to node within a network and the specific techniques or algorithm used for routing is usually highly dependent on the topology and requirements of the system. To this end, the routing algorithm has been removed directly from NSP and resides in a user level process within each node. The routing algorithm, the code that adapts or changes routing paths depending on the state of the links and nodes in the net, has been put at this level for ease of change and independence from NSP. Thus, some nodes in a network may use a highly adaptive scheme, whereas others, perhaps on one end of the network with very few alternate paths, may use a somewhat more static scheme at the same time. With this structure, many routing algorithm processes can be created for inclusion in a node system. The user again chooses the appropriate building blocks for the nodes and total system. To date, all NSP implementations are in software, but nothing precludes their implementation in hardware at a later date as has been done with DDCMP.

ARPANET end-to-end transport protocol routing features. The ARPA Network is a distributed heterogeneous network of large hosts supported by an independent packet-switched communication subsystem composed of IMP's,* which are Honeywell minicomputers. The routing control of the ARPANET is provided by the IMP communication subsystem. The unit of information being transferred is the packet that represents a fixed subset of a message.

The algorithm directs each packet to its destination along a path for which the total estimated transit time is smallest. This path is not determined in advance. Instead, each IMP individually decides which line to use in transmitting a packet addressed to another destination. This selection is made by a simple table lookup procedure. For each possible destination, an entry in the routing table designates the appropriate next line in the path.

Each IMP maintains a network delay table that gives an estimate of the delay it expects a packet to encounter in reaching every possible destination over each of its output lines. This table and other tables mentioned below are shown in Figure 3-23 as kept by IMP 2, for example. Thus, the delay from IMP 2 to IMP 5 using line 3 is found to be 4 in the Network Delay Table. Every $\frac{2}{3}$ sec (faster if the network is lightly loaded), the IMP sends its minimum delay table to each of its immediate neighbors via the communications links. Of course, before the minimum delay table is transmitted to the neighboring IMP's, the IMP sets the minimum delay to itself to zero.

Since all the neighbors of an IMP are also sending out their minimum delay tables every $\frac{2}{3}$ sec, with their own entry set to zero, an IMP receives a minimum delay table from each of its neighbors every $\frac{2}{3}$ sec. One can think of the receiving IMP reading in each table over the rows of the delay table as they arrive. The row to be written over is the row corresponding to the communications line that the arriving minimum delay table came in over. After all the neighbors' estimates have arrived, the IMP adds the local IMP delay table to the neighbors' estimates. This is done by adding to each column of the delay table the contribution of this IMP to the total

*IMP = Interface Message Processor.

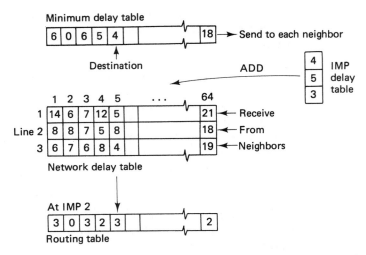

Figure 3-23   An example of a delay table maintained by an ARPANET IMP.

delay to each destination. Thus, the IMP has an estimate of the total delay to each destination over the best path to that destination. Actually, the algorithm does not need to keep all the neighbors' tables in memory; it is sufficient to keep the current overall minimum on each line. Then, whenever a neighbor's table is received, a new minimum delay table is immediately calculated.

In parallel with this computation, the IMP's also compute and propagate shortest path information in a similar fashion. This information is used only in the determination of connectivity. An upper limit of the number of lines in the longest path in the network is used as the cutoff for disconnected or nonexistent nodes.

From a performance point of view, this algorithm explicitly determines the connectivity of the network, since all IMP's are continuously exchanging the length of the shortest path from each IMP to each other IMP. Information travels quickly from IMP to IMP, so that changes in topology are recognized by the whole network in a matter of a few seconds. This figure is probably acceptable if one assumes that the network connectivity does not change too often. Furthermore, the algorithm also explicitly calculates the path of least delay; however, here the approximations, due to the frequency of routing update, mean that the estimated delay for traffic at one instant is a function of the traffic of several seconds before. This could potentially lead to oscillations and poor line utilization. The ARPANET algorithm attempts to head off this class of problems by biasing delay heavily toward the shortest path; that is, delay is measured by the number of packets on an output queue, plus a fixed increment, so that even an empty queue represents additional delay.

The algorithm has several deficiencies, some of which are relatively simple to cure, whereas others are more fundamental in nature. The strong bias in the algorithm toward the shortest path leads to stable flows near optimum values; however, the bias makes the algorithm somewhat insensitive to changes in traffic patterns, so that global optimization of delay and throughput is not likely as network loading increases. A second deficiency is that the algorithm maintains only one route per destination, updated every $\frac{2}{3}$ sec. This means that no load splitting is possible, at least not on a short-term basis. Finally, the algorithm is designed to find the least delay path and does not take into account such factors as optimizing total throughput or preventing congestion (except indirectly).

Perhaps the most appealing feature of the ARPANET routing algorithm is that it is simple. The IMP does not have to know the topology of the network or even the identity of its neighbors. When IMP's and lines go down, the algorithm functions as usual, and the new routing information propagates through the network by a process of exchanges between neighbors. The service provided by the algorithm is, therefore, relatively reliable.

Finally, the algorithm has a modest cost in terms of IMP and line resources. The calculation is proportional to the number of IMP's in the network and the number of lines connected to each IMP. The routing computation takes up about 5% of the CPU bandwidth of the IMP. The delay and node hop information is packed into a single 16-bit word per IMP, so that the routing message sent out on each line consists of 67 words, one for each IMP in the network, plus some header information. This amounts to about 3% of the bandwidth of a 50-Kbps line. At these low-bandwidth rates, added node delays and line delays are not appreciable. The IMP reserves a triple buffer of storage (shared by all lines) for receiving, updating, and transmitting routing messages. These tables, together with its own directory of the "best" lines to each destination, amount to about 3% of the main memory storage in an IMP. In summary, the IMP routing algorithm is a simple, inexpensive algorithm that performs well in steady state and in reacting to small changes in traffic.

The ARPANET algorithm is delay-oriented and works poorly under high load, however, because it does not gracefully distribute available line bandwidth under heavy traffic demand. For example, in cases with equivalent alternate paths, the total bandwidth remains restricted to little more than that of one of the paths.

The ARPANET routing algorithm was designed for a network with homogeneous nodes and circuits; that is, it assumes that the circuits have equivalent bandwidth and delay characteristics, which leads to degraded performance in areas near circuits with dissimilar characteristics. For example, a high-delay satellite circuit to Europe is treated as the equivalent of a low-delay land line in delay computation, leading to unrealistic routing decisions. Also, congestion may build where lines of different speeds meet. There are simple techniques for adaptively measuring circuit bandwidth and speed-of-light delay, which could be used by the packet switching nodes.

The ARPANET routing procedure sometimes adapts too slowly to changes that occur in the large ARPANET topology. The algorithm was originally designed for a much smaller network, so that response times to network changes are now sometimes too slow for existing traffic patterns, causing severe congestion in local areas. For example, data about a line outage on a busy route is sometimes not propagated with sufficient speed to prevent a large amount of traffic from entering this path and becoming bottled up.

Current multiple computer systems employ end-to-end protocol level transport schemes that vary widely in the amount of their sophistication. The sophistication of the end-to-end protocols will depend on the particular system goals and environment. For a dedicated real-time system involving minicomputers in close proximity to each other, an end-to-end protocol that is message-based, has fixed routing, and contains no error control, fragmentation, or sequencing should be used since performance rather than flexibility is of major importance. For large, multipurpose, geographically distributed systems, however, end-to-end protocols encompassing many of the previously described transport functions may be needed.

3.3.3   The User Level Control Layer

Transferring information is only a tool toward the achievement of some practical goals, e.g., interaction between process and terminal or file transfer. These are typical examples of high-level functions that are so commonly used in networks that they are worth packaging in some standard form. They are also termed *protocols*, such as *virtual terminal protocol* or *file transfer protocol*. A high-level protocol such as file transfer may involve more than two computers. It is no longer a simple end-to-end protocol. Actually, a high-level protocol is a set of rules defining the working of a distributed system of minis and/or micros that is designed for handling a particular application.

The goal is, therefore, to create a mechanism for the movement of application or user data between communicating processes and/or resources. This entails communications with, for example, I/O devices, disk files, system loaders, and the distributed programs of a user application.

A distributed mini- or microcomputer system must thus be able to accept commands, input or output data, and transfer information among its various components. These exchanges may carry data or commands as well as state variables (discussed in more detail in Chapter 5) necessary for the synchronization of the entire system.

Although data can be altered intentionally as part of a system task (e.g., data conversion or reformatting), communication mechanisms between the distributed components ideally should be transparent. Thus, an end-to-end protocol may be used as a building block to carry out any information transfer required by a higher level protocol.

Consequently, function or user level control consists of a number of different protocols, each appropriate for a particular class of resources. Some are user created protocols; others may already exist off-the-shelf, such as the DECnet Data Access Protocol (DAP), the Hewlett-Packard Distributed System Network (DSN) Access Method, the TELENET Terminal Access Protocol, and the French Cyclades Virtual Terminal Protocol.* (Other functional level control protocols exist for remote job entry, graphics, voice communication, mail facilities, and maintenance.)

---

*"Terminal Access in the Cyclades Computer Network," International Computer Symposium 1975, Juan-Les-Pins, France, North-Holland/American Elsevier Ed., June 1975, pp. 97–99.

These protocols can also be viewed as subroutines that provide the users with high-level access to all network resources. They typically include remote program management, remote command processing, file transfer, automatic dialing, and peripheral access. The selection and use of these protocols are, in general, determined by the requirements of the specific application.

In order to illustrate some typical functions performed by a user level protocol, the DECnet DAP file transfer protocol is described in the following section.

The DECnet data access protocol.　　The DECnet Data Access Protocol (DAP) is concerned with record and file formats and access requests. Its communicating process accesses the network using the same communication mechanism available to user-written programs. Unlike many other file transfer protocols, however, the DAP protocol also provides a virtual terminal capability.

The design of the Data Access Protocol (DAP) required that particular attention be paid to heterogeneity of the file systems with which DAP would interface (e.g., file systems with different access modes, formats, and capabilities). Within any given network configuration, these systems may exhibit considerable variety. To this end, the protocol was designed to be maximally efficient between like systems. Moreover, it should provide full functionality with the DEC Record Management Services (RMS) standard file system.

Record Management Services (RMS) provides a set of general-purpose file-handling capabilities for a number of operating systems in the DEC family. The service allows user written application programs to create, access, and maintain data files in a variety of organizations and accessed in several ways. RMS files can be organized sequentially, relatively, or indexed. Based upon these file organizations, records maintained by RMS can be accessed in the following ways:

1. Sequentially: Records are processed in consecutive order.
2. Randomly: Records are accessed either by relative record number or by indexing on one or more keys (access by relative record number permits retrieval of a record anywhere within the file without previous accessing of any other record).
3. Dynamic access: The combining of several access methods to permit access such as ISAM (indexed sequential access method).
4. Directly: Allows access to physical blocks.

In addition, RMS supports several record formats (fixed and variable length) and provides a protection and sharing mechanism.

DAP also contains the necessary protective facilities to ensure that files on a DECnet node are no less secure from unauthorized remote access than from unauthorized local access.

Furthermore, although DAP provides remote file access at the record level, it addresses file transfer through file retrieval and storage operations. Some of these features, such as message efficiency, error recovery, and security, are discussed in the following paragraphs.

Message efficiency.   In an effort to obtain efficient line use, several techniques are employed. First, in the messages that are exchanged between systems, a set of default values are described to allow for the possibility of not sending the information, thus making the messages shorter. Secondly, an (optional) length field is included in every message so that several messages can be included in one network message envelope. This message blocking strategy allows several DAP messages to be transmitted with the overhead of only one network transmission.

Further, attributes of individual records, such as records containing FORTRAN carriage control, COBOL carriage control, and implied Line Feed (LF)/Carriage Return (CR) envelopes can be represented, allowing the records to be shipped without these characteristics explicitly included in the data.

Although access is being provided at the record level, it is also necessary to optimize the protocol for file transfer. The optimization efficiency is accomplished during transfer access, by allowing data records to be transmitted sequentially without waiting for any specific DAP record request control messages; that is, the protocol can be operated in such a way so as not to include the use of the normally required control messages for each record transferred, thereby eliminating the overhead associated with each record. Flow control is performed implicitly by the network, thus optimizing the protocol.

Error recovery techniques.   The recovery strategies available within DAP can be either of two types:

1. Recovery from errors due to unaccessible records in the remote file.
2. Recovery from failures in the network, e.g., node failures or links going down.

The first type is handled by the skip/retry and continue facility. When an error is incurred, while either reading or writing a record from a remote system, the protocol is capable of retrying the operation with the record that generated the error, or skip that record and continue the transfer with the next record.

The second type of recovery is relevant only for sequential retrieval and storage of a file to allow continuation following network link reestablishment. In the retrieval case, the current file pointer or record number is sent to the remote file system on link reestablishment, and sequential retrieval starts at that point. In the storage case, the remote file system returns the record number last written and opens the file for append and storage continues.

Security and protection.   As stated earlier, DAP attempts to provide the same degree of file security and protection over the network as is available locally. This is accomplished by requiring that a user of DAP be a registered user of each system holding files to be accessed. To initiate access to a file, the user's identification information is used to authenticate the user (not necessarily logging the user on but providing sufficient information to allow that), and then file access is allowed to proceed under the normal rules for file access applicable to a local user.

DECnet DAP operating examples.   To illustrate the role that DAP messages play in providing data access, two typical operations, sequential file and record retrieval, are described. The current DAP messages are listed in Figure 3-24. Briefly, the pro-

Message	Definition
Configuration	Used to pass system configuration information between the systems involved in a DAP exchange. This message is sent immediately following link establishment by the system and contains information indicating various configurations of operating systems and file systems, version number of the protocol for determining compatability, and generic system capabilities to aid in the translation between unlike systems.
User Identification	Passes the user's identity, a password, and accounting information to the accessed system. Message is used for security and/or accounting purposes.
Attributes	Details the representation of the data in the file being accessed. This message contains information pertaining to file organization, data type, format, record attributes, record length, size, device characteristics, and other information relevant to protection and characterization of the file systems involved.
Access	Specifies the file name and type of access requested. The information indicates type of operation to be performed (e.g., open new file), the file specification (in the format required by the remote node), access mode (sequential, keyed, etc.), access operation requested (get, put, etc.), optional file and record processing features, and sharing options for this access.
Control Device/File	Used to send control-type information to a device or a file system. Control information may indicate, for example, get a record, find a record, rewind magnetic tape, or set loadable tabs for line printer, along with information indicating the particular record (or device) that is being controlled. This message allows the access mode to be changed from the previous setting.
Continue Transfer	This message includes information to allow the various recovery strategies such as try again, skip, or abort.
Acknowledge	Used to acknowledge access commands.
Access Complete	Conveys termination of access to the remote system. This message also is involved with recovery procedures for record transfer.
Data	Transfers the file data over the link established for the access.
Error	Used to report abnormal conditions on the status of DAP messages or data transfers. Soft errors are recoverable by using protocol recovery procedures.

Figure 3-24   DAP message definitions.

cedure for accessing remote files can be described as occurring in three phases: setup, transfer, and termination. The setup phase involves establishing the connection, exchanging the information necessary to authenticate the user, and accessing the file. Transfer of the actual file data occurs after the setup phase is complete and is followed by the message sequence used to terminate an access.

Sequential file retrieval.   The protocol operation for sequential file retrieval is optimized such that there is no overhead for control messages and the entire file is transferred subject only to the flow control mechanism of the network. It is shown in Figure 3-25 and described below.

After the logical link is established, the two systems exchange Configuration messages. Following this exchange, the system requesting access (hereafter called the accessing system) sends a setup sequence consisting of a User Identification message, an Attributes message, and an Access message. At this point, the system being accessed responds with an Attributes message (if access is being requested for an existing file) and an Acknowledge message. Data messages are then transmitted for each record until one of the following occurs:

1. The end-of-file is reached on the accessed system.
2. An error occurs on the accessed system.
3. The accessing system decides it has completed the access.

In the first case, the last record sent in a data message is followed by an Error message with the end-of-file error code. It sends an Access Complete command message and waits for an Access Complete response. It then either disconnects or initiates another access by sending a setup sequence without the Configuration or User Identification messages (the user is already validated for access).

In the second case, an error message will be sent when an error occurs in accessing the original file. The accessing system may either send an Access Complete command message and wait for an Access Complete response (which terminates access) or try to recover using a Continue Transfer message.

If the accessing system decides to terminate access prior to end-of-file, it sends an Access Complete command message and waits for an Access Complete response in return.

It may then disconnect or access another file. In the retrieval case, all error messages are sent synchronously over the logical link using the transmit command to the network.

In some implementations where buffer space is plentiful, an accessed process may buffer messages ahead via the network such that there is a queue of messages waiting to be sent as soon as receives are posted for them at the accessing end of the link. In such cases, an accessing system issuing an access complete command may still receive one or more records of the file or even an end-of-file indication or an error indication due to the pipelining delay in the system. It should pass over these until an Access Complete response is received.

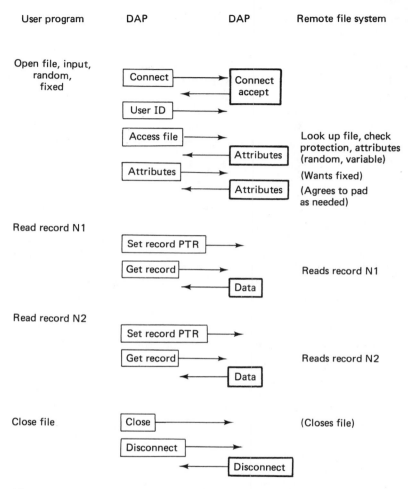

Figure 3-25 Intersystem File/Device Access using DECnet Data Access Protocol (DAP). DAP is used to transfer data to and from I/O devices and mass storage files independent of the I/O structure of the system being accessed. Shown above are interactions between a user program and remote file system (From: DECNET EA 06087 20/77 04A 07.5, Digital Equipment Corporation, Maynard, Mass. 01754).

Record retrieval. Transfer for the record retrieval case is similar to the sequential file retrieval case except that a Control Device/File message (with a record key for random retrieval) must be sent by the accessing process for each record accessed. Here, after the initial setup phase, data is transmitted only when the accessed process receives the required Control Device/File message (i.e., get record with Key *n*), and then it returns the record as a Data message (whose Key is *n*). In addition, if the user had specified record retrieval by sequential access, the Control Device/File message would indicate "get sequential" (without a specific key) and the appropriate response from the accessed system would be to send the next record.

Error recovery for sequential record retrieval is identical to error handling for sequential file retrieval. When End of File (EOF) is reached while accessing a file sequentially, the accessed process sends the Error message "end of the file detected."

The Continue Recovery option, which is used for sequential file retrieval, is not used for record retrieval. When a Control Device/File request specifies a nonexistent record while doing random record retrieval or an error is detected during access, the accessed process will return an appropriate error message, e.g., record number out of range, record not found, error during reading. The next random record may then be requested as if no error occurred.

3.4 INTERPROCESS COMMUNICATION IMPLEMENTATION APPROACHES

As pointed out in the previous sections, central design consideration in multi-minicomputer systems, based on message communication, is the hierarchical ordering of protocol layers, where each layer is composed of the necessary functions required to satisfy application requirements. The control functions may be implemented either on a centralized or distributed concept. (The distributed approach to control is discussed in Section 3.5.)

Message-based multiminicomputer interprocessor communication schemes are usually based on one of two implementation approaches:

1. Building on top of existing operating system that may be either homogeneous (identical) or heterogeneous (i.e., PDP-11's using RSX-11D, RSX-11S, RSX-11M, IAS, RT-11, etc., or minicomputers from different manufacturers such as Data General using the Eclipse, Perkin-Elmer using Interdata 8/32, Modular Computer Systems using the Modcomp IV, etc., each with its own, unique, operating system).
2. Building a completely new system where portions of the interprocess communications protocol capabilities are made available in hardware.

A third alternative is, of course, to build a completely new system. Both of the approaches above are discussed in the following subsections.

3.4.1 Software Implementation Approaches for Message Communications

Design choices available for implementing protocol levels on top of an existing operating system depends to a large degree on the structure of the operating system. As an example, a short description is given of how the DECnet protocol DDCMP and NSP have been incorporated into two different DEC operating systems (RT-11 and RSX-11M). RT-11 is, basically, a single user, real-time operating system. The

NSP layer of the DEC Digital Network Architecture* (DNA) exists, in the implementation, in the form of a collection of subroutines that are linked to the single user task when the task is built. The interface to NSP, as seen by the assembly language user, is a collection of macros†, each of which corresponds to an NSP interface function (e.g., CONNECT or TRANSMIT). The macros expand into appropriate subroutine calls to the NSP subroutines that are built with the task. The DDCMP layer of DNA exists as the front end of the device handler which controls the (single) physical link which connects the RT-11 system with the remainder of the network. The interface between the data link control protocol layer and the hardware layer (the latter consisting of the physical hardware plus that portion of the device handler that is device-dependent) exists as a collection of subroutines, internal to the device handler, that allow the data link protocol (DDCMP) layer to control the device. NSP communicates with DDCMP as any user program would communicate with an I/O driver.

RSX-11M is a multiprogramming, real-time operating system. The NSP and DDCMP layers of DNA have been combined into a process that fits into the RSX-11 operating system structure as the file system does. There are close parallels between a file system and the network process, making it a logical way to interface into the system. A file system adds a structure to a basic block-oriented disc in order for a user to be able to access logical files. The network process adds a structure to a communication channel so that a user can access logical links over that channel. The user issues I/O calls to the network processor, which in turn issues I/O calls to device drivers for actual transmission.

Another implementation approach to protocol layering is to have the user issue I/O calls to a pseudodevice driver. This pseudodriver is actually a communication executive dispatcher, which passes the I/O call to the appropriate module within a communication process subsystem. In this structure, NSP, DDCMP, and device drivers are all modules within the communication subsystem that pass information among themselves via local calls. The assembly language user sees the interface as a collection of macros that are equivalent to the set that the RT-11 user has. These macros expand, however, into appropriate operating system directives that cause functions to be requested from the pseudodevice driver.

This example shows that the implementation of the same protocols will differ widely. Each is tailored to be requirements of their specific operating system, but their basic hierarchical structure is maintained.

The protocol layer implementation is obviously also performance sensitive. If,

---

*DECnet includes a set of network protocols, each of which is designed to fulfill specific functions within the network. Collectively, these protocols are known as DNA. The major protocols are DDCMP, NSP, and DAP.

†"A macro is an "open routine" that is defined in a formal sequence of coded instructions and, when called or evoked, results in the replacement of the macro call by the actual body code that it represents. The use of a macro statement does not result in saving memory locations but rather in saving programmer time." Richard H. Eckhouse, Jr., *Minicomputer Systems: Organization and Programming (PDP-11)*, Prentice-Hall, Inc. Englewood Cliffs, N.J., 1975.

on one hand, lower level protocols are implemented in a way resulting in excessive operating system overhead, total system performance will degrade. If, on the other hand, lower level protocol functions (i.e., data link and end-to-end data transfer control) are removed from the various protocol layers and imbedded in the operating system in order to improve total system performance, however, the clarity and flexibility associated with the strict hierarchical layering will be lost.

Tradeoffs of the two approaches above must be performed based on existing operating system capabilities.

3.4.2 Implementation Approaches for Message Communication Utilizing Hardware

A second means of implementing message communication-based systems is to include portions of the message communication protocol into hardware. This is not an uncommon approach to the design of both shared bus and loop-based systems, and, in fact, several such design approaches were detailed in Chapter 2. Also, much activity has taken place in terms of incorporating data link control protocols either into separate microprocessors or into data link control LSI designs (see Appendix). Another example of this is the implementation by DEC of the DDCMP protocol of DECnet using a high-speed bipolar microprocessor called the DMC 11. Additional examples of the hardware implementation approach is the Honeywell Experimental Distributed Processor* or HXDP (described below) as well as a large number of off-the-shelf, microcomputer manufacturer-developed hardware elements discussed in detail in Chapter 4.

The objective for the HXDP project was to develop hardware and software technology for distributed computer systems where the executive control is fully distributed (decentralized). One of the major goals of the system designers was to perform tradeoffs in the area of system control implementation in hardware versus software, in order to free the latter to concentrate on policies rather than run-time management.

The system was designed for applications where the maximum distance between any of the computers in the system would be limited to 1000 m.

The system contained in 1977 five processing elements but could be expanded into 64 processor/memory pairs. Each of the processor/memory pairs is connected via a bus interface unit to a bit-serial, shared bus consisting of a shielded balanced twisted pair of wires. The data rate on this bus is 1.25 Mbps. The HXDP hardware architecture is shown in Figure 3-26. In HXDP all messages in the system are transmitted over the bus including those between processes that reside in the same processing element. A message may contain up to 255 data words. The bus interface unit hardware addresses messages by message destination name, which is defined by soft-

---

*E. Douglas Jensen, "The Honeywell Experimental Distributed Processor—An Overview," *Computer*, Jan. 1978.

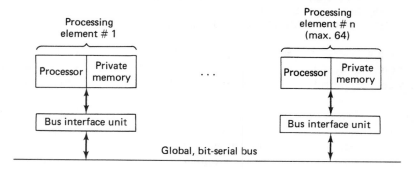

Figure 3-26   The HXDP hardware architecture.

ware. Each bus interface unit can recognize and receive messages for up to eight unique destination names.

Messages are transmitted and received through circular first-in–first-out queues, where each processing element has one output queue and up to eight input queues. The lengths and locations of all queues in each processing element's memory are software defined. To send a message, the software merely places it in the output queue. Messages are subsequently transmitted on the bus, by the bus interface units. The bus interface unit that recognizes the message destination name receives the message, adds it to the corresponding input queue, and makes available to the software a flag and pointer to that queue.

Bus access is controlled by a binary valued circular vector in each bus interface unit. All indexes into the vector (a circular register containing up to 256 bits) are initialized at system power-up time, thereby synchronizing all bus interface units connected to the bus. When one of the bus interface units has a "1" in the indexed position of its vector, it will be able to transmit on the bus. The bus is immediately released after a message has been transmitted and all the indexes in the bus interface units are incremented. The allocation of bus bandwidth to each bus interface unit is set at system configuration time according to anticipated needs of each processing element and cannot be changed dynamically on demand. In order to maintain synchronization of the indexes by each bus interface unit, the current index value of the source bus interface unit is included in the message header, which is received, saved, and used by all bus interface units in the system.

A large number of error-handling features are also incorporated into the system design, such as cyclic redundancy checks, modulation and word count error checks, monitoring of insufficient input queue space, and the detection and recovery from numerous types of message protocol errors.

The implementation of protocols and message handling features into HXDP hardware consequently extends through the data link control layer and into the end-to-end protocol layer.

3.5 MULTIMICRO- AND MINICOMPUTER SYSTEM CONTROL AND THE "HIGH-LEVEL" OPERATING SYSTEM

Having established means of controlling interactions between the major multi-minicomputer system elements such as processors, files, terminals, and other peripheral devices, a control language is subsequently needed to specify types of total system resources and jobs, control their allocation, and specify their environment. The term *process* has been used to signify a basic functional unit of computation. A job can be considered to be a higher level computational unit where it may contain one of more processes that execute either sequentially or concurrently.

Such a language is referred to as a Command Language or Job Control Language. It will be referred to here as a Network Control Language. A Network Control Language relies upon an underlying hierarchy of (1) distributed services provided by the uses of functional or user level protocols representing distributed processors and (2) a transport service provided by the end-to-end message protocol or by direct shared memory techniques. An example of such a language is the Distributed Processing Executive Base (DPPX/BASE) announced in 1978 for the IBM 8100 Information System. Special data areas called *profiles* contain information used by DPPX to control user programs and system resources. A user at a terminal connected to an 8100 minicomputer uses commands for editing data sets, creating and deleting profiles, starting and terminating application programs, and activating and deactivating peripherals and other network resources. A command name in DPPX consists of one or two words that describe a request. Examples of DPPX Base commands are listed in Figure 3-27.

A Network Control Language is more important in distributed systems where the job and resource requirements are dynamically changing.

Such would always be the case in a network development system where user processes are continually being created and terminated. In dedicated real-time application systems, where the Job and Resource requirements are well defined, a Network Control Language is not necessarily needed.

Existing minicomputer operating systems presently provide a variety of control languages that offer the following categories of functions:

- *Initialization:* Includes such functions as defining or deleting logical device assignments, installing tasks, and bootstrapping system.
- *Informational:* Includes display functions of items such as active tasks and online devices.
- *Task Control:* Includes functions such as activating, terminating, and resuming tasks.
- *System Maintenance:* Includes functions such as saving the operating system image and passing control to the system debugger.

Normally each individual function corresponds to a separate command. Systems such as DEC's DECnet and Modular Computer Systems' MAXnet allow these com-

ACTIVATE.NET	Inform DPPX that a network resource is to be prepared for subsequent use
ACTIVATE.NGROUP	Inform DPPX that multiple network devices are to be prepared for subsequent use
ASSOCIATE.CNAME	Establish the source or destination of a program's data
CALL.CLIST	Execute a list of commands immediately
D 2741	Create a profile that characterizes a 2741 Communication Terminal
DEFINE.NET	Create a profile that characterizes an SDLC link, a physical unit, a logical unit, or a request
DISPLAY.NETWORK	Display the status or characteristics of a network resource
SWITCH.OPERATOR	Change the system operator role from a terminal user to an application or another terminal user or an application to a terminal user or another application

Figure 3-27   Examples of IBM DPPX Base commands for the IBM 8100 series of minicomputers. (From: Distributed Processing Programming Executive Base, IBM, General Information, GC27-0400-0 File No. 8100-36, 1st ed., Oct. 1978.)

mands to be sent to a remote processor node. In case of DECnet, a command file is sent to be executed at the remote node. This command file includes the appropriate control commands. In MAXnet the individual commands are remotely executed. DECnet provides a set of network management commands included in NSP that can be separately sent to a remote node. These include commands to extract link and node information, set access control to nodes or links, and perform down-line loading. A command is also available to initialize a loop-back mode on a physical link for purposes of testing. The problem (and challenge) in developing a user-oriented service is thus how to utilize the command primitives and associated protocols mentioned above. Ideally it should be possible for users to develop their own control framework utilizing facilities of off-the-shelf executive software.

Currently, "high-level" operating systems are highly computer-dependent, particularly for heterogeneous multiminicomputer systems. They generally require the design and development of N unique operating systems for N heterogeneous computers.

Research has been directed toward defining a conceptual approach to the design and development of multiminicomputer, real-time operating systems.

For an understanding of the issues involved in developing such a system, the TRW developed layered approach to structuring a Real-Time Operating System (RTOS) for heterogeneous computers is described.

The application performance criteria for such a system includes the following:

1. Full operating configuration under peak load conditions to meet task deadlines of all priorities or meet deadlines of tasks of the highest priority and of the next n lower priorities.
2. Full operating configuration under normal load conditions with the capability to meet deadlines of tasks of all priorities.

The functional implications of the criteria above include the need for complex scheduling and resource allocation routines and clock interrupts. Consequently, the applications processes that RTOS has to support include:

1. Large number of priorities.
2. Event driven processing with repetitive processing of a single chain to tasks and unpredictable event triggers.
3. Task scheduling of real-time tasks according to a priority sequence, repetitively at a fixed frequency relative to both predictable and unpredictable events and repetitively at variable frequencies relative to predictable event occurrences.
4. Interacting processes (tasks).

The design of RTOS to support these requirements is, therefore, based on a layered architecture that segregates major classes into capabilities, as shown in Figure 3-28.

Each layer in the hierarchy represents an abstract virtual machine (a well-defined set of capabilities) with the upper layer being the most abstract and least hardware-dependent. Lower layers are less abstract with the bottom layer (Process Management) being the most specific in terms of machine dependence (computer hardware and machine-oriented language). Lower layers cannot call for service from higher layers, but such services can be invoked for a process by a lower layer by setting an appropriate (hardware or software) interrupt and placing data into a file used by the higher layer function.

A second dimension of layering is along RTOS implementation. Using executive kernels and a microprogrammed interpreter, the applications software, the operating system executive, and the system executive kernels can be made portable and independent of hardware on which they run. An example of kernel layering for a generalized form of RTOS is shown in Figure 3-29. The layering is obviously more extensive

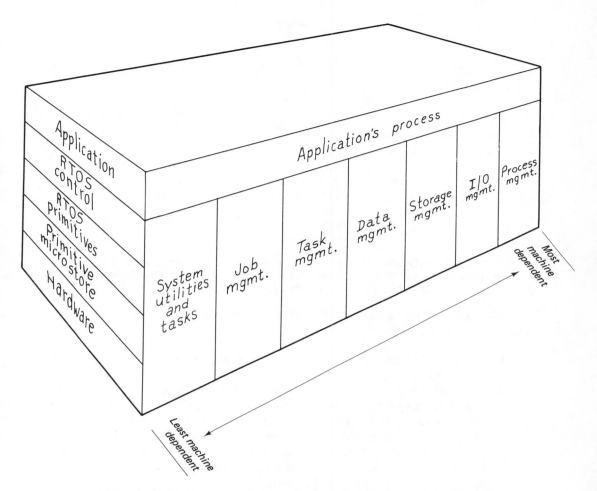

Figure 3-28 RTOS conceptual approach (From: "Distributed Data Processing (DDP) Technology Program," M. P. Mariani, **1**: Final Report #30451–000, 31 Dec. 1977, Redondo Beach, Calif.)

than that offered in DECnet and approaches RSEXEC* and its supporting network operating system for large-scale computers that is beyond the scope of this book.

An approach similar to RTOS has been developed by Univac, called the Distributed Processing Systems (DPS).

---

*RSEXEC or the Resource Sharing Executive System has been developed as a collection of software and associated protocols that allow a set of internetted large computers (PDP-10's) to be used much in the same way as a single-host-based system. See also Harry C. Forsdick, Richard E. Schantz, and Robert H. Thomas, "Operating Systems for Computer Networks," *Computer*, January 1978.

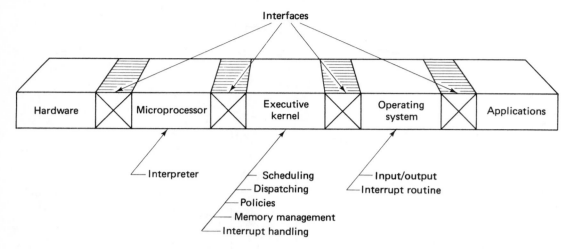

Figure 3-29 Overview of kernel layering for general RTOS (From: "Distributed Data Processing (DDP) Technology Program," M. P. Mariani, 1, Final Report #30451–000, 31 Dec. 1977, Redondo Beach, Calif.)

The basic building block of DPS is the Kernel Exec (KE). The KE has three basic functional sections:

1. Resource Management where the kernel manages processors, storage, semaphores, and events.
2. Primitives Execution where the primitives can be thought of as a process control language (see Figure 3-30 for a summary of primitive formats and some indication of the vocabulary). Primitive operators can be used for a process to execute, permitting/discontinuing the sharing of resources between processes, conveying/recalling to other processes the authority to execute description primitives, and coordinating activity and occupancy in shared resources between concurrent processes.
3. Inter-Kernel Cooperation where a KE collaborates with other kernels for the purpose of executive primitives requested from remote processes, performing load balancing (processes reassignment), or resource reassignment.

A confederation of separate and independent but interlocking KE's are used where each one serves a group of processes described by a Process Description Table (PDT) that becomes part of a Kernel's name space at the time the process is created.

The Distributed Processing System is based on four Univac 16-bit minicomputers interconnected by a memory-level serial transmission ring called the Memory Multiplexing Data Link. Not unlike the previously discussed Honeywell HXDP, the Univac DPS is used for system studies of distributed architectures and "high-level" operating

Figure 3-30 format table:

```
PROGRESS PRIMITIVES
  BLOCK/RELEASE             PROCESS (N)
  SEMAPH, BLOCK            PROCESS (N)
  SEMAPH RELEASE
  REQUEST STATUS FROM/    PROCESS (N)
  UPDATE STATUS OF, RELEASE

DEFINITION PRIMITIVES
  CREATE/DESTROY       PROCESS (N)
  DEFINE/MODIFY        ATTRIBUTE (N)   of PROCESS (N)
  DEFINE/RELINQUISH    RESOURCE (N)    of PROCESS (N)
  DEFINE/MODIFY        ATTRIBUTE (N)   of RESOURCE (N)
  DEFINE/MODIFY        SHARING         of RESOURCE (N)   of PROCESS (N)
                                                         betw. PROCESSES (N) (N)

AUTHORITY PRIMITIVES
  DELEGATE/RESCIND  authority for  CREATE/DESTROY     of PROCESSES   to/from PROCESS (N)
  DELEGATE/RESCIND  authority for  DEFINE/MODIFY      of ATTRIBUTE   to/from PROCESS (N)
  DELEGATE/RESCIND  authority for  DEFINE/RELINQUISH  of RESOURCE    to/from PROCESS (N)
  DELEGATE/RESCIND  authority for  DEFINE/MODIFY      of ATTRIBUTE   of RESOURCE (N)   to/from PROCESS (N)
  DELEGATE/RESCIND  authority for  DEFINE/RELINQUISH  of SHARING     of RESOURCE (N)   to/from PROCESS (N)
```

Figure 3-30 Univac DPS kernel executive primitive formats, where the verbs have the following meaning:

- BLOCK/RELEASE—used to stop another process, or remove the stop making it eligible for entry into a dispatch queue.
- SEMAPHORE BLOCK/SEMAPHORE RELEASE—the P(S) & V(S) operators of Dijkstra. Used to stop conditionally, or release from a semaphore queue.
- REQUEST STATUS—used to request status from the PDT of a process suspended by an event.
- RETURN STATUS & RELEASE—used to update status of PDT and release the suspended Process.
- CREATE/DESTROY—used to build or purge a PDT.
- DEFINE—used to add a resource to the PDT together with some or all of its attributes.
- RELINQUISH—used to delete an object from the PDT and return it to the kernel for disposition.
- MODIFY—used to change an attribute.
- DELEGATE/RESCIND—used to convey or recall authority to execute any of the verbs above.

(From: Thomas O. Wolff, "Improvements in Real-Time Distributed Control," Digest of Papers, *Fall Compcon*, Sept. 1977.)

systems for multiminicomputer systems, an area that is subject to intensive research and experimentation.

Chapter 6 includes examples of various multimicro- and minicomputer systems illustrating the application of the multilevel hierarchical software structures and high-level operating system approaches discussed in this chapter.

PROBLEMS

3-1 What alternatives exist to data link control protocols as discussed in Sec. 3.3.1? What are the tradeoffs?

3-2 What are the drawbacks with the layered approach to protocols in distributed systems?

3-3 Hewlett-Packard has developed a minicomputer-based network known as DS/1000. The software architecture of DS/1000 is similar in structure to those discussed in this chapter (i.e., general nodal addressing scheme and, within each node, a layered software architecture).

Transfer rates, as shown below, have been determined by Hewlett-Packard* for a star configuration with from one to five HP 1000 satellite minicomputers, where each node in the distributed system contains an HP 1000 minicomputer system with an HP Real-Time Executive (RTE) operating system and full-duplex 9600-bps bit-serial lines to the central switch (see also Figure 2-37).

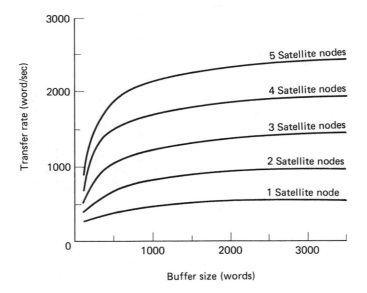

*Robert R. Shatzer, "A Minicomputer-Based Resource Sharing Datagram Network," Trends and Applications: 1978 Distributed Processing, IEEE Computer Society, IEEE, New York, N.Y. 1978.

Assuming 2000 words have been allocated in each mini for program-to-program communication transfers, determine the percentage operating system/network protocol "overhead" as the number of satellite minis are increased from three to five.

3-4 HP has determined the relationship of configurations similar to those described in Problem 3-3 but based on remote file access requests.

Determine the percentage reduction in throughput from theoretical maximum bit-serial line input rates (9600 bps) caused by the operating system, network protocol, and disc controller, file directory, and data control block contention overhead, using information from HP shown below:

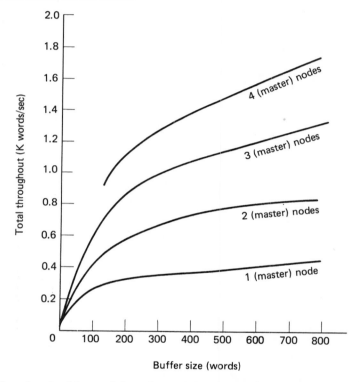

Buffer size (words)

Note that data in this graph have been plotted as total (aggregate) throughput versus throughput on a per satellite-node basis as in the graph used in Problem 3-3. Also, each satellite node is a master or host node for interconnected, remote terminals.

What percentage increase in processing time is incurred by remote file access software for a three- and four-node network compared to a similar configuration with program-to-program transfer software (see Problem 3-3)?

What conclusions can be made with regard to the message processing assumptions used in Problem 2-8?

3-5 Show in a matrix form the most attractive flow control scheme(s) for (a) loop-based systems, (b) bus-based systems, and (c) hierarchical systems.

Which one of these schemes would be the most cost effective to implement? Why?

3-6 Discuss system level tradeoffs for the three methods of process synchronization in a real-time environment.

3-7 Develop a logic diagram showing the HXDP global bus control technique and explain its operation.
    (Include Address Counters, Limit Check, and Control Schedule Memory.)

4

Off-the-Shelf
Multiminicomputer Hardware

4.1 INTRODUCTION

Several factors enter into the decision whether to purchase off-the-shelf system hardware (and supporting software) or to develop, in-house, interconnecting elements. In most commercial applications where cost effectiveness and minimum development cycles are of prime importance, the selection of micros or minis and design of a multimicro- or minicomputer system are generally dictated by the availability of appropriate system building blocks. Several of the configurations described in Chapter 2 can be implemented with off-the-shelf elements.

Microcomputers can usually be interconnected into loosely coupled distributed systems based on either a master-slave or master-master relationship. Interconnect schemes based on master-slave relationships can be implemented where the master and slaves are interconnected point to point or using a shared bus. The bus may be either bit- or byte-serial.

If a master-slave configuration is used, the master usually maintains control of the bus and information is transmitted in one direction only (master to slave) or the slave transmits on the bus only upon request by the master.

When more than two micros are connected into a master-master configuration, additional off-the-shelf elements can be used such as a bus access arbitrator and link controller.

Multiple minicomputer systems are often interconnected into more complex configurations and can be tightly coupled using multiported, shared memories or configured into a limited-distance, bus-based system using Multicommunications Adapters from Data General or Parallel Communications Links from Digital Equipment Corporation (DEC). Data General Corporation also provides hardware for star configurations. Furthermore, DEC offers an off-the-shelf interbus channel for inter-connecting two or more PDP-11's. Hierarchical and point-to-point interconnected systems can be implemented with off-the-shelf hardware using practically any mini-computers presently on the market.

This chapter includes descriptions of available hardware to implement a large variety of multimini- and microcomputer architectures.

4.2   SHARED MEMORY DEVICES

Shared memory multiminicpmputer configurations were discussed in Section 2.2 in terms of the following physical interconnect schemes:

- Time-shared Common Bus
- Crossbar Switch
- Multibus/Multiport Memory

As far as it is known, no off-the-shelf hardware is presently available to configure a crossbar switch-based multiminicomputer system. This section will contain descriptions of time-shared, common bus systems (DEC MA-11 and GA-16/550 Shared Cache Bus), a multibus, and two multiported memory systems: the first one based on core (Modcomp IV/35) and the second based on disk (Data General Interprocessor Bus-IPB with shared disk). None of the interconnecting systems above can be used with computers made by other manufacturers.

Digital Equipment Corporation (DEC) manufactures the MA11-F and MA11-M series shared memory units. These units are supplied with 16K, 32K, 48K, or 64K words of core memory that is addressable through two or four ports. The memory can be selected for two- or four-way interleaved or noninterleaved operation. The MA11 consists of basically three functional units:

- Memory control units
- One or more modules of core memory
- Optional control panel

The memory control unit provides the two- or four-Unibus ports to the computers and multiplexes memory references to the appropriate memory modules via an internal high-speed memory bus, as shown in Figure 4-1.

The unit allows individual address definition for each port and block of memory and provides port arbitration in the event of simultaneous requests. There can be as many as four banks of shared memory seen by a port.

The optional control panel (MA11-FL or M11-HL) contains selector switches that control the operation of each port and block of memory. The Unibus starting address of the memory blocks is individually selected for each port on 16K- or 8K-word boundaries using one set of switches. Another set of switches controls the mode

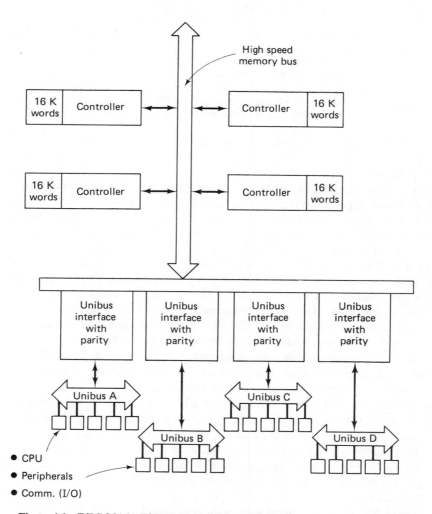

Figure 4-1 DEC MA11-F/H multiport memory for PDP-11. (Courtesy, Digital Equipment Corporation, Maynard, Mass. 01754)

of memory interleaving between memory blocks in a MA11 or between multiple MA11 units. Individual ports can also be disabled by switch action.

The MA11 is transparent to all ports when in operation. The unit recognizes and responds to all memory references to its block of memory. No special programming is required for the unit. The MA11 memory access and cycle time is a function of the mix of transactions occurring but, in general, is on par with standard DEC PDP-11 core memory, as shown in Table 4-1.

Table 4-1   MA11 access and cycle times*

Access time to store data	250–450 nsec
Access time to read data	550–875 nsec
One-port data storage cycle time	400–980 nsec
One-port data read cycle time	700–1400 nsec

*MA11—F/H Multiport Memory for PDP-11, DEC Document No. CSS-MO-F-103.06 (Preliminary), December 22, 1975.

It is not possible for the use of shared memory by a port to be totally blocked by other ports using the memory; however, the access time through a port does depend on the amount and type of activity through all ports of the MA11-F/H. Under certain conditions, the access time for a particular transfer may exceed the normal BUS ERROR time-out period of the device accessing shared memory. This can happen even though the average access time is well below that of the normal time-out period. This condition can be corrected for the processors by lengthening the time-out period.

Any memory bank may be interleaved with any other bank or banks of memory within the MA11 or within any other MA11 connnected by a common Unibus. Interleaving memory can yield an increase in effective memory cycle speed. In some applications, however, a better speed advantage can be gained by not interleaving the memory addresses. This is a consequence of the MA11's tendency to interleave port usage of shared memory. For example, under heavy usage of shared memory, a two-port MA11 will honor the memory requests from the two ports in an alternate sequence. If the two ports are using segments of memory located in different stacks, the effect of interleaved operation can be realized even though the address assignments of the respective memory segments are not interleaved.

The Multiplexer Control Module (See Figure 4-1) controls the timing of the memory transfer through the multiplexer section of the multiport memory. The sequence of events taking place for a data transfer is shown in Figure 4-2.

The General Automation GA-16/550 shared cache bus system differs from the DEC shared high-speed memory bus system in that each memory bank can be accessed through two memory ports and the system can be configured with up to eight processors. Also, rather than interfacing through a central CPU bus (i.e., DEC UNIBUS), each GA-16/550 processor interfaces memory controllers through a 1K-word cache memory, as shown in Figure 4-3.

Two to eight processor systems can be configured by interconnecting a CPU-interfaced cache memory to two cache buses as shown in Figure 4-3. One to four 550's can be connected to each cache bus. Memory capacity can be expanded by adding up to four Dual Port Memory Controllers per cache bus and/or adding up to eight 64K-word memory modules to each Dual Port Controller.

The cache is a limited-capacity (1024 word), 120-nsec memory that automatically maintains a copy of recently used portions of main memory. To the 550 CPU, the cache memory appears to be a much faster 550 main memory.

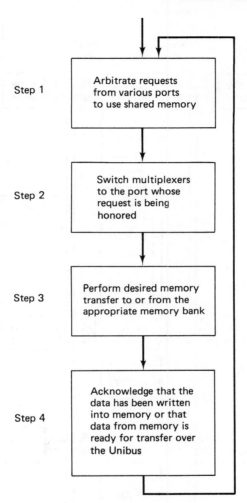

Figure 4-2 Sequence of events for data transfers to or from DEC shared memory.

The patterns of program behavior make the cache memory system work. Most programs have a tendency to make accesses in the locality of recent accesses.

The main memory is mapped into 1K-word segments. Memory map tables are maintained in hardware in the Memory Management system (See Figure 4-3). These maps are set up by the executive program prior to executing applications programs. Since the GA-16/550 is a 16-bit minicomputer, the maximum address space is limited to 64K words. Hence, 64 1K-word segments constitute the directly accessible part of virtual memory space where a segment is stored in cache.

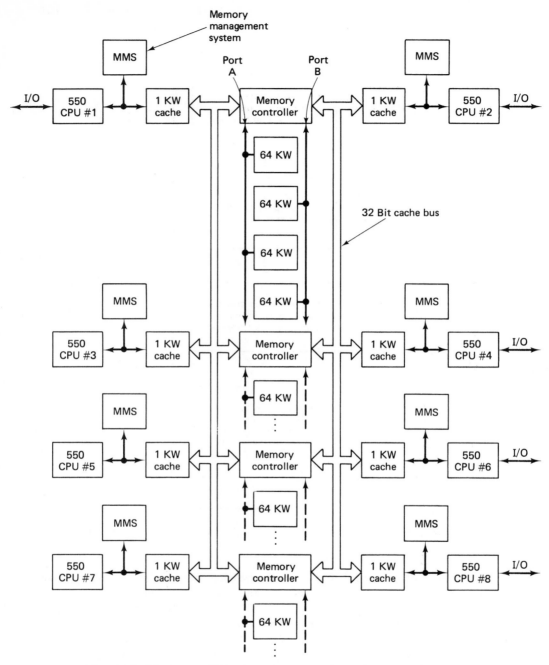

Figure 4-3 Maximum CPU General Automation—16/550 multiprocessor system configuration based on 8 CPU's and 2 Mbytes of main memory (From: General Automation, Inc., GA-16/550 Product Description, 7/16/76, 82S00590A, Rev. A).

If a word is not found in cache memory, two 16-bit words will be fetched from main memory and stored in the cache memory. The cache thus supports the memory mapping scheme providing an instruction access time of 480 nsec for register-to-register instructions (with mapping).

The corresponding instruction time for words not found in the cache memory is 1180 nsec. There are two features of the cache memory design that also support multiminicomputer systems:

1. A TEST and SET memory operation can be performed that bypasses cache memory.
2. An invalidated all-cache command is available to "flush" the cache before inter-CPU buffers are accessed. This command thus invalidates the whole cache if another cache has been updated.

The Systems Engineering Laboratories SEL 32/35, SEL 32/55, and SEL 32/75 computers may be configured in multiminicomputer shared memory configurations based on multibus/multiport hardware. Dual processor SEL 32/75 computer systems may be configured from any two SEL 32/75 computers, a Dual Processor Shared Memory Option and the memory to be shared, as shown in Figure 4-4.

In systems with more than two CPU's sharing memory, SEL 32/75 computers may be joined by Multiprocessor Shared Memory Options, Memory Ports, and Memory Modules to form multiminicomputer configurations. Common blocks of memory may be shared by up to 20 CPU's, and a single CPU may access up to six common blocks of memory. Figure 4-5 shows 18 CPU's connected through 18 Memory Ports to a Multiprocessor Shared Memory Option. A second Memory Port Carriage must be included when more than 18 memory ports are required. A Memory Port is required for each CPU that is to access shared memory.

The 2350 Memory Modules may be interleaved either zero-, two-, or four-way. These memory modules are organized in 36-bit words: 32 data bits plus 4 parity bits (1 parity bit per byte). A memory access request can be accepted every 150 nsec due to overlapped memory design. A SEL 32/75 computer will support both 600- and 700-nsec Memory Modules, if they are not intermixed within a Memory Carriage.

A somewhat similar design has been developed by Modular Computer Systems for the Modcomp IV/35, which is based on Four-Port Memory Interfaces as shown in Figure 4-6. The four memory ports available enable up to four memory accesses to be made at the same time. Modcomp IV/35 offers up to 512K bytes of memory that is expandable in 32K-byte increments. Memory addresses are interleaved on a 16-bit even-odd basis to permit time-overlapped memory accessing. The memory speed permits information to be accessed at rates up to 16 bits every 400 nsec. Because overlapping does not occur with each access, the effective cycle time has been determined to be 500 nsec per 16 bits of information accessed.

Both CPU's and Direct Memory (I/O) Processors (DMP) can be connected to the Four-Port Memory Interface. The DMP contains eight multiplexed, block transfer channels connected to memory. An I/O access can, consequently, be made to one

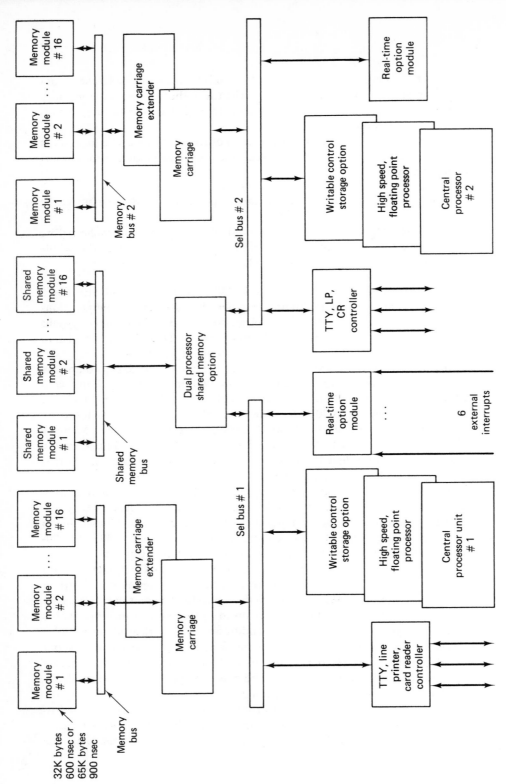

Figure 4-4 SEL 32/75 Dual Processor System architecture.

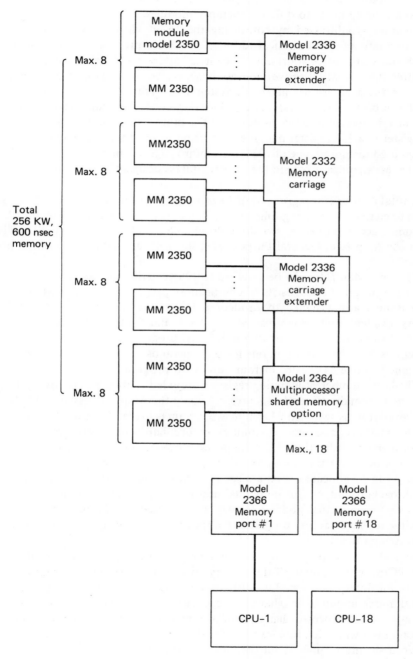

Figure 4-5 SEL 32/75, 18 CPU shared memory configuration.

memory module at the same time that CPU accesses (from a maximum of three CPU's) are being made to different memory modules.

Memory is addressed by converting the 16-bit virtual address defined by the instruction into an 18-bit physical address. The 18 bits provide the capability for up to 256K 16-bit words to be addressed. The virtual address is the effective address.

After the virtual (effective) address is generated, it is mapped into the physical address in the Memory Management System (see Figure 4-6).

The 16-bit virtual address, after all indexing and indirecting operations have been performed, is divided into two 8-bit bytes. The more significant byte is used to address one register in a 256-register map file. The 10-bit page address contents of this register are then used to address one of 1024 (maximum) pages in memory.

The less significant byte in the virtual address designates a word in the addressed page.

A total of four 256-register Map Files are provided in the Memory Management System to enable several programs to remain mapped concurrently. Switching between programs is accomplished by switching Program Status Doublewords (PSD). The PSD defines the Map File, General-Purpose Register File, and all other required program context.

The four Map Files can be assigned to 128K-, 64K-, or 16K-word program sets, where each program set consists of one or more programs link-edited together. Map File 0 is normally assigned to Modcomp IV/35 operating system, MAX IV, and memory resident user programs. Map Files 1 and 2 (and all other pairs) can be assigned to one 128K-word or two 64K-word program sets. In the former case, all instructions must be mapped in one file and operands in the other file. Map File 3 can be assigned to one 64K-word or four 16K-word program sets.

The large number of mapping registers provided enables all or most high-priority programs to remain mapped concurrently. Only the Map File assigned to the lowest priority program is switched when a new program is loaded from disc.

The memory mapping capabilities reduce hardware overhead, provide more efficient memory utilization (512-byte pages allows even small tasks to be loaded into memory without wasting many locations), allow for noncontiguous page allocation (memory can be allocated from a large pool rather than partition memory into foreground, background, and/or individual user areas), permits programs to be stored on disc in the same virtual address format as that used in memory, and provides the capability to have several programs mapped simultaneously resulting in minimum task switching times.

Several minicomputer manufacturers, among them Digital Equipment and Data General Corporation, offer off-the-shelf multiported disc systems. The latter company markets an Interprocessor Bus (IPB) system used for interconnecting two Data General minicomputers in shared disc environments, where agreements must be made as to which processor has control over which files at any one point in time. The IPB contains a watchdog time-out facility allowing it to be used in applications where one processor must know about the failure of the other processor.

In full-duplex communications each mini looks like a high-speed teletype to the

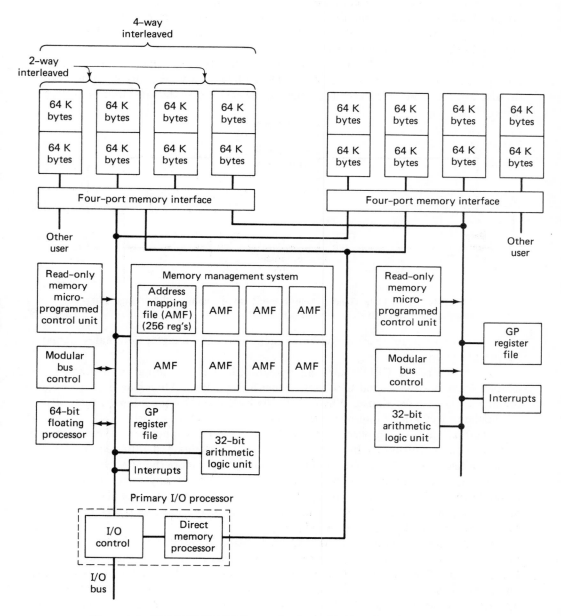

Figure 4-6 MODCOMP IV/35 organization with shared memory and two processors.

171

other computer. When one computer transmits a word, the word is placed in the holding buffer of the other mini's receiver. The transmitting computer is not signaled that the transmission is complete until the other mini has read the word from its holding buffer into an accumulator.

Figure 4-7 shows two Data General Eclipse Minicomputers, interconnected through an IPB and sharing a disc system. Depending on what disc drive unit is used, the disc controller and adapter may or may not be enclosed in the same unit as the disc drive.

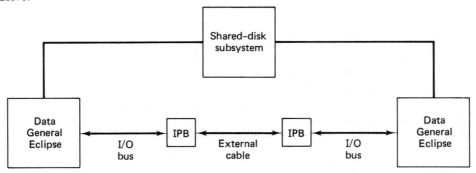

Figure 4-7 Two Data General Eclipse minis share common disc storage and communicate through an Interprocess Bus (IPB).

For moving-head disc subsystems, each subsysem adapter alternates access between the two CPU's.

When one of the CPU's starts an operation (seeking, reading, or writing), the adapter locks out the second CPU until either a Read/Write Done flag is set to 1 for the first CPU or 6 sec elapse. When a CPU is locked out by the adapter, that CPU can neither select a drive unit nor read a valid status word for any drive.

The 6-sec lock-out procedure ensures that one CPU cannot seize the disc subsystem to the exclusion of the second CPU. This prevents a malfunctioning CPU from interfering with the operation of the second CPU for more than 6 sec.

In addition, since either CPU can position the heads on any drive, the position of the heads in the selected drive is unknown to a CPU when it gains access to that drive. Therefore, each data transfer operation should be preceded by a Seek operation to the desired cylinder on the selected drive.

If the adapter is in use when this Seek operation is initiated, the operation commences as soon as the adapter becomes free, and the other CPU is then locked out. If a Seek Done flag for the selected drive is set to 1 and a program interrupt request is initiated, the program can read a valid status word and perform a Read or a Write operation. As soon as the Read/Write Done flag is set to 1, the adapter is free to service any requests from either CPU.

Although the adapter might transfer control to the other CPU once the Read/Write Done flag is set to 1, the error-indicating flags in the status register of the first computer are valid for the operation just completed.

In a system with two minicomputers, it is advantageous, in terms of disc space, to have the operating systems of these processors share the systems disc pack. This is known as a *shared-disc environment*. It is conceivable that the systems would share not only system disc space but also user disc space. In this way, only one copy of a file would be on disc and either processor could access it. This sharing presents a problem, however. If both processors were to read the same record of the same file at the same time, update the record, and then write it back, information would be lost. The updating performed by one processor would be overlaid by the updating performed by the other processor. This is clearly an undesirable situation.

Another version of the problem has to do with disc allocation. If both systems wish to allocate new disc space on the shared disc at the same time, it is conceivable that they would both allocate the same space. The result of this would be both systems writing on the same space of the disc, thinking that this space belonged to them.

In order to prevent these events from occurring, an "interlock" facility is required.

The interaction of the IPB Busy flags of the two processors gives a simple way to accomplish this interlock. One of the many ways to perform interlocking is described below. Let us call the computer wishing to establish a lock on a file "Computer A" and the other computer in the system "Computer B."

To start the lock procedure, Computer A tries to set its IPB Busy flag to 1. Computer A does this by issuing a REQUEST BUS instruction. Computer A then checks to see if its IPB Busy flag is 1. If the flag is 1, Computer A can continue with the procedure of establishing the desired lock. If the IPB Busy flag of Computer A is 0, it means that the IPB Busy flag of Computer B is 1, and Computer B is about to do something in connection with either locking or unlocking a file. Computer A cannot continue the lock procedure until Computer B completes its procedure.

Each computer keeps a table containing information about files in which it is interested. Each entry in the table has indicators that say whether or not this file has a lock on it and which computer has the lock. Once Computer A succeeds in setting its IPB Busy flag to 1, Computer A looks in its table to see whether or not Computer B has a lock on the file that Computer A wants. If the name of the desired file appears in this table, Computer A must wait until Computer B gives up its lock on the file. Note that Computer A does not look in this "lock table" until it is successful in setting its IPB Busy flag to 1. If Computer A looked in the table before attempting to set its IPB Busy flag to 1, it would be possible for Computer B to establish a lock on the desired file between the time that Computer A finished looking in the table and the time that Computer A succeeded in setting its IPB Busy flag to 1.

After Computer A has determined that Computer B does not have a lock on the desired file, Computer A sends a code to Computer B that means "I want to establish a lock." Computer A does this by issuing a WRITE DATA instruction. The code word must be in the specified accumulator. When Computer A issues this instruction, the IPB Done flag of Computer B will be set to 1, signaling Computer B that there is a word in its transmitter/receiver buffer waiting to be read.

Computer B reads this word by issuing a READ DATA instruction. This instruction sets the IPB Done flag of Computer B to 0. The instruction also sets the IPB

Done flag of Computer A to 1, signaling Computer A that Computer B has read the word and is ready to receive another. This sequence continues until all information pertaining to the lock desired by Computer A has been transferred to Computer B. After the last word has been transferred, Computer A issues a CLEAR FLAGS instruction to set its IPB Busy and Done flags to 0. The system is now ready for another lock or unlock procedure to begin. The procedure for unlocking a file is the same as the procedure described above, except that the code word sent is the code word for unlock.

4.3 SHARED BUS HARDWARE

Shared bus systems are available, off-the-shelf for both homogeneous and heterogeneous multiminicomputer systems. Both Digital Equipment and Data General Corporation offer a 16-bit parallel TDM bus-system. Bit-serial coaxial bus systems are available from Interactive Systems, Inc., and Network Systems Corporation. The former system is based on TDM, whereas the latter is using a multiple access technique. Both systems can be used in a heterogeneous environment, with minis from different manufacturers, and both use coaxial cable.

Several manufacturers provide systems based on CAMAC and IEEE Standard 488 (see Chapter 1). CAMAC provides both a bit-serial and a parallel bus approach, whereas the IEEE Standard 488 is based on a parallel-bus approach. The U.S. Department of Defense-approved MIL-STD-1553A, again, is based on a bit-serial TDM bus. Bus systems, based on this last standard, have been developed by Mitre Corporation and Delco Electronics Division of General Motors Corporation. This section contains comprehensive descriptions of the systems above as well as comparisons among them.

The Digital Equipment Corporation Parallel Communications Link (PCL11) allows the interconnection of up to 16 PDP-11 minis to the system. The system is composed of a number of Parallel Communication Link Units (PCL 11-A) and H337 TDM BUS DISPLAY/JUNCTION panels. The number of PCL11-A units must equal the number of PDP-11 minis that are to communicate with each other over the TDM bus. The H337 panel provides a junction point by which cables connecting up to four PCL11-A units may "tap" into the TDM bus (Figure 4-8). It also provides the display/ control area for the Master Sections of these four units. One of the PCL11-A's must be designated the TDM bus Master and a different unit may be designated as a Secondary or Backup Master. This is accomplished by pushing the appropriate switches in the display panel. One of these Master Sections must be enabled in the system to allow communications to take place. The Master Section will then generate transmitter addresses and a clock pulse for the bus. The Secondary Master will automatically become a Master, in case of Original Master Section failure. Any PCL11-A unit may be powered down and/or disconnected without permanent effect on other transmissions, since the unit connects to the TDM bus with a T-style junction.

No two units in the system may have more than 100 ft of TDM bus between them. Each H337 "counts" as $\frac{1}{2}$ ft.

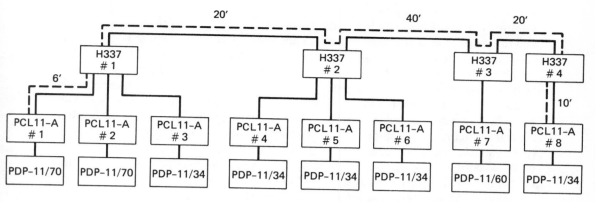

Figure 4-8 An eight-multiminicomputer configuration based on the DEC Parallel Communications Link (PCL11).

The two farthest units in the configuration shown in Figure 4-8 are

$$6' + \tfrac{1}{2}' + 20' + \tfrac{1}{2}' + 40' + \tfrac{1}{2}' + 20' + \tfrac{1}{2}' + 10' = 98'$$

This distance is 2 ft less than the maximum allowable. The maximum transfer rate for 100 ft is 330 Kwords/sec. The maximum transfer rate for a 50-ft bus is 500 Kwords/sec with a maximum of 250 Kwords/sec per unit.

The bus bandwidth can be divided between the nodes in either of two ways: The default allocation simply divides the bus bandwidth equally among the PCL11 nodes on the bus. Time slots on the bus are thus available to each PCL11-A on a round-robin basis.

The second approach available is to set and vary the TDM time slices under software control. PCL11 transmitters can thereby be assigned to handle data rates ranging from a maximum of half of the bandwidth to zero.

At distances over 100 ft, a differential driver must be used for the TDM bus, and the bus bandwidth is reduced as a function of the bus length. Multiple PCL11 units can be attached to any one mini, to implement multiple bus systems. A processor may have more than one PCL11 node either on the same TDM bus or on different TDM buses. The use of two nodes from the same bus might be used for minis having large amounts of traffic. The two nodes can operate independently and concurrently, thus allowing for double the throughput on that processor.

The PCL-11 is used to build local networks in a variety of applications. These include distributed processing, distributed data-base management, industrial data collection and control systems, simulation systems, transaction processing systems and scientific data processing systems.

The transmitter transfers a 16-bit data word at a time from the mini's I/O bus via the data channel to a transmit data register. When a data word has been loaded into the transmit data register, the transmitter requests the use of the bus. Subsequently, when the transmitter is given access to the bus, the transmitter places its identifying number, the identifying number of the receiver to which it wants to trasmit the data, and the status of its word count register on the status portion of the bus. The transmitter then reads the status of the specified receiver from the status portion of the bus.

If the receiver is not busy, data will be transmitted during the next cycle. If two or more transmitters interrupt a receiver at the same time, the priority is determined based on physical location on the bus. If a transmitter attempts to transmit data to an unavailable receiver, a time-out interrupt will occur approximately 10 msec later, after the transmitter has made several thousand attempts to transmit the data. If the receiver is unavailable because it is locked to another transmitter, a lock-out indicator will be set when the time-out interrupt occurs. The transmitter may then be restarted for further attempts or the data may be routed to a different receiver.

Unlike the PCL11 system where the maximum message length is limited to 32K words, messages on the MCA system can be of any length. Also, as can be recalled, bandwidth allocation on the PCL11 system can be either fixed or under software control. In contrast, on the MCA bus, bandwidth allocation is based on the instantaneous number of active transmitters and receivers. With one Nova transmitting and a second Nova receiving, the maximum throughput is limited to data channel speed (175 Kwords/sec). With two Nova's transmitting simultaneously, the maximum aggregate throughput can be 350 Kwords/sec. Time slots on the bus are thus time-shared on a dynamic, load varying basis. An MCA network can operate in one of two jumper selectable modes: either normal mode or fast mode. The maximum bus cable length for normal mode operation is 150 ft. The maximum number of processors is 15 and the maximum data rate is 312,500 words per second. A network operating in fast mode can transmit up to 500,000 words per second but is limited to a maximum of four minis and a bus cable length of only 40 ft. The maximum data rate is achieved when a large number of minis is active concurrently.

Unlike in the DEC PCL11 System, where any PCL11-A or H337 unit can be removed without affecting system operation, if an MCA in the Data General System is removed from a computer chassis, the empty slot must be jumpered to maintain bus continuity. Although any mini can be powered off in the system without affecting the overall operation, a minicomputer cannot be removed from the system due to its daisy-chain architecture, as shown in Figure 4-9. (Data General does, however, provide several alternatives to the 4206 Series MCA—the 5898 series MCS and the DDN —discussed in the following section.)

Unlike the PCL11 or the MCA, the Interactive Systems, Inc. (ISI) bit-serial, coaxial TDM bus-based system can be used to interface minicomputers from several different manufacturers, such as Control Data Corporation (Cyber 17), Digital Equipment Corporation (PDP-11), Texas Instruments (960B), and General Automation (SPC-16/45). The ISI bus system, also termed Videodata TDM, is based on centralized control by a preprocessor channel control unit that is responsible for providing the enabling signals to modems on the coaxial bus, to allow them to transmit information back to the channel control unit at the proper time. This control unit provides line discipline and maintains the communications protocol.

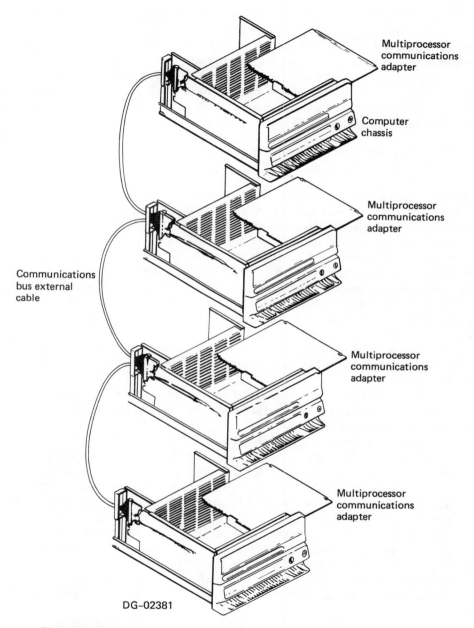

Multiprocessor
communications
adapter

Computer
chassis

Multiprocessor
communications
adapter

Communications
bus external
cable

Multiprocessor
communications
adapter

Multiprocessor
communications
adapter

DG–02381

Figure 4-9 Data General Corporation MCA-Based Multimincomputer System.
(Courtesy, Data General Corporation.)

The Videodata TDM protocol is based on a technique termed *autopolling*. Rather than continuously polling from the central control unit to see if an I/O unit attached to the bus has information to send, Videodata cable devices are automatically transmitting data to the central control unit, in their prearranged time slot.

In typical Videodata TDM autopoll systems up to 248 user devices can share a single TDM channel that operates at rates up to 300,000 bps in each direction. The forward and return channel are each assigned their own frequency. There are presently two series of basic building blocks in the ISI Autopoll system:

1. ISI 300 series modem/controller
2. ISI 800 series modems

The ISI 300 series units are designed to interface central or application computers to a coaxial cable network. This interface is available in two forms: (1) the ISI 310 head end modem and (2) the ISI 320 head end data concentrator/communicator package.

The ISI 310 modem handles all the radio-frequency (RF) transmitting and receiving, logic functions, and serial/parallel conversions required at the head end of the cable network, as shown in Figure 4-10. It can be connected directly to an application computer, host processor, or an ISI 320 by means of an interrupt-driven interface.

The ISI 310 performs logic functions that include appending data received on the reverse channel with the proper modem address and interrupting the processor to which it is connected.

It interrupts the processor for each word but interrupts only when there is meaningful data to pass on. For more complete message formatting, an ISI 320 package will be required.

The ISI 320 is a minicomputer-based data controller/concentrator/communicator with an ISI 310 interfaced to it. The ISI 320 can be connected to an application computer or directly to a host mini.

The ISI 320 performs the role of a data concentrator (buffered storage) and a data communicator (formatting and control). The ISI 320 assembles complete data messages received from devices on the cable and sends them to the host mini via direct memory access (DMA) channels. In the forward direction, the 320 receives a message from the host processor via DMA, formats it, and retransmits the message to the appropriate modem(s).

ISI 800 series modems are used as data acquisition and control devices or in conjunction with communications devices. In the communications mode, they interface digital devices (keyboards, CRT's, printers, minis, etc.) to the coax cable; and each modem is capable of handling from one to four such devices. In the data acquisition and control mode the modems monitor and control "points" in groups of 8-bit blocks.

The 800 series modems operate in a full-duplex mode, simultaneously in both directions. The modem accepts digital data, serializes it (if necessary), and converts the data to RF for transmission to the 300 controller on the reverse channel. On the

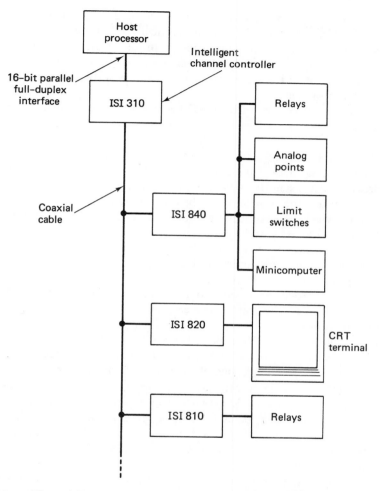

Figure 4-10   Interactive Systems, Inc., Coaxial TDM Network.

forward channel the modem accepts serial RF transmissions, converts the information to digital, and formats the data for serial or parallel transmission to the I/O device.

Within each modem is a phase counter that is synchronized with the 300 series controller. The controller continuously outputs words, data, or idle on the forward channel. Each modem tuned to this channel, upon conversion of the word, increments its phase counter. A comparison is then done by the modem. When its phase counter equals its hardwired address, any data queued for transmission is serialized and transmitted on the reverse RF channel. In this manner each 8-bit modem address is given access for transmission on the reverse channel one "byte-time" per cycle.

The phase counter in all units thus keeps incrementing with each data word, address word, or "idle" word received. Assuming a full 248 address system, each time the phase counter reaches 248, the 310 automatically sends out a control code word that resets all phase counters to zero, and the process starts all over again. If the number of addresses is less than 248, the user sets the highest address on the link via a set of switches on the 310 and does not have to modify software programs each time a remote modem is added.

The 310 modem is connected to the 320 controller via an interrupt-driven 16-bit duplex interface. The 310 will only interrupt the controller when a data word is received.

The ISI 310 modem has a phase counter, too, and because its logic knows the phase counter number at the time data is received on the reverse channel, it knows which address (modem) sent the data. The 310 then appends the data with the proper address and interrupts the controller to which it is connected. Thus, the computer is interrupted only when there is meaningful data to be received. In addition, the computer knows which address sent the data without the address being sent over the cable.

If the 310 modem is connected to an ISI 320 controller, the 320 performs the role of data concentrator/data communicator. It assembles complete messages from devices on the cable and then sends them at high speed via direct memory access (DMA) channels to the host processor. In addition, if a special protocol is required to talk to remote devices, such as industrial controllers, the 320 performs the conversions and executes the protocol.

The advantage of the ISI Videodata TDM bus over both the MCA and PCL11 systems lies in the use of coaxial cable that provides a wide frequency span and superior noise immunity. The physical dispersion of minis, rather than being limited to less than 150 ft, can easily be extended to thousands of feet. Furthermore, unlike twisted pairs of wire, coaxial cable networks can be used in industrial environments where arc welders, motor starters, and AC noise present in a plant cannot affect data transmission. This noise immunity is sufficiently high to allow 60-cycle power for amplifiers used on large cable runs to be sent along the same cable as the RF signals, without causing interference.

In comparison, data transmission on a twisted pair is low frequency and therefore susceptible to 60-cycle and other noise sources. Twisted-pair cabling must be isolated and carefully shielded in most industrial environments, to ensure data transmission validity.

Furthermore, using the ISI Videodata TDM system, minis from different manufacturers can be interconnected. The major drawback of the ISI system is its vulnerability to failures in the central controller that could disable the entire multiminicomputer system.

Network Systems Corporation provides a shared bus system, which, like the ISI system, is based on a shared coaxial bus where minicomputers from different vendors can be interfaced to the bus. The similarities do, however, end there. The NSC bus, not unlike the Ethernet described in Chapter 2, is based on a multiple access technique where an adapter interfacing the bus is allocated bus access on demand basis. Once an adapter acquires the bus, it has full use of it until it is released. Bus allocation is accomplished by blocking an adapter from transmitting on a coaxial bus when a transmission is already taking place. Following the end of a transmission, other adapters continue to be temporarily blocked from transmitting, giving priority to a responding adapter. Variable delays in each adapter give each adapter a time slot in which it may initiate transmission when the coaxial bus becomes free. Each adapter can be interfaced to a maximum of four separate coaxial buses and up to four minicomputers can be connected to any one adapter.

The bus transmission is buffered at each end. This buffering decouples the data rate at each minicomputer I/O channel from the bus data rate. The length of the NSC bus and the number of drops is related to the bus data rate and the quality of the coaxial cable. Table 4-2 gives typical bus length and number of drops for a low- to medium-quality coaxial cable at the available bus data rates.

Table 4-2 NSC system performance

Data Rate (bps)	Bus Length (feet)	Number of Drops
50,000,000	1000	16
25,000,000	1500	16
12,000,000	2000	16
6,000,000	3000	16
3,000,000	4000	32
1,500,000	5000	64

In addition to a processor adapter that interfaces a host processor to the bus and is driven by host software, NSC provides a device adapter that interfaces a device or control unit to the bus and drives the device or control unit. The control unit can be a magnetic tape or disk controller and the device can be an intelligent terminal or a display system.

Each adapter contains three common sections:

1. A bus or trunk interface which consists of hardware and firmware which sends/ receives messages on the trunk.
2. Control memory consisting of 1K 8-bit bytes of adapter memory used for buffering messages to and from other adapters.
3. Buffer memory consisting of 4K or 8K 8-bit bytes of memory where data is buffered to and from other adapters.

In addition, each adapter contains either a processor or device interface containing hardware and firmware for message transmission or receipt from the host, attached devices, or control units.

Figure 4-11 shows a typical NSC system with two adapters and attached minicomputers.

Each adapter has an 8-bit physical bus address. This address is selected by switches on each adapter, such that each adapter is assigned a unique system address

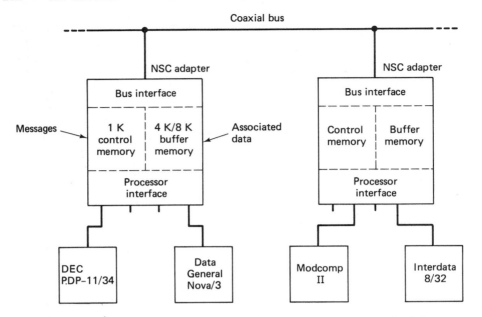

Figure 4-11 NSC system configuration using four different types of minis. (Courtesy, Network Systems Corporation.)

to reduce system complexity. Also, each adapter has a 16-bit physical access code that is set by switches on the adapter independent of the physical bus address. All frames transmitted by an adapter contain this access code as the first frame field. An adapter will not accept or respond to frames which contain an access code which does not compare to its physical access code, regardless of the system address.

When directed to transmit, an adapter contends for the use of the coaxial bus. There are three mechanisms involved in allocating a trunk to multiple transmit requests.

If a coaxial bus is busy, the bus interface hardware will sense it and not initiate a transmission.

Each bus interface hardware unit contains a timing device providing a predetermined delay from the time it senses that the bus is no longer busy and until it is enabled to transmit. This delay allows a response frame transmission, or following transmissions by the adapter that had the bus it allows a response frame to take priority on the bus. The fixed delay is the same in all adapters and depends on the length of the coaxial bus. This delay is 4 nanoseconds per foot and, for a 1000-ft bus, it is therefore 8 μsec, it being necessary to account for the trailing edge of the transmit to travel the full length and for the leading edge of a response to also travel the full length.

Following the bus going "not busy" and the fixed delay, each adapter generates a time pulse at which time it may initiate transmissions on the bus and therefore capture the bus.

The time following the end of the fixed delay at which bus interface n generates a pulse enabling transmission initiation is referred to as "n-delay."

n-delay $= [(n-1)$-delay$] + (4$ nsec$)($distance between $n - 1$ and n in feet$)$

The selection of n-delay is performed as follows. For a six-adapter, 750-ft bus configuration, as shown in Figure 4-12, the delay times are

Adapter n	Delay Time (n-delay)
0	0 nsec
1	0 + (4 nsec)(750') = 3.00 μsec
2	3.00 μsec + (4 nsec)(730') = 5.92 μsec
3	5.92 μsec + (4 nsec)(30') = 6.04 μsec
4	6.04 μsec + (4 nsec)(200') = 6.84 μsec
5	6.84 μsec + (4 nsec)(400') = 8.44 μsec

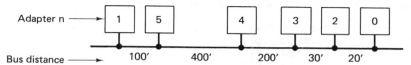

Figure 4-12 Six-adapter configuration used to calculate n-delay.

In summary, the NSC system provides a wider bandwidth, exhibits a greater degree of fault tolerance due to decentralized control, and is more flexible (since each adapter contains both buffer storage and a microprocessor) than the ISI system. The latter may, however, satisfy overall system requirements with considerable cost savings.

The four bus-based systems described above are all available from various vendors. None of them are designed to meet any particular standards and are, in fact, vendor-unique and proprietary. There are, however, several systems developed to various bus standards. Three such systems are described below.

The first successful attempt at standardization of a bit-serial bus was MIL-STD-1553, (Military Standard) "Aircraft Internal Time Division Multiplex Data Bus," released in August 1973 by the U.S. Department of Defense. This standard was thought of as a "strawman" and represented the best thinking within the U.S. Air Force and industrial community at the time it was issued. This specification was updated in 1975 to become MIL-STD-1553A and is currently the Department of Defense approved standard.* Multiplex systems designed in 1973–1974, such as on the F-16, typically used MIL-STD-1553 rather than MIL-STD-1553A. These two specifications are so similar, however, that a well-designed receiver/transmitter pair could be used in either system.

MIL-STD-1553 defines a main bus, which is composed of a twisted shielded pair of wires called a transmission line. This line or cable is terminated in its characteristic impedance. Stubs of the same cable are used to connect the controller and remote

*MIL-STD-1553A has been extended to MIL-STD-1553B which includes additional subaddress modes, broadcast capability, improved noise rejection, and error rate specifications.

terminals to the main bus as shown in Figure 4-13. The standard defines data formats, rates, and the overall operational concept as well as details of the portion of the remote terminal that interfaces to the multiplex bus, that is, the Multiplex Terminal Unit (MTU). The remaining portion of the remote terminal, the Subsystem Interface Unit (SSIU), which contains the control and timing functions and the signal conditioning functions, is not defined in MIL-STD-1553.

The bus controller, as shown in Figure 4-13, issues commands and monitors traffic on the bus, including parity checking and terminal nonresponse time-out. The data bus employs three modes of information transfer:

1. Bus Controller to MTU transfer
2. MTU to Bus Controller transfer
3. MTU to MTU transfer

A maximum of 32 MTU's can be interfaced to the bus and a maximum of 32 16-bit data words can be transmitted or received in any one message block.

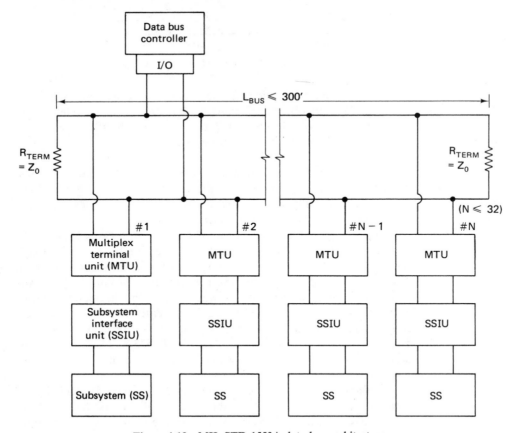

Figure 4-13   MIL-STD-1553A data bus architecture.

For Bus Controller to MTU transfers, the Controller issues a transmit command followed by the specified number of data words.

After message validation, the MTU transmits a status word back to the controller. The command and data words are transmitted in a continuous fashion, without any interword gaps.

For MTU-to-controller transfers, the latter issues a transmit command to the MTU. After command verification, the MTU transmits a status word back to the controller followed by the specified number of data words.

For MTU-to-MTU transfers, the controller issues a receive command to MTU A, followed by a transmit command to MTU B. MTU B subsequently transmits data to MTU A.

Up to 32 stubs, each less than or equal to 20 ft long, may be used to connnect the main bus to the controller on to the remote terminals. The presence of the stubs sets up impedance mismatches that can result in signal reflections. Too low a stub impedance can also cause high transmitter to receiver power losses for the receivers most distant from the transmitter. (The details of a stub are shown in Figure 4-14.) Furthermore, there are a large number of variables such as number of stubs, stub length, main bus length, spacing of stubs, isolation resistors, cable characteristics, receiver/transmitter impedances, and transformer parameters, that make every possible bus configuration unique.

Unlike the previously described bus systems, careful attention must therefore be given to the use of the MIL-STD-1553A bus for each particular application. The MIL-STD-1553A bus-based system differs from the two previously described serial-bus systems in data rate (1 Mbps compared to 300,000 bps for ISI and up to 50 Mbps for NSC) and cable length (300 ft versus thousands of feet for the two others), as well as its lower noise immunity, due to the use of twisted wires rather than coaxial cable. The MIL-STD bus is similar to the ISI system in the use of centralized rather than distributed control.

A recent application of data bus technology based on MIL-STD-1553A has been

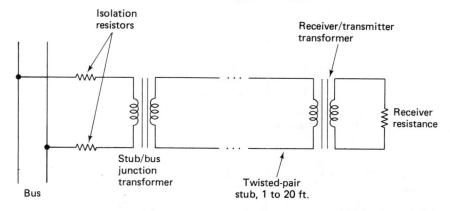

Figure 4-14 Details of a MIL-SPEC-1553A stub.

performed by the Delco Electronics Division of General Motors Corporation.* Stores management refers to the control, monitoring, and release of stores (weaponry) from combat aircraft. Traditionally, stores management systems have been hardwired between the store stations and the cockpit onboard the aircraft.

The system operation was left to the pilot with an occasional assist from a lead computing element. Inventory, status, switch functions, station selection, and operational restrictions had to be memorized and updated, often under hazardous conditions. As weapon complexity increased, this approach became less and less satisfactory and the systems themselves became difficult to install, maintain, and retrofit.

To overcome this, stores management systems have been computerized and bus structured.

Illustrated in Figure 4-15 are bus structured avionics and stores management

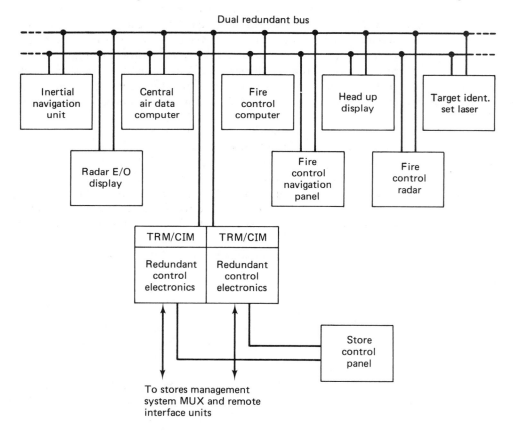

Figure 4-15 F-16 avionics based on dual redundant MIL-STD-1553 avionics bus.

*William J. Sternberg, "Stores Management and Data Bus Systems," NAECON '77 RECORD, pp. 907–913.

interfaces used in the F-16 aircraft. This sytem is based on a dual redundant MIL-STD-1553 bus. Traffic on the bus is regulated by the fire control computer (FCC), a Delco M362. The FCC bus controls 255 unique data parameters at rates varying between 8 and 64 times per second for each parameter. The utilization of the bus is about 33%. The primary bus controller function is to supervise and command all data bus transmissions and manage the data bus redundancy. DMA accessed command table data provides bus redundancy control. The entire data bus controller and its dual redundant transmitter/receiver electronics are packaged on three half-sized ATR standard avionic circuit boards resident in the F-16 FCC.

As far as known, the MIL-STD-1553A has been limited to use in militarized, avionic environments. The most widely used bus standards in the commercial world are Computer Automated Measurement and Control (CAMAC) Instrumentation and Interface Standards, briefly discussed in Chapter 1. In the mid to late 1970's, over 1000 CAMAC products were being manufactured by more than 60 companies worldwide.* A sample list of CAMAC suppliers in the United States is shown in Table 4-3. CAMAC products range from powered card cages (CAMAC Crates), cable assemblies, equipment enclosures, blank printed circuits boards, minicomputer interface controllers, input/output modules, displays, counters, pulse generators, and modem adapters to microcomputers and microcomputer memories.

Table 4-3   Sample list of United States suppliers of CAMAC equipment (From: "CAMAC: A Modular Standard," Dale Horelick, and R. S. Larsen, *IEEE SPECTRUM*, April 1976).

• BI-RA Systems Inc.
    Albuquerque, N. M. 87107
	• Kinetic Systems Corp.
	    Lockport, Ill. 60441

• Digital Equipment Corp.
    Maynard, Mass. 01754
	• Lecroy Research Systems Corp.
	    West Nyack, N.Y. 10994

• EGG/Ortec, Inc.
    Oak Ridge, Tenn. 37850
	• Nuclear Enterprises, Inc.
	    San Carlos, Calif. 94070

• General Automation, Inc.
    Anaheim, Calif. 92803
	• Nuclear Specialities, Inc.
	    Dublin, Calif. 94007

• Joerger Enterprises
    Westbury, N.Y. 11590
	• Standard Engineering Corp.
	    Fremont, Calif. 94566

• Jorway Corp.
    Westbury, N.Y. 11590
	• Tektronix, Inc.
	    Beaverton, Oreg. 97005

	• Packard Instrument Co., Inc. Downers Grove, Ill. 60515

The basic building block for any CAMAC system is the module. The CAMAC standards specify the physical dimensions of the module, including its Dataway connector, the signal and power contact allocation on the Dataway connector, the signal levels for Dataway drivers and receivers, and the required response to commands that are implemented within a particular module.

*CAMAC 1977, Kinetic Systems, 11 Maryknoll Drive, Lockport, Ill. 60441.

The Dataway is an internal bus, usually a printed multilayer motherboard, connecting modules within a CAMAC crate. The latter provides the physical mounting, power, cooling, and Dataway connections for the modules.

The crate contains up to 25 connectors to receive up to 25 modules, which may be of multiple width to accommodate varying complexities or to provide varying front-panel space. What is inside the module is not specified; only the interface to the Dataway is standardized. The simple interface to an external computer controller or additional crates is via a module inserted at the right side of the crate. This interface is termed the CAMAC Crate Controller. The crate controller must address the modules, provide them with appropriate commands, transfer data and status information, and monitor interrupt lines.

The basic crate controller module interface is shown in Figure 4-16.

The Dataway is composed of bused connections except for the station lines N, and look-at-me (LAM, or service request) lines, which are individual point-to-point connections between each of the module stations and the crate controller. The N line, when active or "1," indicates to the respective module that the command on the command bus pertains to that module. Likewise, the L line, when active, indicates to the crate controller that the respective module requires service. The use of individual lines for N and L permits simultaneous actions in many modules.

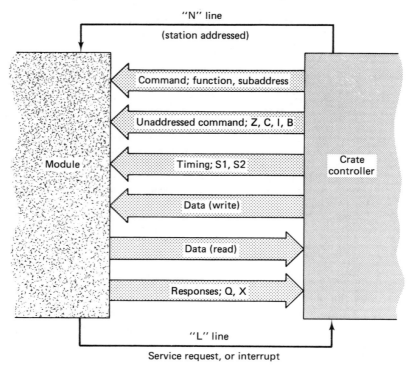

Figure 4-16 CAMAC module and crate controller interfaces.

The entire crate acts as a multiplexer when modules are controlled by the respective N lines. For data transfer from the Dataway to the module, the crate acts as a "distributor." In this case, the N lines control which module or modules accept the data.

The command lines include five function code and four subaddress lines. The five function code lines are coded into 32 function codes, of which about half are defined to achieve a degree of operational compatibility between modules. For example, F(0) is defined a "read data from a module"; F(16) is "write data to a module." The four subaddress lines are used to subdivide the module into 16 entities, referred to as "registers," but in a broader sense they are simply "subdivisions." To give an example, F(0), A(0) reads data from one register, where F(0), A(1) reads data from another register in that module. The subaddress entitites need not be parallel arrays. For example, F(25), A(0) means "execute" (which might mean send out a pulse) on channel 0; F(25), A(1) means execute on Channel 1 (send out a pulse on Channel 1).

Commands are addressed; that is, they are performed only in those modules where the N line indicates to do so. There are also unaddressed commands, sent as single line commands, which apply to all modules; these in particular are Initialize (Z), Clear (C), Inhibit (I), Busy (B). The first three have obvious meanings, the last signifies that a Dataway cycle is in progress or an unaddressed command is being sent.

A Dataway cycle includes two timing signals, S1 and S2, usually generated by the crate controller. S1 is used as a strobe to accept data from the Dataway; S2 is used for initiating actions that may change the state of the Dataway read or write lines. Thus, it is apparent that the CAMAC cycle is a synchronous two-phase timing sequence where data are read or loaded (transferred) on S1 and changed (cleared or sequenced) on S2. There is no standard cycle time, but a minimum of 1 μs is specified, and all modules must meet this specification to achieve full interchangeability of modules in systems.

All data are transferred within a crate in parallel format. There are 24 read lines and 24 write lines; thus, up to 24-bit parallel transfers are handled. Although there is no specification on a "preferred" word size or type of coding, it is suggested that crate controllers handle the full 24 bits so that all possible modules can be serviced.

As mentioned previously, the L line is the source of an interrupt request from a module. The use of individual L lines allows immediate identification of a request. In the general case, however, many different interrupt requests may be generated within a module, all OR'ed onto the single L line. The standard provides guidelines for the control and rapid identification of these multiple interrupts.

There are three basic approaches to the interface between CAMAC crates and a computer. In addition, a crate can be used on stand-alone basis with one or more microcomputer modules.

The crates can be interfaced to a minicomputer such as the DEC PDP-11 using a Bus Crate Controller that provides the complete interface between a PDP-11 Unibus and a CAMAC crate. Using the Kinetic System Model 3911 Crate Controller, control commands and 16-bit read and write cycles require only one PDP-11 instruction. Several crates can thereby be interfaced to a single PDP-11.

A multicrate system using the alternate standard CAMAC parallel branch is shown in Figure 4-17. This system is limited to seven crates. Because of transmission considerations using a 66-pair twisted-wire cable, the branch approach is limited to moderate distances.

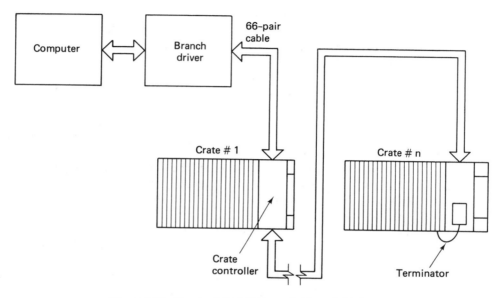

Figure 4-17   Standard CAMAC parallel branch highway.

The most flexible approach is based on bit- or byte-serial interconnect. An example of this is shown in Figure 4-18. Up to 62 crates can be separated several miles. Bit-serial data rates can be selected between 1 Kbps and 5 Mbps. The operating clock frequency is usually selectable from a variable-frequency clock available on a Serial Highway Driver Module.

Crates can also be interconnected using standard bit-serial modems operating at data rates up to 19,200 bps. The bit-serial bus is, however, unidirectional, as shown in Figure 4-18.

What are then the key differences between the MIL-STD-1553A and the CAMAC standard? Both provide bit-serial communications between elements attached to the bus. CAMAC modules are, however, available off-the-shelf in great quantity and for a wide variety of applications. Whereas the data rate on the avionic bus is fixed at 1 Mbps, CAMAC data rates can be selected over a wide range. A failure in the central host or a crate controller will disable the entire system. A failure in any devices attached to the MIL-STD-1553A bus will have no effect upon the rest of the system (unless the central bus controller fails). Furthermore, the avionic bus is limited to a maxi-

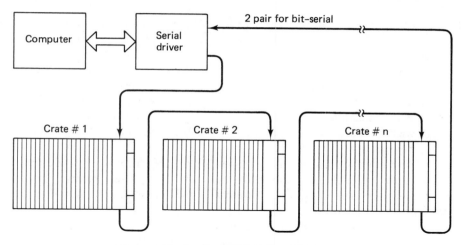

Figure 4-18   Standard CAMAC serial highway.

mum of 300 ft, whereas the serial CAMAC system physical distribution is virtually unlimited (if modems and phone lines are utilized).

The CAMAC bit-serial communications link is, however, in many respects similar to the ISI system. CAMAC can also be used with a coaxial cable (rather than a twisted pair of wires). Both systems interface a central host computer and both systems can be interfaced to a variety of devices. The advantage of the ISI system over CAMAC is again its immunity to individual device failures.

The standard CAMAC Parallel Branch Highway is also, in some respects, similar to the Data General MCA. CAMAC is, however, limited to a maximum of seven crates versus 15 multiple minis for the MCA. For applications requiring substantial processing power at each node, both the Data General MCA and the Digital Equipment Corporation PCL11 offer increased capability. The latter are also software supported by operating systems, which is not the case of a CAMAC-based multimicroprocessor system.

A second parallel bus standard, the IEEE 488 Digital Interface Bus has reached wide acceptance in the instrumentation field. Based on this standard, up to 15 devices can be interconnected on an eight-signal line bus. These devices can be a mix of bench-type instruments, controllers, desk top calculators, and minicomputers. Computer-controlled test systems, such as Fairchild's Logic System VII using multiprocessor techniques, employ the 488 bus to simplify the addition of programmable instrumentation. The SMPU Test Assembly by Rohde & Schwarz, Fairfield, N.J., is a microprocessor-controlled IEEE bus-compatible automatic test set for transceiver measurements. Many instruments, physically incompatible with CAMAC modular hardware systems such as programmable attenuators, digital voltmeters, and displays, are available with 488 interfaces.*

---

*Jim McDermott, "The IEEE 488 Bus Plays a Major Role in Programmable Instrument Systems," *Electronic Design*, November 22, 1976.

The maximum speed of this standard is 1 Mbyte/sec with three-state drivers and 250 Kbytes/sec with open-collector drivers. Transfer of one 8-digit word (eight characters) takes about 32 μsec.

The specified cable has both male and female connectors, so that plugs can be stacked in piggyback fashion, thus saving space on instrument back panels. The IEEE 488 standard is identical to ANSI Standard MC 1.1. These two standards are based on the Hewlett-Packard Interface Bus (HP-IB). The present, off-the-shelf HP Interface Bus is Hewlett-Packard's implementation of the IEEE Standard 488. The HP-IB is described below.

All active interface circuitry is contained within the various HP-IB devices, and the interconnecting cable (containing 16 signal lines) is entirely passive. The cable interconnects all devices in parallel, whereby any one device may transmit data to one or more other participating devices.

Every participating device (instrument, controller, accessory, module) must be able to perform at least one of the roles of TALKER, LISTENER, or CONTROLLER. A TALKER can transmit data to other devices via the bus, and a LISTENER can receive data from other devices via the bus. Some devices can perform both roles (e.g., a programmable instrument can LISTEN to receive its control instructions and TALK to send its measurement).

A CONTROLLER manages the operation of the bus system primarily by designating which devices are to send and receive data, and it may also command specific actions within other devices.

A minimum HP-IB system configuration consists of one TALKER and one LISTENER, but without a CONTROLLER. In this configuration, data transfer is limited to direct transfer between one device manually set to "talk only" and one or more devices manually set to "listen only" (e.g., a measuring instrument talking to a printer, for semiautomatic data logging).

The flexibility of the HP-IB becomes more apparent, however, when one device which can serve as CONTROLLER/TALKER/LISTERNER (e.g., calculator or computer) is interconnected with other devices which may be either TALKERS or LISTENERS, or both (e.g., frequency synthesizers, counters, power meters, relay actuators, displays, or printers), depending on the application. An HP-IB computing controller participates in the measurement by scheduling measurement tasks, setting up individual devices so that they can perform these tasks, monitoring the progress of the measurement as it proceeds, and interpreting the result of the measurement.

As shown in Figure 4-19, the 16 signal lines within the passive interconnecting HP-IB cable are grouped into three sets, according to their function.

Eight DATA lines carry coded messages in bit-parallel, byte-serial form to and from devices, with each byte being transferred from one TALKER to one or more LISTENERS. Data flow is bidirectional in that the same lines are used both to input program data and to output measurement data from an individual device. Data is exchanged asynchronously, enabling compatibility among a wide variety of devices. All interface messages (to set up, maintain, and terminate an orderly flow of device-

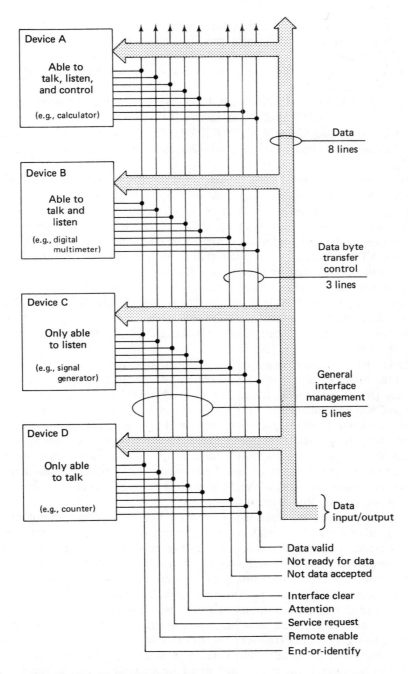

Figure 4-19 Hewlett-Packard Interface Bus connections and structure.

193

dependent messages) are 7-bit coded. Device-dependent messages may be from 1 to 8 bits; however, the codes containing printable characters of the ASCII (American Standard Code for Information Interchange) code set are most commonly used, and messages containing numbers are typically presented in scientific notation (FOR-TRAN-type) format.

Three DATA BYTE TRANSFER CONTROL (handshake) lines are used to effect the transfer of each byte of coded data on the eight DATA lines.

The five remaining GENERAL INTERFACE MANAGEMENT lines ensure an orderly flow of information within the HP-IB system. One of these is called ATTEN-TION line.

The controller dictates the role of each of the other devices by setting the ATTEN-TION line low (true) and sending talk or listen addresses on the DATA lines. (Addresses are manually set into each device at the time of system configuration, either by switches built into the device as shown in Figure 4-19 or by jumpers on a PC board). When the ATTENTION line is low, all devices must listen to the DATA lines. When the ATTENTION line is high (false), only those devices that have been addressed will actively send or receive data, while all others ignore the DATA lines. Several listeners can be active simultaneously, but only one talker can be active at a time. Whenever a talk address is put on the DATA lines (while ATTENTION is low), all other talkers are automatically unaddressed.

The total transmission path length for the HP-IB is 2 m times the number of devices or 20 m, whichever is less.

The HP-IB is, in some respects, more flexible than either the MCA or PCL11 since it allows the interconnection of a larger variety of devices, not being limited to only computers (from one manufacturer). Its daisy-chain interconnect scheme makes it similar to CAMAC and the MCA. In terms of physical dispersion of equipment, it is the most restrictive of all the previously described bus-based systems.

One compelling reason for using microcomputers in distributed systems is to minimize both software and hardware complexity and thus recurring cost when the system is reproduced in large quantities. This is particularly true for stand-alone single-chip microprocessor networks where the standards or interconnect schemes mentioned above are neither easy nor efficient to implement.

The least complex approach using micros is based on point-to-point configura-tions with either parallel or serial interconnects where one of the micros serves as a master. A typical example of this is shown in Figure 4-20 where the Intel 8085 serves as a master and the Intel 8041 and 8049 are slaves. The parallel interface to the 8041 contains 16 address lines, 8 data lines, and 4 control lines. The control lines access a 4-bit status register that is used to provide handshaking between the master and slave processors and to prevent contention between the two micros.

For bit-serial interface, a serial data output line must be connected to a serial data input to signal a data transfer. The I/O interface may be expanded to include additional handshaking signals such as Ready to Send and Clear to Send.

A more complex hardware scheme where up to 8 slaves can be connected to a

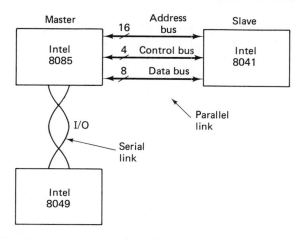

Figure 4-20   Distributed processing configuration based on point-to-point serial and parallel links using Intel 8-bit microprocessors.

shared bus has been developed by Texas Instruments (TI). This scheme involves the use of a bus link controller and an arbitrator that provides access to the bus for up to 8 TI TMS 9940 microcomputers on a priority basis. The bus link controller and bus link arbitrator can be assembled using off-the-shelf TI chips.

Others than the bus interconnect schemes described above, using micros are often more software-oriented. The Mostek MK 3870 microcomputer has a handshake strobe that is under control of the computer's input-output system enabling the designer of the distributed system to use an interrupt-driven approach as shown in Figure 4-21.

As the number of slave processors in the system are increased, the complexity of

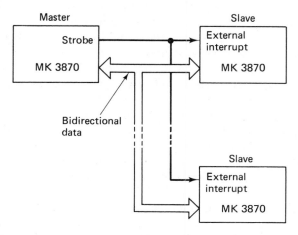

Figure 4-21   Master-slave configuration using the Mostek 3870 microprocessor.

the software will, in most cases, increase accordingly. The designer is therefore well advised to use a message protocol that, as a minimum, uses the command, start, quantity, data, and error check fields as explained in Chapter 3.

The message frame should identify the master and slave(s), the operation to be performed (Load, Store, Status, Execute, etc.), the identification of the location in memory (or register) of the first byte of data, and the number of bytes in the message and it should include an error checking code such as the Longitudinal Redundancy Check (LRC). A typical 250–300 byte memory overhead per micro is incurred executing such a relatively simple protocol.

4.4 STAR CONFIGURATION HARDWARE

Multiminicomputer systems can be configured into star configurations using a bit-serial, synchronous or asynchronous lines where the central node is a mini- or micro-computer. It is then up to the systems designer to decide how the system will be controlled and how much data buffering will be provided by the central host. Two such systems will be described in this section. Both are available from the same manufacturer and both include all necessary hardware and software providing the user with an off-the-shelf multiminicomputer star configuration based system.

The first system is called Type 5898 Multiprocessor Communications System (MCS), developed by Data General Corporation, and the other one, also manufactured by Data General Corporation, is called the Data Distribution Network (DDN).

The 5898 Data General Multiprocessor Communications System is based on a radial bus system where up to 15 NOVA and/or ECLIPSE line minicomputers can be interconnected. A 5898 system, as shown in Figure 4-22, consists of adapters, repeaters, and a common, central communications bus switch chassis.

The communications bus is time-division multiplexed among the adapters. Each minicomputer contains a 5898J adapter board that mounts into any I/O slot of the computer chassis. Each adapter has a unique jumper-selectable number from 1 to 15 that is used to identify it in data transfers to and from other minis in the multimini-computer system. A 5898I repeater consisting of a 7 × 9 in. circuit board mounted in a bus switch chassis connects a single adapter board to the bus switch chassis. The interconnection between each adapter and repeater is via a 45- or 20 ft 5898K cable. The 45-ft cable is used for 312,500 words per second transmission; and the 20 ft cable, for 500,000 words per second transmission. The major difference between the previously described 4206 series MCA (see Section 4.3) and the 5898 series MCS is the mini-to-mini interface via the communications bus switch rather than directly, over a shared bus. In the star-configured system any one of the interconnected minis can be stopped or have their power switched off without affecting the other computers still in operation. Similarly, a failure in any of the links will have no effect on the rest of the system (except for the mini that it is connected to). In all other respects, the operations of both systems are identical, except that the farthest distance between two minis using the MCA is 150 ft, while the MCS limits it to 90 ft.

Where more than 15 minis have to be interconnected and longer distances are

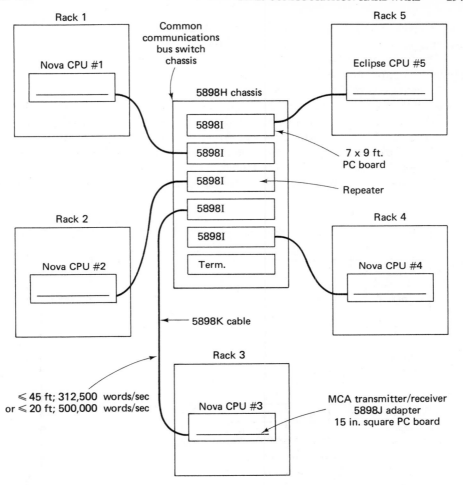

Figure 4-22 Typical five-processor radial, type 5898, Data General, Multi-processor Communications System.

required between minis in a system, Data General offers an off-the-shelf star configuration called the Data Distribution Network (DDN).

The DDN connects up to 253 Nova and/or Eclipse-line minicomputers via a serial, radial bus system. The basic DDN system consists of a microNova-controlled adapter for each computer in a network and a central matrix switch unit to which all adapters are connected. Each adapter is located in a rack adjacent to its host processor and is capable of transferring data at up to 5 million bits per second over a maximum of 1000 ft of cable, to the central matrix switch. The DDN adapter contains two independent interfaces: a transmitter and a receiver that allow for simultaneous transmission and reception of data. Each interface is connected separately to the minicomputer data channel. The program needs only to set up an interface for sending and receiving and all transfers to and from memory are then handled by the Data General minicomputer data channel hardware.

The DDN central matrix switch contains up to 24 full-duplex links that may be connected to any processor pair in a system.

Since the control for the DDN adapter is a programmable microNova, connection of the DDN may be made to a variety of non-Data General minis. The DDN relies on ADCCP communication protocol with CRC, which is transparent to the host minicomputer. (ADCCP is described in Appendix). Each adapter consists of a 4K word, 9-slot microNova with the addition of 4K words of PROM and battery backup.

A block diagram of the central matrix switch with interfacing adapters and minis is shown in Figure 4-23. The central matrix switch is composed of three func-

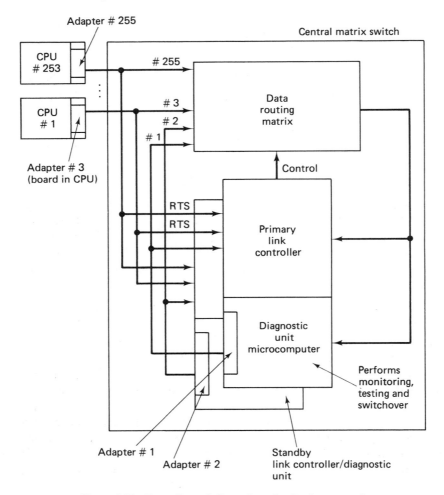

Figure 4-23   Data General Corp. data distribution network.

tional parts; a Data Routing Matrix, Link Controller, and Diagnostic Unit. The Link Controller and Diagnostic Unit are combined into one entity. The central matrix switch contains a primary and a standby Link Controller/Diagnostic Unit to enhance system availability. The Data Routing Matrix (DRM) contains the interconnection circuitry that physically closes the circuit between the transmit portion of one Adapter and the receive portion of the other Adapter. The DRM can also connect the Diagnostic Unit within the Central Matrix Switch to any Adapter in the system.

The Link Controller controls the DRM. The Diagnostic Unit, a microNova, performs online fault detection, and online and offline fault isolation for the DRM and Link Controller. On failure of the latter units, automatic switchover to the standby Link Controller and Diagnostic Unit occurs.

In order to transmit data over the DDN bus, the Adapter first places a series of ADCCP frames on the bus called *request to send* (RTS) commands. The destination Adapter may acknowledge the RTS with a Ready to Receive message or it may indicate a congested condition with a Not Ready to Receive message. The transmitting Adapter will, upon receipt of Ready to Receive, send the message. If a Not Ready to Receive message is received, the transmitting Adapter will send idle characters causing the central switch matrix to break the connection. After an appropriate time period, a transmission retry may be attempted.

Of all the off-the-shelf multiminicomputer systems previously discussed, the DDN allows for the largest number of computers to be interconnected into a single system. Because of the individual links between each of the minis and the central switch matrix as well as the built-in redundance in the switch, this system is, in all probability, the most reliable (but also one of the more expensive) of all the off-the-shelf multimini-computer systems.

4.5 BUS WINDOW HARDWARE

Digital Equipment Corporation offers a bus-to-bus connection device called the UNIBUS window* that allows communications between any two devices on the two buses.

The UNIBUS window allows a PDP-11 mini- or microcomputer system to access addresses on a companion system's UNIBUS as though they (the addresses) were on its own UNIBUS. It does so by automatically translating requests to a designated part of the bus-address space into requests on the other bus. Since all synchronization is done internally by the window hardware, the operation is completely transparent to the operating software.

Any unused block of addresses on the UNIBUS may be designated as the window. Normally, it is placed directly above the last memory module. Thus, on a system with 64K words of memory, an 8K window would be placed from 64K to 72K. Once this window is initialized, any access to location between 64K and 72K will be translated automatically into an access to an 8K address area on the companion sys-

---

PDP-11 Peripherals Handbook, Digital Equipment Corporation, Maynard, Mass., 1976.

tems's UNIBUS. A window operation involves both the UNIBUS on which the access was requested and the bus on which the access is actually performed. Any type of address access (instruction fetch, data fetch, data write, or DMA-type block transfer) may be performed through the UNIBUS window. Once the window is set up, the interbus transfer is completely transparent.

Any device capable of being bus master may originate an access through the window. A processor on one side, for example, can execute code that is contained in the other computer's memory, or a disk or magnetic tape unit can transfer data to memory on the opposite bus. An individual processor is not limited to a single UNIBUS window; multiple windows allow intercommunication between several PDP-11 processors.

Each processor is given complete control over accesses to locations on its own bus. A programmable control unit within each port governs the use of the channel that originates on the opposite bus. The processor on the bus where accesses are performed can disable transfers through the window, restrict them to read only, and decide which addresses on its bus the window may have access to.

The window thus implements two independent paths between busses. Having both window paths enabled for reading and writing allows each system connected by the UNIBUS window to have shared access to part of the other systems memory.

Great care in system design should be taken to avoid deadlock conditions from occurring (see Section 5.7.2 for discussion of deadlock).

4.6 MISCELLANEOUS INTERFACES FOR POINT-TO-POINT AND HIERARCHICAL SYSTEMS

A wide variety of standard interfaces are available off-the-shelf from most minicomputer manufacturers. These interfaces allow the system designer to interconnect two or more minicomputers over both bit-serial and parallel lines. The serial interconnection can be made long distance using modems and telephone lines or locally using point-to-point interconnections. Data transfer can be made in an asynchronous, one-character-at-the-time mode, where each character is preceded by a start bit and proceeded by one or more stop bits or in a synchronous mode, where blocks of information are transferred bit-serially. These interfaces are usually packaged onto a single circuit board that can be strapped for desired character size and stop code length, 20 mA or EIA RS-232C output levels, and operational full modem control. Other features available are bit rate selection (typically from 75 to 9600 bits per second), synchronization character programming, full- or half-duplex operation, parity generation on transmit and parity check on receive automatic answer, direct memory access, and buffering of characters.

Asynchronous and synchronous single-board line controllers are available that include multiplexers for multiplexing 4, 8, or 16 lines. Many asynchronous and synchronous multiplexed line controllers can also be programmed for separate data rates on each line, ranging from 75 to 9600 bps.

Single line controllers are available that can transfer data up to 1 Mbps over coaxial cable (Digital Equipment Corp. DMC11).

It is also feasible to interconnect minis over 16-bit parallel links using interface controllers such as the DEC DR11-B Direct Memory Access Interface that operates directly to or from memory, moving data between the DEC PDP-11 Unibus and the user device, which may be another minicomputer. A similar device, which also transfers data a half-duplex parallel mode between two PDP-11 Unibuses, is the DA11-B, PDP-11 interprocessor link. Data transfer is initialized under program control and proceeds via DMA until an entire block of characters has been transferred.

Some of the line interface controllers, such as the DEC PDP-11, DUP11, are capable of handling a wide variety of protocols including byte-oriented protocols, such as DDCMP and BISYNC, and bit-oriented protocols, such as SDLC, HDLC, and ADCCP (see Appendix). This relieves the PDP-11 processor of a significant amount of overhead associated with interrupt handling, character processing, and error checking.

Many semiconductor firms have introduced single-chip, large-scale, integrated circuits that perform the same functions as the interface boards described above. An example of such a device is the National Semiconductor Asynchronous Line-Control Element (ACE), which can interface a microprocessor to a modem via an RS-232C connector or a 20-mA current loop, or bypass the modem completely interfacing directly to a second microprocessor. A built-in interrupt system in the ACE allows for flexibility in interfacing to all popular microprocessors on the market. The ACE performs parallel-to-serial, serial-to-parallel, and bit-rate error detection and features built-in modem control functions. Even more powerful communications chips are the 2651 and 2652 manufactured by both National Semiconductor and Signetics. The 2651 is a programmable Universal Synchronous/Asynchronous Receiver/Transmitter (USART) chip contained in a standard 28-pin dual-in-line package. It can be programmed to receive and transmit either synchronous or asynchronous serial data. It performs serial-to-parallel conversion on data characters received over a serial line or from a modem and parallel to serial conversion on data received from a CPU. The CPU can read the complete status of the 2651 at any time during the functional operation. Status information reported includes the type and condition of the transfer operations being performed by the device, as well as error conditions such as parity, overrun, or framing.

The 2652 Multi-Protocol Communications Controller (MPCC) transmits and receives synchronous data up to 500,000 bps while supporting bit-oriented or byte control protocols. The chip can interface to a processor with an 8- or 16-bit bidirectional data bus.*

The emergence of these low-cost standard interface chips makes it cost effective to link multiple micros into point-to-point or hierarchical networks.

The single- or multi-line minicomputer communications interface controllers

---

*Sam Travis, "Communications Chip Interfaces with Most Microprocessors," *Electronics*, March 16, 1978.

are, in most cases, supported by software drivers and vendor supplied operating systems and, in some cases, by network software (i.e., DECNET, MAXNET, etc.). This type of support software is usually not available for microcomputer communications interfaces, such as the ACE or the 2651, 2652 communications chips. The complexity of such software is discussed in Chapter 3 and Appendix.

PROBLEMS

4-1 Shown below is a geographically dispersed minicomputer network based on Hewlett

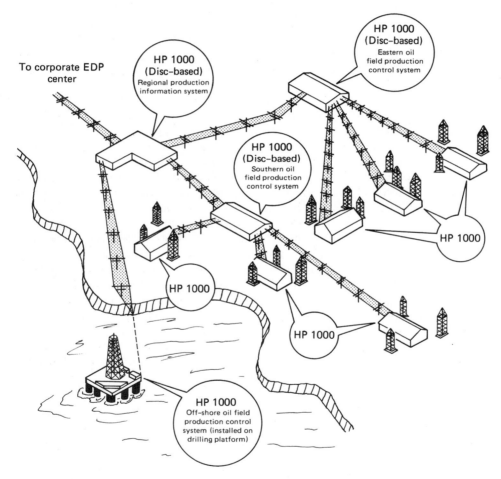

Packard minicomputers used to monitor and control oil production. Its major features are the capability to provide unattended monitoring of oil production from wells, to control flow through pipelines and support the unattended nodes, and to summarize management data for transmission to the company's data processing center.

Propose three alternate approaches to this system using different interconnect structures and hardware elements, described in this chapter. Draw a block diagram of each proposed solution and a summary list of unique advantages and disadvantages of each approach.

The distances between each of the nodes are in the tens of miles and the lines used in the system as shown are limited to 4800 bps.

4-2 Shown below is a small engineering research facility where equipment cost is reduced

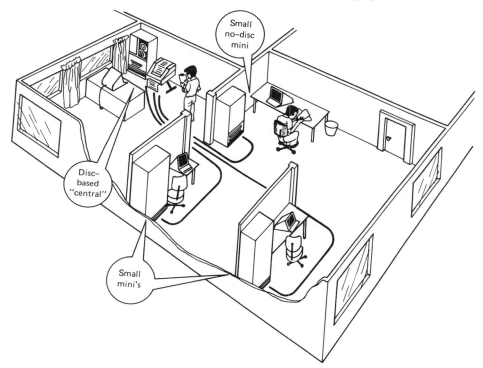

through peripheral sharing and the capability exists to store new test programs at a disc-based "central" without disrupting activity at the other systems.

Propose a hardware solution for interconnecting the minis shown in the figure. What parameters must be known in order to configure a system?

4-3 What system parameters would dictate the choice between a NSC-type and an ISI-type approach?

4-4 Reconfigure the hierarchical system in Problem 2-8 using the NSC adapters. What is the maximum delay that can be expected in the reconfigured system, between the various nodes? Show a block diagram of the NSC-based system.

4-5 Perform a vendor survey of existing distributed minicomputer communications hardware for loop- and bus-based systems.

5

Design Based on
Process Characterization

5.1 INTRODUCTION

The multimini- or microcomputer system design process is approached in a sequential fashion by identifying the type of application functions to be automated: environmental, geographic, user and resource constraints, and knowledge of the application. This initial problem definition phase will prompt the designer to ascertain awareness or understanding of the application (i.e., is the application such that requirements can be defined in great detail during the early design stage or must its characteristics be determined by trial and error after a first version of the system has been developed).

The process identification phase is followed by a problem decomposition phase which includes a functional breakdown of the application into a structured set of data-flow primitives which are combined into a process architecture tree. The value of the functional breakdown lies in the fact that the designer will develop an understanding of the major subtasks to be performed by the system.

The third phase or task includes a determination of process interaction. Analytic tools available to develop an understanding of the various interrelationships between subprocesses include state exchange diagrams, process interaction diagrams, and N^2 charts. Up to this point the design process has been on what is termed a *virtual level**.

According to Mariani, "the virtual level describes an abstract set of data structures, computational processes, and communication channels which implement the functional system ... the virtual level description reveals the inherent architecture

*M. P. Mariani, "Distributed Data Processing (DDP) Technology Program," TRW Defense and Space Systems Group, Redondo Beach, Calif., 31 December 1977.

structure of the computations but does not consider resource limitations or geographical location of processes."

Following the problem decomposition and process interaction analysis, performance requirements can be defined in terms of physical technology choices. Performance requirements analysis to a physical level can be pursued when performance requirements are clearly defined.

Performance requirements analysis includes sizing of tasks, defining the time relationships between tasks, and system control in terms of information movement and processing. The latter will, in turn, determine the choice of transfer strategy, transfer control method, and desired transfer path structure as well as shared and dedicated system resources (computers, peripherals, people, etc.). The performance analysis will culminate in a performance requirements definition.

Once performance requirements have been established, the optimal system architecture can be determined. This includes the selection of interconnect scheme, processing levels, and computers. In many cases two or more competing solutions or "strawman" configurations are developed. These configurations can subsequently be analyzed in terms of cost, reliability, ease of development, and other pertinent trade-off criteria. The result of this analysis is a baseline system design. The design methodology described above is summarized in Figure 5-1.

The following sections detail each of the six design process steps shown in the figure.

5.2   PROCESS IDENTIFICATION

As a starting point in the design process, an informal tentative working document should be produced. This document should state the user's needs in as clear and complete a fashion as possible with enough detail to allow the preliminary design process to begin. Great care should be taken in developing this document not to presuppose an implementation.

The informal requirements specification can later be modified to serve as system specification that may be used regardless of whether the system is developed in-house or procured from an outside source.

Examples of such informal requirements specifications are shown in Tables 5-1, 5-2, and 5-3. The first example is for a patient monitoring problem and is incomplete in many respects. Obviously information is missing on the number of patients involved, the permissible range on cycle rates, the period of time over which data is to be retained, the number of nurse's stations, the size of patient files, etc.

Similar quantitative information is missing on the Wind Tunnel System (Table 5-2) and the Online Credit Authorization and Point-of-sale System (Table 5-3). This information is determined during the performance requirements phase (Step IV in Figure 5-1).

The process identification phase is illustrated using one of the requirements specifications above: the Patient Monitoring System. The methodology described has

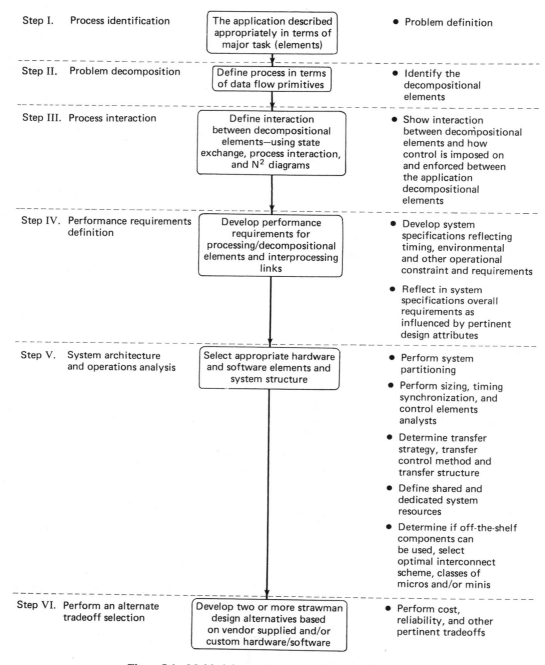

Step I.	Process identification	The application described appropriately in terms of major task (elements)	• Problem definition
Step II.	Problem decomposition	Define process in terms of data flow primitives	• Identify the decompositional elements
Step III.	Process interaction	Define interaction between decompositional elements—using state exchange, process interaction, and N^2 diagrams	• Show interaction between decompositional elements and how control is imposed on and enforced between the application decompositional elements
Step IV.	Performance requirements definition	Develop performance requirements for processing/decompositional elements and interprocessing links	• Develop system specifications reflecting timing, environmental and other operational constraint and requirements • Reflect in system specifications overall requirements as influenced by pertinent design attributes
Step V.	System architecture and operations analysis	Select appropriate hardware and software elements and system structure	• Perform system partitioning • Perform sizing, timing synchronization, and control elements analysts • Determine transfer strategy, transfer control method and transfer structure • Define shared and dedicated system resources • Determine if off-the-shelf components can be used, select optimal interconnect scheme, classes of micros and/or minis
Step VI.	Perform an alternate tradeoff selection	Develop two or more strawman design alternatives based on vendor supplied and/or custom hardware/software	• Perform cost, reliability, and other pertinent tradeoffs

Figure 5-1 Multiminicomputer system design methodology.

206

Table 5-1 Problem description summary, patient monitoring system for intensive care

Description / Requirement	Patient Monitoring Problem for Intensive Care in Hospitals and Medical Centers
1.	A patient monitoring program is required for a hospital's intensive care unit.
2.	Each patient is monitored by analog devices that measure factors such as heart rate, systolic and diastolic arterial pressure, temperature, central venous pressure, arrhythmias per minute, and skin resistance.
3.	These factors are read on a periodic basis, as specified for each patient, and stored in a data base.
4.	For each patient, safe ranges for each factor are specified, such as valid temperature range, heart rate, and blood pressure.
5.	If a factor falls outside the patient's safe range, or if a monitoring device or sensor fails, the nurse's station is notified.
6.	The nurse's station is able to add and delete patients, to set up and change sensor cycle rates and safe factor ranges, and to obtain listings of patient history files including names of physicians, medication lists, and responses to drugs and other treatment.
7.	Growth features: System functions can be expanded to include fetal and pediatric monitoring.

been developed by Barton De Wolf,* and is based on the notion of an *abstract process.*

An abstract process is defined informally† as *the activity resulting from the execution of a program with its data by a sequential processor.* This definition has been rephrased by De Wolf in terms of concepts from state machine theory where the execution of a process is characterized as a sequence of transitions on certain state variables. The state of a process may be defined by assigning values to each of the variables in the state variable set. The set of all possible states for a given set of state variables is designated the *state space* of the process. A process can thus be represented by a state transition function that maps any given state into a successor state. A process can be associated with both computer hardware and software, with clocks and timers, with objects in the environment, and with human operators who

---

*J. Barton De Wolf, "Requirements Specification and Preliminary Design for Real-Time Systems," The Charles Stark Draper Laboratories, Inc., Computer Software and Applications Conference, November 1977.

†Alan C. Shaw, "*The Logical Design of Operating Systems,*" Prentice-Hall, Inc., Englewood Cliffs, N.J., 1974, p. 58.

Table 5-2 Problem description summary for a data acquisition system

Description / Requirement	A Wind Tunnel Model Instrumentation, Data Gathering, Processing, Display, and Data Recording System
1.	A wind tunnel model test facility is required for avionic system design and development.
2.	A computer operated and controlled system that can process digitally both static and low- and high-speed transient data.
3.	Sensors used in the wind tunnel model instrumentation are thermocouples and bridge circuits such as strain gage pressure transducers, resistance thermometers, load cells, strain gage accelerometers, and bonded strain gages. Some discretes are used for mechanical and thermal limits with pulse rate generators for rotary velocity and flow.
4.	The system will gather the sensor data, record it, process it, and display it. Each of these functions will be performed independently of the other.
5.	In addition to data gathering, the system will perform closed-loop model control.
6.	Key parameters and synthesized parameters that would assist in the evaluation of the online test meeting its objectives are made available to experimenters and wind tunnel operators in real- or near-real-time.
7.	Test data reduction is performed offline at the wind tunnel facility.
8.	An English language interactive graphics type of menu display is available at operators CRT terminals.
9.	Quick look data is provided in real-time graphic form.
10.	The quick look data is displayed graphically as one or more parameters on a time base, one or more parameters as a function of another parameter, a parameter overlayed on the same parameter from a previous test or on an expected curve.
11.	The system produces engineering report-quality hardcopy of raw or synthesized performance curves, developed for display on a graphics terminal with editing capability.

interface with the system. De Wolf offers the following guidelines for process identification:

1. A process should represent a coherent functional entity both within the system and in the environment.

Table 5-3 Problem description summary for a retail store online credit authorization and point-of-sale system

Requirement \ Description	Online Credit Authorization, Point-of-Sale System
1.	A point-of-sale (POS)/Credit Authorization system is required for a department store chain.
2.	The retail clerk enters essential information related to a pending sale from a cash register keyboard.
3.	A magnetic-stripe credit card is read by the sales terminal. This card contains the customer's name, address, account number, and credit-authorization information.
4.	The POS terminal transmits all pertinent transaction information to a customer file.
5.	If the sale is approved, the POS terminal will generate the appropriate copies of the sales draft and update the customer's authorization file as well as the file on the card.
6.	The POS terminal will also store locally the daily transactions.
7.	Information on daily transactions are periodically transmitted from each POS terminal to a central file which contains a merchandise inventory list and to a file which contains information on all sales clerks.
8.	The merchandise inventory list is processed for sales statistics and reorder information.
9.	The central personnel file is updated daily for sales commissions. This information is sent weekly to the payroll department.

2. Processes should be assigned to manage the various input/output interfaces at the system/environment boundary both within the system and in the environment.

3. For multimini- and microprocessor systems, process functions should be broken into logical subunits where possible. Such subdividing should be postponed until the full nature of the performance problem is evident.

The process identification step is illustrated in Figure 5-2 using the previously described patient monitoring problem (Table 5-1). Processes are shown as circles and have been associated with activities both in the system and environment (i.e., sensor sets associated with each patient are shown interacting with sensor monitor processes in the system).

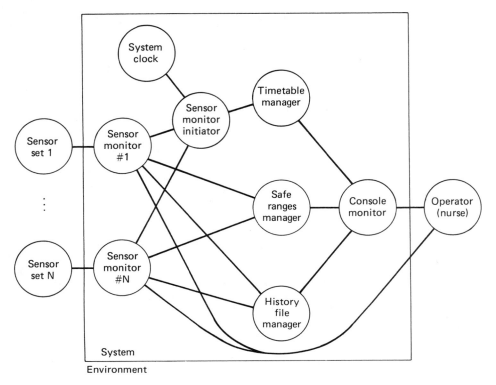

Figure 5-2   Process identification example using the patient monitoring problem.

Each sensor monitor compares the sensor data with "safe range" values stored for each patient in a table and notifies the nurse of any sensor or data exception conditions.

The operator, also represented as a process, enters commands to the system via a Console Monitor. The individual Sensor Monitors are initiated at the proper times by a Sensor Monitor Initiator, which gets the current time from a system clock process and compares it with time-to-go values stored for each sensor set in a system timetable.

The accessing of shared data values—the system timetable, the safe ranges table, and the data history file—is referred by three manager processes, as shown in Figure 5-2.

It should be recognized that this is only one of many possible process identifications for this example and most likely embodies the experience of the designer. Furthermore, the monitors above should not necessarily be equated to the Concurrent Pascal Monitor Construct, discussed in Subsection 3.2.2. However, there is no reason why the Concurrent Pascal Monitor concept could not be applied to structuring the software design for the Patient Monitoring System above (see also Problem 5-10.) Furthermore, no assumptions have been made regarding the actual number of processors to be used in implementing the system. Each process could conceivably have its own processor; however, the hardware-related architectural issues should not be resolved until performance requirements have been determined. This activity is, however, preceded by problem decomposition and the definition of process interaction. These two steps address the problem of specifying the details of both the processes and their interactions.

5.3 PROBLEM DECOMPOSITION

The problem decomposition can be approached in a multitude of ways. The most common approach is the use of block or flow diagrams showing one or more inputs, a process, and one or more outputs. Each block is thought of as a "black box" performing a distinct, definable subtask or function. The conditional relationship is, however, often lost even for systems with very limited complexity. The data-flow description has been approached by researchers in a more concise way using a variety of notations such as "data-flow primitives," "precedence graphs," and "data-flow graphs," to name a few.*

The algorithmic data flow approach used in this section has been developed at Charles Stark Draper Laboratory.† It utilizes a set of four primitives to construct algorithmic structures in a hierarchical fashion. This method allows the designer to uncover possibilities for parallelism or, more broadly, activities for which the ordering is not important and less arbitrary than the strictly sequential system block diagram approach mentioned earlier.

The data-flow primitives labeled Sequencer, Selector, Coordinator, and Iterative Sequencer are shown in Figure 5-3 together with their respective definitions that are based on three elements: manager nodes with or without a predicate (P) and two subfunctions labeled A and B. Subfunctions may also be manager nodes.

In addition, the Selector can be extended from its basic form to a DO CASE, the Sequencer and Coordinator definitions can be extended to include more than two subfunctions, and each of the subfunctions can have multiple inputs and can produce multiple outputs.

The definitions thus include the three basic primitives of structured programming, i.e., SEQUENCE, IF-THEN, ELSE, and DO-WHILE augmented with a primitive for parallelism (the Coordinator).

The usefulness of these data-flow primitives is illustrated by the ability to nest them in a hierarchical fashion to define complex algorithms. Such hierarchical structures have been designated "process architecture trees" by De Wolf.

A process architecture tree is a graph in the form of a tree where the nonleaf nodes consist of manager nodes and the leaf nodes are elementary functional trans-

*J. B. Dennis, and J. B. Fosseen, "Introduction to Data Flow Schemes," Computation Structures Group Memo 81-1, Project MAC, Massachusetts Institute of Technology, September 1973.

†B. DeWolf, and R. Principato, "A Methodology for Requirements Specification and Preliminary Design of Real-time Systems," Charles Stark Draper Laboratory Report C-4923, July 1977.

Symbol	Definition
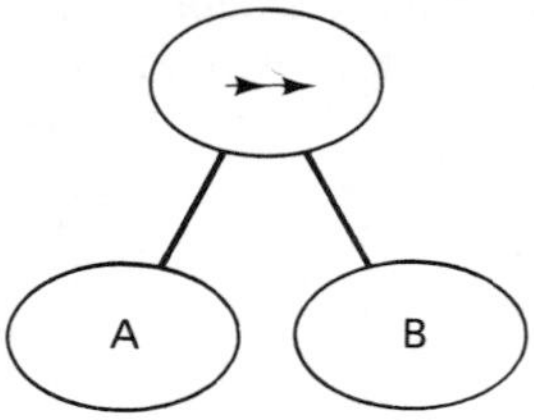	<u>Sequencer</u> Do A and then B. At least one of the outputs of A is required by B. B can also have direct inputs, and A can produce direct outputs.
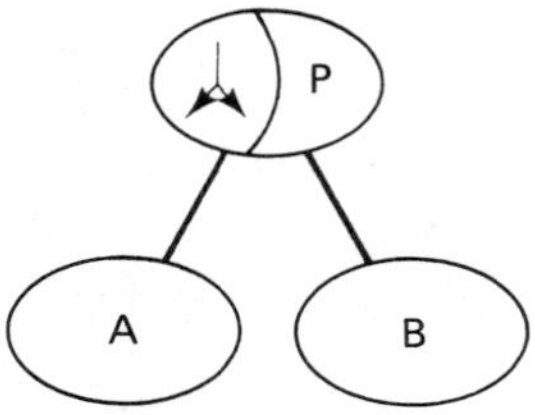	<u>Selector</u> Do A if P is true, else do B. Data inputs are required by the predicate P, as well as by each of the branches.
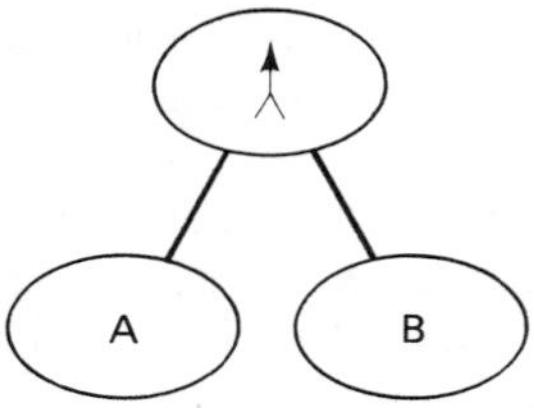	<u>Coordinator</u> Do A and B in any order or in parallel. Data inputs are required by both A and B, but no outputs of one are required as inputs to the other.
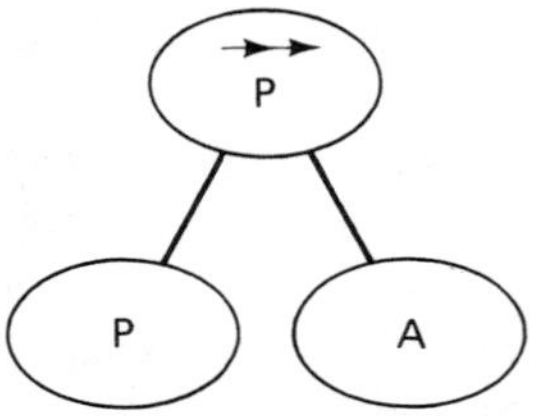	<u>Iterative sequencer</u> While P is true, do A. Data inputs are required by both P and A.

Figure 5-3   Definition of data-flow primitives used for problem decomposition.

formations termed *components*. The links or branches of the tree represent a control structure, whereas the tree as a whole represents the functional transformation of the process and is assumed to be cyclically repetitive unless wait or halt conditions are expressly indicated.

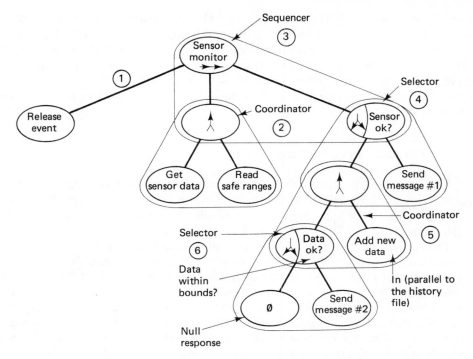

Figure 5-4 An example of a process architecture tree applied to the patient monitoring problem.

The use of data-flow primitives is illustrated using the patient monitoring problem but with a single sensor set (however, a separate sensor monitor process typically exists for each sensor set).

An example of how data-flow primitives are used is shown in Figure 5-4 where a part of the patient monitoring problem is translated into a process architecture tree. The solution depicted in the figure is for a single sensor set (see Figure 5-2). It should be understood that a separate sensor monitor process exists for each sensor set. The diagram in Figure 5-4 is obviously a composite of the Sequencer, Coordinator, and Selector and is based on a nested tree of five data-flow primitives.

The three symbols have the following significance: Initially a release event will occur (1). The sensor data is subsequently obtained and the safe ranges for that sensor set are read in parallel from a table under control of the Safe Ranges Manager (2). Armed with this information, the Sensor Monitor checks first to see if the sensor is OK (3). If the available sensor data is interpreted as invalid due to sensor failure, Message #1 is sent the Operator* (see Figure 5-2). If the sensor is OK (4), the Sensor Monitor proceeds to check to see if the data is OK (within bounds) and to add new data in parallel to the history file (5) (which is under the control of the History File

*The operator being a nurse can then verify sensor failure by visiting the patient.

Manager as shown in Figure 5-2). If the data is OK (6), a null response (ϕ) is indicated that can be interpreted as "do nothing." If not, Message #2 is sent to the Operator.*

Similar process architecture trees may be constructed for the Sensor Monitor Initiator, Console Monitor, and Operator (see Figure 5-2). When using the approach above, the designer should intentionally avoid excessive detail in order to maintain a high-level system view, sufficient to show basic input-output relations and data-flow requirements.

5.4 PROCESS INTERACTION

Using data-flow primitives, interprocess communication and coordination can be specified. Process interactions may occur at several points in the system. These interactions may be of the data-exchange type requiring communications or event type requiring coordination.

The concept of an exchange function is illustrated in Figure 5-5, using process architecture trees. This concept has been developed by Fitzwater and Zave.†

An exchange function, $XC_1(\alpha)$ (eXchange to communicate with an index of 1 and an argument of α) is shown as a component node of Process 1 (Figure 5-5). This is interpreted as when, in the course of its execution, Process 1 reaches the exchange function, it will wait unless and until some other process in the system has executed and is waiting on an exchange function having the same index value. When two exchange functions match, they exchange argument values and then proceed. Thus, the evaluation of the function $XC_1(\alpha)$ in Figure 5-5 eventually produces the value β and the evaluation of the functions $XC_1(\beta)$ (Process 2) eventually produces the value α. Exchange functions having null arguments can be used to accomplish synchronization without data transfer.

Also, more than two exchange functions can exist in a system, where both have the same index, on the condition that only two functions can exchange values at any one time. Furthermore, matching exchange functions can be used within the same process.

Again, using the patient monitoring problem as an example, the exchange functions for interprocess interaction is illustrated in Figure 5-5. The first step in specifying interprocess communications and coordination is to review the interaction requirements of each of the trees (only two are shown in Figure 5-5), adding request/release interactions for shared variables, where needed.

After each of the process architecture trees has been completed and modified (if necessary), a state exchange diagram can be developed for the whole system.

The complexity of such a diagram grows rapidly with the number of process

---

*The message can also be used to provide an audible alarm for rapid nurse or doctor response.

†P. Zave, and D. R. Fitzwater, "Specification of Asynchronous Interactions Using Primitive Functions," Computer Science Department, University of Maryland, 1977.

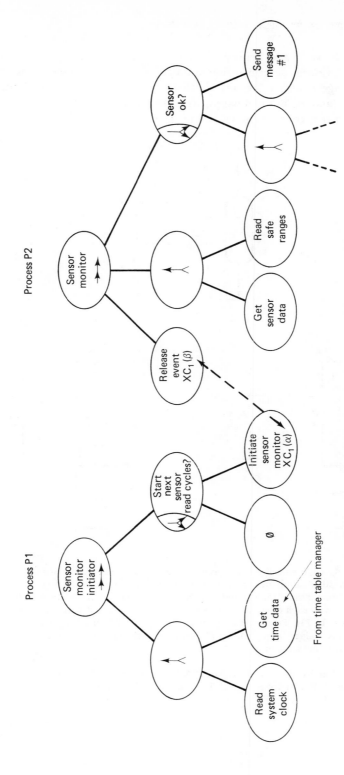

Figure 5-5 The exchange functions are shown for interprocess interaction using two process architecture trees for the patient monitoring problem. (See also Figure 5-4 for description of process P2.)

Process P2

Process P1

Sensor ok?

Send message #1

Sensor monitor

Read safe ranges

Get sensor data

Release event $XC_1(\beta)$

Start next sensor read cycles?

Initiate sensor monitor $XC_1(\alpha)$

Sensor monitor initiator

∅

Get time data

Read system clock

From time table manager

215

architecture trees. DeWolf and Principato* have, therefore, developed an alternate approach to the previously described diagrammatic form, for expressing exchanges.

A state exchange diagram for this alternate approach is shown in Figure 5-6 where processes P1 and P2 are compared, with their equivalent form, based on the process architecture tree concept shown in Figure 5-5.

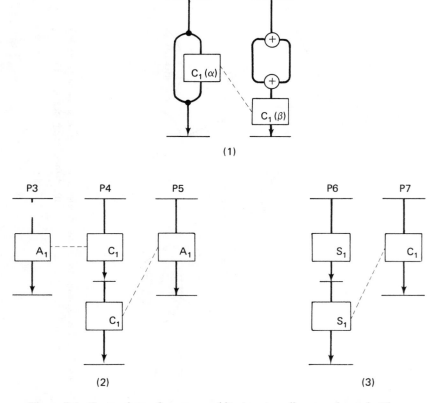

Figure 5-6   Comparison of process architecture tree diagram, shown in Figure 5-5 with equivalent, alternate form (1) for expressing state exchanges. Also shown are two additional varieties [(2) and (3)]. Note that in (2) XA's exchange with XC's but not with each other [many processes (P3 and P5) interact with a single process (P4)]. In (3), P6 proceeds without waiting for P7 supplying its own argument as its value. As shown, it will, however, exchange with a waiting XC (or XA) having the same index.

*J. Barton DeWolf and Robert N. Principato, "A Methodology for Requirements Specification and Preliminary Design of Real-Time Systems," The Charles Stark Draper Laboratories, Inc., Report #C-4923, Cambridge, Mass., July 1977.

Included in this figure are two additional representations of the exchange function. The function XA (e*X*change *A*synchronous) exchanges with XC's in the system having the same index but not with other XAs. XA is thus the same as XC except that XA's cannot exchange with each other. XA is used when many processes must interact with a single process (P3 and P5 with P4).

In the last diagram (3), the function XS (e*X*change *S*ynchronous) will exchange its argument with a waiting XC (or XA) having the same index but will otherwise proceed without waiting, supplying its own argument as its value. It is used to represent processes that cannot or do not wait: processes in the environment such as clocks. (Since, in this scheme, two processes can never read the same clock twice, real-times can be used for conflict resolution.)

A state exchange diagram, for the example problem, shown in Figure 5-2 is illustrated in Figure 5-7 using this more compact notation. It is described in more detail below. The designer should be cautioned, however, not to go directly to this notation until he is thoroughly familiar with the concept of process tree architecture.

The diagram in Figure 5-7 represents the dynamic behavior of the system and its environment in a very clear fashion.

As shown in this diagram, the system clock interacts with the Sensor Monitor Initiator (XS_8—XC_8). Each XS step of the clock represents a tick; data (in this case, time) is exchanged with the initiator only on certain ticks of the clock. The Sensor Monitor Initiator does request/release interactions with the Time Table Manager (XA_9—XC_9), and on certain passes sends initiation signals to the appropriate Sensor Monitor (XC_{2i}—XC_{2i}). Upon initiation, the Sensor Monitor receives data from the Sensor Set, performs request/release interactions with the Safe Ranges Manager (XA_3—XC_3, XA_4—XC_4), adds data to the History File controlled by the History File Manager (XA_6—XC_6, XA_7—XC_7), sends messages to the Operator (XA_5—XS_5), and then waits to be initiated again. As seen from Figure 5-7, the Console Monitor is the most complex process in the system.

For highly complex process configurations, the processor interaction may be difficult to determine. The N^2 chart* can be used for an overall understanding of internal flow, before a more detailed pictorial state exchange diagram is developed.

The N^2 chart is a fixed-format structure that graphically displays the total bidirectional interrelationships between individual functions and/or components within a given system or structure. Interfaces external to the structure may also be identified in a flexible format.

The application of the N^2 chart to the Patient Monitoring System is shown in Figure 5-8. Inputs to each element are on the upper right-hand side, and outputs from the key elements are on the lower left-hand side of the diagonal. There is no predetermined order for listing the elements. It is, however, important to show all the known elements on the chart.

---

*R. J. Lano, "The N^2 Chart," TRW Software Series, TRW-SS-77-04, November 1977, TRW Defense and Space Systems Group, Redondo Beach, Calif.

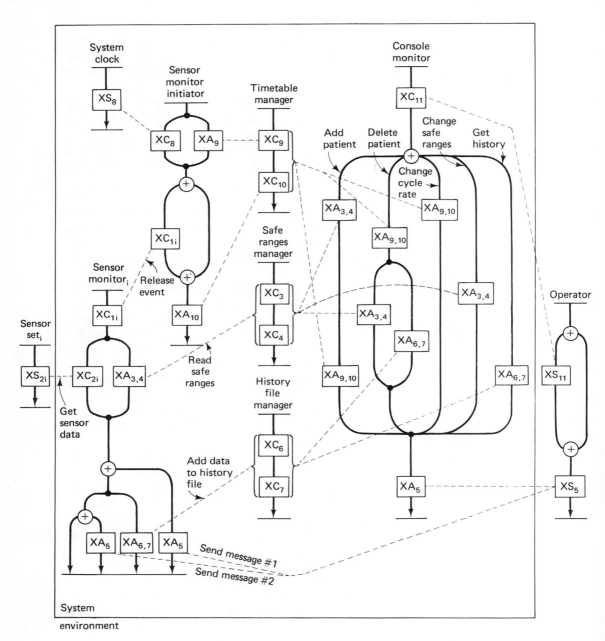

Figure 5-7 State exchange diagram for Patient Monitoring Problem (see also Figure 5-5).

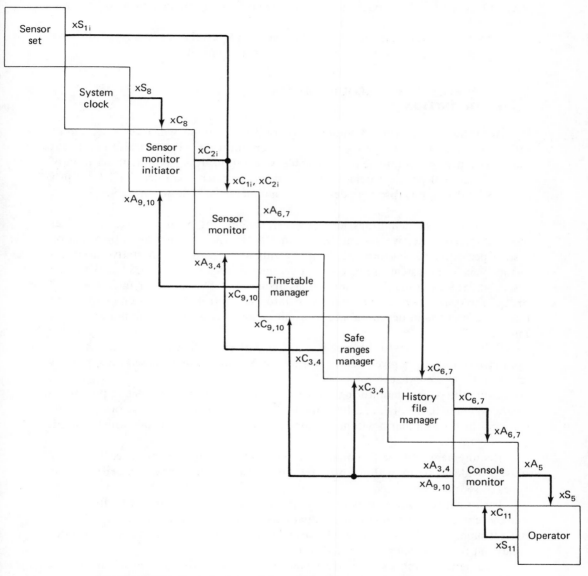

Figure 5-8 N^2 chart depicting information flow/process interaction in the Patient Monitoring System. All functions are on the diagonal, whereas all outputs are horizontal (left or right) and all inputs are vertical (up or down).

The N^2 chart can be used to show the system data flow as well as the exchange interactions without too much detail, which may initially detract from the overall understanding of system interfaces.

Sufficient information should now be available to establish system performance requirements for quantification, allocation, and management.

5.5 PERFORMANCE REQUIREMENTS DEFINITION

According to Thurber,* "requirements are the constraints which the system must satisfy. The requirements specify what the system must do." Thurber also points out that "the source of requirements is a problem definition. It is from the translation of the . . . functional problem definition that the requirements are derived." Examples of problem definitions (problem description summaries) are shown in Tables 5-1, 5-2, and 5-3.

These problem definitions are, however, insufficient by themselves if used as baseline for cost-effective system design since very little information is provided on system performance. Performance requirements are generally quantitative measures against which the system can be tested. Examples of such measures are ". . . less than 3 second response time for sensor signals acquired at the computer interface . . . ," or ". . . the system must be able to process information from a maximum of 100 input lines, interpret the information and transmit commands with a maximum delay of 1 minute . . ."

Performance may also be specified in terms of processing rate such as "X thousand instructions for a given instruction mix or Y output signals based on Z priority levels and a Q second scan rate, etc."

Using the patient monitoring problem as an example, performance requirements can be stated in terms of ". . . a 100 patient system able to measure pulse rate pressure, etc., and provide an alarm within 5 seconds of receipt of input signals which exceeds safe range."

Requirements can be formulated in more detail where, for instance, the system must provide an alarm, within a predetermined time limit that may vary depending on types of sensors being used.

Performance requirements can also include visual alarms for ward patients and audiovisual alarms for intensive care patients, including display messages indicating patient name, bed location, type of alarm condition, medication, and recommended treatment for a particular alarm condition.

Additional examples of performance requirements for this problem are the maximum size of a patient's history file, the size of timetables, the maximum number of display functions on the operator console, the maximum amount of information displayable on any one console, the maximum information retrieval period from

---

*Kenneth J. Thurber, "Techniques for Requirements—Oriented Design," Proceedings of the National Computer Conference, 1977.

time-of-request and maximum wait time for print-out requests for such items as patient history between time a and time b, the listing of doctors treating patients in the system, and medication to be given to a patient.

A key element in many real-time systems is overall system reliability and availability. Performance requirements may include values such as MTBF = 1000 hrs and Availability = 0.995.

Performance requirements are quite often also related to the "man-in-the-loop" or the human operator. Such requirements may define response time for certain inquiries or information transfer times between several people interacting with or using the system.

A typical example of this is "display handover" where, in command and control environments, one operator may ask another operator (also interfacing the system) to provide comments on information displayed on his CRT display surface. The operator message may have to be interpreted and reformatted by the system, sent to a display processor and inserted into a display refresh memory buffer, all within a specified time.

Another equally important performance requirement is the operational environment specified in terms of locations, temperature ranges, physical space, maximum power availability, and other constraints.

The examples of performance requirements above are usually defined in a System Specification. System specifications are, of course, extremely important regardless of whether the system is single or multiminicomputer-based. Is is very difficult, if not impossible, to assess the merits of various design approaches or even determine whether a particular system design will provide a satisfactory solution to a problem, without a concise system specification.

Obviously, well-defined performance specifications are particularly important for multimini- and microcomputer system design where the level of complexity (and room for design errors) usually exceeds that of a single processor system.

What then are the key elements of a multiminicomputer system specification? DeWolf and Principato* suggest at least three aspects for real-time systems that can be specified:

1. Interaction Event Structure
2. Absolute Timing
3. Functional Requirements

Events, being defined as an indivisible operation of a process (i.e., initiating and terminating events associated with each node in the process architecture tree or the execution of an exchange function), either are ordered with respect to each other or may occur simultaneously (concurrently). Ordered events generally follow each other in a time sequence. The specification of ordered events fall into several categories:

1. Input events precede output events within a process cycle.

*See footnote on p. 211.

2. A predetermined number of system cycles may or may not occur before system parameters are changed.
3. User (interactive) commands may follow a predetermined sequence.
4. A series of events may be mutually exclusive in a system (i.e., simultaneous retrieval from and updates to a file).

Time can also be specified in absolute terms. Events may be specified in terms of when they (should) occur or response times could be related to certain input occurrences (such as Console Monitor response time to a sensor message, using the patient monitoring problem as an example). These examples are by no means exhaustive and should be assessed in terms of each individual problem. Finally, functional requirements specifications can be developed using some of the design methodologies described above.

The performance requirements emphasis is also influenced by the relative importance or weight of design attributes.

In complex applications, data processing requirements may have to be partitioned into subsets based on decomposition of data or processing requirements. Each partitioning rule corresponds to a property of the multiminicomputer system that is desirable in terms of one or more system objectives. Some of these properties were briefly mentioned in the overview in Chapter 2. These properties, or attributes, are defined in greater detail in the following paragraphs.

The key design attributes, which also have been termed *design payoff measures* by Mariani, are, in addition to performance, availability, reliability, fault tolerance, life-cycle cost, modularity for growth, form factor, ease of development, physical dispersability, and survivability in hostile environments. Clearly many of these attributes are interrelated, such as availability, reliability, and fault tolerance. Each of the design attributes will be described in the following paragraphs.

5.5.1 Performance

Performance has been discussed in terms of throughput and response using the patient monitoring problem, for example, where performance at the system level was quantified in terms of major functional threads such as patient monitoring, display and recording of sensor values, and the performance of patient-related information management. Throughput performance can also be quantified at the computer level, as measured by the number of calculations or processes performed per unit time (i.e., number of patients concurrently being monitored), and at the communications level as measured by the number of discrete information elements (or words) being communicated over interconnecting computer links per unit time.

Furthermore, response performance may be quantified in terms of processing or communicating an instance of data under a given load condition (i.e., 100 patients monitored concurrently with an alarm condition response of less than 5 secs).

Finally, in certain kinds of applications, performance can also be quantified in terms of throughput and response for a set or range of values (i.e., 50 patients, 1-sec response; 100 patients, 5-sec response; and 150 patients, 10-sec response) where the system saturates within an "envelope" of values (i.e., performance envelope).

5.5.2 Availability

Availability is defined as the percentage of time a multimicro- or minicomputer system is up (available). Availability (A) is defined as follows:

$$A = \frac{\text{MTBF}}{\text{MTBF} + \text{MTTR}} \tag{5-1}$$

where MTBF = mean-time-between-failures (used to express reliability)
MTTR = mean-time-to-repair, which includes preventative maintenance time but usually excludes design uncontrollable aspects of down time, i.e., logistics and administrative times

From this equation, it can be seen that availability can be improved by increasing the MTBF and/or decreasing the MTTR. Means of improving the MTBF are discussed in Subsection 5.5.3.

Reduction of MTTR can be accomplished having spares in stock nearby; providing fast ways of identifying, locating, and correcting failures; and using modularity for improved accessability, testability, skilled maintenance personnel, ample facilities, good documentation, and standardization. The ultimate in low MTTR can be achieved by having spare units wired into the system either as hot or cold standbys. This, combined with automatic fault detection devices and an automatic reconfiguration capability that switches failed units out and backup units in, reduces MTTR to virtually zero (failed units can be replaced or fixed while the redundant units assure continued system availability).

Such fault-tolerant design requires additional critical components, however, that are in turn subject to failure.

5.5.3 Reliability

Reliability has been defined as the probability of performing a specified function or mission under specific conditions for a specified time.* Multiminicomputer systems may be required to carry out more than one type of mission (e.g., a military aircraft may be used for a reconnaissance, bombing, intercept, or strafing mission or a computerized hospital system may be used for intensive care, patient admittance, drug control, bed allocation, payroll, or other administrative functions). Separate reliability models for each of these functions or missions may be in order to make the problem more tractable. Reliability is also a function of the conditions under which the system must perform its function or mission, that is, the stresses imposed on the system play

---

*C. G. Davis, and C. R. Vick, "The Software Development System," *IEEE*, **SE-3**, No. 1, pp. 69–84, January 1977.

an important role in the reliability that can be achieved. The stresses are environmental such as ambient temperature, humidity, vibration, and shock and are related to internal load such as power, voltage, and current as well as operational such as duty cycle. Also, for large, complex multiminicomputer systems, some parts may experience different stresses depending on location as well as at different time segments during operation.

For example, complex satellite communications systems may use micro- and minicomputers both in spacecraft and ground stations. Each of these environments poses different stress levels.

In summary, reliability models must take into account different stress levels for multimission systems, systems concurrently operating in different environments, and systems seeing different stresses during a mission (for instance, aircraft flying through different altitudes and temperatures or satellites operating during boost, orbit, reentry, and recovery phases).

5.5.4 Fault Tolerance

Fault tolerance can be defined as the capability of a multimicro- or minicomputer system to overcome hardware failures and/or software errors without human intervention. Depending on a particular interconnect scheme, various levels of fault tolerance can be achieved. Fault tolerance can be implemented using system reconfigurability where failures can be allowed to occur without performance degradation (i.e., fail-safe operation). Reconfigurability can be obtained using either partial or full redundancy, depending on total system architecture. Redundancy, of course, provides fault tolerance by adding duplicate components.

Two categories of redundancy implementation exist: static and dynamic redundancies. Static redundancy techniques, often referred to as *fault masking* or *parallel redundancy* employ multiple, identical micros, minis, and/or buses, operating simultaneously in parallel/series configurations to protect against failures and failure-caused errors. This way the effects produced by faulty elements will be masked out by properly functioning elements. Examples of static redundancy architectures are multiple (usually triple) line voting schemes. The advantage of static redundancy is that it is simple. The disadvantage is that if applied massively, everything is at least doubled if not tripled. It is thus expensive and impacts the form factor heavily by increasing drastically volume, weight, and power. The nature of multiminicomputer architectures (as described in Chapter 2) is such, however, that they offer redundancy as an inherent property when the task loading does not demand the use of all processors of a multiprocessor configuration.

Dynamic redundancy, also referred to as *standby sparing*, consists of providing extra micros, minis, and communications links that automatically replace defective ones. One of the advantages of dynamic over static redundancy is that only failed units are duplicated rather than all units; i.e., it is selective rather than massive. Dynamic redundancy will require more sophisticated system design approaches using fault-detection methods, real-time recovery procedures, hard-core protection of those parts of the system that provide the fault-detection and recovery capabilities and are required to function correctly before a recovery can take place, and, finally, interprocessor communications using either a bus, loop, or point-to-point path.

There is a necessary and important technical bond and relationship between fault-tolerance and multiminicomputer system maintainability. Both deal with the properties of the entire system under the appearance of classes of faults and/or failures. Both technical areas deal with the detection and location of faults or failures. After detection and location, fault tolerance is concerned with recovery procedures, whereas maintainability is concerned with repairability. In fact, the relationship is so close that fault tolerance should necessarily be considered a part of maintainability or vice versa. Whereas the application of fault tolerance is an attempt to design a system that strives to correct or "heal" failures when they do occur, fault intolerance is a design approach based on preventing failures from occurring. It is accomplished mostly at the part or subassembly level in the form of decreased inherent failure rates. Careful attention to design, selection of materials, manufacturing techniques, quality assurance provisions, test methods, and a priori elimination of weak parts by burn-in lead to parts possessing inherently low failure rates.

Applications requiring high availability, fault tolerance, and fault intolerance may be traded off; fault tolerance typically requires more hardware, whereas fault intolerance requires more expensive hardware. Cost tradeoffs may have to be performed to determine what approach is more desirable. In certain applications where weight, size, and power also greatly affect the total system cost, fault intolerance may be the more attractive choice (such as in aircraft or spacecraft). It may also be possible that a combination of the two will yield the best design solution.

In addition to reliability and maintainability aspects, fault tolerance is related to the ease and rapidity with which a failed multiminicomputer system or minicomputer in the system can be restored to operational status following a failure. For example, if there is a single redundancy in a multiminicomputer system, and there is one failure, the system then becomes fault intolerant (assuming the system is designed based on a combination of both philosophies) until the repair is completed. This fault-intolerance period is a characteristic of design and installation that is expressed as a probability that an item (such as a faulty circuit board in the failed mini) will be replaced within a given period of time when prescribed recovery techniques are performed.

This fault-intolerance measure shown in Figure 5-9* can be expressed either as a measure of the time (T) required to cover a given percentage (P) of all failures or as a probability of restoring the system to full operational status within a period of time following a fault or failure.

5.5.5 Life-Cycle Cost

Life-cycle cost for a multimicro- and minicomputer system covers the time period from initial system conception, design, installation, and use until final replacement (or disposal). It has been defined by Mariani as ". . . the cumulative cost to design,

*W. Dejka, Private Conversations, Naval Ocean Systems Center, San Diego, Calif.

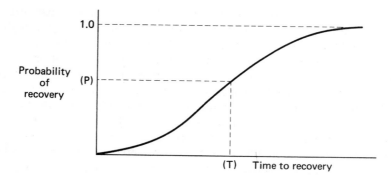

Figure 5-9   Fault-tolerance measurement.

develop, validate and maintain the software and hardware. . . . ." A total cost model is shown in Figure 5-10. At the first level, life-cycle cost is obtained by summing costs incurred during design, development, verification and validation (V&V), and the operational and maintenance (O&M) phases. The development phase cost involves documentation test and implementation of hardware and software (Level 2). Hardware implementation cost is shown to consist of the cost of acquisition, manufacture, and installation of minis or micros and interconnecting link(s).

Cost of data processing is the sum of items shown on Level 4, which includes the cost of peripherals and facilities. The interconnecting network cost breaks down into cost of links and possible traffic switches (depending on architecture) that may reside either at computer locations or intermediate facilities for relaying and/or switching.

Software cost is generally much more difficult to assess than hardware cost. Software cost models exist for the development phase but should be used with caution. Virtually all require estimation of the number and type of routines and instructions per routine expected, as well as subjective determinations of routine complexity and personnel productivity and competence.

The development of reliable and usable software cost models is greatly hampered by the lack of good data especially in the operations and maintenance phase. Yet, this phase may cost the user up to many times (hardware and software together) the cost of acquisition, over a life cycle of perhaps a decade.

All costs associated with the four phases on Level 1 can be expressed as follows:

$$C_{\text{MMCS}} = \sum_{i=1}^{4} (C_{\text{HW}} + C_{\text{SW}})_i \tag{5-2}$$

where C_{MMCS} = total life-cycle cost of multimicro- or minicomputer system
C_{HW_i} = hardware costs associated with the ith life-cycle phase
C_{SW_i} = software costs associated with the ith life-cycle phase

The annual cost of the last phase, O&M, can be expressed as a fraction of the

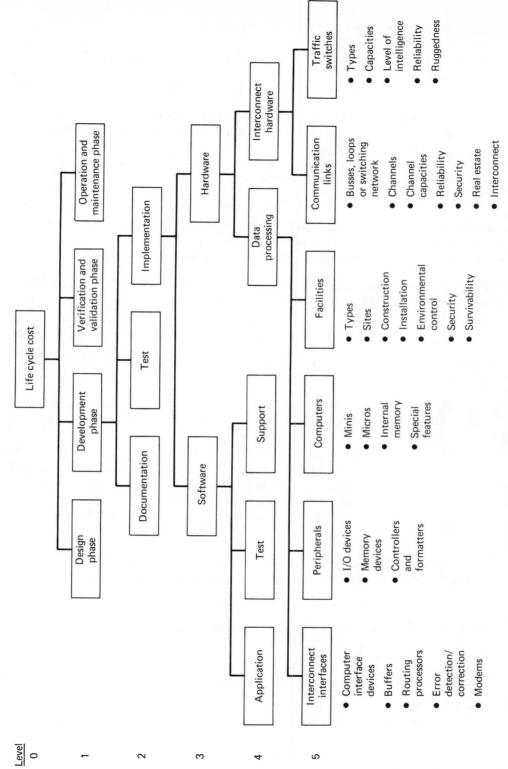

Figure 5-10 Life-cycle cost associated levels and elements at each level for a multimicro- or minicomputer system.

sum of the total costs of the first three phases. Doing this changes Eq. (5-2) to

$$C_{\text{MMCS}} = (1 + fY) \sum_{i=1}^{3} (C_{\text{HW}} + C_{\text{SW}})_i \tag{5-3}$$

where f = annual O&M cost (expressed in "per-year" terms)

Y = multimicro- or minicomputer system life-cycle time period of operational service, number of years

The hardware costs can be decomposed as follows:

$$C_{\text{HW}_i} = (C_{\text{DP}} + C_{\text{FAC}} = C_{\text{NET}})_i \tag{5-4}$$

where C_{DP_i} = data processing hardware cost associated with Phase i

C_{FAC_i} = facilities cost associated with Phase i

C_{NET} = communications/interconnect cost associated with Phase i.

The total computer hardware cost associated with the implementation aspect of the development phase (Phase 2 in Figure 5-10) is as follows:

$$C_{\text{DP}_2} = \sum_{j=1}^{G} C_{\text{DP}_2,j} \tag{5-5}$$

where G = total number of minis or micros used in the system

$C_{\text{DP}_2,j}$ = the total computer hardware cost

Software cost can be decomposed into the cost of developing real-time (RT) and non real-time (NRT) code; i.e., the software cost term of Eq. (5-2) becomes

$$C_{\text{SW}_i} = C_{\text{NRT}_i} + C_{\text{RT}_i} \tag{5-6}$$

where C_{NRT_i} = cost of nonreal-time machine language instructions (NRT MLI's) during Phase i (note that the equation is equally valid using higher level language for programming)

C_{RT_i} = cost of real-time machine language instructions (RT MLI's) during Phase i

The cost of developing NRT MLI's can be expressed by the following equation (the subscript i has been dropped for convenience in the following equations):

$$C_{\text{NRT}} = c_{\text{NRT}} I_{\text{NRT}} \tag{5-7}$$

where C_{NRT} = cost per nonreal-time machine language instruction

I_{NRT} = number of NRT MLI's

Similarly,

$$C_{\text{RT}} = c_{\text{RT}} I_{\text{RT}} \tag{5-8}$$

where c_{RT} = cost per RT MLI

I_{RT} = number of RT MLI's

The total software required during the development and life cycle of the system can be divided into three major categories (as shown in Figure 5-10) as follows:

1. *Application Software.* This is the operational software that supports user requirements (i.e., the Sensor Monitor Initiator, Sensor Monitor, Time Table, Safe Ranges and History File Managers, and Console Monitor software in the Patient Monitoring System example).

2. *Test Software.* This software serves to test the applications software at various levels of development (from algorithm through routine task, sub-program, program, subprocess to process) and during integration and validation testing (system level testing). Test software may consist of simulation software used to exercise and test the applications software during the development phase by simulating the data processing subsystem, environment, and sensor subsystem and of data reduction and analysis and similar test tool programs depending on the particular system application.

3. *Support Software.* The software consists of programs specially developed in support of a particular system and could include programs for configuration management, requirements tracing and test evaluation, program management, system maintenance, logistics, etc.

Hence, all the software required for a multimicro- or minicomputer system can be expressed as follows:

$$SW = SW_{APPLIC} + SW_{TEST} + SW_{SUPPORT} \tag{5-9}$$

Similar to previous groupings, each element can be further broken into real-time and nonreal-time software.

The cost per machine language instruction has been found, from practical experience, in 1977 to be typically as follows:

$$C_{NRT} = \frac{\$42}{NRT\ MRI}$$

$$C_{RT} = \frac{\$120}{RT\ MLI}$$

for nonreal-time and real-time MLI's, respectively. The rates above include the following charges:

- Direct Labor
- Overhead
- General & Administrative
- Fee
- Computer time
- Documentation
- Travel

The rates apply to the following major development phases:

- Requirements definition and analysis
- Preliminary design
- Code and debug
- Testing (algorithm, routine, task subprogram, program, system integration, evaluation and validation, and acceptance by user)

5.5.6   Modularity

Modularity for growth is synonymous with adaptability, enhancement, extensibility, changeability, upgradeability, and modifiability. Growth can often be equated to design specifications and, in particular, design specifications for systems where the exact future needs are difficult to predict. Growth needs are often based on "educated" guesses and, as such, are tempered by the desire to minimize the baseline system cost. Growth requirements are nevertheless imposed to minimize the system life-cycle cost. This is best illustrated by an example.

As shown in Figure 5-11 the cost of developing a baseline system using approach *A* is $a. Doubling the performance of *A* will also double the cost (to $2a). If the baseline performance capability of *A* is tripled before the system reaches saturation and

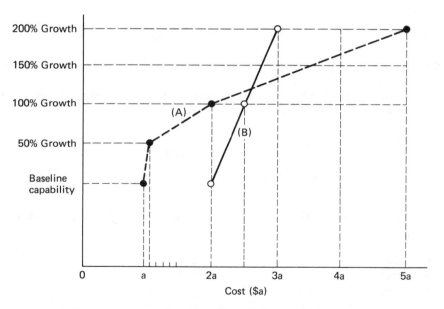

Figure 5-11   Comparison of two potential distributed minicomputer systems, *A* and *B*, where the baseline cost of *A* is $a and the baseline cost of *B* is $2a. System *A*, when expanded to three times its original performance level, is 67% more costly than *B*.

cannot be expanded further, however, the baseline cost will have grown by a factor of five. Approach *B* with an initial cost twice that of *A* is, in spite of this, more attractive from a life-cycle cost point of view than *A* if a growth requirement of 200% has been specified.

In many applications, system design should be based on the selection of an interconnect structure, hardware, and software that not only minimizes the development cost but also allows for expansion with minimum disruption. An attempt has been made to relate cost and downtime to modularity and growth but with limited success (see Problem 5-8). It is, however, difficult to quantify growth in a general form since the relative importance of, and the interrelationships between, cost of upgrading a system, downtime resulting from this upgrade, the number of unique upgradeable components, and the feasibility of updating any of these components, be they interfaces, peripherals, micros, minis, communication links, software modules, etc., is highly dependent on the particular application. Growth in an aircraft or a missile may be limited by external factors such as space, weight, and power, whereas growth in a commercial application may be limited by the maximum extensibility of a bus or the maximum memory expansion capability of a particular minicomputer.

5.5.7 Form Factor

Form factor may be defined as the collective volume, weight, and power characteristics of multimicro- or minicomputer system components at the hardware level (Level 5 in Figure 5-10).

The form factor is of lesser importance in most commercial environments compared to military systems used in mobile, ship-based, airborne, or space environments. For very large multiminicomputer systems where several inputs and/or outputs as well as interconnected minis are used, however, the cabling problem becomes a significant consideration.

The form factor is a function of a large number of parameters such as

- Fault tolerance since it involves redundancy that adds to volume and weight and, if of the static variety, also to power and, of course, cost.
- Modularity, which enhances growth and maintainability but, on the other hand, tends to increase volume and weight.
- Processing speed, which relates directly to all three form factor parameters; i.e., increasing speed increases volume, weight, and power. It has been determined, however, that, in general, faster machines tend to be more "form factor efficient."

It has been determined by Mariani that computer volume, weight, and power for militarized computers can be related to computer speed based on a given execution mix where

$$\text{Speed} = (0.7t_{\text{add}} + 0.3t_{\text{mult}} + 2k_m t_{mc})^{-1} \tag{5-10}$$

where t_{add} = short operation execution time in microseconds (addition)
t_{mult} = long operations execution time in microseconds (multiplication)
k_m = degree of memory transparency (look-ahead)
For total transparency: $k_m = 0$
For no transparency: $k_m = 1$
t_{mc} = memory cycle time in microseconds
Speed = millions of instructions per second (MIPS)

Based on information on 93 ruggedized or militarized small computers, the resulting equation for volume as function of speed was determined as

$$V = 1.89(MIPS)^{0.503} \qquad (5\text{-}11)$$

where V is in cubic feet.

The equation was derived from regression analysis performed on discrete data points representing speed and volume and covers processors having speed values mostly between 0.05 and 0.5 MIPS.

Similarly, using regression analysis on data from the same computers,

$$W = 86.3(MIPS)^{0.536} \qquad (5\text{-}12)$$

where W is weight in pounds, and

$$P = 0.165(MIPS)^{0.275} \qquad (5\text{-}13)$$

where P is in kilowatts.

Finally, a kilowatt per million of instructions (MIP) was obtained:

$$\frac{P}{MIP} = 0.649(MIPS)^{-0.169} \qquad (5\text{-}14)$$

Equations (5-10) through (5-14) should, however, be used with great caution since they are based on computers developed in the 1970 to 1977 time frame where a great reduction in computer packaging size and an even greater increase in processing power has taken place. [A subset of the computers used to derive Eq. (5-11) through (5-14) is listed in Figure 5-12].

5.5.8 Ease of Development

Ease of development or the speed with which a multimicro- or minicomputer system can be designed, developed, and produced is related to system deployability, where the latter is measured as the time required for the system to reach operational capability. Deployability is thus measured as the length of the critical path through the development cycle that is taken to start with the allocation of requirements and process identification (see Figure 5-1).

MANUFACTURER	Model	Year	Word Length (bits)	Memory Cycle Time (μsec)	Instruction Times (μsec) ADD	MULT.	DIV.	Speed (MIPS)	Volume (cu ft)	Weight (lb)	Power (kw)
ARMA	1808LSI	1977	18	1.0	2.0	6.8	13.6	0.225	0.028	—	—
AUTONETICS	D216	1972	16	1.5	2.5	13.8	23.8	0.136	0.255	15	0.048
CDC	AN/UYK-14	1977	16	0.4	0.8	4.4	4.4	0.439	—	—	0.500
DELCO	4016	1976	16 + 1	0.4	3.75	11.8	12.0	0.153	0.051	3	0.024
GARRETT AIRRES	ADAPT RF-20	1971	20	1.2	2.5	12.5	13.8	0.149	0.180	9.75	0.037
HARRIS	/5R	1972	24	0.95	0.95	7.6	14.3	0.257	6.3	230	1.8
HONEYWELL	HDC-701	1975	32	0.6	2.4	10.8	10.8	0.181	1.20	50	0.270
HUGHES	HCM-230	1972	24	1.0	2.0	5.5	15.0	0.247	1.00	45	0.350
	HMP-1670	1977	16 + P	0.6	0.8	5.0	8.0	0.376	2.20	85	0.260
IBM	4π/SP-1	1971	16 + 1	0.6	2.7	5.7	8.0	0.238	0.340	18.1	0.072
	4π/AP-1	1970	32	0.45	2.0	6.8	10.8	0.257	0.872	36	0.230
LEAR SIEGLER	LS-52-D	1973	16	1.0	1.75	4.3	12.0	0.212	0.560	30	0.200
LITTON	L-30	1975	16	0.9	0.9	5.0	7.0	0.330	1.1	55	0.180
NORDEN	11/34M	1976	16	0.9	1.9	9.0	12.9	0.203	0.880	58	0.410
NORTHROP	TOP 20	1972	16	0.9	0.6	6.8	6.8	0.298	0.270	15	—
RAYTHEON	RP 16	1974	16,8	0.18	0.65	9.7	12.4	0.285	—	16	0.110
RCA	ATMAC	1976	16	0.28	0.24	0.93	17.2	1.378	0.664	30	0.009
	SUM C	1973	—	1.0	1.5	10.0	20.0	0.198	0.517	16	0.030
ROLM	AN/UYK-19	1972	16	1.0	1.0	5.3	9.2	0.304	0.560	40	0.200
	AN/UYK-27	—	—	1.2	1.2	7.7	7.7	0.230	0.873	—	0.150
SANDERS	MIP 16/10R	1972	16	0.2	0.2	4.0	5.0	0.650	—	45	0.200
SINGER	SKC-3000FM	1974	16, 20	1.2	5.6	14.0	49.2	0.107	0.015	1.1	0.027
	SKC-3100	1975	16, 19	1.2	2.2	10.8	13.8	0.167	0.008	0.57	0.019
	SKC-3000	1971	16, 20	1.2	5.6	39.2	42.6	0.059	0.008	0.57	0.016
	SKC-3120	1976	16	1.2	1.3	5.61	11.0	0.264	0.008	0.57	0.020
TELEDYNE	TDY-214	1970	20	3.3	7.5	31.0	39.0	0.056	0.800	4.5	0.040
	TDY-52A	—	—	1.0	2.9	6.2	20.0	0.205	0.002	0.188	0.007
TEXAS INSTRUMENTS	2502T	1970	16	2.0	4.0	10.5	—	0.126	0.370	25	0.100
UNIVAC	AN/UYK-15	—	16 + 2	0.75	0.75	3.75	3.75	0.417	4.45	170	—
	AN/UYK-20	—	16	0.75	0.75	3.8	6.8	0.417	5.28	2.20	1.0
VARIAN	RV 75	1976	16	1.07	1.32	5.94	7.92	0.075	0.311	50	0.200
WESTINGHOUSE	Millicomputer	1976	16	1.0	3.0	8.66	—	0.176	0.600	29	—

Figure 5-12 Computer characteristics for several militarized computers manufactured in the 1970–1977 time period. From M. P. Mariani, Distributed Data Processing (DDP) Technology Program, **2**: Research Appendices, TRW Defense and Space Systems Group, Final Report No. 30451-000, 31 December 1977.

233

The development cycle is highly dependent on hardware elements such as

- Number and types of computers
- Computer availability (delivery schedule)
- Hardware interfaces
- Interconnect structure/architecture

It is evident that deployability is closely related to the level of off-the-shelf components used in the system (see Chapter 4). Equally important are software and software-related considerations such as

- Staffing (number of personnel) and mix (percent programmers, managers, quality assurance, etc.)
- Implementation language used
- Number of software modules
- Ratio of real-time to nonreal-time programs
- Data base size and complexity
- Documentation (number of pages) required
- Implementation technologies (i.e., structured code, top-down programming, chief programmers, code reviews, etc.)

5.5.9 Physical Dispersability and Survivability

Physical dispersability and survivability are closely related. Survivability is defined as the probability that a multimicro- or minicomputer system can sustain hardware losses due to hardware failures, software errors, and hostile action and continue to carry out the nominal mission objective, as spelled out by the performance requirements, without degradation. Survivability is thus related to the probability that a system will fail during a particular time interval based on a certain system availability. This attribute is important for systems that may be subject to destruction (i.e., vandalism, sabotage, or other forms of hostile action such as in military environments). Survivability can be achieved using redundant, dispersed computers and transmission links between computers that are less susceptible to damaging effects or events, e.g., by operating in ways that reduce the probability of damage and by using redundancy techniques to increase the probability of maintaining the required connectivity of the system.

Survivability in bus-based systems can be improved using a dual-bus system (Figure 4-15) or in a loop-base system by using a dual loop (see Chapter 2, Loop Reliability). Survivability is also improved by duplicating micros or minis in a dual-bus or loop system and physically dispersing the computers.

The purpose of the review of all key design attributes has been to provide the reader with an understanding of the importance of these attributes and the influence they have on the system specifications. Figure 5-13 summarizes the relative importance of the key design attributes in some typical multimicro- and minicomputer application areas. Obviously, parameters such as performance, availability, reliability, form factor, physical dispersability, and survivability can be specified. The designer must, however,

Attributes \ Application areas	Automotive, control	Space, avionics, shipborne, control	Medical, monitoring	Business, point-of-sale, electronic funds transfer, transaction processing	Laboratory, scientific data processing	Industrial, process control	Data acquisition, file management	Military, tactical command, and control	Simulation, training
Performance (throughput, response, etc.)	M	H	M	M	H/M	H/M	H/M	H	H
Availability	M	H	H	M	L	H	H	H	M
Reliability	M	H	H	M	L	H	H	H	M
Fault tolerance (path, switching elements, nodes, etc.)	L	H	H	H	L	H	M	H	L
Life-cycle cost (off-the-shelf hardware, software, ease of developments, etc.)	H	M	H	H	H	H	H	M	M
Modularity/growth	L	M	M	H	H	H	H	H	H
Form factor (volume, weight, power)	H	H	L	L	L	M	L	H	L
Physical dispersability and survivability (failure reconfigureability)	L	H	M	M	L	H	M	H	L

Figure 5-13 Examples of potential application areas and the relative weighting of attributes for a distributed micro- or minicomputer system (H = very important; M = moderately important; L = unimportant or inconsequential).

understand the impact of such specifications on interrelated areas such as life-cycle cost, ease of development, and deployability. It is also clear that detailed life-cycle cost analysis cannot be accomplished until a well-defined design has been developed (Step VI in Figure 5-1). This must, however, be preceded by a definition of system architecture.

5.6 SYSTEM PARTITIONING, SIZING, TIMING, AND INTERCONNECT STRUCTURE

The analyses described in the previous sections support the development of an inherent architectural structure for data processing but do not consider quantitative performance needs, resource limitations, or the geographical location of processes, to use some examples. A detailed, hardware/software design cannot be performed, however, until both qualitative *and* quantitative performance requirements are defined. Once detailed performance requirements have been developed, the physical, quantitative system design can proceed.

A system architecture definition is based on deliverable components that implement the system. During the definition phase, the limitations of components are analyzed and imposed, geographical distribution decisions are made, and necessary redundancy requirements are induced. The system architecture definition is concerned with which type of computer to use, what size memories are required in each one, what system synchronization and control method to be implemented, the information transfer strategy to be used between micros or minis, the type of intercomputer transfer path to be selected, and what resources are to be shared or dedicated in the system.

Finally, it must be determined if off-the-shelf hardware and software will satisfy the architectural and operational requirements or whether new hardware and software must be developed.

This section will, therefore, explore approaches to multiminicomputer system partitioning, timing and sizing, and system topography.

5.6.1 System Partitioning and Partitioning Criteria

The system partitioning process was initially discussed in terms of the process identification phase and described in greater detail for the problem decomposition and process interaction phases based on the exchange function, process architecture tree, state exchange diagram, and N^2 chart concepts. Following this, the quantification process was discussed for the system design specification task where events could be ordered into parallel and sequential steps. The primary system objectives driving partitioning of data processing are performance-related payoffs such as throughput, response, form factor, reliability/fault tolerance, reconfigurability/growth and other attributes, also described in this section.

Partitioning rules can be developed to support the system architecture analysis. These rules will improve the opportunity for meeting system objectives and constraints. Such rules should be developed individually for each application, however, since design attributes are, to a great extent, application dependent (i.e., survivability, failure reconfiguration, fault tolerance, and form factor are more important in a military/tactical environment than ease of development or physical dispersability—on the other hand, physical dispersability, growth/modularity, and availability may play a more key role in a process control environment than form factor or survivability).

For example, system partitioning can be performed to improve on performance, increase overall system reliability and growth potential, lower the life-cycle cost, and reduce the form factor, to use examples.

When partitioning for change and growth, it may be advantageous to insulate the multiminicomputer system from external changes, as much as possible. This can be achieved by confining specific interface details, such as message formats and header data to designated interface modules with one module per distinct interface. For example, the patient monitoring system, if properly partitioned and depending on the development of new types of sensors, could be expanded by simply adding a sensor interface module or microprocessor, without having to make major changes to the rest of the system.

The major objective of partitioning for change is, therefore, to confine the impact of changes within a single partition or, at worst, within a minimal number of partitions.

When partitioning for reliability, steps must be taken to assure that computation errors or single-point hardware failures do not lead to corruption of data bases or dangerous output responses to the external environment. An example of this is a distributed minicomputer system on board an aircraft that is performing a multiplicity of tasks such as navigation and guidance and display of radar data, where a failure in the display system may impact the navigation system with perhaps serious implications in terms of passenger safety.

Failure-effects analysis must, therefore, be used during the system design/partitioning activity to project consequences of failures, define containment points, and develop recovery algorithms. The containment points define partitions in the processing and induce design requirements for validity checking, fault detection, and recovery procedures.

Partitions can also be performed by segregating micros or minis that can be allocated to different computer/processor architectures, to permit geographical distribution, and to enhance reconfigurability and reliability. This type of partitioning has been termed *vertical*. It is generally desirable to locate partitions at points in the data flow where a minimum of data must be stored or communicated. Such points are often associated with major events or decisions about the data.

Using the Patient Monitoring System as an example of vertical partitioning (Figure 5-7), where predecessor-successor relationships stemming from data dependency (i.e., Time Table, Safe Ranges, History File), and mandatory control-flow considerations (i.e., between Sensor Monitors—Sensor Monitor Initiator and Console Monitor—Time Table, Safe Ranges, and History File Managers) exist, may be the partitioning of sensor-related functions (Sensor Monitors) and operator-related functions (information Managers and Console Monitor) within separate micro- or minicomputers. Vertical partitioning is, of course, also closely related to the occurrence of time-sequential events as described in Section 5.5. (A typical example of vertical partitioning is the Bank of America system described in Chapter 6).

In many applications, data processing functions can be performed concurrently or without regard to order. In these types of applications, horizontal partitioning applies. Most obvious candidates for horizontal partitioning are those processing steps that are completely disjoint, i.e., have no data relationship or mandatory predecessor-successor control-flow relationship. Another type of permissible concurrency is instance independence: Processing of each instance is uncorrelated with other instances.

An example of the former is the On-Line Credit-Authorization, Point-Of-Sale

(POS) System (Table 5-3) where each POS terminal operates independent of all other POS terminals or the Production Control System (Figure 2-41) where each Production Control Mini (PCM) collects data from, and issues control signals to, its dedicated devices.

Instance independence is illustrated by the branch and rejoin nodes in a control-flow graph, wherein the AND branch is an explicit indication of parallelism. As shown in Figure 5-7, processing along each branch by the Sensor Monitor (Get Sensor Data and Read Safe Ranges) may proceed independently until a rejoin node is encountered. An OR node, on the other hand, indicates that only one branch will be executed, dependent on the outcome of the branch-selection test (Console Monitor: Add Patient or Delete Patient or Change Cycle Rate or Change Safe Ranges or Get History).

If the processing on different branches indicates radically different hardware-architecture solutions, the branches could be horizontally partitioned to execute on different processors. (The Ford Motor Co. LNA and the NASA POCCNET discussed in Chapter 6 are good examples of horizontally partitioned systems.)

Functional partitioning, whether vertical or horizontal, must eventually resolve questions of data interaction and sharing between parallel processes and the impact on hardware selection. A multimicro- or minicomputer system is, obviously, a collection of independent processors and, of equal importance, a collection of memories, except for the case where several minis may communicate with each other using a single shared memory. Concurrently running programs in a multicomputer environment (except where a shared memory is used) communicate with each other through common data blocks. Figure 5-14 illustrates how multiple processes distributed spatially across a set of processors might be linked with a set of data blocks in a sys-

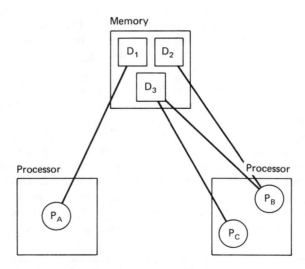

Figure 5-14 Multiprocessors with shared memory.

tem with centralized memory. It is assumed that data blocks D_1 and D_2 are used by processes P_A and P_B, respectively, and that data block D_3 is shared by processes P_B and P_C.

Unless a restrictive paging system is used, any memory allocation scheme that does not split up data blocks can be used in a shared memory system as long as the total memory available is large enough. Processes may be scheduled or moved from processor to processor without regard to the memory location of the data used by the process. Thus, process P_B may be moved to the other processor in the multiprocessor example by moving a few program and data pointers.

In a distributed system, memory module size may dictate that the data be partitioned into at least two groups, D_1 and $D_2 + D_3$. As long as processing deadlines allow process P_A to be assigned to one processor and processes P_B and P_C to another processor (as shown in Figure 5-15), all is well—in fact, the partitioning of the memories protects data D_1 from incursions by processes P_B or P_C.

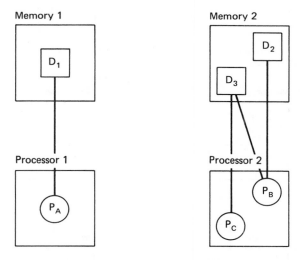

Figure 5-15   Multiprocessors with dedicated memory.

If process P_B requires the exclusive use of a processor because of time constraints, etc., however, then process P_C must be moved to another processor where it can no longer directly address the data block D_3 that it shares with process P_B. Process P_C can, however, be provided the needed access by using one of four schemes. In the first scheme, P_C negotiates with a new process, P_D (possibly a portion of the executive), which accesses data block D_3 in response to messages and data transmitted from P_C via a bus or loop system. As shown in Figure 5-16, P_B continues to access D_3 directly.

In the second scheme, data block D_3 may be relocated with P_C so that process P_B accesses D_3 by communicating on the system bus or loop with an additional process P_F, as shown in Figure 5-17. The difference between this and the previous scheme is that P_F also serves as a common process that both P_B and P_C can access.

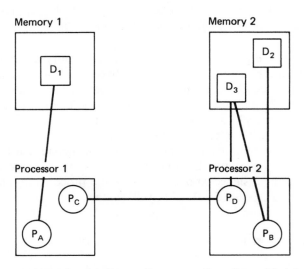

Figure 5-16   Alternative #1, Process-Processor scheme for multiminicomputer system partitioning.

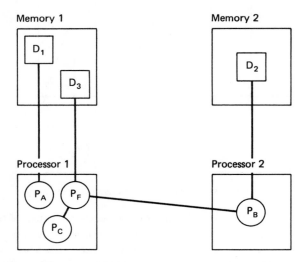

Figure 5-17   Alternative #2, Process-Processor scheme for multiminicomputer system partitioning.

Based on the third scheme, the data block D_3 may be split into two blocks, D_4 and D_5, with intercommunication processes P_D and P_F used to provide interprocess transfers or data argument exchanges. Actually, the first two cases are special cases of this case with D_4 and P_F or D_5 and P_D allowed to be of zero size (Figure 5-18).

Finally, in the fourth scheme, the data block D_3 may be split into two blocks, D_4

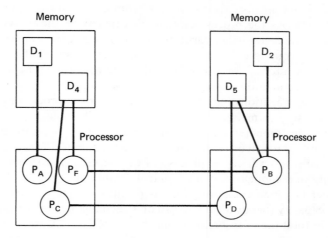

Figure 5-18   Alternative #3, Process-Processor scheme for multiminicomputer partitioning.

and D_5, with a pair of processes, P_G and P_H, cooperating to transfer data from one block to another in accordance with a preestablished criterion.

For example, if process P_C used data block D_3 only as input, then data block D_5 could be the current copy of the D_3 information and data block D_4 could be a copy of the portion of D_3 relevant to P_C. Processes P_G and P_H would communicate as shown in Figure 5-19 to maintain D_4 to the degree of currency and precision required by P_C. Thus, even if D_5 were updated frequently by P_B, D_4 may be updated at a slower rate if the lack of time lines does no harm to process P_C.

Clearly, processing power is wasted if each processor has a large margin of com-

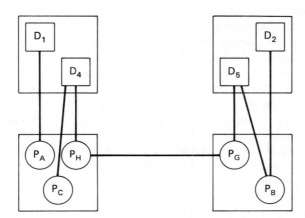

Figure 5-19   Alternative #4, Process-Processor scheme for multiminicomputer partitioning.

putational power and memory space over the requirements for the function or functions assigned to it. As the processing/memory capacity of the individual minis or micros decreases, however, further partitioning with a subsequent increase in the interprocessor traffic is required to meet processing deadlines. As the subdivisions become finer, the volume of information transmitted between the processors increases as well as the degree of coordination required between processors.

Eventually, the partitions may become so fine that the processors must be synchronized in lock step to maintain coordination and still meet processing deadlines. Thus, in a multiminicomputer system with homogeneous processors, a reduction in processor capacity entails an increase in interconnect capability. This impact is reduced to a negligible level if a variety of processors can be used in a system albeit with a resulting penalty in reconfiguration and control flexibility.

The manner in which computing load is partitioned not only impacts on interprocessor link capacity (bandwidth) but also on the configuration of the Input/Output of the system in total (i.e., sensors, man-machine interface, external control devices, actuators, etc.).

If I/O devices for the system are, for instance, serviced by a global bus so that they are accessible to all processors in the system, then processing function involving these units will be much more amenable to partitioning than if only one or two processors have access to the device.

Software for a multiminicomputer system is typically organized into programs and subprograms (or processes) that perform specific functions. Such a program or programs may be small enough to share a processor with other programs or, if a single program, so large that it must be broken down into several cooperating co-routines running in several processors. Thus, the partitioning of a computational task developed by the applications programmer may not coincide with the partitioning dictated by the hardware. If the partitioning of the software does match processor/memory boundaries, however, the outputs passed between processors are more likely to be well defined, well documented, and physically meaningful than in a system with arbitrary partitions. It is considerably easier to debug a system in which variables passed between partitions have some physical meaning since, typically, a problem analyst has considerably more knowledge of the limits and expected values of such data.

Finally, system partitioning is related to the allowed functional variability and processing element computer power and speed (performance) for a particular system. Individual computer performance is closely related to a particular instruction set and instruction execution speed, amount of instruction and CPU overlap capability, I/O rates, software efficiency, memory access time, etc., whereas functional variability is related to the choice of a single type of micro or mini (homogeneousness), mixed (but dedicated) micros and/or minis in a system (heterogeneousness), or dynamically assigned mixed types of computers.

The homogeneous multimicro- or minicomputer system, where all computers are identical, is probably the simplest to develop from a hardware and interconnect point of view, since all interfaces can be made identical and a degree of symmetry can be applied to system architecture. In such a system, fewer problems also present themselves from a fault-tolerance point of view, since any processor could (theoretically, at least) assume the function of any other processor due to compatibility.

The heterogeneous system may be functionally more effective since each micro or mini can be oriented toward being optimum for a class of functions. Such systems are, however, considerably more difficult to design due to possible differences in word size, communications control hardware, software protocols, and timing, to name a few areas. The dynamic reassignment of micros and minis of different design and internal architecture, including operating system software, compounds the problem even further.

Some interconnect structures are, however, more suitable for homogeneous architectures than others. We will return to communications between partitions and interconnect structures after the following discussion on individual micro- and mini-computer performance.

5.6.2 Micro/Minicomputer Timing and Sizing

Computer sizing and timing analyses are typically based on the identification of each processing task, determination of the task rate, number of CPU instructions per task, number of I/O accesses per task, number of I/O buffer words needed per access, and the assessment of memory size for executive and applications program storage, including unexecutable data and tables as well as time or storage constraints. If no particular micro or mini has been targeted for processing tasks, the results of problem sizing are dependent on hardware assumptions that are unavoidably imbedded in the sizing methodology employed.

Furthermore, if the exact and entire set of operations associated with each processing task (that is, detailed programming flow-chart-level information) were known, a relatively accurate task sizing could result. In most applications, however, this kind of information is not available until very late in the design process.

On the other hand, it should be realized that underestimates in sizing are less critical in multiminicomputer system design than they are in single processor system design. As shown in Chapter 2, most multiminicomputer systems can readily be expanded when more processing power (throughput capability) is needed (assuming the partitioning job has been performed correctly). It should also be kept in mind that, for many of today's micros and (in particular) minis, memory can readily (and with relatively limited cost increase) be expanded if initial design estimates have proved to be too conservative.

The classical methods of evaluating throughput of computers are based on mix estimates and benchmarks. The utility of these methods is closely related to the level of understanding the problem environment and the number and ratio of instructions required to process the information. When sizing, based on instruction mix estimates, is performed, it should be remembered that, in addition to applications programs, most systems incur systems processing overhead for the executive or control program.

Sizable discrepancies may also be introduced where applications programs are written and compiled in higher level language (i.e., Fortran, Basic, Cobol, RPG, etc.). Compiler efficiencies (or inefficiencies) are difficult to assess and a more accurate (but also more time-consuming) approach may be to write and run benchmark programs.

The actual memory sizing is often nothing more than guess work with accuracy or correctness being closely related to the experience level of the designer (or programmer). The difficulty is further compounded by the great variation in programmer "skill" or approach to software development (flow charting, coding, etc.). In many applications, it is not unusual to have variations in lines of code for an identical function as large as 1 to 10. Furthermore, the use of instruction mixes for throughput estimates may result in discrepancies or errors due to computer differences in word size, internal data paths, addressing logic, and other CPU-unique features, such as the instruction repertoire.

Theoretical evaluations of program execution times as well as benchmark tests should include the effects of data communications, internal to the system. The following parameters have, in this case, the most impact on CPU utilization:

- Number of messages sent and received per second.
- Size of the messages.
- Multimicro- or minicomputer system topology and communications links hardware.
- CPU instructions available to handle communications.

Examples of the effect on CPU utilization for various message rates and message size are shown in Figures 5-20 and 5-21, respectively, for the Digital Equipment Corporation PDP-11/34 and PDP-11/70 using DECnet (see Chapter 3). It is clear that a micro or mini can saturate for high traffic levels without being able to perform any applications program processing. (Note also that where the ratio of data-to-protocol information becomes large, constant CPU utilization is reached). In spite of all the pitfalls and uncertainties involved in using instruction mixes and vendor supplied instruction times, the technique provides a relatively simple way of sizing memory and throughput needs and is useful as a rough estimate of performance requirements.

The instruction mix approach should be based on a basic unit of CPU throughput measure. For purposes of sizing validity, this unit must be a legitimate representative of basic processing operations encountered in all areas of the problem. For easy translation and application to various differing CPU characteristics, this basic unit should be readily expressed or converted in units related to a given processor's execution speed. The average instruction execution time for basically computational (arithmetic) types of programs is generally equivalent to that of a basic arithmetic instruction (ADD/SUBTRACT) operating on a direct memory referenced operand (i.e., operand resides in memory and must be directly addressed by the instruction). This contrasts with data management/manipulation types of programs where a large percent (perhaps half) of the total instruction mix consist of LOAD/STORE instructions. However, execution time for load/store instructions is generally equivalent to that of ADD/

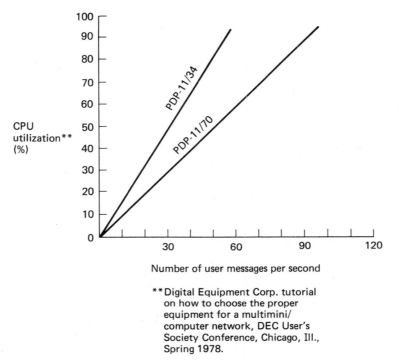

Figure 5-20 CPU utilization versus number of user messages/second for the Digital Equipment Corp. PDP-11/34 and PDP-11/70.

SUBTRACT instructions when both classes of instructions use memory referenced operands. Hence, an ADD direct memory referenced instruction (or equivalent) adequately fits the requirements of a "basic instruction" unit for sizing purposes.

In order to translate all processing operations to this basic instruction unit, various execution weights have to be assigned to all instructions. This execution weight is thus proportional to the basic instruction unit. Texas Instruments has proposed a set of weights and associated memory storage requirements for present day avionics and other military applications as shown in Figure 5-22.

Complex arithmetic instruction or operation (for example, square root, sine, cosine, and arctangent) weighting factors assumed in the sizing methodology obviously reflect some assumptions with respect to the relative execution times of these operations. Assumptions employed in this area usually become quite important in computational or "number crunching" applications; however, in data-manipulation-type applications, these assumptions are of little, if any, importance.

Assumption dependency is directly related to the amount of overhead (or housekeeping) operations associated with performing basic application-related functional operations. Operations in this class usually include data retrieval and storage (loads/ stores), data formatting or conversions, multiple-precision arithmetic considerations,

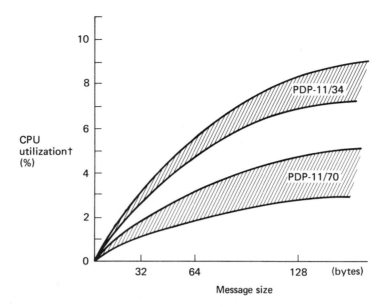

†All CPU utilization percentages include
operating system and DECnet software overhead
plus overhead for execution of the performance
measurement programs themselves.

Figure 5-21   CPU utilization versus user's message size, as seen by the user
program. (Segment size: 256 bytes of user data plus 34 bytes for DECnct protocol.)

and functional program flow control (branches, loops, etc.). Computational applications may be significantly impacted by assumptions such as scaling and multiple-
precision capabilities. On the other hand, data manipulation applications may be
significantly affected by assumptions of data extraction and bit manipulation.

Using a base instruction (BI) unit equivalent to ADD-type instruction and
assuming a 5 to 1 ratio of control (housekeeping) to arithmetic operations, the following sizing expressions have been developed by Texas Instruments for sizing:

$$\text{MIPS} = \frac{\text{BI}}{i} \times (i_r) \times 10^{-6} \qquad (5\text{-}15)$$

where MIPS = throughput requirement in millions of instructions per second.

$$\text{BI} = c_1(\text{BI})_a + c_2(\text{BI})_c + c_3(\text{BI})_{I/0} \qquad (5\text{-}16)$$

where c_1 = operation weight for arithmetic units and typically unity.
  c_2 = operation weight for control units and typically 5 for control operations assuming the CPU architecture nonfile-oriented (most opera-

Operation	Execution Weight	Instructions Memory†
ADD/SUBTRACT/LOGICAL*	1	2
MULTIPLY*	4	2
DIVIDE*	5	2
DOUBLE-PRECISION MULTIPLY	36	114
DOUBLE-PRECISION DIVIDE	72	122
SQUARE ROOT	41	49
SINE	28	51
COSINE	31	57
ARCTANGENT	34	72
ARCSINE	66	46
ARCCOSINE	68	54
EXPONENTIATION	65	60
MATRIX ADD	$18 + 4mn$	18
MATRIX MULTIPLY	$mnl(6) + 5 + m(8 + 10l)$	36
MATRIX SCALAR MULTIPLY	$15 + 4mn$	10
MATRIX TRANSPOSE	$18 + 4mn$	18
MATRIX INVERSE	$(5 + 46n + 70n^2 + 23n^3 + 4n^4) + 2(3n + n^2 + n^3) + 3(2n^2 + n)$	232

*Primary, hardware operations.

†16-bit words.

[*Note:* m, n, l are matrix dimensions: $A = (m \times n)$, $B = (n \times l)$.]

Figure 5-22   Arithmetic operation execution weights/storage requirements.

tions require a load/store sequence to be associated with them). This ratio is modified somewhat (7.5 %) because of an assumed 50/50 mix of short/long control instructions.*

c_3 = operation weight for Input/Outupt operations. An I/O operation is assumed to be associated with each processing task input parameter (independent variables) and each output parameter from the processing task (dependent variables). A weight of 10 allows for I/O data scaling, converting, formatting, validity checking, etc.

$(BI)_a$ = total arithmetic operations in base instruction units.

$(BI)_c$ = total control operations in base instruction units.

$(BI)_{I/0}$ = total I/O operations in base instruction units.

i = iteration per BI (typically unity).

i_I = iteration rate—function of how many times a particular instruction

*Control operations for logic type (Boolean) operations typically have a control-to-logic ratio of 3 : 1. This overhead accounts for data retrieval/storage for each operation and partial word/bit handling.

sequence must be repeated per second (i.e., a display image may have to be recomputed for every refresh cycle, or 30 times per second or navigational updates may have to be provided 100 times per second. In a patient monitoring system, pulse rates and other critical functions may have to be analyzed every 10 sec per patient).

The instruction memory (M_I) size is determined using the following equation:

$$M_I = k_1 I_a + k_2 I_c + k_3 I_{I/0} + k_4 s \tag{5-17}$$

where

$$
\begin{aligned}
M_I &= \text{instruction memory (16-bit word) required in number of words} \\
k_1, k_2, k_3, k_4 &= \text{multipliers dependent on number of instructions required} \\
&\quad \text{within each category (i.e., arithmetic, housekeeping, I/O)} \\
I_a &= \text{number of arithmetic instructions} \\
I_c &= \text{number of control (housekeeping) instructions} \\
I_{I/0} &= \text{number of I/O instructions} \\
s &= \text{subroutines}
\end{aligned}
$$

The data or temporary storage (M_D) memory size is determined using the following equation:

$$M_D = q_1 P_I + q_2 P_o + q_3 M_i + q_4 M_c \tag{5-18}$$

where

$$
\begin{aligned}
M_D &= \text{data memory (16-bit word) required in words} \\
P_I &= \text{input parameters} \\
P_o &= \text{output parameters} \\
M_i &= \text{intermediate computations} \\
M_c &= \text{stored constants} \\
q_1, q_2, q_3, q_4 &= \text{multipliers where multiple copies are needed for temporary} \\
&\quad \text{stored data (generally unity)}
\end{aligned}
$$

The use of the equations above is illustrated by the following example taken from the Texas Instruments' DAIS study where task sizing is performed for a wind estimate process that is part of a navigational software program. The various terms in Eq. (5-16) are determined as follows:

Arithmetic operations in base instruction units $(BI)_a$ using weights in Figure 5-21 are

$$
\begin{aligned}
4 \text{ ADD/SUBTRACT} &= 4 \times 1 = 4 \\
4 \text{ MULTIPLY} &= 4 \times 4 = 16 \\
1 \text{ SINE} &= 1 \times 28 = 28 \\
3 \text{ COSINE} &= 3 \times 31 = \underline{93} \\
&\qquad\qquad\qquad 141
\end{aligned}
$$

Control or housekeeping units $(BI)_c$ are

$$\text{Arithmetic instructions: 4 ADD/SUBTRACT} = 4 \times 1 = \ \ 4$$
$$\text{Housekeeping instructions: 4 MULTIPLY} \quad = 4 \times 4 = \underline{16}$$
$$20$$

Input/Output base instruction units are

$$\text{No. of input parameters (independent variables)} = 6$$
$$\text{No. of computed outputs (dependent variables)} \ = \underline{2}$$
$$8$$

Solving Eq. (5-16) we obtain

$$BI = (1.0)(141) + (0.75)(5)(20) + (10)(8) = 296$$

The solution to Eq. (5-15) is thus

$$MIPS = \left(\frac{296}{1}\right)(10)(10^{-6})$$
$$= 0.00296 \text{ million instructions per second}$$

The instruction storage using Eq. (5-17) is determined as follows:

$$M_I = k_1 I_a + k_2 I_c + k_3 I_{1/0} + k_4 s$$
$$= (2 \times 8) + [1.5 \times (5 \times 16)] + (10 \times 8) + (1 \times 108)$$
$$= 324 \text{ words}$$

Note that $s = 108$ was well known. This is usually not the case and an "experienced guess" must be made (call it a "fudge factor").

The temporary data storage is determined using Eq. (5-18) for

$$q_1 = q_2 = q_3 = q_4 = 1$$
$$M_D = P_I + P_O + M_i + M_c$$
$$= 6 + 2 + 17 + 0$$
$$= 25$$

Note that $M_i = 17$ is an approximation and also a function of "best engineering judgement."

An example of total throughput and memory requirements for an avionic multiminicomputer application (the Digital Avionics Information System—DAIS) arrived at using the methodology above is provided in Figure 5-23. This processing summary for a baseline avionic system does not consider processing interdependencies between

Function/Subfunction	Instruction Memory	Data Memory	Iteration Rate	MIPS
Navigation				
Inertial	1,350	250	100	0.0904
Air Data	385	50	10	0.0041
Wind Estimate	324	25	10	0.0030
Air Mass	380	25	10	0.0037
Flight Control	4,615	745	512	0.69
Stores Management	8,870	50	25	0.1170
Power Management	6,502	50	25	0.0813
Fire Control				
Missile Envelope (Helmet Sight)	1,310	100	30	0.0971
Gun, lead pursuit	2,945	150	30	0.0878
Missile, lead pursuit	2,945	150	30	0.0878
Missile, lead collision	2,650	150	30	0.0794
Gun, snapshot	2,995	200	30	0.0894
Bomb, navigation	1,935	100	30	0.0626
Electronic Warfare				
RHAW	16,600	6,000	100	0.8300
Electronic Counter Measures	2,000	100	40	0.04
Displays				
Vertical Situation Displ.	8,000	8,000	30	0.2400
Horizontal Sit. Displ.	8,000	8,000	30	0.2400
Head-Up Displ.	8,000	8,000	30	0.2400
MPD 1	4,000	4,000	30	0.1200
MPD 2	4,000	4,000	30	0.1200
Fuel Management	1,440	500	2	0.0023
CITS				
Intermittent	3,100	585	—	—
Continuous	1,500	500	40	0.0600
TOTAL	93,846	41,930		3.3859

Figure 5-23   Base line processing requirements for avionic system derived using base instruction timing and sizing methodology. From "A Conceptual Definition Study for a Digital Avionics Information System (DAIS), Approach II, Vol. 1, Texas Instruments, Inc., Prepared for Air Force Avionics Laboratory, March 1974, #AD-780 581).

individual tasks and each task is sized according to the amount of processing required to execute only that particular task. In spite of this, a total of approximately 136K words of memory and a throughput of 3.4 MIPS are required where the latter, in terms of single processor capacity, puts it in the big league with large main frames. (Note that most of today's 16-bit word micros and minis are in the 0.300- to 0.800-MIPS range). However, partitioning the various functions into navigation and flight control, stores and power management, fire control, electronic warfare, and display processing elements with each element allocated to a micro or minicomputer, individual memory sizes and throughput requirements can be handled by a mini or even a microcomputer.

So far, very little has been said about *benchmarking*.

It is, however, at this point that benchmarking proves to be a useful tool in determining what class of micro- or minicomputer should be used. A benchmark, of course, is an existing program that is coded in a specific language and executed on the machine being evaluated. Great care should be taken in running the benchmark to make sure that the period of the clock used in measuring the time it takes to run the benchmark is significantly (orders of magnitude) shorter. (If this is not the case, close to a 50% inaccuracy can result—assuming, for example, that a clock period of 100 msec and total program run time is 51 msec, run time will be measured by the closest clock cycle, i.e., 100 msec).

A properly written and run benchmark or series of benchmarks will provide the designer with a fairly good indication of the relative processing power of micros or minis being considered for the system (see Problem 1-3). Once timing and sizing analysis and benchmark tests have been completed, interconnect structures can be evaluated.

5.6.3 Interconnect Structure Analysis

Several basic design alternatives are available for developing a multimicro- or minicomputer interconnect structure. Information between computers can be transferred from source to destination either directly or indirectly. If an indirect transfer strategy is employed, one or more switching entities may be employed. This intervening switching entity may perform and address transformation or route the message onto one of a number of alternative output paths. Examples of systems based on indirect transfer are loops, buses, or star configurations, or packet-switched systems. The major difference between direct and indirect transfer strategy lies in the distribution of message transfer "intelligence." Indirect transfer methods require more complex communications capability but also increase the fault tolerance of a system.

Indirect transfer methods are based on either centralized or decentralized routing of messages.

For centralized routing, a single switch is used such as in the case of a star configuration, or bus or loop with a central switch. If decentralized routing is selected, two or more switches may be used to control the transfer of messages between micros or minis. The centralized routing approach is more vulnerable in terms of the single-switch failing, thereby causing the entire system to fail, than if two or more switches are used, such as in a packet-switched system where redundant switches (and paths) exist between all computers in the system.

A third design alternative exists in terms of selecting the message transfer path between computers. It may be dedicated as in the case of the loop, star, or completely interconnected system or shared as in the case of bus, packet-switched, or shared memory systems. It may also be a combination of both as in hierarchical systems, where the computer at the top of the pyramid receives messages from several computers, whereas computers at the bottom of the hierarchy have a single path to the computer "above" it.

A system based on a dedicated path structure is generally more fault tolerant than a system using shared paths. If a path (accessible from more than two points) fails, no alternate way exists to transfer data between computers in the system. As discussed in Chapter 2, however, systems with redundant paths can be used to minimize the effects of single-point failures on the total system.

Anderson and Jensen* have developed a taxonomy based on transfer strategy, control method, and path structure, as discussed above. A modified diagram of this well-known taxonomy is shown in Figure 5-24. Each of the system architectures listed in Figure 5-24 have been discussed in Chapter 2.

Based on information provided in Chapters 2, 3, and 4, some generalized observations can be made regarding each type of architecture in the areas of cost, modularity/flexibility/expandability, reliability/availability/fault tolerance, performance/throughput, ease of development/"off-the-shelfness", and form factor (design attributes).

The various types or groups of interconnect methods are listed in Figure 5-25 in descending order in terms of reliability. This ordering is based on the assumption that no redundancy techniques are employed (i.e., multiple buses or loops, dual switches, etc.).

Cost of various interconnect schemes depends on whether a system can be developed using off-the-shelf hardware and/or software or whether the design must be performed "from ground up." Cost is also related to the number of micros or minis to be used in the system, the amount of memory required in each node of the system, and the bandwidth of communications links between computers. The cost of completely interconnected systems tends to be high compared with loop- and bus-based systems. Throughput capacity is as much a function of interconnect structure as it is of link technology. Use of a twisted pair of wires limits data rates to a few megabits per second over a distance of a few thousand feet. Even at this distance, problems are encountered with too many drops if we are dealing with a bus-type system. The bandwidth can, however, be increased using parallel lines, coaxial cable, or fiber optics links. It is, of course, possible to use dial-up or leased telephone lines, but that limits the maximum bandwidth typically to a range of 4800 to 50,000 bps. Higher bandwidths are also possible with the use of microwave or satellite links, but this will today have a profound impact on total system cost.

Depending on how the various design attributes are weighted (which is application-dependent), one or more desirable interconnect structures can be selected. Obviously, for geographically distributed applications, a shared memory-based system is totally unacceptable. On the other hand, in a local point-of-sale environment, where the whole system is limited to one building (store), a packet-switched network would probably not make sense.

*George A. Anderson and E. Douglas Jensen, "Computer Interconnection Structures: Taxonomy, Characteristics and Examples," *ACM Computing Surveys*, **7**, No. 4, December 1975.

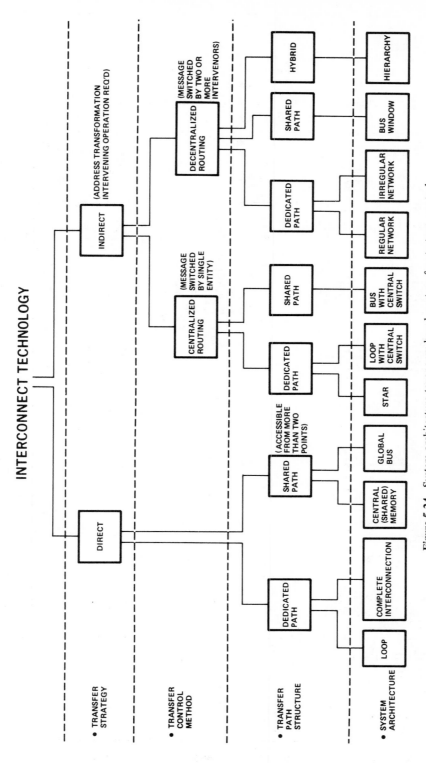

Figure 5-24 System architecture taxonomy based on transfer strategy, control method, and path structure.

INTERCONNECT TECHNOLOGY	RELIABILITY
COMPLETE INTERCONNECTION - THE COMPLETELY INTERCONNECTED ARCHITECTURE IS CONCEPTUALLY THE SIMPLEST DESIGN. IN THIS DESIGN EACH PROCESSOR IS CONNECTED BY A DEDICATED PATH TO EVERY OTHER PROCESSOR. COMMUNICATIONS COST BECOME PROHIBITIVE AS THE NUMBER OF PROCESSORS AND DISTANCES INCREASE.	ONLY LOCAL PROBLEM IF MINI FAILS REDUNDANT PATHS FOR SINGLE LINK FAILURES — MAXIMUM
PACKET SWITCHED NETWORK - MESSAGES BROKEN INTO PACKETS AND TRANSMITED VIA AVAILABLE NODES. AT LEAST TWO PATHS EXIST BETWEEN ANY TWO COMPUTERS IN THE SYSTEM.	ONLY LOCAL PROBLEM IF MINI FAILS
REGULAR NETWORK - EVERY COMPUTER IS CONNECTED TO ITS TWO NEIGHBORS AND TWO COMPUTERS ABOVE AND BELOW IT. THE NETWORK GETS COMPLICATED IF THERE ARE VERY MANY COMPUTERS. THE "TREE" IS A HIERARCHICALLY STRUCTURED VARIATION WITH ANY PROCESSOR ABLE TO COMMUNICATE WITH ITS SUPERIOR AND ITS SUBORDINATES AS WELL AS ITS TWO NEIGHBORS.	ONLY LOCAL PROBLEM IF MINI FAILS REDUNDANT PATHS FOR SINGLE CONNECT FAILURE
IRREGULAR NETWORK - THIS CONFIGURATION HAS NO CONSISTENT NEIGHBOR RELATIONSHIPS. IT IS COMMON IN GEOGRAPHICALLY DISPERSED NETWORKS WHERE COMMUNICATION LINKS CONTROL THE DESIGN.	PARTIAL REDUNDANCY FOR LINK FAILURES
HIERARCHY - THIS CONFIGURATION IS USED IN PROCESS CONTROL AND DATA ACQUISITION APPLICATIONS. THE CAPABILITIES ARE SPECIALIZED AT LOWER LEVELS AND MORE GENERAL PURPOSE AT THE TOP.	SYSTEM OPERABILITY REDUCED WITH SINGLE POINT FAILURE. MORE SERIOUS THE HIGHER UP THE FAILURE OCCURS.
LOOP OR RING - LOOP ARCHITECTURE EVOLVED FROM THE DATA COMMUNICATIONS ENVIRONMENT. IN THIS CONFIGURATION, EACH COMPUTER IS CONNECTED TO TWO NEIGHBORING COMPUTERS. THE TRAFFIC COULD FLOW IN BOTH DIRECTIONS, BUT CIRCULATING TRAFFIC IN ONE DIRECTION IS LESS COMPLICATED.	SYSTEM UNAFFECTED WITH SINGLE LOOP FAILURE FOR TWO-LOOP SYSTEM - CATASTROPHIC FOR SINGLE-UNIDIRECTIONAL LOOP
GLOBAL BUS - THE USE OF A COMMON OR GLOBAL BUS REQUIRES SOME ALLOCATION SCHEME FOR SENDING MESSAGES FROM ONE COMPUTER TO ANOTHER.	ONLY LOCAL PROBLEM IF MINI FAILS CATASTROPHIC WITH BUS FAILURE
STAR - THIS CONFIGURATION HAS A CENTRAL SWITCHING RESOURCE. EACH COMPUTER IS CONNECTED TO THE CENTRAL SWITCH. TRAFFIC IS IN BOTH DIRECTIONS. (SWITCH)	ONLY LOCAL PROBLEM IF MINI OR BUS FAILS. CATASTROPHIC IF SWITCH FAILS. SWITCH POSSIBLY LESS RELIABLE THAN BUS OR LOOP
LOOP WITH SWITCH - THIS REFINEMENT OF THE LOOP PROVIDES A SWITCHING ELEMENT THAT REMOVES MESSAGES FROM THE LOOP, MAPS THEIR ADDRESSES, AND REPLACES THEM ON THE LOOP PROPERLY ADDRESSED TO THEIR INTENDED DESTINATION. (SWITCH)	CATASTROPHIC IF EITHER SWITCH OR LOOP FAILS
BUS WINDOW - THIS CONFIGURATION HAS MORE THAN ONE SWITCH. MESSAGES MAY BE TRANSMITTED ON THE PATH THEY ARE RECEIVED OR ON ANOTHER. THE SWITCHES PROVIDE "WINDOWS" FOR PASSING MESSAGES BETWEEN BUSES.	SERIOUS CONTENTION PROBLEMS. PARTIAL SYSTEM FAILURE IF SWITCH OR BUS FAILS
BUS WITH SWITCH - THIS IS MORE LIKE THE GLOBAL BUS BECAUSE EACH COMPUTER IS CONNECTED TO THE CENTRAL SWITCH, AND TRAFFIC FLOWS FROM THE ORIGINATING COMPUTER TO THE SWITCH, AND FROM THE SWITCH TO THE DESTINATION COMPUTER. THE COMPUTERS SHARE THE PATH (BUS) TO SHARE ACCESS TO THE SWITCH. (SWITCH)	CATASTROPHIC IF BUS OR SWITCH FAILS
SHARED MEMORY - THE MOST COMMON WAY TO INTERCONNECT COMPUTER SYSTEMS IS TO COMMUNICATE BY LEAVING MESSAGES FOR ONE ANOTHER IN A COMMONLY ACCESSIBLE MEMORY. THE KEY CHARACTERISTIC IS THAT THE MEMORY IS USED AS A DATA PATH AS WELL AS STORAGE.	CATASTROPHIC IF MEMORY FAILS — MINIMUM

INCREASED RELIABILITY — REDUCED RELIABILITY

Figure 5-25 Interconnect technology comparisons based on design attributes.

COST	GEOGRAPHIC DISTRIBUTION	MODULARITY, EXPANDABILITY	PERFORMANCE	SOFTWARE SUPPORT	OFF-THE-SHELF SYSTEMS	MANUFACTURER
HIGH- FUNCTION OF DISTANCE BETWEEN MINIS AND NR. OF MINIS IN SYSTEM	UNLIMITED	FAIR - NUMBER OF PORTS ON EACH MINI; = N - 1;	TYPICALLY 2400-4800 bps 50 Kbps AND 1,544 Mbps POSSIBLE	DECNET, MAXNET (FAIR - GOOD)	NONE	ANY MINICOMPUTER MANUFACTURERS SYSTEM CAN BE DEVELOPED INTO A COMPLETELY INTERCONNECTED MULTIMINI COMPUTER SYSTEM
HIGH- EACH NODE REQUIRES ROUTING CONTROL	UNLIMITED	GOOD	TYPICALLY 50 Kbps	ARPANET SOFTWARE	ARPANET TELENET	BOLT BERANEK AND NEWMAN
HIGH - FUNCTION OF NUMBER OF MINIS IN A SYSTEM	CAN BE UNLIMITED; TYPICALLY VERY LIMITED (10'S OF FEET)	POOR	TYPICALLY 3-5 Mbps	CUSTOM	NONE	NONE (HYPERCUBE NEVER MATERIALIZED)
MEDIUM - FUNCTION OF DISTANCE BETWEEN MINIS	UNLIMITED	FAIR	TYPICALLY 2400-9600 bps	DECNET MAXNET HP DS 1000	NONE	ANY MINI COMPUTER SYSTEM CAN BE USED TO DEVELOP ANY IRREGULAR NETWORK
MEDIUM - FUNCTION OF DISTANCE BETWEEN MINIS	UNLIMITED	GOOD	TYPICALLY 2400-9600 bps DECNET	HP DS 1000 DECNET	NONE	ANY MINICOMPUTER SYSTEM CAN BE DEVELOPED INTO A HIERARCHICAL SYSTEM
MEDIUM - MAIN COST ADAPTORS	LIMITED (100'S-1000'S OF FEET)	GOOD - LIMITED BY MINI ADDRESSING CAPABILITY	PARALLEL: UP TO 500 KILO WORDS/SEC SERIAL: 1-3 Mbps	HEWLETT PACKARD, DS/1000 DATA GENERAL RDOS OR SIMILAR	MULTICOMMUNICATIONS ADAPTER (MCA)	DATA GENERAL CORP. HEWLETT PACKARD
MEDIUM - MAIN COST BUS ADAPTORS	LIMITED (1000'S OF FEET)	GOOD	UP TO 50 Mbps, TYPICAL 1-3 Mbps	CUSTOM	NSC-BUS CAMAC BUS IEEE-488 TDM & FDM PC-11	NETWORK SYSTEMS CORP KINETIC SYSTEMS HEWLETT PACKARD ISI DIGITAL EQUIPMENT CORP.
MEDIUM TO LOW - MAIN COST ITEM IS SWITCH	LIMITED (1000'S OF FEET)	GOOD UNTIL SWITCH SATURATES	UP TO 3 Mbps	DATA GEN RDOS OR SIMILAR	DISTRIBUTED DATA NETWORK (DDN)	DATA GENERAL CORP
MEDIUM - MAIN COST ITEM IS SWITCH	LIMITED (100'S-1000'S OF FEET)	GOOD - FAIR UNTIL SWITCH SATURATES	1-3 Mbps	CUSTOM	SPIDERNET	CUTLER HAMMER BAILEY METER BELL LABS
LOW - MAIN COST ITEM IS SWITCH	VERY LIMITED (10'S OF FEET)	POOR	200-500 KILO WORDS SEC	RSX-11M RSX-11D	DEC BUS WINDOW (DA11)	DIGITAL EQUIPMENT CORP.
LOW - MAIN COST ITEM IS SWITCH	LIMITED (1000'S OF FEET)	GOOD - FAIR UNTIL SWITCH SATURATES	UP TO 3 Mbps FOR SERIAL BUS	CUSTOM	MITRIX	MITRE
LOW - MAIN COST IS MULTIPORTED MEMORY	VERY LIMITED (10'S OF FEET)	POOR - LIMITED TO NR OF MEMORY PORTS	MEMORY SPEED 500 KW/SEC TO 3 MW/SEC	MOST VENDOR O.S.	MULTIPORTED MEMORY MULTIPORTED MEMORY MULTIPORTED MEMORY CACHE-BUS INTERPROCESSOR BUS (IPB)	MODCOMP SEL DEC GENERAL AUTOMATION DATA GENERAL

Figure 5-25 Continued

Traditionally, point-of-sale, banking, data acquisition, and process control systems have been based on hierarchical architectures. This does not necessarily mean that a loop or bus system should be ruled out.

Associated with interconnect technology are the subjects of resource sharing and equalization of processing loads. Sharing communication facilities is obviously one form of resource sharing. This can be extended to information and system peripheral sharing. The subject of information sharing and distributed data bases is discussed in Chapter 7. Peripheral sharing is related to the degree of physical dispersion of the system. In a shared memory-type system, where computers have to be relatively close to each other, it quite often makes sense to share peripherals such as line printers, card readers and magnetic tape units. Peripherals can be switched either under computer control or manually, thereby reassigning them to different processors.

The segmentation or partitioning of the overall baseline system processing loads into equal-size processing segments will make it possible to use only one type and size computer in the system. The benefits of this approach are several. Using only one type of computer reduces the number of spares and simplifies logistics and training. Also, since all processors are functionally identical, the system may be implemented in a way where an idle micro or mini is always available and can be switched online to perform the tasks of any other processor in the system that may be inoperative due to failure or maintenance performed on it.

5.7 SYSTEM TRADEOFF ANALYSIS

The system design methodology described above is illustrated using data acquisition as an example. In a "typical" data acquisition environment, a multitude of sensors collect information. This information must be converted into computer-readable format, time annotated and analyzed. The analysis may be performed in real-time under interactive operator control or offline, in a batch mode (see Table 5-2 for a Wind Tunnel System description and Table 5-3 for a Point-Of-Sale System). The boundary between data acquisition and process control is often quite fuzzy. As implied by the nomenclature, however, process control involves, in addition to data acquisition, a significant amount of feedback whereby a system operates in a closed-loop mode (feedback is provided to effect system operation—usually in real-time).

As indicated in Figure 5-13, key attributes in the typical data acquisition system are performance, reliability, availability, and modularity.

The consideration of all possible architectures (see Figure 5-24) is generally not necessary. The pros and cons of transfer strategy, control method, and path structure usually provide a clear indication of the most attractive solutions.

Conventional data acquisition systems are generally based on a single large host or main frame (IBM 370, Honeywell Level 66, Univac 1110, etc.) with one or more front-end processors/multiplexers interconnected to sensors. The front-end processors typically contain input-output conversion circuitry. An example of such a system is shown in Figure 5-26. One or more levels of multiplexing may exist, depending on the

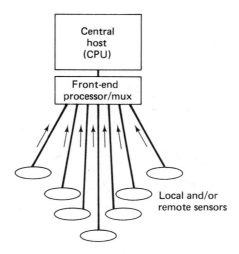

Figure 5-26   Conventional data acquisition system.

geographic dispersion of sensors and data rates for communications links. Analog and digital sensors may be added anywhere in the system at the expense of interconnecting links and additional ports into the multiplexer. When all ports are filled, an additional multiplexer is required. If the computer is fully utilized, the addition of a sensor may require an upgrade to a more powerful processor. If the central processor fails, the entire system is down; however, the advantage of this architecture is its simplicity.

Since data acquisition systems are distinguished by the fact that sensor and input devices do not have to communicate with each other, hierarchical or centralized systems are usually the most attractive design approaches when single, large hosts are used. Also, message routing tends to be fixed and thus does not warrant the use of indirect transfer schemes that usually are logically complex and expensive. In direct transfer-type systems (see Figure 5-24), the transfer path structure may be either dedicated or shared. For data acquisition systems, complete interconnection is not needed, thereby reducing such architectures to a loop. Neither is the centrally shared memory architecture applicable, reducing shared path approaches to the global bus architecture. The hierarchical loop and global bus architectures are thus explored in more detail.

The hierarchical system, using multiple micros and/or minis can be implemented with a large host being a main frame computer or a large minicomputer (midi). It is also possible to implement this architecture with two or more hosts sharing memory, where one of the hosts serves as a front-end processor. (Hierarchical multiminicomputer performance is discussed in Section 2.6.) The disadvantage of hierarchical systems are the same whether a large main frame or minicomputer host is used.

One of the major disadvantages, availability, is often improved by providing a large amount of redundancy, as shown in Figure 5-27. Such redundance may double

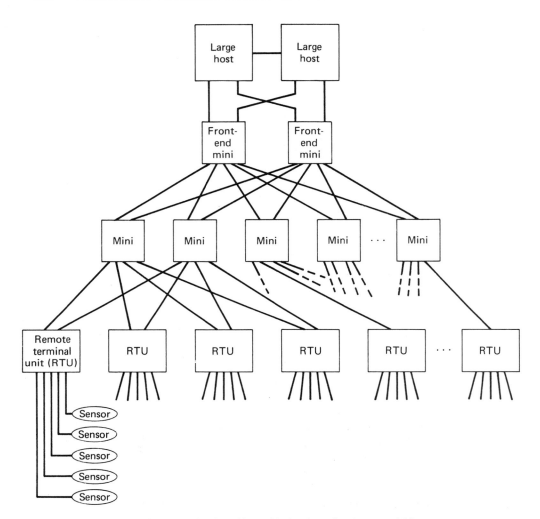

Figure 5-27   Redundant hierarchical system for data acquisition.

the hardware cost and also increase software cost depending on how failures are detected and the speed of switchover. Redundancy is, in some applications, not carried out to the bottom (sensor) level, in order to minimize cabling complexity. Switchover and reconfiguration, in case of failure, may be accomplished by the next higher level in the hierarchy, or at the same level. The latter approach may be more difficult to implement since a failed element, depending on the type of failure, may not be able to accomplish the switchover. Schemes exist where the standby processor receives a periodic interrupt to a time-out device. If this interrupt does not occur, time-out will occur and the spare will start transmitting received and processed inputs together with a message notifying the level above (and the system operator) about the nonreceipt of the time-out-inhibit interrupt. Voting schemes are also possible but this is even more costly, requiring, as a minimum, triple redundancy.

Loop architecture, applied to data acquisition, is attractive from a modular point of view. A sensor may be placed anywhere on the loop with a simple interface and may, if necessary, communicate with a node connected to the loop. Since messages are passed from node to node successively, the failure of a single node or path between two nodes can bring down the entire ring. Thus, for unidirectional, active repeater loops, the failure effect and failure reconfiguration attributes are poor. Loop systems are, however, available to improve system fault tolerance (passive repeaters or bypass relays).

The primary advantage of loop systems are their relatively low cost and high modularity. Node processor failures can be masked by load sharing among the remaining minis or micros if task addresses are kept in tables in each node and checked by the communications software in each computer. The loop approach is particularly attractive when wide-band coaxial or fiber optics buses are used to interconnect the nodes. (For more on fiber optics, see Chapter 7.)

The global bus is also very attractive for mini- or microprocessor-based data acquisition systems. Access to the bus is shared by the computers by some allocation scheme and messages are sent directly to the destination node. Computers can be connected to the bus via a standard interface anywhere on the bus. Furthermore, the fault tolerance of a bus-based system is relatively high, provided that a failure does not disable the bus. Performance of bus-based systems is discussed in Section 2.3.

More off-the-shelf hardware exists today for shared bus systems than for ring-type systems (see Chapter 4).

The choice among the three architectures above is determined by the number of sensors in the system, their physical location, and the amount of data collected by the sensors for transmission to the system processor(s). Where the number of sensors is extremely large and data rates are very high, the hierarchical system approach may be the most practical and cost effective. Since most data acquisition systems require relatively low sampling or input rates from sensors, however, the global bus or loop architecture may be preferable. Their vulnerability to communications path failures can be mitigated using redundant paths.

The problems inherent in any approach are interprogram communication and data-base considerations, potential deadlock, and error recovery. Each of these multimicro- and minicomputer system design problem areas are discussed in the following sections.

5.7.1 Interprogram Communications

Interprogram or intertask communication was discussed in Section 5.4 in terms of the Exchange Function. All communication involves the transmission of data and synchronization through the exchange of message between tasks and between tasks and the operating system and I/O devices. Data is thus communicated by inserting it into a message that is then sent to the task needing the data, over a loop or global bus.

One or more of the processors attached to the bus or loop may be connected to a storage device such as a disc. A task wanting data from a data base stored on the disc will send a message to a task responsible for maintaining that data base on the disc, with a request for specific data. This data is subsequently returned in a reply message to the requesting task. Since all accesses to the data base are through one task, the problem of simultaneous access is essentially eliminated.

A set of primitives associated with this scheme allow synchronization of multiple tasks, preventing lock-out of high-priority tasks by lower priority tasks and release of resources in the event of premature task abortion.

When tasks or processes are colocated in the same micro or mini, the message discipline requires only knowledge of the source (task) and destination (task) name.

For noncolocated tasks, the program should also know the eventual location of each task in the system. Distributed processing protocols (see Chapter 3) must, therefore, be used where the actual task distribution is defined by separate, task-independent process tables under control of each micro- or minicomputer operating system in the hardware communications interface. Messages to local tasks are thus simply turned around by the protocol handler and passed back to local tasks, whereas messages to tasks located in remote processors are forwarded via the loop or bus. The data acquisition system configuration is, therefore, quite flexible, allowing for dynamic reconfiguration.

For loop or bus schemes, based on synchronous transmission, one master is needed to send a synchronization signal to other micros or minis in the system. In a sense, synchronization is a special case of communication during which no data is transferred. Rather, the act of signaling is used to "wake up" a task executing in another processor. A task may be "dormant" and waiting for a synchronization signal, until it receives a wake-up signal that enables it to continue execution. Manipulation of synchronization signals requires a mechanism to guarantee that asynchronous accesses to resources (also data bases and peripherals) shared by two or more tasks in the system are controlled, in order to protect information from simultaneous change by two or more tasks.

This mechanism has been termed *mutual exclusion*. Mutual exclusion must, thus, be provided in a multimicro- or minicomputer system to enable one processor or task to lock out access of a shared resource by other processors or tasks when it is in a critical section. A *critical section* has been defined by Adams and Rolander* as "a code segment that once begun must complete execution before it, or another critical section that accesses the same shared resource, can be executed."

Adams and Rolander suggest that a Boolean variable be used to indicate whether a processor is currently in a particular section (True) or not (False). The testing and setting of this variable must be performed as a single, indivisible operation since two or more micros or minis may test the variable simultaneously and then each set it. This would allow them to enter the critical section at the same time.

---

*George Adams and Thomas Rolander, "Design Motivations for Multiple Processor Microcomputer Systems," *Computer Design*, March 1978.

The test-and-set instruction is, therefore, critical in micros or minis used in multiprocessor applications, provided it is indivisible for all micros or minis operating on the shared variable (see also the discussion on these issues in subsection 3.2.4). When an entire file or record is transferred to another processor on the bus or loop for update and eventual rewrite, or when update data is accrued remotely over an extended period, however, the lock-out scheme based on mutual exclusion is unworkable. To deny real-time processes access to existing data, even for short periods of time, may be unacceptable. On the other hand, to allow tasks to compute and act on data that is no longer current may also not be acceptable.

Transferring raw data to the site of the data base and computing updates there will place an additional load on the loop or bus. This can be avoided by having some of the micros or minis in the system acquire data, convert the data into engineering units, perform an alarm check, and reduce the data in their own local data bases. Only summary information or alarm conditions would subsequently be transmitted to the processor and/or data-base processor that controls the logger and operator communications. In this case, each local data base would be independent of the

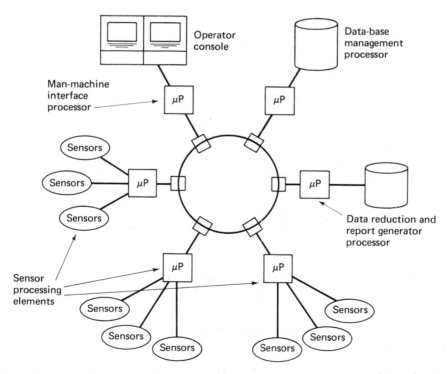

Figure 5-28   Proposed loop-based data acquisition system configuration.

"global" history file. A proposed configuration* for implementing this scheme is shown in Figure 5-28 based on a loop configuration.

5.7.2 System Deadlock

Unless appropriate care is taken during the design process, system deadlock problems may occur. Deadlock involves circular waiting where one or more tasks are waiting for resources to become available, and those resources are held by some other tasks that are, in turn, blocked until resources held by the first task or tasks are released. This is illustrated in Figure 5-29 where process P_A in processor A is accessing data block D_1 in memory and will not release it until data block D_2 becomes available. Access by P_A to data block D_2 is blocked by process P_B in processor B, however, until data block D_1 becomes available. Chen† proposes three ways of dealing with deadlocks:

1. Deadlock Prevention
2. Deadlock Avoidance
3. Deadlock Detection and Recovery

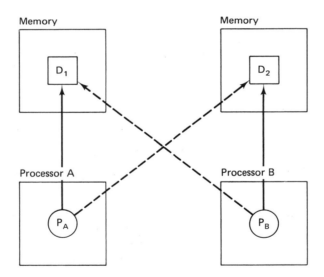

Figure 5-29   Deadlock occurs when process P_A will not release D_1 until D_2 becomes available while, concurrently, process P_B will not release D_2 until D_1 becomes available.

*Charles W. Rose and James D. Schoeffler, "Distribution of Intelligence and Input/Output in Data Acquisition Systems", International Telemetering Conference Proceedings, Vol. XII, 1976, Los Angeles, Calif.

†Robert Chia-Hua Chen, "Bus Communication Systems," Ph.D. Dissertation, Department of Computer Science, Carnegie-Mellon University, Pittsburgh, Pa., Jan. 1974.

Deadlock prevention algorithms can be used to certify that a given loop or bus system design is deadlock-free. In order to assure this, the resources that the messages may request must be known beforehand in some way. It is also assumed that the resource requirements do not change during the actual operation of the system (in a dynamic environment). Deadlock prevention is, therefore, used mainly in the design phase and the algorithms apply to systems with alternate routing [i.e., two-way loops or redundant loops or buses as well as systems based on indirect, decentralized routing with two or more paths (see Figure 5-24). These topologics do, however, provide poor utilization of resources due to the redundancies].

Deadlock avoidance algorithms are used as part of the online operation. These algorithms may restrict the number of messages in the system if risk for deadlock exists. The deadlock avoidance algorithms may also make sure that messages are not released (or transmitted) until resources needed by the messages have been reserved. These algorithms generally impose additional overhead on both processing time and channel capacity.

Finally, deadlock detection and recovery algorithms rely on time-outs where when a message is blocked for a length of time exceeding a predetermined limit, the message is assumed to be deadlocked and recovery procedures are put into effect.

Deadlock recovery may be time-consuming and require extra hardware for back-up message storage.

The PDP-11 Unibus window described in Section 4.6 is an example of a multi-

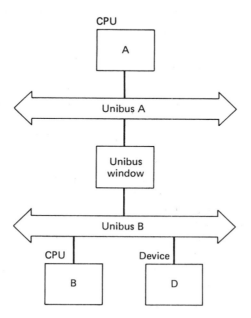

Figure 5-30   Digital Equipment Corporation PDP-11 Multiminicomputer configuration using Unibus Window.

minicomputer systems approach prone to deadlock problems. Figure 5-30 shows a typical multiminicomputer configuration using the Unibus window. In normal operation, a mini accesses its main memory or peripheral devices via its own Unibus. The Unibus window is used when mini A wishes to access device D, which is connected to the PDP-11 B's Unibus but not to A's.

Processor A acquires its Unibus and addresses the Unibus window, which then requests processor B's Unibus. If it acquires processor B's Unibus, a path is then established whereby A can access D. In case A has acquired its Unibus, but not yet B's Unibus and, concurrently, B has acquired its own Unibus and also accesses the window requesting A's Unibus, however, both A and B will wait for the other Unibus, and a deadlock state will exist. Fortunately, the window has a time-out feature to alert each processor of this occurrence.

It is, however, possible to design synchronous systems where the existence of a circular loop of requests may not result in a deadlock situation because the requests may be granted in a synchronized way. Synchronized systems are discussed in Chapter 2 (the U.C. Irvine DCS loop and the Pierce-type loop).

Within each loop, message sending is synchronized so that, even when the "buffers" in the loop are filled, deadlock does not occur.

5.7.3   Error Recovery

Deadlock recovery is a special case of error recovery. In conventional systems, input-output transfers are completed using a "handshaking" synchronization scheme, and data errors on point-to-point communications links are generally rather infrequent. In distributed data acquisition systems, however, errors are more likely due to repeaters, signal attenuation, and bus or loop electrical discontinuities, etc. Error correction schemes are, therefore, needed. Error correction codes often occupy too great a fraction of the message bandwidth to be cost effective. For many data acquisition environments, retransmission of erroneous messages are, therefore, chosen rather than error correction features.

Messages can be numbered to prevent the loss or duplication of messages in the event of communication errors. This is of great value in data acquisition applications in which, for example, counting of events is critical as is the control of a stepping motor. Error recovery is generally accomplished by the detection of "crashes" by other processors as a result of time-out conventions on messages and the passing of "are you OK?" messages. Thus, hot restart can be effected by resetting all message synchronization bits to their initial states after the crashed micro or mini is reinitialized. This assumes, of course, that the bus or loop is passive (using transformer coupling) since a crashed node or interface to the shared communications facility will disrupt communications around the loop or on the bus in an active, repeater system.

For CPU failure detection in a multiminicomputer system, the following approaches have typically been taken:

- A processor trap or interrupt when the CPU detects an invalid instruction, operand address, parity check, etc.
- A software signal when a reply to a transmitted message has not been received within a specified time.

The attitude that component failures are temporary and that normal network operations can always be resumed when a failed component is repaired gives rise to the concept of transient fault. A transient fault occurs when a failure occurs in a hardware component of the network, such as a processor, storage medium, or input-output device. A transient fault also occurs when an error on the part of one software component is detected by another software component, perhaps in a different host.

When a transient fault occurs, an attempt is usually made to recover the environment of each affected process and to regenerate its connections to other components in the system. This requires the assumption that certain features of the environment, such as system catalogs, dictionaries, and virtual channel or link assignments stored on direct-access devices, survive the fault or are duplicated.

This can be achieved using a combination of checkpoint operations and appropriate message transmission protocols. It may also be possible to use appropriate synchronization algorithms to avoid deadlocks and violations of mutual-exclusion conditions causing failures; however, the latter approach is presently poorly understood.

Checkpointing involves the periodic storage in a checkpoint file of state variables, virtual channel information, and file names currently in use during the operation of a process or task. The time at which checkpointing is performed is determined by the process and normally occurs after a critical variable is changed but before decisions are made based on its new value.

PROBLEMS

5-1 Redraw Figure 5-1 using the N^2 chart approach. Identify each of the inputs (vertical) and outputs (horizontal).

5-2 Develop a process architecture tree diagram for the Wind Tunnel System as defined in Table 5-2.

5-3 Develop a process architecture tree diagram for the POS system summarized in Table 5-3.

5-4 Use the process architecture tree diagram for the POS system (Problem 5-3) for developing an N^2 chart.

5-5 Complete process architecture tree diagrams for the Sensor Monitor Initiator, Console Monitor, Operator, and Sensor Set based on the Patient Monitoring problem. Use these diagrams to verify the State Exchange diagram shown in Figure 5-7. The Sensor Monitor tree should be amended with the Exchange Functions.

5-6 Provide an example of how you would map the diagram developed in the previous problem into a hardware configuration. Explain your rationale.

5-7 It has been proposed* that cost and downtime can be related to modularity and growth as follows:

$$G = \frac{1 - e^{-pn_p}}{n_p} \sum_{i=1}^{n_p} w_i e^{-dDT_i} e^{-cC_i}$$

where G = growth can range from 0 to 1 (= 100%)
n_p = number of unique upgradeable components out of a total of N_p components
w_i = absolute importance of Component i out of all known system components
DT_i = multimicro- or minicomputer system downtime resulting from upgrading Component i
C_i = cost in dollars of upgrading Component i
p, d, c = constants that serve as curve scaling factors and as a means to weight the various attributes shown in Level 5, Figure 5-10. d is in the inverse of hours; c is in the inverse of thousands of dollars.

The numerator in the first term of the equation above gives a particular distributed micro- or minicomputer system credit for having upgradeable components (i.e., interfaces, peripherals, micros, minis, communications links, etc.). The next to last term reduces the growth value for a system requiring long downtimes when changes are made. The last term does the same for high change-over costs.

In order to show growth behavior using this equation, assume that there is only one upgradeable component in the system (i.e., $n_p = 1$) and that this component is a very important one so that the absolute importance weight of the component has a value of one (i.e. $w_i = 1$). Show growth (G) in terms of cost of upgrading (C_i) in thousands of dollars for the following downtimes:
(a) 1 hour
(b) 1 day
(c) 3 days
(d) 1 week
(e) 1.5 weeks
using the following arbitrary values for the constants in the exponential terms:

$$p = 0.05$$

$$d = 0.02$$

$$c = 0.11$$

Show the results in graphic form with logarithmic scales for G and C_i.
Are the growth values high or low and, if so, why?
At what point does cost become very dominant?

5-8 Use the growth equation in Problem 5-7 and determine the growth factor using the same values for the constants (p, d, and c), for a 1-hr downtime but for systems having

*See footnote on page 204.

2, 5, and 10 upgradeable components. Does this equation truly reflect increased (or decreased) growth as a function of increased number of upgradeable components?

What corrections (if any) should be made to this equation to reflect the dependence of growth on the number of upgradeable components?

5-9 Use the hierarchical configuration shown in Figure 2-41 to determine the growth factor (see Problem 5-8) with the following costs for the upgradeable elements:

$$PCM: \qquad \$400$$
$$\text{Level 1 mini:} \quad \$1,000$$
$$\text{Level 2 mini:} \quad \$10,000$$
$$\text{Assume } w_1 = 0.42 \text{ for Level 2 mini,}$$
$$w_2 = 0.1 \text{ for Level 1 mini,}$$
$$w_3 = 0.04 \text{ for each PCM}$$

For $p = 0.05$, $d = 0.02$, and $c = 0.11$, and 50% growth capacity, determine the acceptable downtime.

Are the constants used in the equation "reasonable"? Would a different set of constants provide a more reasonable answer? If not, why?

5-10 How would you structure the Patient Monitoring system in terms of software. Explore issues of concurrency, deadlock, and the use of software described in Chapter 3.

6

Application Examples

6.1 INTRODUCTION

The number of local and global networks of micro- and minicomputer systems has been proliferating in the mid-to-late 1970's. The most common types of multi-minicomputer systems have been based on off-the-shelf hardware such as the Multi-communications Adapter (MCA) from Data General (described in Chapter 4) as well as directly interconnected systems using either hardwired links or voice-band telephones lines with modems.

The earliest versions of distributed minicomputer systems were usually based on hierarchical structures and used in process control and transaction processing environments. These systems were characterized by large "fan-outs," i.e., several hierarchical levels of minicomputers, with each level tailored to perform one or more well-defined tasks. Some of these systems were also based on hybrid interconnect schemes combining hierarchical structures with buses or loops. An example of such a system is the Bank of America Distributed Computing Facility, described in the following section.

In applications requiring a diversity of processing capabilities, systems based on other types of interconnect structures have evolved. One of the earlier distributed systems using bus technology in an industrial nonacademic or research environment is the Ford Motor Company distributed micro- and minicomputer system that is based on the Local Network Architecture (LNA). This system is based on multi-layered protocols similar to those described in Chapter 3.

An entirely different approach to distributed system design has been taken by the National Aeronautics and Space Administration (NASA) with their POCCNET, which is based on packet switching.

268

Finally, a fourth approach to multiminicomputer design using a unidirectional loop and all off-the-shelf hardware has been developed by TRW.

Each of these four approaches are discussed in this chapter in terms of unique system requirements and the particular design approach taken by the system designers, including error-handling philosophy.

Furthermore, to illustrate the application of concepts described in previous chapters, each of the four examples is discussed with emphasis on different aspects of the design process; system architecture and interconnect structure for the Bank of America system (Chapter 2), protocol layering in Ford Motor Company's LNA (Chapter 3), and design methodology and system structuring for POCCNET and TRW's Experimental Signal Processing System, respectively (Chapter 5).

These systems range from homogeneous to heterogeneous, dedicated to general-purpose, hardwired to packet-switched, partially connected (using resource sharing distributed computing networks), well-bounded, and defined applications to open-ended, multipurpose computing facilities. They have been, or are being, developed for commercial applications (banking), scientific processing, real-time data acquisition and control (automobile manufacturing), and signal processing.

The purpose is to provide some examples of approaches that may be applicable to other design problems.

6.2 THE BANK OF AMERICA DISTRIBUTED COMPUTING FACILITY

The following description of a multiminicomputer system application in a commercial (banking) environment is based on a system chiefly developed in-house by Bank of America in California. This system is based on polled, multidrop, multiplexed links connected to central clusters of minis.

6.2.1 System Requirements

Bank of America has developed two interconnected data processing centers, each with several interconnected clusters of minicomputers that serve more than 1100 branch offices distributed throughout California. More than 9000 teller and administrative video terminals in the branch offices provide access to a segmented (and distributed) data base for inquiry and update transactions for the bank's Demand Deposit Accounts (DDA) and Savings Deposit Accounts (SDA). In addition to serving checking and savings accounts, the system is designed to provide data capture for new accounts and to allow record changes and, eventually, Bank Americard credit inquiries and loan processing. The requirement is to support a minimum of 4 million checking accounts and 4 million savings accounts. The DDA and SDA applications systems are required to process approximately 100 inquiry and update transactions per second and a minimum of 300,000 transactions per day.

Basic requirements dictating the system design were

1. Reliability

2. Throughput
3. Ease of hardware and software maintenance
4. Ability to accommodate geographic dispersion
5. Ability to respond to 95% of all inquiries in less than 6 sec

These requirements were derived from the following needs: The system was to be based on a relatively conservative design approach, however, the traditional hierarchical, master-slave approach was to be avoided. Furthermore, the design should be based on redundant processors with "hot" standby spares; if one of the processors would go down, the other one would automatically assume the full workload, via switching or bridging of communications lines into the system. Also, failure of one computer or component should not bring down the entire subsystem or cause failure of service to the network of users.

6.2.2 System Design Approach

The basic hardware subsystems are called *modules*. A module consists of two message-handling processors (MHP's) and two file management transaction processors (FMTP's). The processors consist of General Automation GA-16/440 Mini-computers each with 128K bytes of main memory where the load is shared between the processors; in the event of failure, automatic switchover provides for uninterrupted operation.

In a basic processing module, each FMTP has direct access to the entire module data base. The FMT's contain system software needed to load, retrieve, and update the module data base and communicate with the MHP's plus application software to process inquiries.

The MHP's route inquiries and responses to one of three locations:

1. The associated FMTP if the required data/account is resident in that module
2. Another module where the required data-account is resident
3. To the unit/terminal originating the inquiry/message

All messages passing through an MHP are also recorded on its associated logging device, as shown in Figure 6-1.

FMTP's and MHP's, in a module, are interconnected point to point using General Automation's 1579 Controllers operating at 1.2 Mbps via a local bus.

Modules are specialized to three different applications:

1. Network Operations Center (NOC)
2. Demand Deposit Accounts/Savings Deposit Accounts (DDA/SDA)
3. Online Data Capture (ODC)

Two data processing centers exist, one in San Francisco and one in Los Angeles. Each of the two centers has a complement of one NOC module, one ODC module, and three DDA/SDA modules.

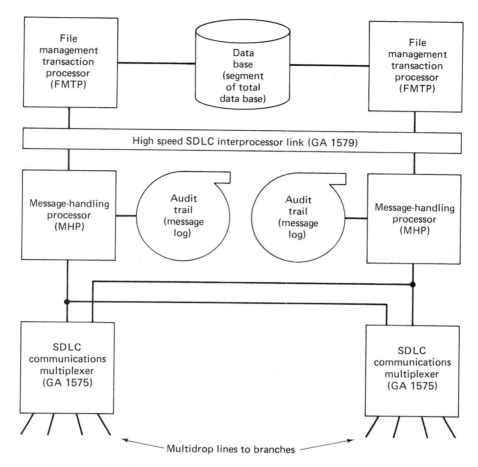

Figure 6-1 Distributed Computing Facility Module, Bank of America System using four General Automation GA-16/440's. (From: John D. Foster, "The Development of a Concept for Distributive Processing," Compcon 1976, San Francisco, Calif.)

All five modules in each center are interconnected via the GA 1579's, operating at 1.2 Mbps.

The centers in San Francisco and Los Angeles are also interconnected via GA 1579's operating in a full-duplex mode at 9600 bps.

The DDA/SDA modules can each handle up to a maximum of 32 SDLC communications lines (each with a maximum of 12 drops to branch offices). As shown in Figure 6-1, these communications lines are handled by two multiplexers (GA 1575's) that each can handle up to 16 lines operating at data rates up to 9600 bps.

These communications lines are connected to remote programmable control units (PCU's) that are polled by the MHP and perform the following six functions:

1. To act as a branch controller for up to 32 single-station–single-line port teller terminal connections.
2. Perform data concentration.
3. Prebuffer up to 270 characters of CRT screen data.
4. Store screen formats and edit routines.
5. Format data into standard MHP transmission format.
6. Interface the MHP units utilizing multipoint SDLC line protocol.

The NOC module, as shown in Figure 6-2, provides a facility for operator control, monitoring, and statistics gathering for the network resources. In addition to the DDA/SDA modules, it has a CRT terminal for operator interaction and report generation as well as hardcopy generation capability from a line printer.

Many of the NOC control functions are duplicated in the other application modules in the case that the center's NOC module is not operational.

The ODC module does not have its own communication lines but rather uses an MHP from one of the DDS/SDA modules in the center.

The applications software for the system was implemented by Bank of America

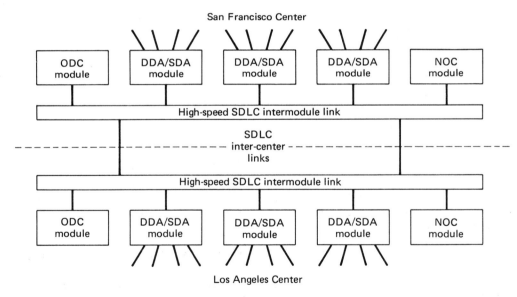

Figure 6-2 The two California centers shown in this figure were started with five modules. More modules were added as applications such as inquiries for loans or for BankAmericard accounts were brought up. Inquiries into time plan loans or real estate loans are handled by a single module. (From: John D. Foster, "Distributive Processing for Banking," *Datamation*, July 1976. Reprinted with permission of DATAMATION® magazine, copyright by Technical Publishing Company, a division of Dun-Donnelly Publishing Corporation, A Dun & Bradstreet Company, 1978, all rights reserved.)

whereas the primary components of the MHP processor, FMTP processor, and NOC module subsystem were implemented with standard, General Automation software as a base.

The components used for the MHP subsystem are the SDLC driver/handler routines for intra/intermodule intercenter and terminal controller communications, line control and task scheduling control routines, message handling and routing package, and switchover/switchback capability of the communications lines in case of processor failure.

The FMTP subsystem was implemented by Bank of America using General Automation's standard CONTROL-III operating system and File Management system. The major components of the FMTP are

- Application support and interface routines.
- Intramodule link-handling routines.
- A switchover/switchback capability for disc storage in case of processor failures.
- A message processing package.
- A data-base load and unload package.
- Transaction processing support routines.
- An operator communication package.

In addition, the NOC was implemented using some 80 operator commands for network control and monitoring such as program and data file transfer, data file display, peripheral status display, system statistics gathering and display, system resource enable/disable operations, remote source enable/disable, and system access control and initialization functions.

6.2.3 Error-Handling Philosophy

In order to satisfy one of the foremost design requirements (i.e., reliability and throughput), several important features have been incorporated into the system design:

1. Each module data base is resident on at least four disc spindles. This spread provides potentially greater accessibility to the data since four concurrent accesses from four CPU's are theoretically possible.
2. Sufficient storage is provided to allow two generations of the module's data to be resident, plus backup copies of programs, tables, etc.
3. Each FMTP has direct access to the entire module data base.
4. Provisions are made to preclude concurrent update of a single record by both FMTP's using the high-speed interprocessor link (see Figure 6-1).
5. FMTP's communicate with MHP's over dual communication links.
6. With all processors in a module aware of the other's status, if one FMTP goes down the other automatically assumes the full workload. Similarly, if one

MHP should go down, the other will assume the communications load automatically via switching of the external communications lines into that processor (and module).

7. The design permits deliberate shutdown of half a module without interrupting service to users. While one half-module is responding to inquiries against "today's" data base, "tomorrow's" data can be loaded into another area of the data base by the other half.

8. A disc failure can be corrected by one half-module while the other half continues inquiry processing against the remainder of the data base.

Component and/or subsystem failure are handled in the following manner: Two modes of message transmission are used: Normal and Error. The normal is the most direct route as established in the MHP routing tables, whereas the error path is the one that is taken as a backup route when there is a failure, either hardware or communication line, which prevents routing via the primary route. Message paths are shown in Figure 6-3. When more modules are added, more complex error routing is required, but the principle is the same. Not only must the alternate paths be verified as operational, but in a cluster-to-cluster transmission that has the intercluster lines down verification must be made that proper indication is provided to the NOC and the inquiring terminal, so that transaction messages do not become lost in the system.

There are four basic types of communication paths for normal messages in this configuration.

1. Terminal → PCU → MHP → FMTP → Disc, where the MHP, FMTP, and Disc are all in the same module.

2. Terminal → PCU → MHP → MHP → FMTP → Disc, where the disc is located in another module from the module to which the terminal is connected. The two modules, however, are in the same cluster (center).

3. Terminal → PCU → MHP → MHP → FMTP → Disc, where either the second and third, or only the third, MHP is in another cluster (intercluster communication).

4. Terminal → PCU → MHP → MHP → MHP → MHP → FMTP → Disc, where the first two MHP's are in one cluster and the second two MHP's are in the other cluster.

Types 3 and 4 occur when the originating MHP must go to another MHP in the same cluster to access the communication line for the other cluster. In case of failure, two modes exist in terms of routing of messages.

The first condition or mode is when the message path fails for messages being transmitted from a terminal to a data base. The second condition occurs when a failure occurs on the message path for a message being returned from a data base to a terminal.

In case of a failure where messages from a terminal cannot reach a data base, all alternate paths will be tried. Only if the data base cannot be reached will the terminal receive a message indicating that the data is inaccessible.

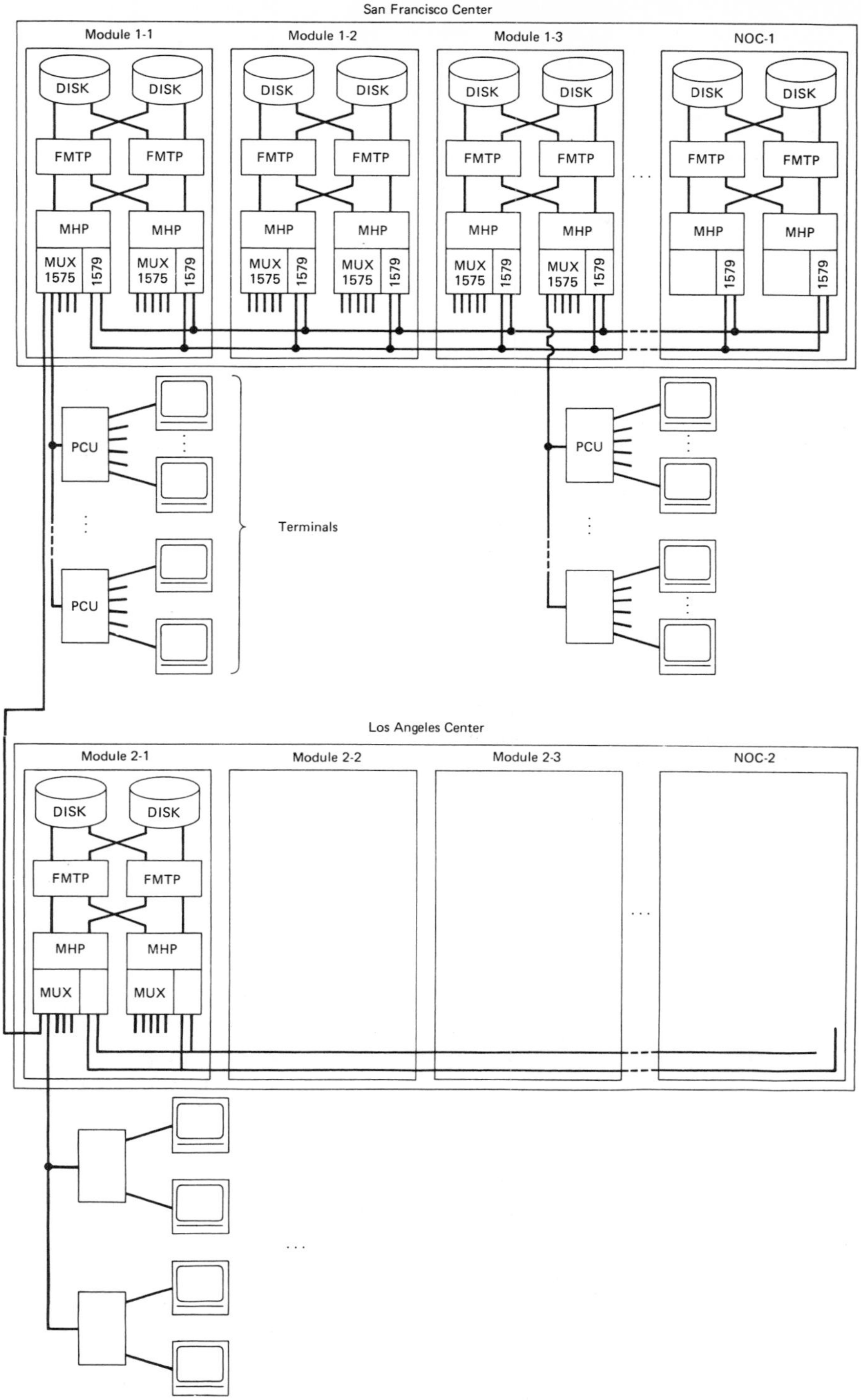

Figure 6-3   Bank of America total system configuration with two centers.

275

In addition to individual component failures, there are instances where multiple failures can occur and still allow partial system operation. System action to such failures have, to some degree, been predefined where alternate routes will be switched in, error messages are sent to terminals, and/or the NOC is notified.

6.2.4   System Advantages/Shortcomings

The advantage of the banking system is the high level of redundancy with multiple levels of fallback (failsoft) in case of failures.

A second attractive feature is the relative simplicity of design where each "dual" processor is functionally dedicated (FMTP's, MHP's).

The penalty paid for this is, of course, more expensive hardware costs as well as more complex interconnect requirements, which translate into a large amount of cabling with inherent degradation in reliability.

The system described in the following section is based on a simplified interconnect scheme, but uses a more complex software control structure since the system contains minis and micros of many different manufacture which perform a large variety of unique functions.

6.3   FORD'S LOCAL NETWORK ARCHITECTURE — (LNA) BASED PROCESS CONTROL NETWORK

6.3.1   System Requirements

Ford Motor Company's Research Laboratory in Dearborn, Michigan, has developed a distributed processing test-bed, with possible applications to Ford Motor Company's product testing, machine and power tool monitoring, product functional control, maintenance dispatching, and energy management environments.

Ford's requirements are for online transfers of various files between a large number of nodes. The local data processing environments range from product manufacturing facilities with end-of-line testing and repairing of products where a common data base is needed that includes information on shifts and occurring quality problems to product line monitoring, computer-based control of robots, and production line flow.

Facilities also exist where signal processing is being explored in terms of signature analysis of various tools such as drills to determine when a tool is worn down and should be replaced.

Unique requirements exist for interconnecting facilities where spot resistance welding is performed and data is logged during various steps in the process for later analysis.

Ford also plans to internet facilities where engine dynamometers are used to simulate road load on vehicles, where data is collected on engine RPM and torque, emission temperature, fuel flow, etc., for subsequent computer analysis.

The primary requirements for this distributed data processing facility are therefore, as follows:

- Minimal impact of networking on existing computer facilities (i.e., operating systems).
- Minimal impact of change-over from local to distributed processing.
- Highly reliable operations to keep plant running continuously, regardless of link or local node failure(s).
- Capability to handle a wide range of computers (large, mini, micro) presently used in various locations in manufacturing plants (Heterogeneous System).
- Extensive expansion capability (in engine plant alone, 192 sites were identified by Ford in 1978 for computer/terminal device control/communication).

Ford's approach has been to develop a prototype system for laboratory automation that serves as test-bed for a larger system to be installed in Ford's manufacturing plants. By late 1978, some 15 active sites (nodes) had been interfaced to the prototype system, including minicomputers such as the Interdata 8/32, Data General Nova, and TI 9900.

The following sections describe tradeoffs and the approach taken by Ford to satisfy the basic requirements above in such areas as computer interfacing, protocol structure, system control, user log-in procedures, and system expansion.

6.3.2 System Level Tradeoffs

One of the primary requirements for the system was to provide highly reliable service to all users connected to the system. This requirement immediately eliminated interconnect structures sensitive to single-point failures, such as star configurations with a central hub that, in case of failure, would bring the entire system down. Eliminated from consideration were also centrally controlled bus systems based on polling (see Chapter 2), where all messages in the system would have to be forwarded via a message flow control computer. Furthermore, systems based on computers interconnected in a loop fashion (also described in Chapter 2) where ruled out, since a single-point failure would stop messages from being passed along the loop via intermediaries.

One of the least problematic interconnect approaches from a reliability point of view (disregarding various redundancy schemes that typically further complicated the design) are systems based on the distributed, multiple access bus (such as Mitrix, Subsection 2.3.3, Ethernet, Subsection 2.3.6, and the Network Systems Corporation bus system, Section 4.3).

Several multiple access schemes were evaluated by Ford, such as Pure Aloha where the contention for the transmission medium (in the case of Aloha, radio frequency) occurs randomly and the slotted Aloha scheme where predetermined time slots for transmission are shared by several computers (see also Subsection 2.3.3). Other schemes considered were the Ethernet (see Subsection 2.3.6), which handles contention based on a carrier-sense-multiple-access approach with collision detection

(CSMA/CD), and the Network Systems Corporation system (see Section 4.3), which also uses carrier-sense-multiple-access but with a message checksum, to detect simultaneous transmissions ("nonpersistent" CSMA).

Based on analytical analysis, it was determined that, for large propagation to message-length ratios (arrival rate of new and rescheduled messages—due to carrier detection—per message time), CSMA/CD is superior to other modes of operation.

Additional tradeoffs of message size, transmission rate, and propagation delay revealed that a packet length for a 1-Mbps line bandwidth of 1000 bits gives a suitable system performance.

A tradeoff was also performed between the use of coaxial or fiber optics cable. Since the cost of fiber optics exceeded the cost of coaxial cable and because of the unavailability of fiber-optic couplers at the time of system implementation, Ford chose to go with coax.

6.3.3 System Design Approach

The Ford local network architecture is an example of multilayered protocol structure applied to a shared bus hardware interconnect structure. The protocol structure, shown in Figure 6-4, is based on six levels ranging from the physical link protocol layer at the bottom to the user level at the top. Several similarities exist between the layering scheme used in DECnet (Chapter 3) and the LNA approach. The physical link carrying both data and link control characters, distinguishes between them. The physical link protocol also performs polynomial error encoding and decoding, synchronization, and information encoding for data transparency. A data link control flag is used for synchronization, and bit stuffing is employed for data transparency (see IBM's SDLC described in Appendix). Since LNA is based on packet transmission (the amount of data carried by one packet varying from 0 to 128 characters), the packet format is defined at the packet protocol level. The packet format contains a link protocol flag (see above), a packet header, a data body, a CRC link protocol check field, and a flag. The header contains the packet destination and source addresses and a control field. The two levels described above are, in several respects, analogous to Levels 1 and 2 discussed in Chapter 3.

Similarly, the LNA Levels 3 and 4 are comparable with the transmission and transport layers, respectively, also discussed in Chapter 3.

The LNA Level 3 connection control layer is based on a connection control function called COM. This function defines a network port and controls port-to-port message transfers. At least one unique job is associated with each port, which it dynamically allocated and deallocated by COM. Other related functions performed by COM are summarized in Figure 6-4.

To communicate with COM, a unique string of commands is used to identify the logic link messages. These commands are followed by a parameter list containing parameters used for specifying initial conditions, finding error conditions, and testing of operations. Parameters are also included that define the maximum packet length, maximum time before sending the data, and a packet delimiter.

USER PROCESS LEVEL (6)
- Applications programs
- Retrieval, storage, and appending of data files
- Use of utility software
- Process-to-process connect/disconnect functions

SYSTEM PROCESS LEVEL (5)
- File control
- Device services
- Task scheduling

LOGICAL LINK PROTOCOL LEVEL (4)
- User definition of data flow, packet routing, and path control
- Error checking

CONNECTION CONTROL LEVEL (3)
- Message-to-packet parsing
- Packet sequencing, buffering, and selection
- Acknowledgement
- CRC
- Initial process connection

PACKET PROTOCOL LEVEL (2)
- Packet format

PHYSICAL LINK PROTOCOL (1)
- Distinguishment between data and link control characters
- Polynomial error encoding/decoding
- Synchronization
- Information encoding for data transparency

Figure 6-4 Functional Layering of LNA. (Reprinted from Data Communications article "Concepts, Strategies for Local Data Network Architectures," R. H. Sherman, M. G. Gable, and G. McClure. Copyright 1978, McGraw-Hill, Inc. All rights reserved.)

The next level, the logical link protocol layer, exhibits several similarities with DECnet's NSP (see Chapter 3) that contains rules for building logical channels, initiating communication sessions, and routing data packets onto logical links. The LNA logical link protocol allows the user to define the data flow, routing, and path control to the COM process.

The data flow and routing is determined by the user who logs in his source network name, LOG1. Connections are then established by assigning the destination network name, ASGN. The source and destination names consist of network addresses based on three bytes;

1. Port Identification

2. Segment Number
3. User Identification

The port name identifies the individual adapter. The segment number identifies the local network.

LNA is designed to permit interconnections of several local bus systems into a global network. In a local LNA bus-based network, no routing is required (all users have access to the packet destination name). When the system is expanded into multiple, interconnected nets of local bus systems, however, a device is needed to interface the bus-based nets. This device is called a Gateway. The Gateway performs path building, address filtering, and fault control. (These functions are discussed in more detail in Subsection 6.3.5.) When two or more local networks are connected through a Gateway, the segment number is used to identify a special local network and an entire route called the *path name*, which consists of port identifiers followed by the final destination name.

Three characters, shown in Figure 6-5, are reserved for network addresses and used to match the destination name of a packet with the name of a user. Packets are only accepted if a unique name or a don't-care name exists. This name is used to establish a packet's destination.

The next protocol layer, the system process level or Level 5 (see Figure 6-4), contains the LOG process that allocates and deallocates processes and files and controls accesses to the network addresses by users, thereby also controlling network security. The LOG command language is summarized in Figure 6-6. Generic names are used for automatic handling of resource allocations. The LOG process translates the generic names into network addresses. The LOG is a dynamic bookkeeping procedure using CATALOG, which contains both the generic names and the network addresses of processes and resources including resource costs, access privileges, and present attachments. A CATALOG-update algorithm is used that deletes network addresses when connections cannot be established. When recovering from a network fault, the LOG restores previous relationships between multiple, replicated copies of CATALOGS.

The topmost protocol layer, the user process level, contains user functions (i.e., applications programs).

---

* = Port Name of the LOG Process (The LOG
process is contained in the uppermost protocol
layers)

? = Don't-Care Name of a Port, Process, or Segment

! = Unassigned Name of a Port, Process, or Segment

Figure 6-5 Characters reserved for LNA network addresses. (Reprinted from Data Communications article "Concepts, Strategies for Local Data Network Architectures," R. H. Sherman, M. G. Gable, and G. McClure. Copyright 1978, McGraw-Hill, Inc. All rights reserved.)

COMMAND	TASK
QU MARY LOCATION	Find the network address of the generic name process, if it exists
QU MARY ENTER	Enter into the CATALOG the generic name process with its network address
QU MARY EXIT	Remove from the CATALOG the network address of the generic name
QU MARY ATT FRED	Attach the named processes to the requesting generic process
QU MARY DET FRED	Detach the generic name process from the requesting process
QU MARY COST	Provide the network resource cost of the generic name process

Figure 6-6   Source of the LNA LOG commands are listed based on two processes generically named MARY and FRED. (Reprinted from Data Communications article "Concepts, Strategies for Local Data Network Architectures," R. H. Sherman, M. G. Gable, and G. McClure. Copyright 1978, McGraw-Hill, Inc. All rights reserved.)

The use of some of the protocol levels is illustrated by the following example of a testing facility which contains an engine dynamometer test stand which uses a microprocessor to collect engine performance data. This performance data is subsequently transmitted to a data acquisition system called Datalogger and a disk storage-based File Computer (see Figure 6-7).

The steps involved in making a normal connection between the processors shown in Figure 6-7 that illustrate the use of COM and LOG are summarized in Figure 6-8.

A normal connection is made by the Datalogger entering the network with the network address:

$$\text{LOG1} = \text{p2S1U1}$$

Source network name—↵
8-bit port name of Datalogger (See Fig. 6-7)
Segment 1 (= Local Network No. 1)
8-bit User Process Name

The Datalogger assigns the destination address for the data as follows:

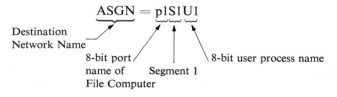

$$\text{ASGN} = \text{p1S1U1}$$

Destination Network Name
8-bit port name of File Computer
Segment 1
8-bit user process name

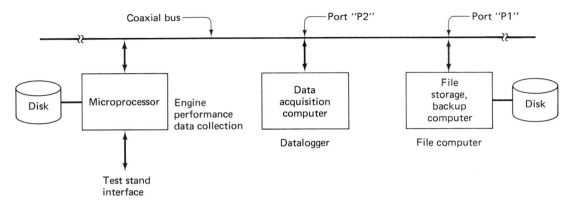

Figure 6-7 A section of the LNA system used for engine dynamometer testing (Reprinted from Data Communications article "Concepts, Strategies for Local Data Network Architectures," R. H. Sherman, M. G. Gable, and G. McClure. Copyright 1978, McGraw-Hill, Inc. All rights reserved.)

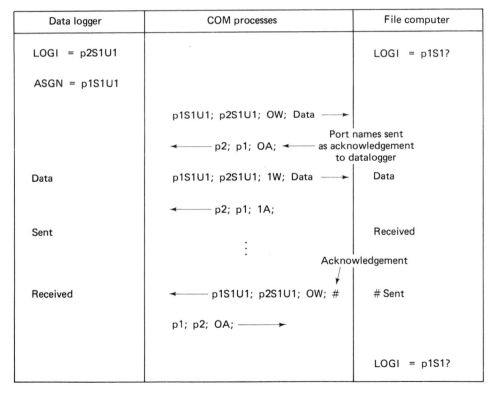

Data logger	COM processes	File computer
LOGI = p2S1U1		LOGI = p1S1?
ASGN = p1S1U1		
	p1S1U1; p2S1U1; OW; Data ⟶	
	⟵ p2; p1; OA; ⟵	Port names sent as acknowledgement to datalogger
Data	p1S1U1; p2S1U1; 1W; Data ⟶	Data
	⟵ p2; p1; 1A;	
Sent		Received
	⋮	
		Acknowledgement
Received	⟵ p1S1U1; p2S1U1; OW; #	# Sent
	p1; p2; OA; ⟶	
		LOGI = p1S1?

Figure 6-8 Command sequence for normal process connection (Reprinted from Data Communications article "Concepts, Strategies for Local Data Network Architectures," R. H. Sherman, M. G. Gable, and G. McClure. Copyright 1978, McGraw-Hill, Inc. All rights reserved.)

The File Computer subsequently enters with its network address:

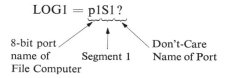

Source and destination names used to identify logical link messages are sent to the COM process that performs the connection control function. Since, in this example, only a single segment is used (S1), the COM process subsequently sends only the port names (p2, p1) as acknowledgement to the Datalogger.

When data is sent, the packet is received by the File Computer since U1 matches the don't care field "?" (see also Figure 6-5).

Following this, the don't care field "?" is converted to the U1 field.

When the data transfer is completed, the Datalogger receives a "#" as an acknowledgement.

As shown in Figure 6-8, the File Computer unassigns itself by entering P1S1?, which allows other users to access the file system.

6.3.4   Error-Handling Philosophy

Error-handling procedures have been incorporated into several of the protocol layers, such as polynomial error encoding and decoding at the physical link protocol level, cyclic redundancy checks (CRC) and acknowledgement procedures at the connection control level, and various forms of error checking at the logical link protocol level (see Figure 6-4). An example of the logical link messages used in automatic fault detection and recovery is given in Figure 6-9. Generally, a backup computer is used in the configuration shown in Figure 6-7. In case a communications fault is sensed by this backup computer, it will immediately rename itself and take on the role of the original file computer. During local switching of this backup computer into an "active" role, end-to-end acknowledgements will protect the system from losing packets.

6.3.5   System Expansion

The Bank of America distributed minicomputer system can be expanded by adding more modules to the centers or by adding more centers beyond the original two in Los Angeles and San Francisco.

LNA can, correspondingly, be expanded by adding micros and/or minis to a bus (upper limit of ports is less than 256) and increasing the number of coaxial cable systems. Coaxial cables in LNA are interconnected via Gateways. These Gateways perform routing using routing tables, provide program buffering, and (if necessary) perform protocol translation. The LNA interconnect scheme based on Gateways is illustrated in Figure 6-10 where Segment 1 is connected to Segment 2 via Gateway 1

Datalogger	File System	Backup
LOG1 = p2S1U1	LOG1 = p1S1U1	
ASGN = p1S1U1		
DATA	DATA	
SENT $\longrightarrow$	RECEIVED	
	"CRASH"	
	$\longrightarrow$	"CRASH SENSED"
		LOG1 = p1S1 ?
DATA		DATA
SENT	$\longrightarrow$	RECEIVED
	"BACK ON LINE"	
	LOG1 = !S1 !	
	ASGN = p1S1 !	LOG1 = p1S1 ?
	FILE SYSTEM UP $\longrightarrow$	DATA
		RECEIVED
		$\longleftarrow$ BACKUP OFF LINE
		LOG1 = !S1 !
	LOG1 = p1S1 ?	
DATA	DATA	
SENT $\longrightarrow$	RECEIVED	

Figure 6-9 Fault recovery (Reprinted from Data Communications article "Concepts, Strategies for Local Data Network Architectures," R. H. Sherman, M. G. Gable, and G. McClure. Copyright 1978, McGraw-Hill Inc. All rights reserved.)

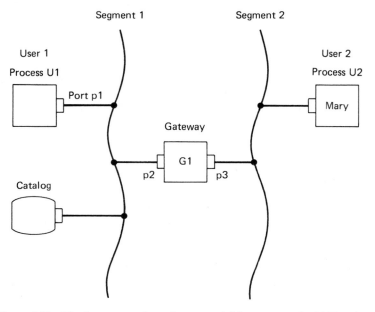

Figure 6-10 The interconnection of two coaxial bus systems in LNA using a gateway. (Diagram Courtesy of Ford Motor Company)

(G1). As shown, user node Fred uses G1 to establish a data path for a message transaction with user node Mary. A message sent from process U1 to process U2 via the Gateway G1 is performed in a sequence of discrete steps whereby the Gateway substitutes path names from Segment 1 to Segment 2 nomenclature thereby performing address filtering.

This address filtering procedure can also handle multiple gateways on the same segment (coaxial bus). Where a series of gateways are used between multiple segments, and where a gatway does not receive an acknowledgement from another gateway along a route, the six-step address filtering technique illustrated in Figure 6-11 can be used.

Gateways perform, in addition to the path building and address filtering techniques described above, fault control. This is provided through error detection using time-outs on positive acknowledgements and by error correction through gateway broadcasts for alternate routes, which are found by exploiting the broadcast nature of the global bus (rather than using routing tables as in the ARPANET System).

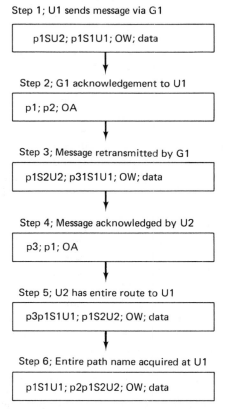

Step 1; U1 sends message via G1

> p1SU2; p1S1U1; OW; data

Step 2; G1 acknowledgement to U1

> p1; p2; OA

Step 3; Message retransmitted by G1

> p1S2U2; p31S1U1; OW; data

Step 4; Message acknowledged by U2

> p3; p1; OA

Step 5; U2 has entire route to U1

> p3p1S1U1; p1S2U2; OW; data

Step 6; Entire path name acquired at U1

> p1S1U1; p2p1S2U2; OW; data

Figure 6-11   Message handling between User 1 and User 2 [(See Figure 6-10). Diagram Courtesy of Ford Motor Company]

It is, however, difficult to predict if delays through multiple parallel gateway paths will cause deadlocks to occur, particularly if the system is expanded into a very large number of interconnected segments.

6.3.6   System Advantages/Shortcomings

The major advantage of the Ford Motor Company's Local Network Architecture is the relative simplicity in terms of system expansion. The system is designed to handle a wide variety of minis and micros and, due to its decentralized nature, provides a high degree of reliability (unless, of course, the coaxial cable is cut). The major disadvantage of the system is the relatively low bandwidth (1 Mbps). This bandwidth is, however, used quite efficiently and may prove adequate for its intended application.

6.4   THE NATIONAL AERONAUTICS AND SPACE ADMINISTRATION (NASA) GODDARD SPACE FLIGHT CENTER PAYLOAD OPERATIONS CONTROL CENTER NETWORK

The Goddard Space Flight Center (GSFC) complex, located in Greenbelt, Maryland, serves as the focal point for coordinating and controlling low earth-orbit spacecraft payloads. A relatively large number of individual Payload Operations Control Centers (POCC's) are used at GSFC to control and monitor status information on various spacecraft, coordinate space experiment evaluations, and process commands that control the spaceraft payload.

Standardization of spacecraft, the use of the Space Shuttle to launch spacecraft, and the use of the Tracking Data Relay Satellites to standardize and simplify the communications links between orbiting satellites and earth-based operations control centers in the 1980's has prompted NASA to also develop a standardized approach to payload operations control centers, hence, the creation of the Payload Operations Control Center Network (POCCNET) concept at GSFC.

Payload Operations Control Centers are anticipated to require interfacing to a multitude of facilities such as the Space Shuttle Launch complex at the Kennedy Space Center in Florida, the Shuttle Mission Control Center in Houston, Texas, and other operations control centers such as the Spacelab* POCC and the operations control center for the Interim Upper Stage (IUS) and the Spinning Solid Upper Stage (SSUS) used to propel payloads from the close-to-earth orbiting Space Shuttle into higher orbits in space. POCC's must, therefore, be able to send messages to the various NASA ground facilities as well as to satellites. Messages to satellites consist, in general, of commands to payloads and experiments. Messages received from satellites by POCC's are termed *telemetry*. Telemetry contains information collected by the satellite as well as information on the health and status of a satellite.

---

*The Spacelab is a self-contained laboratory that is enclosed in the Space Shuttle payload bay and may contain several experiments as well as human experimenters.

A POCC facility is, as a rule, located in a mission operations room that may contain one or more minicomputers with associated peripherals and operations consoles. The typical POCC must be able to handle simultaneously the receiving and processing of real-time telemetry and memory dumps or tape-recorder data dumps and to perform command generation and transmission. Memory dumps from spacecraft are received at the rate of 32 Kbps and must be processed in real-time. Tape-recorder dumps are received at the rate of up to 512 Kbps for later offline processing.

A typical POCC must also perform conversion of telemetry data from a spacecraft into engineering units, display this information, and analyze tape-recorder dumps to ascertain the health and status of various on-board systems such as the attitude control system, the command and data-handling system, the power system, the propulsion, system, and the on-board experiment system.

Examples of tasks that must be performed and graphically plotted in a POCC are bookkeeping of spacecraft momentum for attitude control; propellant bookkeeping, including the recording of spacecraft tank pressures and temperatures; energy bookkeeping such as recording of on-board battery terminal voltages, temperatures, and charge/discharge rates; and calculations of time remaining for tape recording.

Other POCC calculations involve spacecraft maneuver predictions, orbit determination, and power system analyses.

The POCC also has the capability of reading, modifying, transmitting, and receiving data-base information in real-time, performing mission planning which includes the merging of experiment planning and project planning activities which, in turn, results in a predetermined set of spacecraft commands and operations instructions, and scheduling of communications resources between the POCC and the spacecraft as well as the POCCNET Communications and Scheduling System. POCC users, also called Mission Operations Personnel, must, therefore, perform tasks such as information gathering based on requests from experimenters not necessarily located in the POCC, comprehension, decision making, and data transfer (I/O) between experimenter(s) and the POCC system.

Most of the future spacecraft missions will have lower budgets and shorter lead times for POCC development than typical missions of the past. Future POCC systems must, therefore, possess a high degree of flexibility so that they may be reused to save development time and money. The POCCNET approach has thus been taken by NASA to meet these requirements.

The POCCNET, which consists of interconnected POCC's, differs from the Bank of America network in terms of use of a mix of minis and micros of a large variety of different makes (heterogeneous) and interconnect scheme (packet switching). The latter was also implemented several years before the NASA/GSFC POCCNET system.

The POCCNET also differs from the Ford LNA in terms of interconnect structure (although both use gateways) and the kinds of functions performed at the various nodes in each system (process control by LNA versus scientific and telemetry processing in the POCC's).

The reliability aspects have received the same level of attention in the design of all three systems. Failures in the Bank of America system would mean the disruption of customer services in an extremely large customer community; failures in the LNA would mean disruption to automobile production line flow; whereas failures in POCCNET would result in the loss of scientific data from satellites and perhaps even the endangering of one or more spacecraft missions.

6.4.1 System Requirements

Not unlike the previously described LNA, each node in POCCNET may perform unique functions and represents by itself a system. The system requirements for POCCNET are, therefore, twofold:

1. Requirements for each POCC and the elements common in all POCC's.
2. Overall system assurance and the interface between the POCC's and the external facilities, such as other NASA facilities and the spacecrafts themselves.

The system engineering approach followed by NASA in establishing both the POCCNET internal and external requirements is, to a great degree, similar to one or more of the steps discussed in Chapter 5 (see Figure 5-1).

The approach used in developing the POCCNET is illustrated in Figure 6-12.

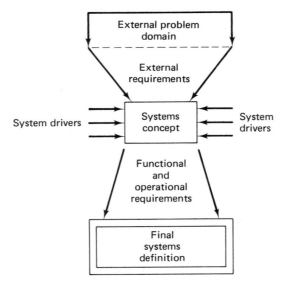

Figure 6-12 Systems engineering approach used by NASA to derive a final systems definition for the POCCNET. [From: "Payload Operations Control Center Network (POCCNET) Systems Definition Phase Study Report," Goddard Space Flight Center, MOD-6SR/0178, TM 79567, January 1978.]

External requirements were identified and described in functional and quantitative terms as appropriate. Next, generic system drivers chosen by technical and management personnel and representing generalized objectives or constraints to be satisfied were applied. These drivers narrowed the field of all possible system concepts down to a small set of candidates.

The external requirements were subsequently analyzed and applied to the system concept candidates. This process generated functional and operational requirements on subsystems of the concept. The system drivers are described in some detail to illustrate this approach.

Seven system drivers were identified by NASA as essential to the success of the GSFC POCC's in the 1980's:

1. Standardized spacecraft, space shuttle and TDRSS orientation
2. Flexibility
3. Low cost
4. POCC autonomy
5. People orientation
6. Advances in computer technology
7. Evolutionary organization and operation

The POCC's had to be oriented to a large number of new standardized elements such as standard spacecraft, standardized launch procedures and vehicles (the Space Shuttle), and a standardized communications capability such as the Tracking Data Relay Satellite System (TDRSS). These are all new NASA systems that will provide more capability at lower cost than their respective predecessors. The POCC's should also provide increased capability at reduced cost by the use of standard hardware, software and implementation, and operations procedures. If standard POCC systems and applications were properly designed and implemented initially, they could be reused with, at most, minor modifications for support of other spacecraft missions. Thus, the cost would be amortized over a number of missions instead of being borne fully by each user.

The second driver was flexibility. Most computing machinery has a useful life in the 10- to 20-year range. But, most NASA/GSFC missions last only from a few months to a maximum of 5 years. Thus, POCC's are forced by simple economics to reuse equipment. The software sometimes costs even more than the hardware, and a substantial amount has approximately the same useful life. Therefore, from mission to mission, POCC's are forced by economics to reuse as much software as they can. For these reasons, designing long-term flexibility into the POCC software and systems initially so that these can be easily and inexpensively reconfigured from mission to mission was a POCC driver.

Low cost was a third driver. POCC's have traditionally cost only a few percent of the cost of the spacecraft series being controlled from ground. In the 1980's, as the cost of the flight systems decreases due to standardization and the complexity of their requirements increases, the POCC's will be under severe cost pressure. The usual technique used to provide low cost and flexibility is to pool resources and draw on them according to need. Opposed to this was the fourth system driver, POCC Autonomy.

A POCC should never have to jeopardize its spacecraft because of the constraints of pooled operation. A project should always be able to operate its POCC as it deems necessary for legitimate spacecraft health and safety reasons. Any POCC system that cannot assure a project that it will have control of the resources it needs for survival of its spacecraft would not be a satisfactory system for conducting space operations. Therefore, POCC Autonomy was an essential system driver.

The fifth driver was people orientation. The direct personnel costs of implementing and operating a POCC for an extended period of time far exceed the equipment costs. The maximum impact that can be made on cost is in the personnel area. Attaching personnel cost head on means that systems should be oriented to the requirements of the people who have to develop, use, and maintain them. A system has to provide the man-machine interfaces and capabilities each user requires to be productive on the system.

The sixth system driver was advances in computer technology. Two effects of advances in this area have been the rapidly decreasing cost of the digital logic elements that make up computers and the rapidly decreasing cost of computer interconnection via high performance bit-serial channels. (The desirability of serial interconnect links was prompted by the existence of computers with word lengths of 16, 24, and 32 bits and character sizes of 6 and 8 bits.) The end result of falling logic prices is that it has become economically feasible to distribute a number of computers to solve complex distribution problems. By solving each subproblem where and as it arises, the overall system problem usually never becomes overwhelming or unmanageable. To make full use of the distributed computing concept, it should be possible to interconnect the distributed computers in the POCC's easily and at low cost.

The seventh and final system driver was evolutionary organization and operation of POCC systems. GSFC has been developing and operating POCC's since the early 1960's. In those days, each series of spacecraft had radically different characteristics and requirements. As a result, each new spacecraft series led to a new POCC development. The GSFC POCC's have been fully utilized over the years, but user requirements and the system drivers described above obsoleted many of the earlier POCC capabilities and features. The level of support in the mid-to-late 1970's strained existing POCC resources far beyond the most optimistic early expectations. Nevertheless, the POCC system of the future must be evolutionary in terms of growth from previously existing systems since the approaches to earlier POCC's worked well in the past and should not be abruptly abandoned. A second evolutionary requirement for systems design was called *modular responsiveness to unknown requirements*, which meant that modest new requirements could be met by small increments in system capability.

By analyzing these seven system drivers along with the external requirements, a systems concept was synthesized. The application of system drivers to the synthesis of a systems concept is summarized in Figure 6-13.

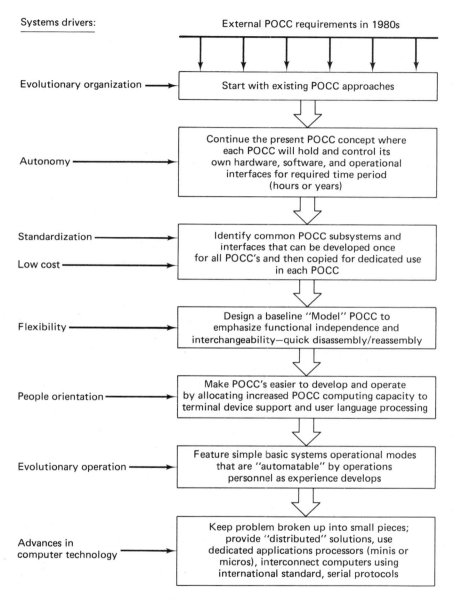

Systems drivers:

External POCC requirements in 1980s

Evolutionary organization → Start with existing POCC approaches

Autonomy → Continue the present POCC concept where each POCC will hold and control its own hardware, software, and operational interfaces for required time period (hours or years)

Standardization →
Low cost → Identify common POCC subsystems and interfaces that can be developed once for all POCC's and then copied for dedicated use in each POCC

Flexibility → Design a baseline "Model" POCC to emphasize functional independence and interchangeability—quick disassembly/reassembly

People orientation → Make POCC's easier to develop and operate by allocating increased POCC computing capacity to terminal device support and user language processing

Evolutionary operation → Feature simple basic systems operational modes that are "automatable" by operations personnel as experience develops

Advances in computer technology → Keep problem broken up into small pieces; provide "distributed" solutions, use dedicated applications processors (minis or micros), interconnect computers using international standard, serial protocols

Figure 6-13 Summary of the application of systems drivers to the synthesis of a systems concept. [From: "Payload Operations Control Center Network (POCCNET) Systems Definition Phase Study Report," Goddard Space Flight Center, TM-79567, January 1978.]

6.4.2 System Design Approach

The systems concept was synthesized from external requirements such as POCC functions to be performed, interfaces and data rates to/from external sources, and the number of POCC's needed in the 1980's as well as the previously described system drivers. Requirements also dictated a larger number of POCC's that should, essentially, be similar to existing, older POCC's, but the average future POCC would have to handle higher data rates and be more complex. The starting point for a POCC systems concept for GSFC was to take a standard minicomputer and dedicate it for a period of time (ranging from 1 hour to a year) to run POCC applications. This applications processor (AP) would host all the POCC applications for a single given payload. The drivers of standardization, flexibility, and low cost implied that there should be a number of identical AP's at GSFC, each one able to run standard command software customized by a data base for a particular payload. In order to maintain standardization of the AP's, nonstandard interfaces would be handled by "virtual interface" processors (VIP's). In this way, each POCC would essentially consist of a core of standard applications software running on a standard AP surrounded by other processors that would handle interface idiosynchracies and present a standard interface to the AP.

Examples of main interfaces to the AP are links to remote POCC's (JSC in Houston), the Space Shuttle Launch complex at KSC in Florida, large-scale mission support computers and other external systems, and Local Mission Operations Room (MOR) devices such as keyboards, CRT's, command panels, hardcopy devices, and strip-chart recorders. Interfaces to other NASA facilities and the spacecraft itself would be provided by an independent telemetry and command (TAC) system that would consist of a stand-alone processor. This processor would, consequently, receive to payload real-time telemetry from the NASA worldwide communications network called NASCOM and put it into a standard form, natural to that payload. The TAC would also format commands from the POCC for transmission via NASCOM that would ultimately be radiated to the spacecraft.

A simplified representation of how the TAC, AP, and VIP processor functions were to be grouped by their degree of interaction and independence is depicted in Figure 6-14. Functions which interact closely via shared data or which are similar and share procedures were grouped together and assigned to a single processor (i.e., mini). The weak interactions between functions, represented by dashed lines in Figure 6-14, were implemented by data flowing between processes performing the functions (i.e., by interprocess communication).

In addition to NASCOM interfaces, a POCC must also access external systems such as large-scale mission support computers, data-base management computers, and the NASCOM Network Control Center (NCC) computers, etc. Each of these systems has unique characteristics that may change from time to time. Hence, for each of these systems, a standard gateway processor was identified that would isolate the details of the system interface from the user POCC. Every POCC had to be able to get at every gateway, requiring either operational patching, tens of channels on

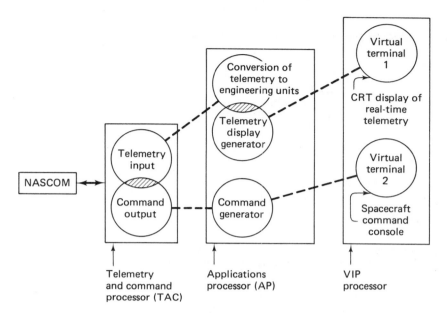

Figure 6-14   Simplified typical process structure for a required POCC. (From: "Evolutionary Distributed Systems Design," Richard des Jardins, IEEE-CS COMPSAC 77, First International Computer Software and Applications Conference, Chicago, Ill., 1977.)

each gateway processor, or a generalized Inter-Process Communication (IPC) system. Only the third alternative was deemed acceptable. A generalized IPC system would, therefore, be required that would be connected to every POCC computer at GSFC and would enable any such computer to talk to any other computer at any time. The model configuration for IPC system and gateways is shown in Figure 6-15.

The previous description of the POCCNET design has generally only dealt with all the elements within a POCC rather than emphasizing interprocess communications. It is, however, felt that a fairly comprehensive discussion of all the elements in POCCNET are needed to understand the reasons for tradeoffs and the approach taken in designing the IPC network. The functional, operational, and performance requirements for the IPC network are listed in Figure 6-16.

Six IPC design alternatives were explored by NASA before selection of the optimal approach. The interconnect structures investigated were as follows:

1. Shared memory
2. Crossbar switching between hosts
3. Global bus based on a twisted pair of wires using simple polling, priority requests, contention, or cyclic time division
4. Global (cable) bus using coaxial cable and time-division multiplexing (TDM) or frequency-division multiplexing (FDM) schemes

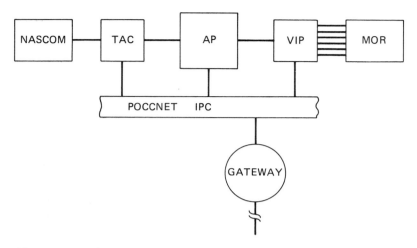

Figure 6-15 A fully interconnected POCC configuration. (From: "POCCNET System Definition Phase Study Report," NASA/GSFC TM-79567, Jan. 1978.)

Functional Requirements	• Flow Control • Error Control • Message Characteristics • Real-Time Host Communication • Expandability • Manufacturer Independence • Serial Communication • Communication Reliability • Geographical Independence
Operational Requirements	• Ease of Management • Ease of Use (Message Contents Transparent) • Fail Soft Characteristics
Performance Requirements	• Channel Speed (2 Mbps) • Message Length (Max. 8192 bits) • Throughput Time ($\leq$ 9.2 msec) • Response Time (Ack. in $\leq$ 10.3 msec)

Figure 6-16 POCCNET Inter-Process Communication (IPC) network requirements.

5. Basic loop design
6. Computer subnet with host computers connected to a subnet of a series of node computers.

(The interconnect schemes above are discussed in greater detail in Chapter 2.) It was determined by NASA that the computer subnet scheme is the only one of the above six alternate design approaches that satisfies all the requirements. The NASA interconnect scheme tradeoff process is summarized in Figure 6-17.

Requirements	Common Access Memory	Crossbar Switching	Common Bus	Cable Bus	Basic Loop	Computer Subnet
Easy to manage—generates loading and status reports and does traces on request, reports problems to a higher authority	No	Yes (with a host in control)	No	No	No	Yes (with a host in control)
Easy to use—minimum or no constraint on message length or content	Yes	No	Yes	Yes	Yes	Yes
Fail soft—no failure in the network will be catastrophic	No	No	No—dual routing or new technique required	No—dual routing or new technique required	No	Yes
Provide real-time host communication	Yes	Yes	Yes	Yes	Yes	Yes
Expandable—will not choke with information volume or message overhead as system is expanded, expansion will not deteriorate system	No—bus overload problems with a large number of hosts	No—switch points increase geometrically with additional lines	No—bandwidth problems with a large number of hosts	No—bandwidth problems with a large number of hosts	No—bandwidth problems with a large number of hosts	Yes (with proper interconnecting channels)
Manufacturer independent—allows hosts from various manufacturers to communicate and even allows the computers making up the network to come from different sources	No—word lengths from sources are different	Yes (with interface)	Yes (with interface)	Yes (with interface)	Yes (with interface)	Yes (with interface)
Geographically independent—allows remote or local hosts to communicate from widely separated geographical locations (hundreds of feet to thousands of miles, which implies serial communication)	No	No—synchronization would be a problem	No—common bus is often parallel	No—typically designed for local environments	No—loop response time would be degraded	Yes

Figure 6-17 Tradeoff summary of POCCNET interconnect alternatives. (From "POCCNET Systems Definition Phase Study Report," NASA/GSFC, TM 79567, Jan. 1978, Goddard Space Flight Center, Greenbelt, Md.)

The selected POCCNET subnet structure performs the basic functions required for two or more processes to utilize the system for transferring programs, control information, and/or data between the processes, usually located in the AP's. Network control is achieved by having a Data Operation Control Center (DOCC) supervise the operation of the subnet node processors, called POCCNET Message Processors (PMP's). The DOCC AP provides a center for POCCNET operations and configuration control, scheduling the use of other host computer systems and allocating resources among the POCC's supported by POCCNET. The PMP subnetwork· with interconnected AP hosts is shown in Figure 6-18.

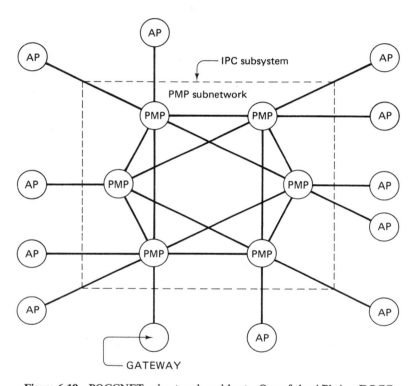

Figure 6-18 POCCNET subnetwork and hosts. One of the AP's is a DOCC.

The PMP's are used by the IPC to transfer message frames through the network, keep performance statistics, and detect failures of equipment that are under PMP control. The DOCC also authorizes the construction of logical channels between processes in the AP's.

The following paragraphs will briefly describe the protocols and command and traffic routing structure, enabling the PMP's to act as decision and control points for configuring all interprocess communication.

POCCNET protocols correspond to the five-level interface structure shown in

Figure 6-19. This structure is similar to the model discussed in Chapter 3. The major difference is that function level protocols are divided into system and user protocols. Levels 1, 2, and 3 correspond primarily with the CCITT X.25 protocol standard. Only the implementation of Levels 3, 4, and 5 are described since the differences are more pronounced at these levels.

POCCNET transport network level protocols (Level 3). The X.25 Level 3 host to network commands are as follows:

Call Setup and Clearing

- Call Request—used to establish a logical circuit.
- Call Accepted—used to accept a Call Request.
- Clear Request—used to refuse a Call Request.
- Clear Confirmation—used to confirm a Clear Request.

Data and Interrupt

- Data—used to transmit frames on a logical circuit.
- Interrupt—used to bypass the normal frame transmission sequence.
- Interrupt Confirmation—used to confirm an Interrupt.

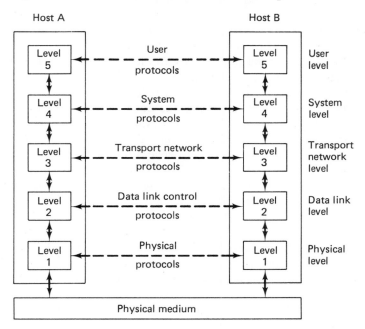

Figure 6-19 POCCNET five-level protocol interface structure. (From: "A Layered Interface Structure for Distributed Systems Based on X.25," Richard des Jardins and Fred Brosi, IEEE-CS/NBS Computer Networking Symposium, Maryland, Dec. 15, 1977.)

Flow Control and Reset

- Receive Ready—used for flow control.
- Receive Not Ready—used to indicate a temporary inability to accept frames.
- Reset Request—used to reinitialize the flow control parameters.
- Reset Confirmation—used to confirm a Reset Request.

Restart

- Restart—used to recover from major failures.
- Restart Confirmation—used to confirm a Reset Request.

The X.25 Level 3 commands, however, do not address certain POCCNET requirements that deal with guaranteed performance of logical channels. One such requirement is that in order to control the allocation of resources and to protect against faulty software, programs will request bandwidth in bits per second. The request will be sent to the PMP, which will control the allocation of program bandwidth. The insertion node will then monitor the usage of the program bandwidth. Bandwidth must be requested for worst case conditions, i.e., a burst of blocks or high-speed dumps. If a program is allocated 20,000 bits/sec, then the operator could transfer four 5000-bit blocks per second or any combination of different size blocks totaling 20,000 bits. Also, if a program requests N bits per second and only M bits per second are currently available, the program will be informed and it will be the operators decision whether to accept the degraded bandwidth or not.

The PMP provides for the storing, forwarding, and ordering of frames between the source and destination host such as an AP. Each frame entering the PMP will be stored in the frame queue, as shown in Figure 6-20.

Once a frame has entered the queue, the node will reset the associated DMA channel to receive the next frame into the next available slot in the queue. The queue will hold up to 70 frames. If the queue becomes filled, Receive Not Ready's will be transmitted to each sending node. Once the queue is emptied to a certain level, Receive Ready's will be transmitted to the waiting PMP's. As the frames enter the queue, the PMP will determine which channel the frame is to be transmitted over and then start the DMA operation on the appropriate channel.

Message routing tables are used to control message flow through the IPC network. Each frame the PMP receives is identified by a logical channel identifier (LCI). As shown in Figure 6-21, three separate LCI's are used. The source LCI is supplied by the source host and is converted by the insertion PMP to the network LCI.

The network LCI is used within the network to route the frame to the destination PMP.

The destination LCI is inserted by the destination PMP before the frame is transferred to the destination host.

Thus, the source LCI is a local identifier for the source host's process, the destination LCI is a local identifier for the destination host's process, and the network LCI is used within the network to route the frame.

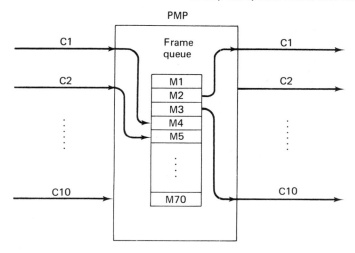

Figure 6-20 Frame queue in the POCCNET PMP where each frame is a maximum of 512 16-bit words. The total queue size can be a maximum of $70 \times 512 = 35,840$ words. (From: "High Performance Local Communications Based on the CCITT X.25 Protocol," A. E. Elenbass and L. L. King, Sixteenth Annual Technical Symposium, Systems and Software, June 2, 1977, National Bureau of Standards, Gaithersburg, Md.)

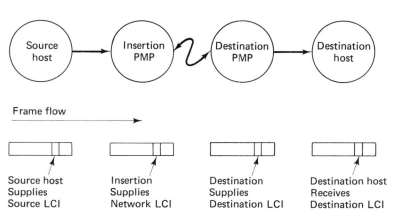

Figure 6-21 Source, network, and destination LCIS. (From: "POCCNET Systems Definition Phase Study Report," NASA/GSFC, TM 79567, Goddard Space Flight Center, Jan. 1978, Greenbelt, Md.)

Certain LCI's (source, network, and destination) are reserved for communication paths between the PMP's and DOCC. If there are N PMP's in the cluster, LCI's 0 through N handle PMP/DOCC communications. Requests to the DOCC are always made via LCI 0. Requests to PMP through N are made via LCI 1 through N.

An example of the routing tables is shown in Figure 6-22. Two hosts (AP1 and AP2) have an established communication path via PMP1 and PMP2. The solid lines

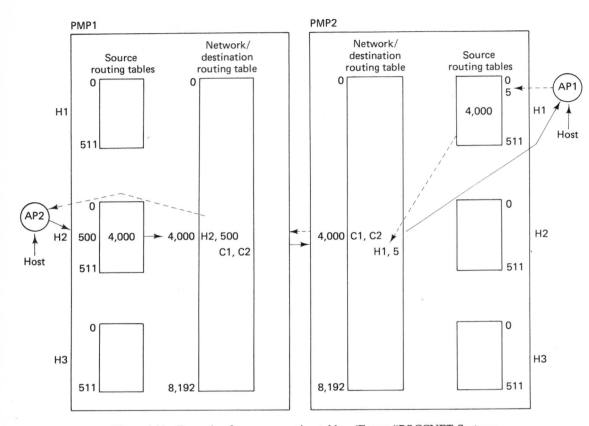

Figure 6-22 Example of message routing tables. (From: "POCCNET Systems Definition Study Report," NASA/GSFC, TM 79567, Goddard Space Flight Center, Jan. 1978, Greenbelt, Md.)

from AP2 and AP1 represent the table path in the return direction. In the example, steps performed are listed in Figure 6-23.

POCCNET system level protocols (Level 4). The Level 4 protocols consist of a number of separate protocols, each appropriate for particular applications. The POCCNET File Transfer Protocol (FTP) is useful for transfer of files between two processes running on different AP's. The Virtual Device protocols provide logically standardized computer I/O devices. Protocols for the POCCNET Virtual User create a Standardized Interactive User, independent of virtual device type. The FTP, Virtual Device, and Virtual User Protocols have the following characteristics:

In FTP, a server file transfer process performs data transfer services for a user file transfer process. Each such process has a protocol interpreter that can make and break connections and can send and receive commands or status messages. The pro-

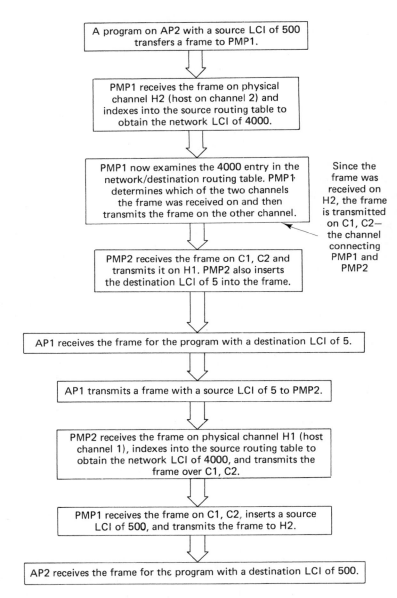

Figure 6-23   Steps performed transferring a frame from AP2 to AP1 as shown in Figure 6-22.

tocol interpreter controls a data transfer process that is responsible for setting up parameters for the transfer of data and for accomplishing the actual transfer. Both file transfer processes have an interface to their local file system; in addition the user file transfer process also contains an interface to the user (human or software).

FTP commands are used to establish and close connections and to control the transfer of data. Capabilities are provided for the user to define the file and record structure of his data and to specify the method to be used for data transfer (e.g., stream of characters, block at a time, or compressed).

FTP access control commands are used to establish control connections, to identify the user and his host, to give accounting information, and to close control connections. Transfer parameter commands are used to change data transfer parameters from their default values. Service commands cause data to be transmitted, received, and stored as a new file or appended to an existing file.

Due to the tremendous variety of terminal devices (e.g., CRT terminals, printers, and card readers, as well as those unknown at the time of the intial POCCNET design that might become available in the future), it is practically impossible to develop one or even a family of device handlers which could interface all the devices which would be required on POCCNET.

POCCNET terminal devices have, therefore, been virtualized, i.e., ideal I/O devices are specified with standard capabilities. Messages exchanged between user application processes and these *virtual terminals* (VT's) are constrained to certain forms, and all process-to-VT communication sequences must obey simple protocols at the system level.

Three classes of VTs comprise all necessary device types: in-string, out-string, and block display.

In-string is a device that is capable of inputting *lists* (i.e., sequences) of strings; a string is a list of characters. As a virtual device, there is no design limitation on the length of the string list or the length of each string in the string list, although any implementation of in-string would have such limitations (e.g., an 80-character input string is a reasonable standard).

Out-string is the complementary device to in-string; it outputs lists of strings. Out-string can be thought of as a line printer that can print an arbitrary number of lines, each of arbitrary length.

Block display is the virtual device that most nearly represents the CRT display terminal. It is defined as a set of fields, where each field is either a string, a segment, or another block display.

The third class of Level 4 protocols, the Virtual User Protocols, is based on the virtual user concept.

A *virtual user* (VU) is a process (which may "own" an external device such as a CRT terminal display and keyboard) capable of interacting with other more general POCCNET processes to simulate a standard interactive human user. The VU process abstracts away the characteristics of real users, replacing them with specifications of their inputs and outputs.

Every VU possesses at least two standard ports, invariably named IN and OUT. The VU also has three predefined subregions accessible through the IN port, whose standard names are PROMPT, ERROR, and INFO. These names reflect the operational significance of these regions, as follows.

- Messages directed to PROMPT are requests for returned information; responses to PROMPT messages are returned via the OUT port.
- Messages directed to ERROR indicate that the previous response from the VU is in error and must be corrected (the previous PROMPT still stands).
- Messages (called *info-blocks*) directed to INFO contain information that the VU may use during the formulation of responses to subsequent PROMPT or ERROR messages (e.g., a menu); info-blocks do not necessarily elicit responses from the VU.

The VU protocols do not specify the meaning associated with PROMPT, ERROR, or INFO messages or the responses to these messages from the VU (that would be for Level 5 protocols); they specify only the permissible order of transmission and reception.

Conceptually the VU provides the means for a general POCCNET process to obtain data or commands interactively; that is, the initiating process solicits a RESPONSE from the VU by means of a PROMPT message; when the RESPONSE is received, it is analyzed by the initiating process. If this response cannot be used directly or if it is incorrect in some sense, the initiating process indicates this to the VU by means of an ERROR message. The VU analyzes the ERROR message and reformulates and returns another RESPONSE. When the RESPONSE is acceptable, the initiating process PROMPT's for further messages that are in turn subject to emendation via ERROR/RESPONSE sequences. The INFO block is used for two-dimensional interaction with the VU, such as for menus* and lightpen selections.

A VU provides an interface between a protocol Level 5 human user and an application program executing on POCCNET host computer. By defining standard operational procedures, some of the human user's tasks can be automated. This is done by coding the VU responses to the application program in a standard Level 5 language. Then, instead of requiring the human user to be physically present, his *responses* can be taken from the predefined procedure file. This *surrogate* VU cannot be distinguished from the real thing by the application, except by an inappropriate or unexpected response. The application program would then issue an ERROR message to the VU, which in the case of an automated surrogate would suspend procedure execution and alert a human operator or execute a contingency procedure.

POCCNET user level protocols (Level 5).   Given the Level 4 system resources, Level 5 defines the exchanges between users of these resources. These exchanges relate principally to the data expected by the user of the resources: a record read from a file, the information displayed on a CRT screen, the dialogue with a conversational virtual user, and the results of a distributed computational process.

---

*Display menus are commonly used to search a data base using a CRT display. A menu can be visualized as a table of contents. When an item is selected from the menu, a lower level menu is displayed describing the selected item in more detail. From this menu, in turn, an even more detailed description can be retrieved, etc.

Level 5 contains user data creation, user level security and end-to-end interaction coordination. Level 5 would tend to be unique to each user group with a limited degree of standardization (i.e., in a mission-oriented network such as an airline reservation system, many of the network-wide services would lie at Level 5).

Communication at the user level of POCCNET is carried out between two processes communicating in a mutually acceptable language. If they want to jabber at each other in a language that is incomprehensible to anyone else (e.g., encrypted messages), they are free to do so. On the other hand, they are encouraged to adhere to a standard syntax and semantics for communicating among themselves, and they are required to do so when communicating with system processes (systems supervisors, data-base managers).

The System Test and Operation Language (STOL) is a specification of a standard syntax and some semantics, but its real power, as in English, is in expandability. As new communication capabilities at the user level are required, users can agree on a dialect of STOL extensions to suit their individual needs. POCCNET, as a system, can expand its capabilities by adding sentences to STOL for common functions provided on more than one system.

The standard STOL syntax has been defined, as well as a set of standard STOL statements for common space payload applications. POCCNET network control directives, network job control language (JCL), and network interprocess communication (IPC) are also expected to be accomplished via user commands to Level 4 in the form of STOL directives.

For example, a user process would use STOL to issue a CONNECT directive to a remote system, define JCL or invoke a predefined procedure on that system, or start up another user process on the remote system. It would then CONNECT to the remote process and begin exhanging user level messages with it. A set of STOL IPC primitives would also be available for synchronizing the execution of remote processes.

The STOL requirements for network user communications, data access, process creation, and control are specified to be compatible with POCCNET host operating systems capabilities. These capabilities are added to STOL as simple extensions of the language.

6.4.3 Error-Handling Philosophy

The design goal of POCCNET was to achieve a mean-time-between-failures (MTBF) of many thousand hours, with a fail-soft capability for the PMP subnetwork (see Figure 6-18). The worst possible single failure should not disconnect more than 10% of the host computers. In fact, it was postulated that if a worst case failure in the PMP subnetwork could disconnect 10% of the host computers when there are 100 host computers in the POCCNET, that same failure could only disconnect 5% of the computers when there are 200 host computers (in the late 1980's or early 1990's).*

*POCCNET Systems Definition Phase Study Report, Appendix 6A, "Inter-Process Communication (IPC) Requirements Analysis," Goddard Space Flight Center, Greenbelt, Md., January 1978.

The POCCNET error-handling philosophy is based on a combination of performance and system status monitoring and fault detection and isolation capabilities. Once a fault area has been pinpointed, bypass procedures will be initiated.

As mentioned earlier, the Data Operation Control Center (DOCC) configures the subnetwork resources. Canned procedures for configuring normal and alternate POCCs and for connecting and disconnecting various devices are defined and stored in the DOCC AP. In case a DOCC AP fails, a standby backup software system, stored in a partition established in a separate data-base storage AP, is used.

The actual virtual channel configuration is also verified by the DOCC on a regular basis, as shown in Figure 6-24. Regular configuration checks are performed for checkpointing purposes and to compare an actual configuration to scheduled configurations. Also, any changes in device status due to hardware or software faults are reported to the DOCC as they occur. The status of the complete set of POCCNET resources are maintained in a DOCC status table.

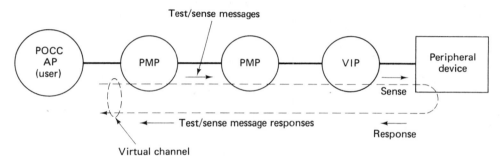

Figure 6-24 Resource assurance test/sense messages are regularly transmitted over virtual channels to verify a connection over a virtual channel.

Faults are detected either through status monitoring or from a fault indication. Fault indications are also provided internally in the PMP subnetwork where a PMP is able to detect the failure of a neighboring PMP when the latter is not transmitting a valid sequence of idle patterns, data, etc., or if a message has been retransmitted three times without a response.

These fault conditions are reported to the DOCC, which then calculates routing paths around the failure and notifies all involved PMP's of the change.

The DOCC will also verify the effect of a fault on the users. If the fault is not catastrophic, the users may prefer to continue in a degraded mode to complete an operation that is in progress.

Fault isolation procedures and tools are used to identify a fault further. Maintenance procedures may be used at this point to correct the problem either by a software command or by physical replacement of a failed unit.

6.4.4 System Advantages/Disadvantages

The system requirements are, if possible, even broader for the POCCNET than they are for the Ford Motor Company LNA. Both are, however, designed to handle a very large number of micros and minis and both are based on a highly structured protocol scheme. The POCCNET approach is probably less attractive when only a limited number of computers are internetted.

The POCCNET subnetwork approach, although more costly, may provide higher fail-soft capability than the LNA, where a cable failure is catastrophic to the system as a whole. Although the cable bus is distance limited, the LNA overcomes this limitation using gateways (also used in POCCNET).

6.5 A SIGNAL PROCESSING SYSTEM DESIGN BASED ON MULTIPLE MINICOMPUTERS

The Bank of America system, the Ford Motor Company LNA, and the NASA POCCNET are examples of approaches taken in developing large distributed networks of micro- and minicomputers. These descriptions included tradeoffs, approaches to interconnecting the computers, and error-handling philosophy as discussed in Chapter 2. They also discuss variations to the hierarchical protocol layering described in Chapter 3. The fourth system description illustrates the approach taken by TRW in designing a small (three minicomputer) distributed system based on existing, off-the-shelf hardware. The description includes an illustration of the design methodology discussed in Chapter 5 (see Figure 5-1), with emphasis on data flow, process interaction (Section 5.4), system deadlock (Section 5.7.2), deadlock elimination, design implementation, and system test. The distributed signal processing system development is an attempt by TRW to build an "intellectually manageable" system with no synchronization or mutual exclusion problems, to avoid deadlock situations and to provide the ability to move functions from one processor to another with no function code modifications.

In contrast to the three previous applications examples, the distributed signal processing system has been developed for experimental purposes. The development of this system and the supporting technology was spearheaded by P. Brinch Hansen of the University of Southern California and Dennis Heimbigner, Roger Vossler, and Frank Stepczyk of TRW Defense and Space Systems Group.*

6.5.1 System Requirements

The system requirements were rather general in nature. An existing signal processing system, which exhibited synchronization and deadlock problems and which did not run very long without producing time-dependent errors, had to be improved upon.

*Frank Stepczyk, "A Case Study in Real-Time Distributed Processing Design," Computer System Application Conference, IEEE, Chicago, Ill., Nov. 13, 1978.

306

It was also impossible to study alternate multiprocess decompositions without a major system rewrite for each decomposition. To understand the system requirements and subsequent redesign based on distributed processing, a brief overview is given of the original, centralized, signal processing implementation. Two Digital Equipment Corporation PDP-11's were used to process a set of signal processing Fortran-written algorithms that performed quality measurements of signals in a low signal-to-noise-ratio environment and classified these signals based on their internal characteristics. (Signal processing and analysis is useful in a multitude of both commercial and military applications. It is, for instance, used by Ford Motor Company in the LNA to analyze acoustic signals from drill presses to determine when drill bits are worn out and must be replaced. Signal processing is also used in sonar applications to analyze signal patterns emitted by submarines and ships.) Certain signal processing systems may use hardwired preprocessors that accept the *raw* signal(s) and perform matched filtering.* Such a preprocessor, the SPS-81 signal processor, was used in the original system, as shown in Figure 6-25.

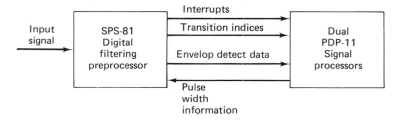

Figure 6-25 Block diagram of original signal processing system.

Each signal input to the signal measurement algorithms in the PDP-11's had two forms. Its first form was that of a digitized signal (ED) that had undergone bandpass filtering and envelope detection in the SPS-81.

The second form of the signal (PMF) was the ED signal above, which had, in addition, undergone matched filtering in the SPS-81 with respect to the current minimum pulse width.

A detailed functional view of the PDP-11 based algorithms and I/O signals is shown in Figure 6-26, where the input (PMF and ED) are two forms of only one signal.

The MS routine formed the mark-to-space transition indices (MST) in the Pulse Match Filtered (PMF) data and sent these indices to PWCON. When the output buffer of the MS routine was filled, the data was sent to the PWCON routine. PWCON performed pulse width and confidence measurements using the signal-dependent thresholds. It used the mark space indices to search the Envelope Detect (ED) data

---

*The signal-to-noise ratio can be maximized using the so-called *matched filter* in cases where signal information is carried only by the absence or presence of a signal pulse and where the signal shape is of secondary importance (see Mischa Schwartz, *Information, Transmission, Modulation, and Noise*, McGraw-Hill Book Co., New York, 1959.)

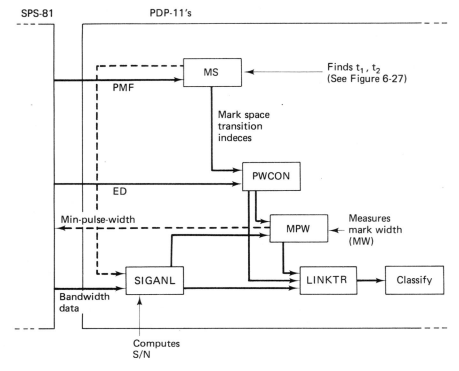

Figure 6-26 Input-Output to and from PDP-11 based signal processing algorithms where

$$PMF = \text{Pulse Match Filtered Signal}$$
$$ED = \text{Envelope Detected Signal}$$
$$MS = \text{Mark Space}$$
$$PWCON = \text{Pulse Width Confidence}$$
$$MPW = \text{Minimum Pulse Duration}$$
$$SIGANL = \text{Signal Analysis}$$
$$LINKTR = \text{Bus Transmission}$$

to compute the pulse widths. Figure 6-27 shows the relationships of the PMF and ED data.

The reason that both PMF and ED data were used was that when operating in a low signal-to-noise environment the PMF data could better reflect a signal lower down in noise. The output of PWCON went to the CLASSIFY routine by way of bus transmission routine called LINKTR. The CLASSIFY routine, which resided on a separate PDP-11, sorted the pulse widths into segments and compared their signatures for the purpose of classifying the signal. The MPW routine received duration measurement data from PWCON and computed new minimum pulse widths, if necessary. This pulse width information was fed back to a pulse width matched filter function in the digital preprocessor (SPS-81).

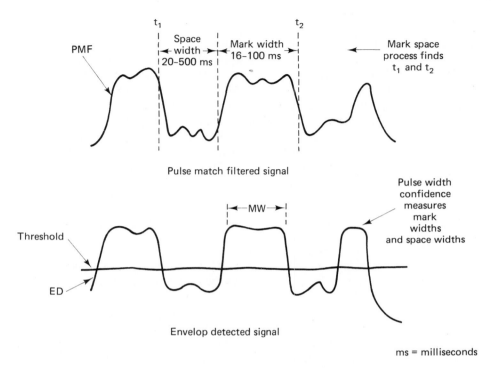

Figure 6-27 Relationship between the PMF and ED data, where MS shown in Figure 6-26 finds t_1 and t_2 and PWCON measures mark width (MW). (The "mark" or time from t_1 to t_2 ranges from 20 to 500 msec and the pulse peak amplitude width of PMF ranges from 16 to 100 msec.)

The SIGANL routine computed signal-to-noise ratios every 3 sec. It received frequency change information (FREQ) from the SPS-81 and output signal/noise information to the CLASSIFY module both through the LINKTR module and the MPW module.

Additional routines included a scheduler, an operator command interpreter, and various initialization routines.

All the major input data to the signal processing algorithms (PMF, ED, FREQ) were triple buffered by the SPS-81. An interrupt occurred after each buffer was filled by the SPS-81. MS, PWCON, PMF, LINKTR, and SIGANL were run one at a time under control of an event driven scheduler. The filling of a buffer caused the buffer to be placed on a buffer queue. A subsequent table lookup (signal function table) resulted in the proper next function(s) for processing the full buffer to be placed on a function queue. The next task to be executed was determined by priority and First-in/First-out (FIFO) examination of the function queue.

The original signal processing routines, except the CLASSIFY routine, were implemented in Fortran and macro-assembler to run with the Digital Equipment

Corp. (DEC) RSX-11S operating system. These four modules were combined into one task as separate subroutines with large common blocks for communication and control. In addition to the input-output buffers, parameter buffers and auxiliary buffers were used. Buffer control was part of the application code. The only performance requirements for the signal processing application was that the first PDP-11 processor had to accept 259 words of data from the SPS-81 processor every second for each signal. The SPS-81 could not be prevented from writing into PDP-11 memory nor could its interrupts be disabled. Therefore, the most important scheduling factor was not to let the SPS-81 output cause buffer overflow. The size of the signal processing code and data including the RSX-11S operating system was approximately 16,000 words; 4000 of these words were attributed to DEC's RSX-11S.

6.5.2 Overall Design Approach

The overall design approach adhered to the following three major guidelines:

1. The provision of structure and discipline in an environment where many concurrent tasks are being performed. It was felt by the design team that the form and structure of a language plays the dominant role in the development of a reliable, well-structured, real-time distributed system. Concurrent Pascal* was, therefore, selected as the implementation language since it has been shown that its constructs and structure worked well in developing structured and reliable systems in a single computer, concurrent environment.† It was felt by the developers of the distributed signal processing system that these same constructs would also be valuable in a distributed minicomputer environment.
2. A ring-type system would offer a high degree of flexibility with limited software complexity in its communication's capability since the routing is relatively simple. The configuration used was, therefore, based on three Digital Equipment Corp. PDP-11's connected via DA11B bus links, as shown in Figure 6-28. The bus links were used unidirectionally, giving the configuration a ring-like appearance.
3. An application system would be constructed rather than one general-purpose, real-time operating system with different applications programs. It was felt by the designers of this system that there is too much emphasis on building large real-time subsystems on top of existing vendor operating systems. Where the vendor operating system does not provide the desired capabilities, much of the operating system is either bypassed or significantly altered. It was also felt that the argument that it takes too long to build the complete system (operating system plus applications) is no longer valid when one utilizes a high-level real-time system language for dedicated applications. For example,

---

*P. Brinch Hansen, *The Architecture of Concurrent Programs*, Prentice-Hall, Inc. Englewood Cliffs, N.J., 1977.

†P. Brinch Hansen, "Experience with Modular Concurrent Programming," IEEE Transaction on Software Engineering, March 1977.

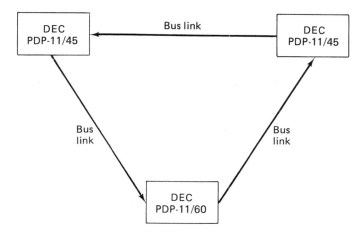

Figure 6-28 Interconnect scheme for the TRW experimental signal processing system.

the signal processing system that was to be implemented did not need the use of a file manager; however, the file system along with associated utilities is a major part of many existing vendor supplied operating systems.

The design methodology formulated by the system design team resembles to a great extent the design approach described in Chapter 5. It was based on (1) Process Identification, (2) Process Interaction and (3) Testing and Process Reassignment.

Given the system requirements, the identification of logical processes was performed. What constituted a process depended on such items as the application's functional entities, the type of algorithms involved, amount of potential parallelism, and the system support functions. There were no assumptions made regarding the exact number of processors at this stage other than perhaps knowing whether there would be only a few (e.g., less than 4) or many (greater than 10). It was felt that the understanding of process input-output relations was key to successful distributed system design. A process interaction graph that shows the data flow characteristics was first formulated (see Section 5.4). Unfortunately, already at this point the detailed design of many of the processes had to be performed. The type and form of process communication and synchronization could not be precisely specified until the interactions of the parallel algorithms were understood.

Having characterized process interactions, an interprocess communication scheme was then formulated that would both guarantee the proper functioning of the system and meet the system performance requirements. Proper functioning meant that no synchronization, mutual exclusion, or deadlock problems would occur. Utilizing the MONITOR construct found in CONCURRENT PASCAL (Subsection 3.2.2) aided in solving synchronization and mutual exclusion problems. The major efforts at this stage were deadlock and performance prediction analyses. Deadlock problems could occur at all levels in the system from a system support process or MONITOR to an application process. It was felt that the precise specification of all process interaction was the key to understanding how to prevent deadlock.

Finally, when the distributed system was to be developed, the ability to test a distributed system on a single processor and the ability to test concurrency was needed.

The other design aspect at this stage was a simple means of assigning and reassigning process to different processors.

It was expected that the guidelines of Steps 1, 2, and 3 would be repeated several times, each step providing valuable feedback to the following step.

6.5.3 System Design

In restructuring the system into a distributed signal processing facility, the SPS-81 signal processor was omitted. At the time of the design, it was not clear how to include special-purpose processors such as the SPS-81 in a distributed environment since they could not support more general-purpose control. A tape recording of PMF and ED digital data obtained from the output of the SPS-81 was, therefore, used.

The following subsections describe the three design phases based on the earlier formulated design methodology.

Process identification. The first step in the redesign of the signal processing system for a distributed environment described above was to select the overall process partitioning strategy. It was decided to maintain the functional decomposition that characterized the original signal processing application. The next step was to identify concurrent processes. Singnal processing algorithms generally lack data-dependent control and the signal flow is characterized by a high degree of parallelism. It seemed that there was sufficient parallelism between the MS routine and the PWCON routine (see Figure 6-26) to warrant making them independent processes. PWCON could be measuring the width of an old mark while MS is looking for a new mark (see Figure 6-27). For a single channel, the amount of parallelism could be up to one mark width, or 100 msec. Communication overhead for sending the data from MS must be subtracted from this value to estimate the actual amount of parallelism.

The SIGANL and MPW routines were computed at intervals depending on either selected thresholds or at set time periods in case of SIGANL. It was decided to make them processes since they represent independent functions.

The "classify" function was designated as a single process. The LINKTR module was replaced by a process named DDP that buffers the pulse width and confidence data from the PWCON, SIGANL, and MPW functions into 16 word blocks, for input to the classify process. The SPS-81 processor function was replaced by an SPS process that read actual SPS-81 output data from tape and sent it to the appropriate signal process. The signal processing scheduler was eliminated. It was felt that the need for sophisticated scheduling would be drastically reduced in a distributed environment. It was estimated that the extreme case could amount to as many as one process per processor.

It was also felt that simple low-level scheduling of the kernel and the use of monitors would eliminate the need for a scheduler. The process data flow graph of the Distributed Signal Processing Application's function is shown in Figure 6-29.

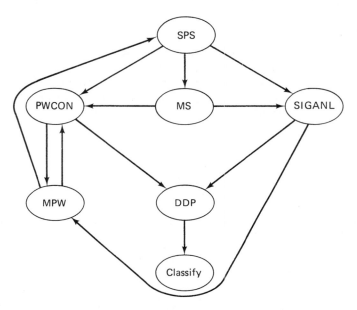

Figure 6-29   Process identification for Distributed Signal Processing System.

Process interaction.   Following process identification, the input-output relationships between processes were analyzed. This was accomplished by separating the control code from the application code. A large amount of code in the original signal processing algorithms was used to control buffers and set up buffer indices. In the new design, a separate interprocess communications scheme based on explicit message exchanges would perform message handling. One of the more difficult tasks turned out to be the separation of data private to each process and data shared between the processes. These difficulties were based on the fact that common blocks of data were extensively used throughout the original signal processing code.

Once these difficulties had been resolved, it turned out to be a relatively simple task to change the amount of data passed between processes such as MS and PWCON. In the original system, MS had to fill up an output buffer of MS indices before sending it to PWCON. This was no longer necessary in the new, distributed system design as MS could send an output to PWCON after finding an MST index.

Since the code for the processes was available from the original system design, the detailed design of the Distributed Signal Processing System's (DSPS's) processes could be performed rather quickly. It also provided a good understanding for exactly what form and type of communications were necessary between the processes.

In the first version of the DSPS, the MS process would not buffer its MST output data but, instead, send each index, when found.

The process interactions and characteristics of data communicated between the DSPS processes are shown in Figure 6-30. The encircled numbers on the interconnect lines are link numbers identifying virtual channels. The use of link numbers and virtual channels is explained in the following paragraphs.

Having characterized the process relationships, an interprocess communication (IPC) scheme was needed to implement the design and provide properties such as deadlock-free operation and system transparency to calling processes.

It was decided to use a Ring Net IPC developed by P. Brinch Hansen.* This would provide the ability to transmit fixed-length messages onto a virtual channel without the use of centralized control.

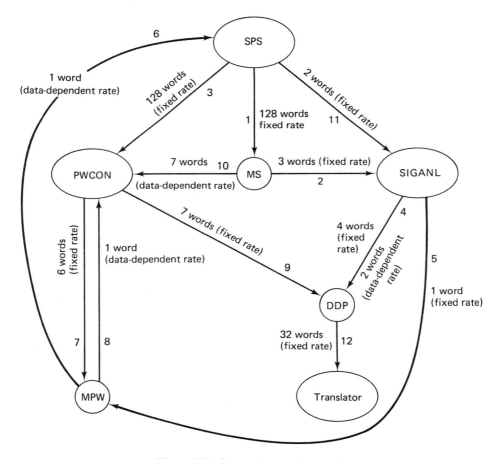

Figure 6-30 Process interaction graph.

*P. Brinch Hansen, "Network: A Multiprocessor Program," IEEE Computer Society Computer Software and Application Conference, November 1977.

A fixed number of virtual channels connecting a fixed number of processes was established at compilation time. These virtual channels were identified by unique link numbers that are shown on each of the links in Figure 6-30. Two of the most attractive features of the Ring Net above are that it is deadlock-free and well-structured. Its deadlock-free property was achieved by the facts that (1) a Send operation on a channel delays the calling process until another process performs a Receive operation on the same channel (and vice versa) and (2) each processor node contains message buffer slots equal to the maximum number of virtual channels $+$ 1. Its least attractive feature is that there is too much communication overhead for messages between processes at the same node. It was decided to have two IPC schemes but only a single-user protocol. In case the Receiver Process would be located at the same node as the Sender Process, a message would be processed by a Message Monitor IPC handler rather than Ring Net IPC handler.

It was also decided that the User Process would only issue Send and Receive messages including variable names of any data to be sent or received. This would make communications more understandable.

The handling of multiparameters and the decision on whether to use the Ring IPC scheme or Message Monitor IPC scheme was implemented by an abstract data-type class called NETWK. The process communication protocol was implemented in two hierarchical layers, as shown in Figure 6-31. The lowest layer consists of two IPC schemes: the Ring Net IPC scheme and the Message Monitor IPC scheme.

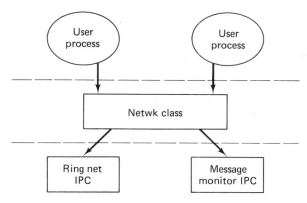

Figure 6-31 Protocol layers in the DSPS.

Testing and process reassignment.   The most difficult problem encountered in the test phase was system deadlock. As described in Subsection 5.7.2, system deadlock problems are usually caused by circular waiting. As shown in the process interaction graph in Figure 6-30, there are several circular chains of processes and cases where these are more than one input message to a process. Deadlock in the Distributed Signal Processing System could be caused by the allocation of message buffer resources.

The Ring Net IPC scheme provides a deadlock-free property at the internode or system level. A technique was still needed to eliminate deadlock at the user process level due to the circularities shown in Figure 6-30. An attempt was made to eliminate deadlock at the process level by incorporating a buffer in each node for sender messages. This buffer was set for different sizes at each node, depending on the maximum amount of messages sent by that node over a time interval; however, this approach made the system time-dependent.

Extreme differences in process run times were measured during system test, mostly due to the large time ratios between terminal and process speeds.

The system would deadlock at different times during testing depending on which of the processes would write to the terminal. Writing to the terminal for purposes of testing was not considered when the buffer sizes were computed for each node. Since it was not known where or how many terminal writes would be involved, it was decided that the creation of preventive or time-independent deadlock algorithms would be the only feasible solution to avoid system deadlocks. The two major problems associated with deadlock were thus the circularity and the nature of the data in the system.

As seen in Figure 6-30, the issue of circularity in which MPW sends data back to SPS and PWCON and SIGANL sends data to MPW had to be resolved. Deadlock problems can be created when a process may receive input messages from two or more different processes. The process could easily become blocked indefinitely waiting for input from one message buffer while another input message buffer would fill with items for reception. One drastic approach would have been to decompose any process with more than one input message buffer into several simpler concurrent processes until each process only had one input message buffer.

It was, however, determined that some other approach should be found.

The nature of the data was important in eliminating deadlock. A distinction was made between shared data and data that was transferred. Shared data had little or no directionality, a number of processes both accessed and altered it, and it had a larger lifetime than transferred data. Status information is an example of shared data. Transferred data had a definite directionality from the producer to the consumer, and its lifetime was relatively short, being processed and discarded soon after reception.

In order to arrive at a deadlock prevention scheme for the Distributed Signal Processing System, the nature of the data was looked at and it was felt that the following data were "shared" data:

- Minimum Pulse Width values from the MPW process to both the PWCON and SPS processes.
- Signal Noise ratio (from SIGANL process) to the DPP and MPW processes.
- Signal Average, Noise Average data from the SIGANL process to the DPP process.

The PWCON, SPS, DPP and MPW processes could still function adequately even if there was a delay in updating the shared data above.

The process interaction graph, shown in Figure 6-30, was, therefore, changed with the incorporation of four auxiliary processes (SPSA, PWCONA, MPWA, DDPA) with associated shared data monitors, as shown in Figure 6-32. The auxiliary

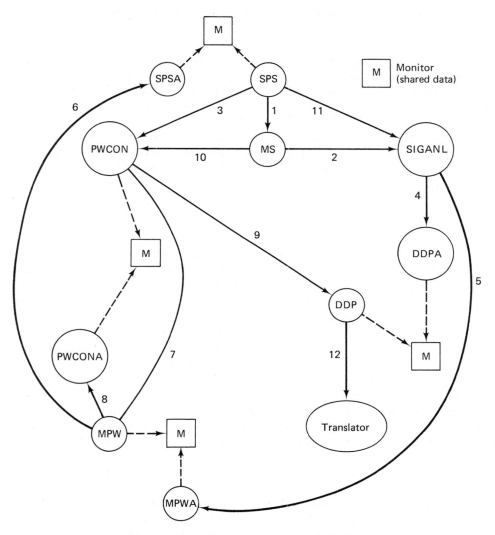

Figure 6-32   Final process interaction graph.

processes should reside on the same processors as their corresponding task process. As an example, SPS and SPSA should be on the same processor. The purpose of the auxiliary process was to provide the ability to utilize the monitor construct in a distributed processor environment.

The possibility of deadlock vanished in the SPS-PWCON-MS-SIGANL part of the graph (Figure 6-32) with the addition of a dummy message sent from MS to PWCON for certain cases. This guaranteed that MS would send one message to PWCON and SIGANL for each message it received from SPS. These processes were cyclically in lock step. The deadlock prevention techniques above also provided a time-independent solution to the deadlock problem.

Testing was accomplished bottom-up as each component was designed. Each component of the Ring Net IPC system underwent extensive testing. All the other system support components underwent individual tests. In testing the application code, a tape of SPS-81 signal output was obtained along with a listing of the output of the PWCON function. Also, a listing of the final output of the CLASSIFY function was obtained for this data. The processes (MS, PWCON, SIGANL, PMF, DDP) were tested first until accurate correspondence was achieved. Following this, the CLASSIFY process was tested. The final output matched the original version quite closely.

The two most difficult aspects of testing a distributed system, based on concurrent processes, were found to be

1. Testing the concurrency
2. Testing several nodes at the same time.

Testing the concurrency involved the use of a special scheduler/monitor and time process. It centered around testing the meaningful states of the monitors, since concurrency problems were related to the monitors and shared data. Once the proper operation of the monitors was known, the processes that used them could be treated as simple sequential programs.

It was concluded by the test team that testing a network was best done on a single processor since difficulties were encountered in synchronizing two or three processors and in obtaining their exclusive use. The test scheme was very simple with the use of the CONCURRENT PASCAL language. All Monitors, Classes, and Processes were system types. It was easy to create new instances of them. The Distributed Signal Processing System was tested by duplicating all the system support components and replacing the bus-link monitors by buffer monitors. The distributed nature of the system was tested utilizing two simulated nodes on one processor. When the system was actually put on three processors, no errors were found to occur.

The following procedure for various process/processor compositions and test runs was used:

A base copy of the Distributed Signal Processing System was maintained. Special update files were created called Mod Sets, which, when applied against the base system, created unique concurrent programs for each node in the cluster. To make a particular process/processor change, all that needed to be done was to have a unique channel INPSET and OUTSET for each node of the Distributed Signal Processing System. Consequently, only processes that would run on a particular processor needed to be initialized by means of an INIT command. The auxiliary processes had to reside on the same processor as their corresponding task process.

The INPSET channel numbers were the link numbers that were input to processes running in a particular processor. The OUTSET channel numbers were the link numbers that were output from processors on that same processor. As an example, consider a three-processor test run in which the process/processor decompositions are as shown in Figure 6-33.

Processor	Process	Channel Sets
1	SPS, SPSA, PMF, PMFA	INPSET = [5,6,7] OUTSET = [1,3,6,8,11]
2	MS, PWCON, PWCONA, SIGANL, DDP, DPPA	INPSET = [1,2,3,4,8,9,10,11] OUTSET = [2,4,5,7,9,10,12]
3	CLASSIFY	INPSET = [12] OUTSET = [ ] – NULL SET

Figure 6-33   Example of three-processor test run decomposition.

This is illustrated by Mod Set for Processor 1, as shown in Figure 6-34.

```
/MODSET: SIGNAL PROCESSING - PROCESSOR 1
/REPLACE 3,4
     SIGNAL PROCESSING PROGRAM
     FOR PROCESSOR 1
/ /
/REPLACE 1764,1765
INPSET:=[5,6,7];
OUTSET:=[1,3,6,8,11];
/ /
/INSERT 1772
INIT  SP(MX,CSET,TTY,INP,OUT,DOTLN1),
      SPA(MX,CSET,TTY,INP,OUT,DOTLN1),
      DT(MX,CSET,TTY,INP,OUT,SGNR),
      DTA(MX,CSET,TTY,INP,OUT,SGNR);
/ /
```

Figure 6-34   Mod Set for Processor 1.

The distributed signal processing base program was modified with the changes shown in this figure. Each of the processes had their own system support, IPC algorithms, and was self-scheduling. The three-processor tests were run and compared against a single processor version of the DSPS. It was found that the three-processor version was 2.3 times faster.

During the three-processor test, it took 137 sec to process all 323 records (259 words) from the SPS-81 input tape, signifying that three-processor version was handling data at 2.35 blocks (259 words) per second, whereas the only performance requirement for the original signal processing application was that it handle at least one block per second.

6.5.4 Conclusions

The following conclusions were arrived at in converting the original Signal Processing System into a distributed, concurrent system:

1. The Language Concurrent Pascal and its construct for concurrency proved invaluable in developing a coherent and reliable system.
2. The deadlock problem was of larger magnitude than originally anticipated.
3. The ability to construct a basic interprocess communication scheme was useful in solving the deadlock problem.
4. It is feasible to develop a multiminicomputer system where functions or processes can easily be moved from one processor to another with no function code modifications.
5. The principle of designing distributed real-time applications based on time-independent multiprograms contributed to the success of this design effort.

PROBLEMS

6-1 The Bank of America system described in Section 6.2 is a mix of interconnect structures, defined in Figure 5-25. Define the structures and list possible, alternative implementations based on a different set of multiple-interconnect schemes. Discuss alternate approaches based on performance, availability, reliability, fault tolerance, life-cycle cost, and modularity, using information provided in Chapter 5.

6-2 Compare the Ford LNA protocol structure with DECnet and NCS discussed in Chapter 3. What are the differences and similarities?

6-3 Do you agree with NASA's conclusions listed in Figure 6-17? Use information provided in Fig. 5-25 to substantiate/refute their claims.

6-4 List advantages/disadvantages of using DECnet in the NASA POCCNET.

6-5 Use the Exchange Function/Process Architecture Tree approach discussed in Chapter 5 to describe the TRW distributed signal processing system. What are the shortcomings/advantages of this approach over the one used by the TRW design team? What other configuration would be suitable for solving the distributed signal processing problem? Why?

6-6 What hardware and software test tools would you propose that would be suitable for failure analysis and detection in the four systems described in this chapter?

6-7 The capabilities of acquiring network addresses from the Ford Motor Company LNA system LOG process at the system process level is illustrated in the following diagram. Using information provided in Figures 6-5, 6-6, and 6-8, clarify each step in this process.

Datalogger	COM Processes	LOG Process
LOG1 = 1S1U2		LOG1 = *S1!
ASGN = *S1!		
QU MARY ATT $\longrightarrow$	*S1!;!S1U2;0W;data	
	$\longleftarrow$!;*;0A;	
		LOG1 = *S1U1
		ASGN = !S1U2
	$\longleftarrow$ p1S1U2;*!U1;1W;data	MARY LOCATION p1S1U2
	*;p1;1A; $\longrightarrow$	
LOG1 = p1S1U2		
QU JOHN		
LOCATION $\longrightarrow$	*S1U1;p1S1U2;2W;data	
	$\longleftarrow$ p1;*;2A;	
	$\longleftarrow$ p1S1U2;*!U1;3W;data	JOHN LOCATION p2S1U1
	*;p1;3A; $\longrightarrow$	
ASGN = p2S1U1		

7

Future Trends

7.1 INTRODUCTION

Several multimicro- and minicomputer system-related technologies are maturing to the point where they will greatly impact system design, development, and operation in the near future. These technologies encompass computer hardware and software as well as data communications. Very Large-Scale Integration (VLSI) is rapidly reducing the cost of processors while providing increased processing power. Concurrently, new storage devices have emerged such as magnetic bubble memories, charge coupled devices (CCD's), and Electronic Beam Addressable Memories (EBAM's). In the software area, new capabilities are being developed such as concurrent operating systems and distributed Data Base Management Systems (DBMS's). In the communications arena, the use of satellites for cost effectively moving data at very high rates over long distances will be feasible and, for short-haul cummunications, fiber optics links may replace conventional two- or four-wire and coaxial lines. The following sections describe these technologies and their impact on multimicro- and minicomputer system design. Finally, areas requiring further research are defined.

7.2 HARDWARE TECHNOLOGY

Semiconductor technology as a whole has made rapid advances in the past and that pace is by no means slowing down. It is clear that the technological acceleration cannot continue unabated forever. As long as we are several orders of magnitude away from the theoretical limit, however, progress will likely continue at the rate shown in

322

Figure 7-1. It has been proposed that the practical limit for Metal-Oxide Semiconductor (MOS) technology for a 5 × 5 cm² chip is a complexity of about 100 million gates. We are obviously very far from this practical limit.

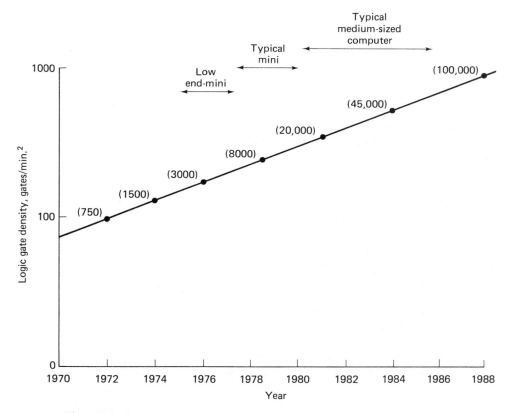

Figure 7-1 Past and predicted logic density increase versus time for microprocessor chip. It is assumed that chip size will increase to 100 mm² by 1988. Numbers in brackets denote gate complexity (i.e., number of gates on a single chip). The first-generation (4-bit) microprocessor chip contained 750 gates. The second-generation (8-bit) microprocessor chip contained some 1500 gates. The third-generation (16-bit) microprocessor contained up to 8000 gates (i.e., TI TMS/SBP9900, Zilog 2800, etc.). (From: Federico Faggin, "How VLSI Impacts Computer Architecture." Reprinted with permission from *IEEE Spectrum*, May 1978.)

Logic circuitry was available in small-scale and medium-scale integration (SSI and MSI) packages and went in the early 1970's on to large-scale integration (LSI). New manufacturing technologies and fabrication techniques brought about drastic changes to semiconductor chip density, speed, power consumption, and the very-large-scale integrated circuits (VLSI).

7.2.1 Microprocessor Technology

These integrated circuits are either sold as separate chips or packaged on printed circuit (PC) boards. These boards are fairly general-purpose computer systems containing a microprocessor, some read/write random access memory (RAM), some permanent read-only memory (ROM), and some type of input-output interface, usually a serial interface and some parallel I/O lines. These PC boards do not include power supplies or switches.

The most commonly available word size for microcomputer boards was 8 bits in the late 1970's, however, both 4- and 16-bit boards were available. It is expected that 32-bit boards will be available in the early-to-mid 1980's. The most flexible instruction sets often come with 16-bit processors since they are, in most cases, reduced versions of available minicomputers (i.e., DEC LSI-11/23, Computer Automation LSI 4/10, Data General microNova, Hewlett Packard 2108K, Texas Instruments TM 990/100M, etc.).

For multimicroprocessor applications, microprocessors with a good mix of I/0 commands in their repertoire should be used. Commands such as bit or byte setting and incrementing or decrementing of data at the port are useful to the system designer. For high-performance applications (two to five times that of MOS μP's), boards using bipolar bit-slice technology are preferable. Bit-slice organization is a multichip arrangement in which elements of the microprocessor are divided among several identical modular chips that can be linked in parallel. The bit slice is available in 2-, 4-, and 8-bit sections. These sections may be linked in parallel to process word lengths of 4, 8, 12, 16, 32 (etc.) bits. This potential for building any word length desired can be advantageous over the set word length of the monolithic processor. Power consumption for bit-sliced processors is high, however, whereas monolithic processors are power optimized for a specific word length (in addition to using the slower but also less power-consuming MOS technology). It has been suggested by Faggin* that future processor development will proceed along two paths: The traditional one with increased number of functions added to a chip and increased chip speed performance (i.e., the chip will eventually include the capabilities of a complete microprocessor board with CPU, memory, and I/O; see Figure 7-2). The other path will entail a reorganization of the processor logic for multichip parallel-operating systems (i.e., the multimicroprocessor system). The future microprocessor must include features that make it possible to use it as a building block in a shared-bus environment. This future microprocessor board would, hence, be self-contained in terms of bus interface logic and "pluggable" to a serial or parallel bus.

7.2.2 Storage Technology

Progress similar to that in packaged logic is being experienced in the memory and storage areas of computer technology. Progress in semiconductors in terms of density (Figure 7-3), performance, and cost has resulted in the displacement of magne-

*Federico Faggin, "How VLSI Impacts Computer Architecture," *IEEE Spectrum*, May 1978.

As Circuit Density Increases, The Following Products Can Be Fabricated:					
Microprocessors		*1979*	*1981*	*1983*	*1985*
ROM Dominant	ROM RAM	4 Kbytes 256 bytes	16 Kbytes 1 Kbyte	60 Kbytes 4 Kbytes	— —
RAM Dominant	ROM RAM	128 bytes 512 bytes	128 bytes 2 bytes	128 bytes 8 Kbytes	128 bytes 32 Kbytes
Relative System Speed		1.5X	2X	4X	5X

Figure 7-2   Projection of microcomputer capabilities (From: "New Single-board 16-bit Chips May Soon Be Challenged by 16-bit Chips," Dave Bursky. Reprinted with permission *Electronic Design*, Vol. 26, No. 11, May 24, 1978, copyright Hayden Publishing Co., Inc. 1978.)

tic cores as the major memory technology. The most widely used technologies for main memory applications are bipolar and MOS. The most recent addition of semiconductor memory technology is the charge coupled device (CCD) memory. Other types of technologies emerging are magnetic bubble memories and electronic beam addressable memories (EBAM). Cryoelectronic memories are still in the research phase but may become the predominant technology in the more distant future.

The most significant differences among bipolar, MOS, and CCD devices are speed, power dissipation, density, and cost. Both MOS and bipolar memories are available with various storage capabilities; Random Access Memory (RAM), Read Only Memory (ROM), Programmable ROM (PROM), Erasable PROM (EPROM), and Electrically Alterable ROM (EAROM). The label RAM is very misleading in that ROM's also are random access devices.

The distinguishing feature of RAM is its read/write capability. Data storage in all semiconductor read/write memories is volatile (i.e., information is lost when power is removed). Most bipolar RAM's operate statically, whereas many MOS RAM's are dynamic, requiring periodic refresh. This refresh necessitates external support circuitry, not necessary with static RAM's. Dynamic chips occupy less space than do static chips of equal memory capacity; and dynamic chips require less power since they do not require the constant power that must be supplied static RAM's. Static RAM's generally are more expensive than dynamic RAM's.

ROM's are nonvolatile and best suited for systems produced in large volume, where tooling charge for a unique fixed-bit pattern mask is relatively small on a percent basis and is counterbalanced by the economics of batch processing.

Information is stored in a PROM after processing and packaging of a system has been completed. PROM's are usually the best choice in low-volume production and in systems having limited useful life, where some degree of system tailoring is required for each installation.

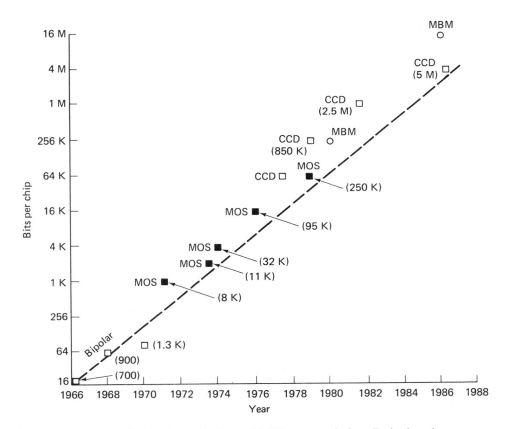

Figure 7-3 Bit densities of bipolar and MOS memory devices. Projection also includes magnetic bubble memories and charge coupled device memories. Numbers in brackets denote bit density per square centimeter. (Note that densities for core memories in 1960's were up to 250 bits/cm².) (From: Erich Block and Dom Galage, "Component Progress: Its Effect on High-Speed Computer Architecture and Machine Organization," *Computer*, April 1978; Dean Toombs, "An Update: CCD and Bubble Memories," Copyright by The Institute of Electrical and Electronic Engineers, Inc. Reprinted with permission from *IEEE Spectrum*, April 1978.)

EPROM's are MOS/PROM's that can be erased using ultra violet radiation and reprogrammed, whereas bipolar PROM's cannot be modified.

EAROM's have the advantage of alterability without the necessity of erasing the entire array.

These programmable erasable memories are useful in developmental systems where design changes are not uncommon and where short turnaround times are essential. Metal-Oxide Semiconductor memories (MOS) are the most commonly used semiconductor memories. MOS leads bipolar devices in both high-density and low-power dissipation. MOS RAM's vary in access times from 50 nsec to 1 sec. This contrasts with bipolar RAM's that can operate with access times below 100 nsec. Compared to MOS memory densities (see Figure 7-3; 64 Kbits/chip in 1979), densities for bipolar devices range from 64 to 1024 bits per chip. Certain bipolar technologies will make it possible, however, to reach complexities of 2K to 10K bits per chip.

The use of lower performance MOS memories in high-performance minicomputer systems has been made possible through the use of the buffer or cache memory concept, thus providing major improvements in memory access time. The cache acts efficiently as a speed-matching device between the high-performance logic circuits in the processor and the lower performance, MOS-based main memory. The cache is obviously, due to its comparatively high cost, extremely small in terms of memory capacity compared to main memory (see Chapter 4, General Automation 16/550 computer architecture).

Charge Coupled Devices (CCD) are another form of semiconductor memory technology. Although the first commercially available 64-Kbit CCD was announced only in 1977, it has characteristics that make it look promising for the future. It bridges the speed and capacity gap between other semiconductor RAM's and magnetic bulk storage such as cassette tapes and floppy disks. CCD's have reduced power consumption also. This is due to the fact that CCD components do not dissipate DC power, leaving total power consumed frequency-dependent.* Lower power, plus the fact that CCD's are solid-state devices, increases the reliability of chips. Some of the disadvantages of CCD's are that CCD's are volatile-type memories, and since they rely on shifting charge from one location to the next in order, they are limited to serial access memory applications.

CCD's fit into special application areas, however, where RAM's are overqualified and costly and where magnetic bulk memories are too large or unreliable to be cost-effective. Furthermore, CCD's have other advantages over head-per-track discs such as 10–50 times faster speeds, the use of solid-state technology, and multiple rather than single "tracks." CCD's may also be of use in telecommunications as hardware-integrated delay lines, filters, and memories. Although magnetic bubble memories (MBM) have been a reality in the laboratory since as far back as 1969, they did not appear on the memory market until in the late 1970's.

Magnetic bubble memories are best suited for use in bulk and auxiliary storage systems. Initial applications have been in microcomputer storage. MBM's are cost competitive with small floppy disks. MBM's have high packing density, unlike CCD's are nonvolatile, have start and stop capability, and can be mounted on the same PC board as the CPU. Also, the manufacturing technology used for production of bubble memory chips is similar to that of semiconductor devices. But, because MBM's are serial devices, and because drive frequency is limited, MBM's have low data-transfer rates and relatively long access times. It is expected that chip capacity for MBM's

---

*Charge Coupled Devices, as their name implies, store information in the form of capacitive charge. This charge decays (or "leaks" out) requiring periodic refresh. The refresh must be performed at certain frequencies at which time power is consumed.

will approximately double every year until 1985–87, when capacity will have reached 16 Mbits per chip (see Figure 7-3).

Electronic beam addressable memories (EBAMS) use the concept of an electron beam accessing a structureless MOS chip. Information is stored in the form of electrical charges. This is accomplished by directing an electron beam of sufficient energy at a storage site that is positively biased. Similarly, erasure of information storage can be accomplished by negatively biasing the metal oxide. Detection of information is achieved by measuring the current flow which results when the electron beam is allowed to strike the storage site which is held at zero bias. The lack of structure is characterized by the fact that bit densities are determined by electron beam size, the deflection mechanism, and the internal characteristics of the memory plane. It is not dependent on the resolution with which bit sites can be fabricated. In the late 1970's, densities of the order of 10^7 bits/in^2. could be achieved.

Access to a memory location involves deflection of the electron beam to the desired memory location. The access time varies from a few to about 30 μsec. Data transfer rates are on the order of 10 Mbps. Other characteristics of EBAMs include low power consumption, extremely low cost, nonvolatility for extended periods of time, insensities to temperature variations, and mechanical ruggedness.

MBM, EBAM, and CCD characteristics are compared in Figure 7-4.

One rather unsual type of microelectronic memory is the superconductive tunnel junction, or cryoelectronic memory. This memory has some very desirable features but also presents difficult problems. It can be switched in 50 to 100 psec* with only 7-nsec memory-cell access times. It also consumes three or four orders of magnitude less power than high-speed transistor circuits. Because of the low power dissipation, circuits can be packed more densely without heating problems. This, in turn, causes large systems signal propagation times to be reduced because shorter interconnect lines are possible. Since cryogenic cells are superconducting, not only is storage nonvolatile, but no power is required in the quiescent state.

Dissipation for a fully populated 16K chip at maximum repetition rate will be only 40 μW. It is estimated by IBM that a full 16-Kbit chip will provide 15-nsec access time and 30-nsec read/write cycle time.

On the negative side, operating tunnel junctions require near 0°K temperature. New packaging and interconnection techniques are needed to achieve the high packing density required for minimum interconnection delays. Also, mechanical stresses generated by differing thermal-expansion coefficients must be dealt with in order to avoid damage when the temperature is reduced from room temperature to nearly absolute zero. Furthermore, a 2-in. cryogenic cube housing several Mbytes of memory and a processor unit creates obstacles; researchers continue to wrestle with interfacing. Fiber optics and LED's may provide the answer. The 1980's will provide a developmental period for cryogenic memories, but they will probably not become available for many years.

*Paul Snigier, "IBM's Search for the Ultimate Computer," *Digital Design*, May 1978.

Memory Characteristics	Magnetic Bubble Memory	Electron Beam Addressable Memory	Charge Coupled Device Memory
Storage Representation	Magnetic domain	Electrical charge	Electrical charge
Bit Density	2×10^6 Bits/in.^{2}	10^7 Bits/in.^{2}	10^6 Bits/in.^{2}
Access Mode	Sequential	Quasi-random	Sequential or block addressable
Access Time	0.5–10 msec	10–20 μsec	Sequential: 5–50 μsec Block access: 5 μsec
Transfer Rate	100–500 Kbps	4–8 Mbps per tube	1–10 Mbps
Power Per Bit (During Memory Operation)	0.4 μW	10 μW	50 μW
Cost Per Bit (1978)	0.2¢	0.005¢	0.05¢
Largest Chip Size Fabricated (1978)	250 Kbit (Texas Instruments, Rockwell International!)	120 Mbits per tube 32 (CDC)	64 Kbit (Mnemonics)
Operational Temperature Range	0–50°C	0–50°C	−10° to 80°C
Susceptibility to Electromagnetic Emanations	Can be shielded	Can be shielded	Can be shielded
Susceptibility to Power Surges	Power must be filtered	Power must be filtered	Power must be filtered

Figure 7-4 Characteristics of MBM's, EBAM's, and CCD's (David K. Hsiao and Stuart E. Madnick, "Database Machine Architecture in the Context of Information Technology Evolution," Proceedings International Conference on Very Large Data Bases, October 1977, pp. 63–84. Also, discussions with Don Smith CDC's Micro Bit Division, Lexington, Mass., and Jerold Cox, Texas Instruments Components Division, Dallas, Texas.)

7.3 COMMUNICATIONS AND INTERCONNECT TECHNOLOGY

The traditional approaches to interconnect computers is based on the use of either serial or parallel links. For tightly coupled systems (shared memory) where maximum distances between transmitters and receivers are in the tens of meters range, parallel cables are typically used with 8, 16, or 32 bits for data and an equal or perhaps larger number of bits for parity check and control lines.

Loosely coupled systems use either parallel cable (see Chapter 1, CAMAC and IEEE-488 Standards), two- or four-wire twisted pairs or coaxial cable. Where a large number of drops (10 or more) are required, discontinuities and impedance mismatch will rapidly degrade the signal-to-noise ratio to a point where high error rates may be encountered (more than 10^{-5}). For limited-distance, point-to-point communications, twisted wire pairs may be used in conjunction with base-band modems (signal amplifiers and receivers). Base-band modems are available, off the shelf, from a number of manufacturers (International Communications Corporation, Codex, Prentice, Tran, Astrocom, etc.) ranging from $750 to $1000 depending on unique features. Data rates achievable using base-band modems are typically in the 2.4- to 19.2-Kbps range. Cable lengths are typically limited to a maximum of 2000 ft (600 m).

For longer distances (i.e., kilometers) coaxial cable must generally be used. For long-haul communications, voice grade terrestrial lines are most commonly used with maximum data rates of 9600 bps. These traditional interconnect methods based on coaxial links or twisted pairs of wires are challenged by fiber optics links for short-haul communications and radio and satellite links for long-haul communications. These new technologies are described in greater detail in the following subsections.

7.3.1 Fiber Optics Technology

Both fiber optics and satellite links offer some unique advantages as well as posing some constraints compared to the more traditional interconnect media such as copper wire and other long-haul terrestrial links.

Optical fibers used in communications are small—typically 0.005 in. in diameter—and lightweight. Data rates as high as 1 gigabit/-sec (1000 Mbps) have been demonstrated.

Furthermore, optical fibers do not conduct electricity and are, therefore, unaffected by electromagnetic interference (lightning can strike the cable without disturbing communications). Also, since light does not radiate through the cable, cross talk—the unwanted coupling of signals from one channel to another—does not occur.

The danger of electrical shorts between conductors is gone, and should the fiber optic cable suddenly be immersed in water from an unexpected flood, the signals will continue to propagate unhampered.

Optical fibers are still more expensive than copper wires, but the price has been declining. So has their high attenuation characteristic, to the point where the losses are now much less than for many standard copper conductors, particularly at high frequencies.

Off-the-shelf fiber optic cable available in 1977 demonstrated losses in the 6-dB*/km range.† Losses as low as 0.5 dB/km have been demonstrated under laboratory conditions.

Shown in Figure 7-5 are three basic types of optical fibers in use today. The first type is known as single-mode step-index fiber. Here the core diameter is extremely small and only a single optical mode is sustained. Practical difficulties of coupling energy into a single propagating mode have prevented acceptance of this type of fiber.

The multimode step-index fiber allows a larger number of propagation modes. This type is bandwidth-limited for long distances.

A third type, the multimode, graded index fiber combines the advantages of both the previous types. In this fiber, the index falls off gradually from the center of the fiber

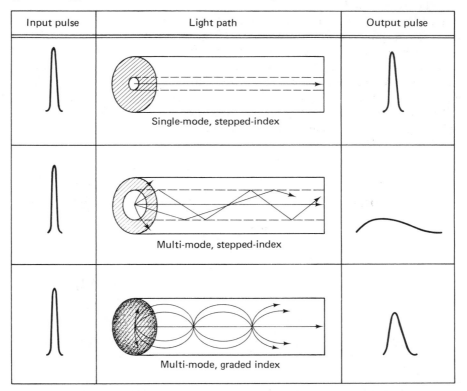

Figure 7-5 Basic types of optical fiber waveguides. (From: Robert E. Brooks, "Fiber Optics: Communicating on a Beam of Light," *TRW/DSSG/Quest*, Autumn 1977.)

*The decibel (dB) is a logarithmic unit of measure used to express the ratio between two power levels. One decibel is 10 times the log to the base 10 of the power ratio. Thus, a power loss of one-half would be a loss of 3.0103 dB (log 2 = 0.30103) or very nearly 3 dB. A gain of 3 dB means very nearly twice the power.

†Premium cable from Siecor Optical Cables, Inc.; bandwidth at 1 km (−3 dB) is 400 MHz.

toward the outside. Tests at Corning Glass Works have demonstrated data transmission at rates up to 100 Mbps over a distance of 10 km using this type of fiber. It is, however, also the most expensive of the three basic types.

Fiber optic cables are available with one or more optical fibers. At least one manufacturer (Siecor) has included a stablizing central member for cables including six or more optical fibers. This support member in the center of the cable is a steel cable. (This type of cable should obviously be avoided in applications where computer security is of importance since the metal cable mitigates one of the key advantages of fiber optics; i.e., eavesdroppers can no longer tap the line by placing a pickup coil nearby, where a metal line may act as an antenna to the computer. In military applications, it may also be desirable to hide the location of the cable, where metal detectors cannot be used to find it.)

Early use of fiber optics in computer-to-computer communications has been limited to point-to-point communications. In the late 1970's, systems were developed to operate in a multidrop environment using optical couplers. Couplers can be used to combine optical energy from two or more waveguides into one waveguide or to split energy from one waveguide into two or more. A block diagram of a developmental fiber optics coupler is shown in Figure 7-6. The coupling between Ports 1 and 2 (P2/P1) ranges from 40 to 75% and between Ports 1 and 3 (P3/P1) ranges from 5 to 40% depending on coupler type being used (Canstar Fiber Optic Directional Couplers, Type #TC4-A,B,C).

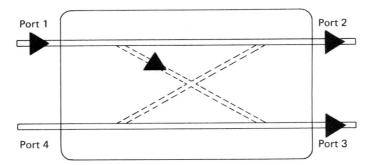

Figure 7-6   Fiber optic directional coupler (Courtesy, Canstar Communications Optical Fiber Products Division, 1240 Ellesmere Road, Scarborough, Ontario, Canada).

In applications where a coaxial bus is used to interconnect multiple minicomputers, the unidirectional characteristics of fiber optics must be recognized. For two-way communications, two fibers must be used. In loop-type architectures, a single fiber is sufficient for communications, as shown in Figure 7-7. This system will obviously fail if any one of the links or nodes fail. The reliability of the loop can, however, be improved using the coupler, shown in Figure 7-6. Other more reliable loop architectures, which can also be implemented using fiber optics, are discussed in Chapter 2.

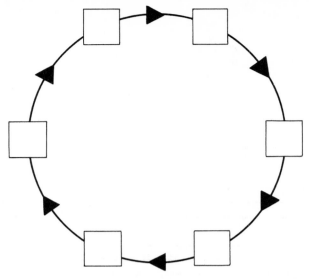

Figure 7-7 Loop-based architecture using a single strand for fiber optics cable.

An experimental 10-Mbps fiber optics data bus has been developed which conforms to the USAF MIL-STD-1553 (see Section 4.3) with the following exceptions:

- This system uses fiber optics rather than a shielded twisted pair for the transmission medium.
- The data rate is 10 Mbps rather than 1 Mbps.

In addition, the traditional multidrop bus architecture is replaced by a starlike radial bus architecture as shown in Figure 7-8.

The system is based on seven simulated Multiplex Terminal Units (MTU's) and Subsystem Interface Units (SSIU's) and a Data Bus Controller termed Control Multiplex Terminal Unit (CMTU) and CMTU Test Set.

The radial data bus, rather than the traditional inline data bus with T-couplers, was used since the fiber optics bus is much more like a constant current system rather than a constant voltage system (such as the metal-wire bus). As pointed out earlier, the power losses using optical couplers is relatively high. A large number of such couplers would, therefore, require extremely high input power levels for optical transmission onto the bus. The radial coupler serves as a common node in the radial data bus and distributes input power from any transmitting MTU or the CMTU uniformly to all the MTU's and the CMTU. The loss in the radial coupler is acceptable since there is only one of the coupler/fiber optics link interfaces in any given transmission path, regardless of the number of nodes in the system.

Research has also been conducted in the area of multiplexing techniques for fiber optics, where different light frequencies (i.e., colors) are multiplexed and demultiplexed, similar to FDM on coaxial cable. These techniques may bring optical multiplexers to the communications marketplace in the mid-to late 1980s.

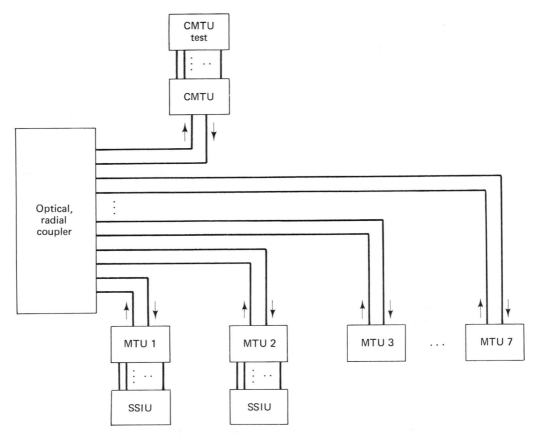

Figure 7-8 Diagram of 100-Mbps experimental MIL-STD-1553 data bus using fiber optic data links and a radial coupler. Coupler is housed in an ITT Cannon D-style connector. (From: J. R. Biard, "Short Distance Fiber Optics Data Transmission," 1977 IEEE International Symposium on Circuits and Systems, April 1977.)

7.3.2 Digital Satellite Communications Technology

In 1977 there were some 42 satellite communication systems in the world, 22 of which included both satellite and terrestrial equipment.* The majority of these systems was based on the use of many different carrier frequencies. This is the technique used for separating radio and television stations. It is also used for point-to-point microwave repeaters and cables and has naturally been adopted for satellites. This technique is called *frequency division multiple access* (FDMA) and is an efficient way of sharing the allocated portion of the radio frequency spectrum.

*"Satellite Communications," Wilbur L. Pritchard, Telecommunications, *1977 Handbook and Buyers Guide*, **II**, No. 13, July 1977.

In a satellite link, however, it leads to some problems because of the need for handling many frequencies simultaneously. Intermodulation between multiple carriers (one carrier influencing another) causes distortion. This distortion can be reduced by operating the satellite transmitter at a lower power output than it is otherwise capable of, which allows the amplifier to operate in the linear portion of its power curve. But this technique is inefficient, since larger ground stations must be used to make up for the lower satellite power, or larger satellites must be built to carry higher power transmitters.

Nevertheless, FDMA was the most popular technique for commercial communication satellites in the 1970's. Services in operation in the late 1970's included video transmission, 3-kHz voice circuits and digital data circuits operating at up to 56 Kbps. The United States domestic carriers, American Satellite Corporation, Western Union, and RCA, could interface at the user premises using terrestrial interconnections from their respective earth stations to the user's facility. In some specialized situations, these carriers would locate their earth station at the user's premises. United States domestic tariffs for satellite, ground links, and local loops and satellite rates United States to non-United States locations have been rapidly declining since the mid-1960's. Already in the mid-1970's satellite communications links compared favorably to AT&T terrestrial links for medium to long-haul communications (see Figure 7-9).

The intermodulation problem characteristic of FDMA can be solved by a technique called *time division multiple access* (TDMA). With TDMA each station uses the entire satellite channel transmitter power for a small fraction of the time, proportional to its communication traffic. By synchronizing their times of transmission and sending their communications as "bursts," many stations can share a single satellite channel. Their bursts arrive at different times with small gaps, known as *guard times*, between them. This technique is illustrated in Figure 7-10.

Frequency guard bands are used between FDMA channels for the same reason guard times are used between TDMA bursts—to avoid adjacent channel interference. TDMA operates in the time domain in a way analogous to FDMA in the frequency domain. The two techniques are compared in Figure 7-11.

TDMA, as illustrated in Figure 7-10, works well if all the satellite down-link signals can be received by all the stations in the system. But sending all the signals to all the stations wastes satellite power and uses up radio-frequency spectrum that could be used for other signals. A newer technique that overcomes these problems is called *spacecraft-switched time division multiple access* (SSTDMA). Advanced satellite antennas can direct all the energy from a transmitter toward a single station. Multiple antenna beams can be generated by a single antenna with enough isolation between beams so that the same frequencies can be used for all channels. A satellite switch rapidly changes the connections between antenna beams so that each beam is connected in sequence to each of the other antenna beams, allowing each station to communicate with every other station. This system concept is illustrated in Figure 7-12. The advantages of this system are that it uses all the available frequency spectrum at each station and concentrates all the satellite transmitter downlink power on the immediate area of the station the signal is intended for. Although this technique is extremely

Satellite Rates—United States to Europe	
Effective Dates	Monthly Half-Circuit Rates
Intelsat Charges to Comsat	
6/27/65	$ 2667
1/1/66	1667
1/1/71	1250
1/1/72	1080
1/1/73	930
1/1/74	750
1/1/75	705
Comsat Charges to Carriers	
6/27/65	$ 4200
4/4/67	3800
7/1/71	2850
Carriers Charges to Customers	
6/27/65	$10,000
10/1/66	8000
10/1/67	6500
8/2/68	6000
4/1/70	4750
8/15/71	4625

Representative United States Domestic Tariffs in February 1975 (Satellite, Ground Links, and Local Loops)			
Between	And	Satellite Single-Channel Rates	AT&T Single-Channel Rates
Chicago	New York	$ 620	$ 760
Chicago	Los Angeles	820	1674
Dallas	Los Angeles	820	1231
New York	Los Angeles	1120	2300
Washington	San Francisco	1120	2292

NOTE: Carrier, Comsat, and Intelsat Rates Are for Circuits to the Midpoint (I.E., Half-Circuit Rates). Carrier Rates Include Terrestrial Haul from Comsat Earth Station to New York.

Figure 7-9 Comparison of satellite and terrestrial links and an example of cost decline for United States-to-Europe satellite rates (from Norman Abramson and Eugene R. Cacciamani, Jr., "Satellites: Not Just A Big Cable in the Sky," Copyright by The Institute of Electrical and Electronics Engineers, Inc. Reprinted, by permission, from *IEEE Spectrum*, September 1975.)

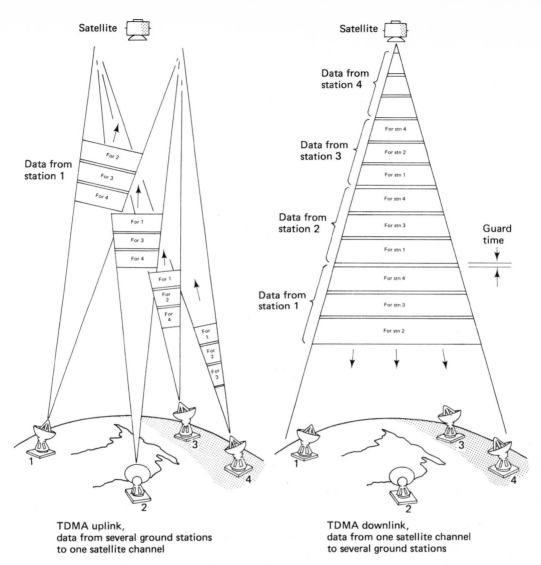

Satellite

Data from
station 1

For 2
For 3
For 4

For 1
For 3
For 4

For 1
For 2
For 4

For 1
For 2
For 3

1
2
3
4

TDMA uplink,
data from several ground stations
to one satellite channel

Satellite

Data from
station 4

For stn 4
For stn 2
For stn 1

Data from
station 3

For stn 4
For stn 3
For stn 1

Data from
station 2

For stn 4
For stn 3

Data from
station 1

For stn 2

Guard
time

1
2
3
4

TDMA downlink,
data from one satellite channel
to several ground stations

Figure 7-10 TIME DIVISION MULTIPLE ACCESS for the case of multiple
stations sharing a single satellite transponder channel. The up-link signal from a
given station consists of a set of "bursts" of digital data, each burst containing
data addressed to a particular receiving station. A burst from a given station is
assigned a time slot. The ground station clocks are synchronized so that all are
using a common set of time slots, one for each station in rotation. The entire
rotation occupies only about 750 msec, which means that the interrupted nature
of the signals is not perceived by users. In the satellite, the incoming signal is
shifted in frequency and retransmitted just as in the case of an FDMA signal. It
still consists of a sequence of bursts from the transmitting stations. The receiving
station receives the burst, reads the addresses on the data within each burst, and
processes only the data addressed to it. (From: Wade White and Morris Holmes,
"The Future of Commercial Satellite Communications," *TRW/DSSG/Quest*,
Spring 1978.)

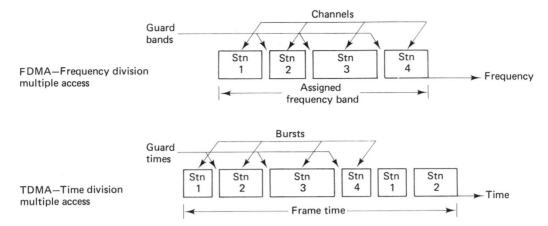

Figure 7-11 TIME SHARING BY TDMA is directly analogous to frequency sharing by FDMA. In FDMA, portions of the frequency bands are assigned to the stations in accordance with their respective traffic volumes. Guard bands are provided between the assigned bands to allow for the fact that frequencies can vary slightly from their assigned values because of tolerances in components. In TDMA, time is allocated to the stations in accordance with their respective traffic volumes. Guard times are provided between the time slots assigned to adjacent stations to allow for imperfections in the timing and synchronization mechanisms. The total time required to sample all stations is on the order of 750 msec, so that the communication appears continuous to the user (From: Wade White and Morris Holmes, "The Future of Commercial Satellite Communications," *TRW/DSSG/Quest*, Spring 1978).

efficient, one satellite transmitter for every ground station, as shown in Figure 7-12, restricts its use to systems with only large communication terminals.

A further modification to SSTDMA that provides service to small stations places many stations in each satellite antenna beam. This concept is called *area-coverage SSTDMA*. The stations communicate with each other by TDMA within the different connection periods of the satellite switch. A simplified diagram of this system concept is shown for two areas in Figure 7-13. In a point-to-point SSTDMA system, all stations can be transmitting and receiving data practically all the time. Station operation in the area-coverage SSTDMA system is intermittent, since all the stations in the area must share a single communication up-link and down-link. In this way, area-coverage SSTDMA operation is similar to basic TDMA operation where all stations in the system share a single communication channel.

All of these TDMA techniques were nearing commercial use in the late 1970's. SSTDMA was incorporated in the Western Union Advanced Westar service; ground-switched TDMA is used by the spacecraft of Satellite Business Systems; and the Bell System will be using beam-switched TDMA on its next generation communication satellite in the 1980's.

All this means that high data-rate links will be available at reasonable cost to

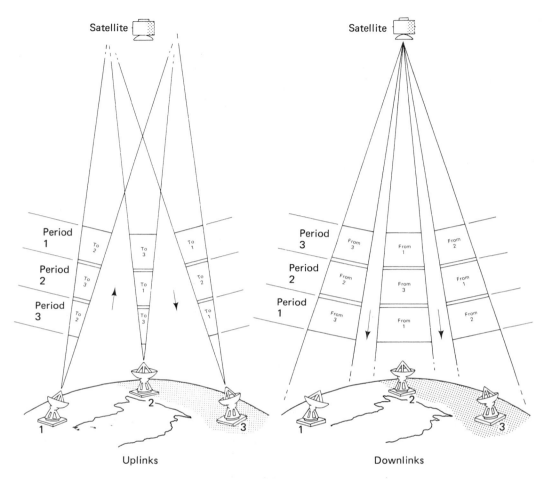

Satellite

Period 1
Period 2
Period 3

To 2 To 3 To 1
To 3 To 1 To 2
To 2 To 3 To 1

1   2   3

Uplinks

Satellite

Period 3
Period 2
Period 1

From 3 From 1 From 2
From 2 From 3 From 2
From 3 From 1 From 2

1   2   3

Downlinks

Figure 7-12 SPACECRAFT-SWITCHED TDMA for the case of point-to-point communications, with separate beams from the satellite for the different receiving stations. This configuration is well adapted to high-traffic links. The bursts from the respective transmitting stations are addressed to particular receiving stations. They are received simultaneously on separate channels in the spacecraft transponder (or on separate transponders). The synchronized switch in the spacecraft routes the signal to the separate beam directed at the addressed station. Switching is usually done in a prearranged repetitive sequence, but in very complex systems the satellite switch may read routing instructions on a burst and switch it accordingly. In this way the bursts from different stations are not interleaved but are processed simultaneously, resulting in a higher data rate (From: Wade White and Morris Holmes, "The Future of Commercial Satellite Communications," *TRW/DSSG/Quest*, Spring 1978.)

339

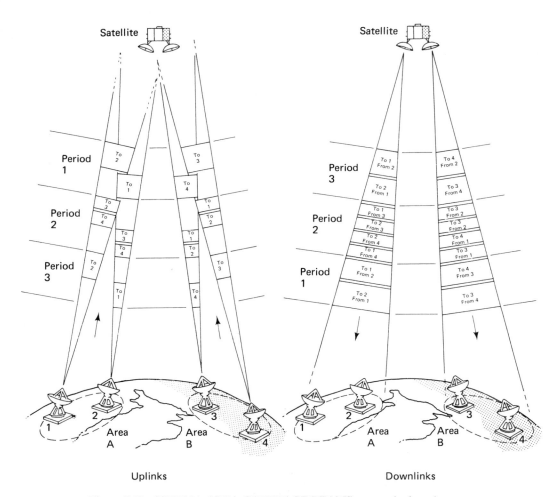

Uplinks   Downlinks

Figure 7-13 SSTDMA AREA-COVERAGE BEAMS are used when there are many small stations. Bursts from transmitting stations are interleaved and switched in the spacecraft to the appropriate beam for retransmission to the ground. Satellite antenna patterns are made relatively broad to cover areas containing several stations.

link computers, with no distance restrictions or penalties. Satellite Business Systems will, in the 1980's, provide users with links operating up to 6.3 Mbps, and Western Union with the Advanced Westar will provide channels ranging up to 50 Mbps and beyond.

The earth terminals for complex satellite communications are coming down in cost, from over 5 to 10 million dollars in the early 1970's to, perhaps, one-tenth of that a decade later.* In spite of area-coverage SSTDMA operation for satellite communications, it is still expected that the cost of an earth terminal will be proportionately large compared to that of the minicomputer facility. It is, therefore, expected that, in most applications, the user will "come to the earth terminal" rather than vice versa. Users will, therefore, have to connect to earth terminals through access lines using cables, microwave facilities, fiber optics links, or radio. One form of digital radio communications, packet radio broadcasting, is a flexible and cost effective way to link users to earth terminals without normal terrestrial communications facilities.

7.3.3   Radio Channel Networks

Packet radio broadcasting is a technique whereby data is sent from one node in a computer network to another by attaching address information to the data to form a packet—typically from 30 to 1000 bits in length. The packet is then broadcast over a communications channel that is shared by a large number of nodes in the net; as packets are received by these nodes, the address is scanned and the packet is accepted by the proper addressee (or addressees) and ignored by others (compare this with Ethernet, explained in Chapter 2). Packet broadcasting, in addition to radio channels or cable, can also be based on satellite communications. The key distinction between radio and satellite communications is the difference in propagation delay that is roughly $\frac{1}{2}$ sec for a stationary satellite located in synchronous orbit at more than 22,000 miles from earth, as opposed to small fractions of a millisecond for line-of-sight ground radio.†

One of the earliest known projects involving packet-switched radio broadcasting was undertaken by the University of Hawaii, in the early 1970's. The system developed in Hawaii, called the Alohanet, is shown in Figure 7-14.

Two 100-KHz channels are used in the UHF band and random access channel for user-to-computer communication at 407.350 MHz and a broadcast channel at 413.475 MHz for computer-to-user messages.‡

The central communications processor of the net is a Hewlett Packard HP 2100 minicomputer called the MENEHUNE, which functions as a message multiplexer/concentrator in much the same way as an ARPANET IMP. The MENEHUNE

*C. Weitzman, "Mission Control Communications Interface Requirements Study, Space Transportation System," TRW Systems Group, NASA Contract NAS9-14709, 1976.

†Because a synchronous satellite is in orbit at an attitude of 22,300 miles, the data transmitted from one computer to another must travel approximately 44,600 miles. Even at the speed of light, this transmission takes approximately 0.24 sec. But the transmission is not really complete until the receiving system acknowledges to the sending system that the transmission was received correctly. Because the acknowledgement must also travel 44,600 miles, a completed data transmission requires a minimum of 0.48 sec and, possibly, longer if an error condition requires retransmission of the original data.

‡R. Binder, N. Abramson, F. Kuo, A. Okinaka, and D. Wax, "Aloha Packet Broadcasting—A Retrospect," AFIPS Conference Proceedings, **44**, 1975 National Computer Conference, May 19–22, 1975, Anaheim, Calif.

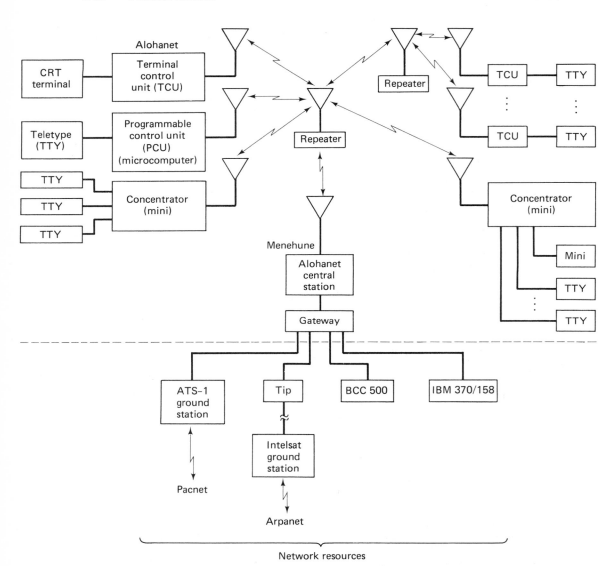

Figure 7-14 The ALOHANET including network resources connected via gateway devices (From: R. Binder, N. Abramson, F. Kuo, A. Okinaka, and D. Wax, "Aloha Packet Broadcasting—A Retrospect," AFIPS Conference Proceedings, **44,** 1975 NCC, AFIPS Press, Montvale, N.J.)

accepts messages from the University of Hawaii central computer (IBM 370/158) or from Aloha's own time-sharing computer, the BCC 500. Outgoing messages in the MENEHUNE are converted into packets, which are queued on a first-in, first-out basis and are then broadcast to the remote users at a data rate of 9600 bps.

The multiplexing technique that is utilized by ALOHANET is a purely random access packet-switching method that has come to be known as a pure Aloha technique; packets are sent by the user nodes to the MENEHUNE in a completely unsynchronized manner—when a node is idle, it uses none of the channel. Each full packet of 704 bits requires only 73 msec at a rate of 9600 bps to transmit (neglecting propagation time).

If two nodes transmit a packet at the same time, a collision occurs and both packets are rejected. A positive acknowledgement protocol is used for packets sent on the random access channel. If an acknowledgement is not received within a predetermined interval, the node will automatically retransmit the packet after a randomized delay, to avoid further collisions.

The choice of radio channels for any communication system is a complex task, requiring tradeoffs of many factors such as desired bandwidth, area coverage, spectrum availability, potential interference and noise sources, regulatory requirements, and equipment costs. The use of wide channel bandwidth tends to force the use of higher frequencies where spectrum crowding is less severe and the availability of bandwidth is greater. Crowded radio bands are undesirable, not only because of interference to other users but also because of interference from them.

When using higher frequencies, however, equipment cost will escalate and the range will decrease. Above 500-MHz equipment cost becomes prohibitive and area coverage becomes more difficult due to more pronounced shadowing effects of the radio waves by buildings and hilly terrain. Above 300-MHz radio propagation tends to be limited to line-of-sight paths. Due to these limitations, the 400- to 500-MHz UHF band was selected as optimum for the ALOHANET radio frequencies. Since most radio equipment available in the UHF bands use frequency modulation, this type of modulation was selected for the RF channels. For a transmitter equipment radiated power of 10 W, a simple whip antenna at a terminal node and an elevated antenna at the MENHUNE (or repeater), the radio range is approximately 17 miles in urban areas and between repeaters; at the MENEHUNE terminal, which is using a well-elevated antenna, the maximum range is 290 miles.

The ALOHANET has also been interconnected to the ARPANET, as shown, in Figure 7-14. The latter involves a 50-Kbps satellite link connecting Hawaii to California. The interface between the ALOHANET and the packet-switched ARPANET was accomplished using a Gateway device. Gateways will be discussed in more detail in the following section.

7.3.4 Gateway Devices

A classic problem, common to many new distributed systems being developed, is to provide the capability to interconnect the system to an existing network of computers having incompatible hardware, communications techniques, operational objectives, and performance characteristics. A related problem is the need to interconnect existing computer systems for data-base sharing, quite often within the same business organization. For example, a department store chain may internally use a network of POS terminals connected to a centralized (but local) computer facility. The same organization may use a separate system for customer credit verification and authorization. In addition, remote locations (stores) may be connected to a regional center for accounting and payroll functions. Furthermore, a network of terminals and minicomputers may exist for inventory, order entry, and warehouse/distribution control. Since functions performed in all these systems are interrelated, a decision may be made, when all these systems are operational, to merge some of the capabilities (i.e., interconnect the various file structures).

The Gateway concept has, therefore, been proposed as a method of interfacing two or more computer networks with differing characteristics in a cost-effective manner, with minimal impact on the internal procedures used in any of the networks or multicomputer systems.

The Gateway may connect two or more bus or loop-type systems (such as in the LNA system discussed in Chapter 6), a loop to a packet-switched system, a packet-switched system to a different packet-switched system (i.e., POCCNET to ARPANET also discussed in Chapter 6) or a fully interconnect system to a bus-based system. Multicomputer systems having different architectures will obviously require different techniques for interconnecting. A Gateway allows a user in one system to access a file or program in a separate, incompatible system.

The Gateway must, therefore, transform the characteristics of one network into those of the other so that a minicomputer in one network or system can communicate with a mini in the other network. This transformation can be a simple task or a complex chore depending on the function being transformed.

The Gateway may have to convert protocols (character or bit-oriented), buffer messages depending on differences between message lengths in both systems, and perform message reformatting (changes in headers and other message characteristics) and error control as well as synchronization and reinitialization. The most difficult problems arise when a function in one network control program does not exist in the other. This requires additions to the program lacking the functions (i.e., control programs dealing with messages or segments, regulating flow of data rather than ensuring flow control, performing error detection only rather than error control, etc.).

Due to the specialized nature of functions that have to be performed by a Gateway device, it is assumed that each design has to be based on the unique requirements of the two systems to be interconnected.

The availability of Gateway devices, wide-band data links (i.e., fiber optics and satellites) combined with the growth in microprocessor throughput capability, and the drastic cost reductions for solid-state memories will profoundly impact on multimicro- and minicomputer design in the next decade. Before some of these future developments are discussed, a review is made of future trends in distributed data-base systems.

7.4 DISTRIBUTED DATA-BASE TECHNOLOGY

A Data-Base Management System (DBMS) is a generalized software system designed to provide facilities for data organization, access, and control. The data base is the collection of logically organized information intended for access by multiple users. Any individual user would typically require only a portion of the entire data base, and the data base constitutes the collective requirements of all users. One may access the data base via several alternative media, application programs, inquire languages, report generators, and DBMS utilities; however, the heart of the system is the data management software which interfaces user-oriented programs to the data base.

The goal of most modern DBMS is to provide a structure in which the typical user is unaware of the data-base organization that has been established by a Data-Base Administrator (DBA). The DBA is, typically, one or more individuals who act as a central control in the management of a DBMS. He implements the data-base design and assigns passwords in the control of system security. He also analyzes system utilization via system accounting and utilities, in order to produce more efficient and effective systems. The DBA establishes a logical view of the data base, which ideally is independent of the storage media (usually disks) which have hardware defined restrictions which must be recognized and complied with by the data management software (DMS). (The DMS is the central software module in a DBMS that handles all input-output between the application programs and DBMS utilities on one hand and the data base on the other.) The access to the disk is accomplished by the computer operating system.

A primary reason for a DBMS is that it provides for an integrated data base controlled by a singular control program—the DBMS. When one particular item is changed or added, all programs that would access that item subsequently would receive the latest version. This is compared to the traditional approach in which one program updates a file and the changed values are eventually transferred to another file for use by another program.

DBMS' are presently available from all of the main frame manufacturers (IBM, Univac, Honeywell, CDC, etc.). Specialized DBMS houses are also marketing their unique DBMS for one or more main frames. The trend set by these vendors is to provide a "total system." This is characterized by a collection of software modules that not only handle the data-base management functions but also satisfy users' requirements for inquiry, accounting and billing, report writing, and other applications-oriented capabilities. As a practical matter, this packaging approach is heavily influenced by marketing considerations. Previously the user had to acquire a DBMS from one vendor and purchase additional software from other vendors, which then necessitated the user to integrate the modules himself. Therefore, some vendors have brought all these components together and renamed their offerings.

An overview of a typical DBMS functional organization is shown in Figure 7-15. Although more than a hundred different DBMS are available, very few have been developed for minicomputer applications. Furthermore, most of the DBMS's for minis have been developed for a centralized, single-CPU facility, as shown in Figure 7-16.

Also, typical current-day "high-performance" DBMS's are capable of handling no more than 10 to 100 requests per second. It has been predicted* that a demand will

*David K. Hsiao and Stuart E. Madnick, "Database Machine Architecture in the Context of Information Technology Evolution," Proceedings, International Conference on Very Large Data Bases, October 1977, Chicago, Ill.

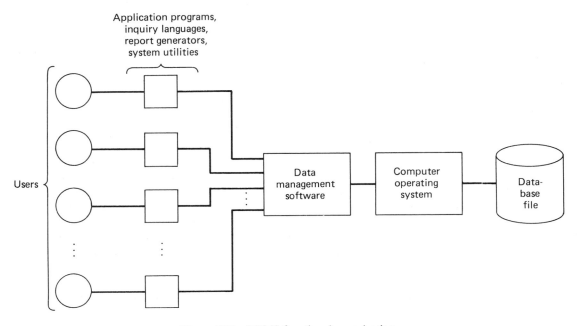

Figure 7-15   DBMS functional organization.

exist in the 1980's for systems with 1000's of users and over 1000 queries generated per second and that the information node or nodes in a system could receive up to a million requests per second under peak load.

This is several orders of magnitude above the state-of-the-art today. One major reason for this discrepancy may be that existing computers have primarily been designed for computational purposes. The architecture of computer systems for high-performance, large-scale information system management is still largely an unsolved problem.

Distributed data-base technology, therefore, shows promise in turns of faster, easier access to data than is feasible with a traditional, centralized DBMS. In addition, due to the increasing geographic dispersion of the end users within an organization, pressures are generated on data processing and corporate management to distribute data processing and storage capabilities to the location of data origin and/or end use of data. According to the CODASYL* systems committee; "The major benefits derived by distributing these functions focus on increased data availability to the end user and reduced exposure to total system failure due to hardware/software failure."†

---

*Conference on Data Systems Languages: a collection of several organizations (Sperry Univac; Hewlett Packard; Universities of Minnesota, Michigan, and Maryland; Dept. of the Navy, Fibreboard Corp., SYCOR, the NCR Corp., etc.) that have established a design standard for DBMS implementation.

†"Distributed Data Base Technology—An Interim Report of the CODASYL Systems Committee," by the CODASYL Systems Committee, Proceedings, National Computer Conference, 1978.

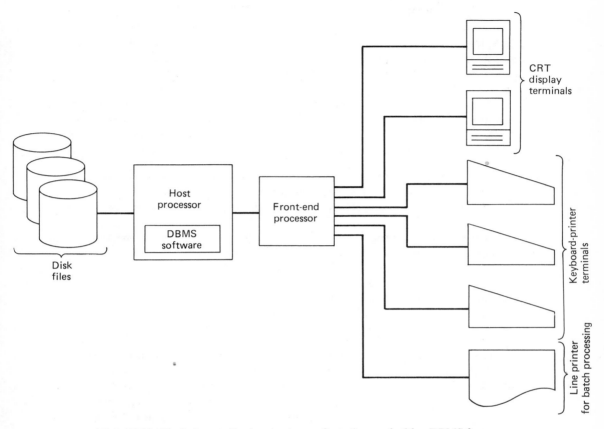

Figure 7-16 Typical centralized computer configuration used with a DBMS for online queries and update as well as batch processing of DBMS requests.

Any data-base management system architecture must address a set of principal issues:

1. The organization of an integrated data base.
2. The storage location(s) for data in the system.
3. The location of data in the system.
4. The control of concurrent addresses.
5. The mechanisms and/or structure to provide security and integrity.

These issues are of even more critical importance in a distributed environment than in the centralized environment and will, therefore, be discussed in more detail in the following sections.

7.4.1 Organization of Distributed Data-Base Systems

Most modern, centralized data-base management systems contain data management software including a definition of the data base (description of its structure) in addition to, of course, the data base itself. A distributed DBMS includes three additional entities: a Network DBMS, a Network Access Process, and a Network Data Directory.

Assuming a DBMS only includes those functions that relate to a local data base, all additional functions needed for a distributed system can be included in a Network Data-Base Management System (NDBMS). Based on CODASYL's recommendations, the NDBMS should include at least the following five functions:

1. Intercept a user request and determine where to send it for processing or what minis in the system must be accessed to satisfy the request.
2. Access the network directory or at least know how to request and use the information in it.
3. Coordinate the processing and response to a user request if the target data exists in multiple minicomputers in the system.
4. Function as the communications interface between the user process and the local DBMS and DBMS's in other minis.
5. Provide data and process translation support in a heterogeneous distributed data-base environment. Heterogeneousness in this context implies differences between hardware (and software) elements in each node in the system.

The Network Data Directory (NDD) contains information indicating the minis at which the various units of data resides within the distributed processing environment. Given the optimal assignment of data files in the network, the first step in making a file in one mini accessible to other minis or terminals in the system is to supply the other mini with the information needed to locate this file. This information can be classified by the level a NDD is maintained in the system, i.e., full NDD or partial NDD (it is, of course, also feasible to design a distributed DBMS without a NDD).

With a full NDD approach, there is at least one directory that lists every file (program) in the network of minis and indicates where each file is physically located.

When a user requests access to a multiminicomputer network file, this directory is scanned in order to locate the mini in which the file is stored. The three major disadvantages of this approach are storage space, search time, and uniqueness of file names. The directory search time for a given file name may become a significant component in the "request-response" cycle when the file directory is large. Furthermore, all files recorded in the directory must have unique names and these names must be known to all the users.

The file directory may be maintained only in one central location, but then the problem of reliability arises. If a "centralized" unique file copy would be destroyed, access to all files in the network would be blocked. If a duplicate file copy was maintained, storage space requirements would double and the update of all directory copies would impact communications overhead.

The main advantages of a full NDD approach are that the file is located by sending only one message from the originating node to the file directory and any request for a nonexistent file is spotted immediately.

With a partial NDD approach, regional directories could be maintained that list only the files in that region and the location of the other regional directories. A request for a file from a given minicomputer node will first search its local region directory and if the file is not found, a query for this file location will be sent to the other regions. This interdirectory inquiry may take several forms. The local region directory can send a query to all the other directories waiting for a positive response.

Another way is to link all directories into a ring structure. Each directory will pass the query to the next directory who can either respond affirmatively or pass the inquiry on. If the query makes a complete circuit of the loop and returns to the original directory, the file does not exist in the system. The advantage of such a system is fast file query response time. The disadvantages are the extra storage cost for storing the regional directories and communications cost for updating these directories.

In the third approach—not using a NDD—the file location would be fixed and the file name itself would indicate the file location by prefixing a location code to the file name. This prefix could be supplied by the software when the file is created and assigned to a given node. The main advantage of this method is that file location is obvious and no processing is required to obtain this location.

Any file movement from one minicomputer to another would, however, require a change to the file name and this change would have to be known to all potential users.

The user would have to remember not only the file name but also the prefix. In case of duplicate copies of files in various nodes, the user would have to determine to which of the copies he wants to route his message.

Combinations of the full versus partial NDD are also feasible: the centralized, extended centralized, localized, and distributed file directories.

In the centralized file directory case, a master directory is located at one of the minicomputers. Should a user require a file that is not stored at his local directory, he consults the master directory. The centralized master directory is updated when a new version of a file or a change in storage location is required.

In the extended centralized file directory case, once a user finds the location of a file in the master directory, he can append this information onto his local directory. Should the user use this again, he can obtain the location of this file from his local directory, thereby reducing the amount of intercommunications between minis, for querying the master directory. When the centralized file directory is updated, however, it also needs to update all the local directories that have appended information on that file.

Localized directory systems do not use a master directory. User queries the local directories of all computers in the system until the location of the requested file has been found. This is, of course, the "pure" partial NDD approach discussed earlier.

Finally, in the distributed directory case, each mini in the system has a master directory. The advantage of such a system is fast file response time, whereas the disadvantages are the extra storage cost and the maximal communications overhead for updating all the directories.

Figures 7-17 through 7-20 show the four types of distributed directories using a hierarchical architecture.

Chu and Nahouraii* have computed the monthly directory operating cost versus probability of directory update after each query, based on a star network configuration with 10 computers. It was assumed that all computers would have identical directory query and update rates. Figure 7-21 shows the monthly operating cost for centralized, extended centralized, localized, and distributed file directories versus the probability of directory update after each query. It was assumed that the storage cost is $C_s = \$7 \times 10^{-5}$ per byte per month, the communications cost is 10 times the storage cost

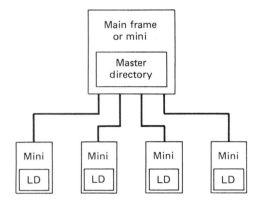

Figure 7-17 Centralized file directory—hierarchical configuration.

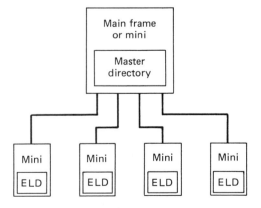

Figure 7-18 Extended centralized file directory—hierarchical configuration.

*Wesley W. Chu and E. E. Nahouraii, "File Directory Design Considerations for Distributed Data Bases," Proceedings, International Conference on Very Large Data Bases, October 1975.

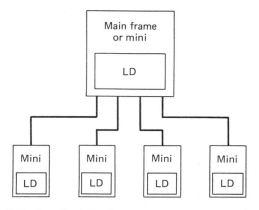

Figure 7-19   Localized file directory—hierarchical configuration.

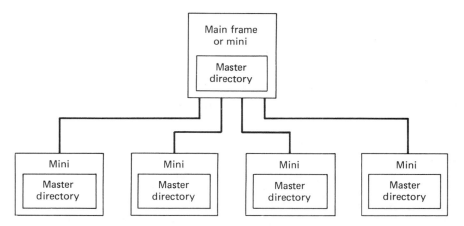

Figure 7-20   Distributed file directory—hierarchical configuration.

(C_s) per byte,* and the code translation cost is equal to 2000 times the storage cost (C_s) per transaction. The calculations were based on a query rate of 1×10^3 per month, an average length of 30 bytes per query, a local file directory size of 6×10^5 bytes, an extended local file directory size of 6×10^4 bytes, and a probability of one-third of a file having transactions with more than one computer.

Since the distributed file directory and the extended centralized file directory do not require communication for querying a file, they yield better file query response time than the centralized file directory and the localized file directory. When a data base consists of multiple master directories, the queries generated by the users are shared by the master directories in the system. Therefore, the file query response time

---

*In this example, it was assumed that all nine computers are 50 miles away from the central node.

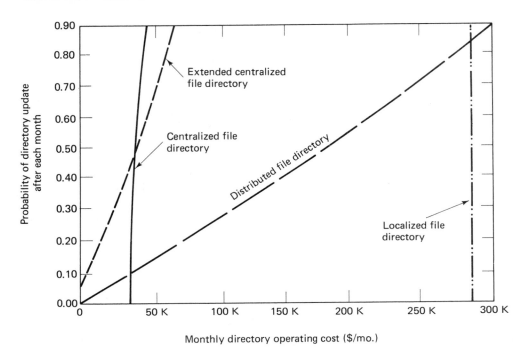

Figure 7-21 Monthly directory updating cost versus probability of directory update after each query for distributed DBMS.

for the multiple directory system is faster than that of the single master directory system.

It is clear that the relationships shown in Figure 7-21 will change for changes in the configuration. It is, however, assumed that, for the distributed DBMS environment, a network access process (NAP) will exist at every node as the interface between processes at the node and the communications facility (the interconnect structure and supporting hardware and software). The NAP is that portion of the communications facility that executes on the mini in a node. The CODASYL recommended relationships among the data bases, DBMS's, NDBMS's, and the NAP are shown in Figure 7-22, which shows a complete data/user node, a data node, and a user-only node.

7.4.2 Deadlock Avoidance

Deadlock in a distributed DBMS occurs when two or more tasks have blocked each other from executing by locking shared portions of the data base. This is an unfortunate side effect of the need for a task to establish temporary exclusion control over a portion of the data base. Deadlock control in a single system is well understood (see Chapter 5), but in a distributed DBMS the locking problem is made more difficult by the existence of multiple minis with individual control. Concurrency must be controlled through cooperating algorithms executed in each mini. The problem is

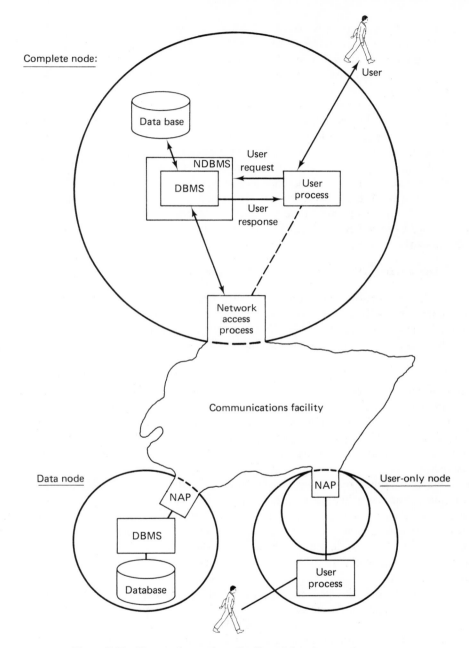

Complete node:

Data base

NDBMS

DBMS

User
request

User
process

User

User
response

Network
access
process

Communications facility

Data node

NAP

DBMS

Database

User-only node

NAP

User
process

Figure 7-22 Data and users in a distributed data-base environment.

to ensure that a data base remains consistent despite attempts at concurrent update from different processors. Objects in more than one minicomputer data base, such as duplicate data or structural information, must be concurrently lockable.

The underlying cause of deadlock in DBMS is the organization of conventional secondary storage media. In order to optimize the utilization of secondary storage, several requests must be processed simultaneously. This organization tends to reduce disk head movement and latency that is often the limiting factor in the performance of a DBMS. The deadlock problem may be minimized if conventional secondary storage is not used. This may be feasible using content rather than location addressing techniques and faster access memories (i.e., MBM's or CCD's).

Further research is presently needed, however, for both deadlock detection and prevention. Very little is presently known about the probability of interference and deadlock in concurrent data-base access. For transaction processing systems, there is a strong reason to believe that interference is rare and that elaborate deadlock avoidance algorithms would not be economical.

7.4.3 Distributed DBMS Security and Integrity

Since many data bases contain private or classified information, the security of a distributed DBMS must be assured before determining what benefits are to be gained by multiminicomputer access. The principal security question in a distributed data base is whether it is inherently more (or less) secure than a single computer system.

The use of the so-called "back-end processor" has evolved partly in order to improve data-base security. The back-end processor is a computer that is dedicated to data-base management and performs this function for one or more computers in a network.* The dedicated back-end machine provides security by screening every data-base request. Furthermore, no application programs execute on the dedicated back-end processor, eliminating the threat of a malevolent program monitoring data-base activity.

The most outstanding security liability of a distributed DBMS is the use of communications lines in a geographically dispersed network of minis. In environments where distance between minis is limited to thousands of feet or perhaps a few miles, line security can be achieved using encryption techniques or fiber optics links. In either case, provisions should be made to be able to ascertain whether the line has been tampered with in terms of tapping it. Line tapping is, however, extremely difficult if fiber optics are used.

Data-base integrity can be compromised by inadequate concurrency control (i.e., deadlock problems), erroneous software, security breaches, or system failure (i.e., "crashes"). Problems can be created by system failures in terms of concurrent file updates where a sudden hardware failure may make it extremely difficult to guar-

---

*One of the earliest back-end processor DBMS's has been developed by Cullinane Corporation. This system is based on a Digital Equipment Corporation PDP-11 mini and a back-end version of Integrated Database Management System (IDMS).

In the initial implementation, all LDM's will be Datacomputers. In the future, it may be possible to use other computers and DBMS's in the role of the Datacomputer.

The logical data model supported by SDD-1 is relational. Most data-base software use tree or plex structures that generally are more complex ways of relating data items. Relational data bases are constructed from "flat" arrangements of data items, as shown in Figure 7-24. This is contrasted with a four-level tree structure illustrated in Figure 7-25 and a plex structure shown in Figure 7-26 that includes links showing relations between data based on simple mapping (one arrow) and complex mapping (two arrows).

Employee number	Name	Sex	Grade	Date	Department	Skill code	Title	Salary
53730	Jones, Bill W.	1	03	100335	044	73	Accountant	2000
28719	Blanagan, Joe E.	1	05	101019	172	43	Technician	1800
53550	Lawrence, Marigold	0	07	090932	044	02	Secretary	800
79632	Rockefeller, Fred	1	11	011132	090	11	Consultant	5000
15971	Ropley, Ed S.	1	13	021242	172	43	Technician	1700
51883	Smith, Tom PW.	1	03	091130	044	73	Accountant	2000
36453	Ralner, Joan C.	0	08	110941	044	02	Secretary	900
41618	Hamburger, Freda	0	07	071230	172	07	Engineer	2500
61903	Hall, Robert Jr.	1	11	011030	172	21	Analyst	3700
72921	Fair, Carolyn	0	03	020442	090	93	Programmer	2100

Figure 7-24 Example of Data Structure in a Relational Data Base (From: James Martin, *Principles of Data Base Management*, © 1976, p. 97. Reprinted by permission of Prentice-Hall, Inc., Englewood Cliffs, N.J.)

The assignment of logical data items in SDD-1 to the physical storage resources of the data modules is based on the partitioning of each relation into subsets called *fragments*. Each fragment is defined to be a "rectangular" subset of a relation using Boolean conditions to define data attributes such as greater than, less than, and equal to. The partitioning of relations into fragments is illustrated in Figure 7-27 where each fragment is defined as follows:

- $Personnel_1$: = Personnel where Salary > \$30,000, projected on Name, Age, Position, TID (for tuple ID).*
- $Personnel_2$: = Personnel where Salary > \$30,000, projected on Supervisor, Department, TID.
- $Personnel_3$: = Personnel where Salary ≤ \$30,000, projected on Name, Age, Position, Supervisor, Department, TID.
- $Personnel_4$: = Personnel projected on Salary, Years-of-Service, TID.

*The tuple identification (TID) is unique for each tuple. The rows in Figure 7-27 are referred to as tuples. (A tuple is a set of data item values relating to one entity.)

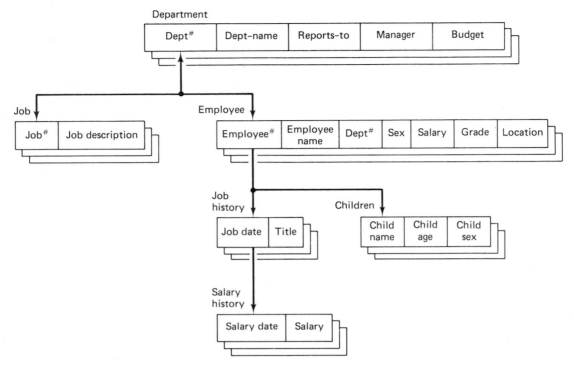

Figure 7-25   Example of Tree Structure. The relations between the various levels are shown in terms of keys, immediately above each relation (From: James Martin, *Principles of Data Base Management*, © 1976, p. 101. Reprinted by permission of Prentice-Hall, Inc., Englewood Cliffs, N.J.)

A fragment is either entirely present or entirely absent at each data module. Each fragment may be stored redundantly at more than one module.

Various alternatives for handling the data-base directory have been discussed. As shown in Figure 7-21 the optimal choice depends on the pattern of transaction traffic between the computers as well as the inquiry versus update ratio.

SDD-1 is treating the directory as ordinary user data where the data that comprise the directory are partitioned into fragments just as all other user data and, like user data, these fragments are stored in a distributed and redundant manner throughout the system. The directory information for determining the location of the directories is factored into separate relations that are stored in every data module. This permits choices regarding the distribution and redundancy of the directory to be delayed until data-base design.

The primary goal in designing SDD-1 is to minimize communication cost. The minimization of local processing costs are considered secondary.

SDD-1 will undoubtedly serve as model for other distributed DBMS's in the future.

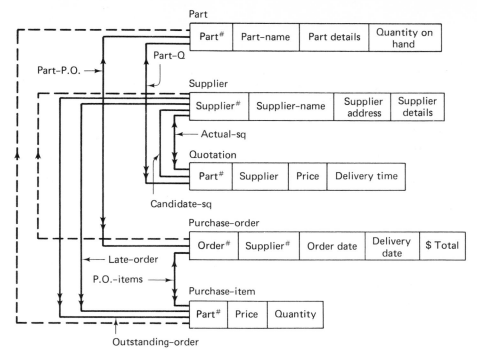

Figure 7-26 Example of Plex Structure. Some of the links show relations among the data (From: James Martin, *Principles of Data Base Management*, © 1976, p. 102. Reprinted by permission of Prentice-Hall, Inc., Englewood Cliffs, N.J.)

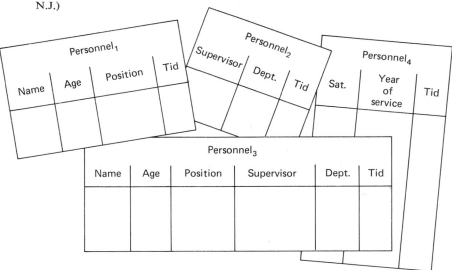

Figure 7-27 Partition of a Relation into Fragments in SDD-1 (From: J. B. Rothnie and N. Goodman, "An Overview of the Preliminary Design of SDD-1: A System for Distributed Data-Bases," 1977 Berkeley Workshop on Distributed Data Management and Computer Networks, Lawrence Berkeley Laboratory, University of California, Berkeley, Calif., May 1977.)

7.5 IMPACT OF NEW TECHNOLOGY ON DISTRIBUTED MICRO/MINICOMPUTER SYSTEM ARCHITECTURE

Advances in hardware, software, and communications technology will greatly impact future multimicro- and minicomputer system architectures.

The combination of low-cost satellite communication links and high-speed fiber optics, loop-based systems will provide the basis for large, complex, hybrid interconnect structures, as shown in Figure 7-28, where information can be shared on a global basis, while the advantages of loop technology can be derived for local systems.

It will also be possible to interconnect existing networks of multiple minicomputers with new designs, using gateway technology. Combinations of loop or hierarchical and point-to-point interconnect technology will make it feasible to develop complex local/remote systems. For instance, it may be feasible to provide security, environmental control, energy management, and smoke and fire detection, coupled with computing service support for personnel management, inventory control, accounting service, scientific processing, etc., all in one network on a per-building

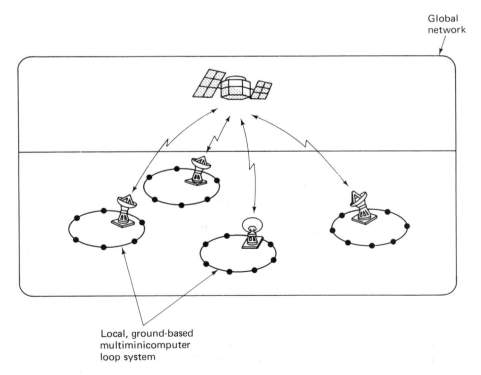

Global network

Local, ground-based multiminicomputer loop system

Figure 7-28 Local-, loop-, or bus-based clusters (nets) interconnected to higher echelon command centers.

360

basis. Each local processing facility/capability may be internetted into regional facilities such as a city fire department, police department, and central office for businesses located in the building. All such facilities could be "wired-in" when the structure is developed. An example of such a multinet is shown in Figure 7-29.

This concept can be expanded for retail business support, banking services, reservation services (airlines, car rental agencies, hotel reservations, entertainment, ticket agencies, etc.) where these systems may share either hardware or software resources or both. Hybrid interconnect technology can be used to optimize both the local and remote system elements.

Areas requiring further research as suggested by Eckhouse, Stankovic, and Van Dam* are network synthesis, network reliability, and redundancy in terms of cost

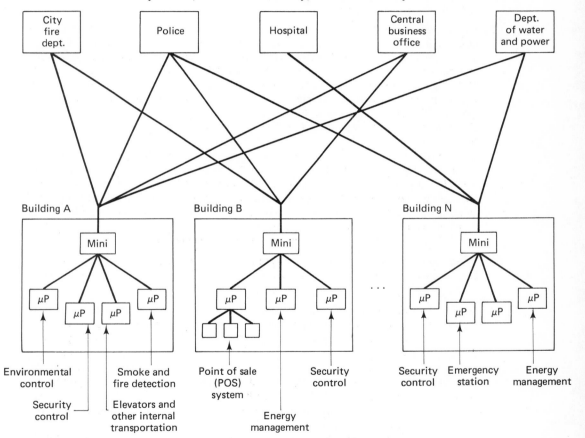

Figure 7-29 Multihierarchical-point-to-point communications link, multimicro- and minicomputer system.

*Richard H. Eckhouse, Jr., John A. Stankovic, and Adries Van Dam, "Issues in Distributed Processing—An Overview of Two Workshops," *Computer*, January 1978.

and performance, reliability, language and measurement tools, network failure detection and recovery, redundancy management, network protection and security, distributed processing, modeling and simulation, program partitioning, decentralized operating systems, automatic load sharing and balancing, interprocess communications, broadcast versus point-to-point communications, protocols, and deadlock resolution. The attempt in this book has been to shed some light on some of these problems and to summarize the state of the art.

PROBLEMS

7-1 Which ones of the interconnect structures listed in Figure 5-23 would benefit the most from fiber optics? Why?

7-2 One of the drawbacks of satellite links is the long delay between two earth stations connected via satellite. The retransmission of packets or message blocks may have a serious effect on response times as well as on overall effective throughput. A sending station has to wait at least 540 msec before it receives an acknowledgement from the receiving station saying that the transmitted message block was received correctly. For extremely wide-band links the significant component of the total transmission time would be the sum of the propagation delays (i.e., 270 msec for no errors, 270 + 540 msec if one retransmission was needed, 270 + (2 × 540) msec if two retransmissions were needed, etc.).

A distributed minicomputer system has been using a terrestrial 4800-bps link interconnecting two nodes. The cost of this link has been $600 per month. An equivalent satellite link with an error rate of one in 10^{-5} bits is, however, available for only $400 per month. Would it be more cost effective to switch to satellite communications, considering the fact that the existing system is based on Continuous ARQ with pullback (see Appendix) and uses 4800-bit message blocks?

What improvements can be made to increase the effective throughput?

7-3 What parameters (see Subsection 7.4.1) have the greatest impact on whether the directory is distributed or stored centrally for each of the configurations shown in Figure 5-24?

7-4 In a modern satellite control center the data base is the interface between the satellite Payload Operations Control Center (POCC) computational system and other elements of the ground support system, including payload experimenters, project planning personnel, external computing facilities, and data storage and cataloging facilities. Often, to make its services continuously available, a data-base system is either implemented as a dual, centralized facility connected to all other host computers in the system or decentralized, where the data base and its user are partly isolated from other data bases in the system, and interaction between one minicomputer configuration and another is relatively restricted.

Explain the differences between these two traditional approaches and the CODA-SYL Network Data Base Management System (NDBMS).

7-5 Develop two "straw-man" alternatives to the system depicted in Figure 7-29 for the case where approximately 20 buildings are interfaced to the city fire department, police department, hospital, etc., and all facilities are located within a 2-mile radius. Assume each building contains on the average some 30 microprocessors and the average data rate between the micros and minis located at the central facilities is equal to 4800 bps. Assess modularity, performance, growth capacity, and other key factors for the two optimal configurations. Indicate what key tradeoffs would have to be performed on the basis of new technologies discussed in this chapter.

What off-the-shelf hardware and software should be used? What kinds of links should be used?

Appendix:
Data Link Control Protocols

A.1 INTRODUCTION

This appendix includes summaries of the characteristics of some of the more commonly used data link control protocols as well as various hardware implementations of these protocols. Each protocol description follows the format used in Subsection 3.3.1 in order to maintain a common baseline for comparison.

The two major classes of protocols are the character and the bit-oriented. The major character-oriented protocols are IBM's Binary Synchronous Communications and DEC's Digital Data Communications Message Protocol (DDCMP). They are sufficiently different to be regarded separately. The bit-oriented protocols have evolved concurrently and are sufficiently similar to be described together. They include American National Standards Institute's (ANSI's), Advanced Data Communications Control Procedures (ADCCP), IBM's Synchronous Data Link Control (SDLC), International Standards Organization's (ISO's), High-Level Data-Link Controls (HDLC), Control Data Corporation's Control Data Communications Control Procedure (CDCCP), Burroughs Corporation's Burroughs Data Link Control (BDLC), and CCITT's X.25 (also adopted by ISO). BSC, DDCMP, ADCCP, and SDLC are described in detail; the remainder are described by pointing out differences.

A.2 BINARY SYNCHRONOUS COMMUNICATIONS (BSC OR BISYNC)

One of the most widely used protocols in the industry is IBM's Binary Synchronous Communications (BSC). BSC, also known as BISYNC, has been in use since 1968 for transmission between IBM computers and batch and video display terminals. Modified BSC is used by Hewlett-Packard Company in their minicomputer-based network architecture, called DS/1000 at the data link control level.* The way in which BSC handles the necessary protocol functions are explained in the following paragraphs.

Data transfer control. The format of a BSC transmission block is shown in Figure A-1. BSC uses control characters to delimit the fields. The header is optional.

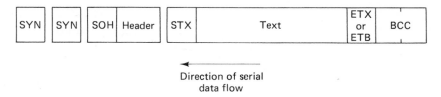

Direction of serial
data flow

Figure A-1   BSC message format.

If it is used, it begins with SOH (Start of Header) and ends with STX (Start of Text). The contents of the header are defined by the user. Polling and addressing on mulipoint lines are handled by a separate control message and not by using the header field. The text portion of the field is variable in length and may contain transparent data. If it is defined as transparent, it is delimited by DLE STX and DLE ETX (or DLE ETB). The trailer section contains only the block character check (BCC).

Rules stipulated by BSC for terminal-to-computer data exchange are shown in Figure A-2.

Error checking and recovery. BSC uses VRC/LRC, CRC-16 (EBCDIC),† or CRC-12 (6-bit Transcode) to detect and correct transmission errors. Retransmission of a block will be requested if errors occur [i.e., the block character check (BCC) transmitted does not degree with the BCC computed by the receiver or if there is a VRC error]. Sequence errors are checked for by alternating positive acknowlegements to successive blocks. ACK0 and ACK1 are sent as separate control messages as responses to even- and odd-numbered blocks in the message, respectively.

Information coding. BSC supports ASCII,‡ EBCDIC, and 6-bit Transcode for coding the information. Certain bit patterns in these codes have been reserved for control characters such as

SOH— Start of Header
STX— Start of Text

*Robert R. Shatzer, "A Minicomputer-Based Resource Sharing Datagram Network, Trends and Applications: 1978 Distributed Processing," *IEEE*, New York, May 18, 1978.
†EBCDIC = Extended Binary Coded Decimal Interchange Code. This is an 8-bit character code primarily used in IBM equipment.
‡ASCII = American Standard Code for Information Interchange. This is a 7-bit plus parity code.

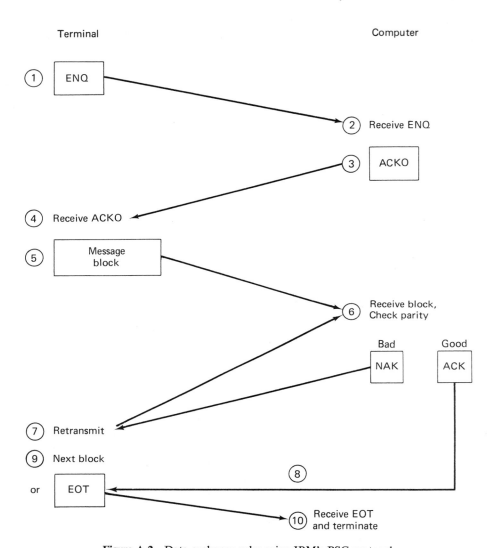

Figure A-2 Data exchange rules using IBM's BSC protocol.

ETX— End of Text

ITB— Intermediate Text Block

ETB— End of Transmission of Blocks Preceding the Last Block Multiple Block
Transmission

EOT— End of Transmission

NAK—Not Acknowledged

DLE— Data Link Escape to Extend the Set of Control Characters

ENQ— Enquiry to Solicit Response from Receiving Station

BSC is also using two-character sequences for control such as ACK0, ACK1, WACK (Wait Before Transmitting Positive Acknowledgement), RVI (Reverse Interrupt—for premature termination of a Transmission), and TTD (Temporary Text Delay, to indicate delay in transmission or to initiate an abort of the transmission in progress).

Information transparency.   The transparent mode is defined by starting the text field with DLE STX. Any data link control characters transmitted in the transparent mode must be preceded by a DLE character. Where a DLE bit pattern occurs within the transparent data, a second DLE must be inserted. When the message is received containing two DLE's, one DLE is discarded and the second DLE is treated as data. This approach is termed *character stuffing*.

Line utilization.   BSC is based on half-duplex communication requiring line turnaround twice between each block and an acknowledgement sequence used with each block (see Figure A-2). BSC can be used for both point-to-point and multipoint lines. Line utilization using BSC is, however, inefficient due to the half-duplex mode, particularly so with satellite communications links that always experience relatively long turnaround times (see Chapter 7).

Synchronization.   Each BSC block must be preceded by a minimum of two SYN characters. Some systems based on BSC perform automatic hardware insertion/deletion of SYN characters.

Communication facility transparency.   BSC was originally developed for bit-serial synchronous transmission but can also be used on asynchronous or parallel links.

Bootstrapping.   IBM does not support bootstrapping with BSC. (However, ARPANET is using a modified form of BSC to allow bootstrapping.)

A.3   DIGITAL DATA COMMUNICATIONS
MESSAGE PROTOCOL (DDCMP)

DDCMP is a character-oriented full-duplex protocol introduced by Digital Equipment Corporation as its standard for simultaneous two-way data transmission between computers and terminals. It accommodates both synchronous and asynchronous modes. The detailed characteristics of DDCMP are as follows:

Data transfer control.   The DDCMP frame format is shown in Figure A-3. Any one node starting a message transfer must initially send an inquiry and receive an acknowledgement before message transfer may proceed. Following the acknowledgement, data is transmitted in the form of numbered blocks, as shown in Figure A-3. A single acknowledgement statement may acknowledge up to 225 previous message

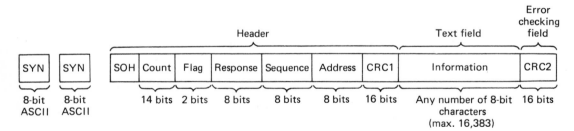

Figure A-3 DDCMP Message Block Format where SOH (start of header) indicates that the block is a data message. This block position can also contain ENQ indicating that the block is a control message or DLE indicating that it is a bootstrap message. Count indicates the number of bytes in the information field, sequence indicates message sequence number, and the cyclic redundancy check (CRC1) is used to verify the header. CRC2 is used to verify the entire block (Block Check Character or BCC.)

numbers. One of the simplest rules for data exchange, based on DDCMP, is shown in Figure A-4 for full-duplex transmission.

Error checking and recovery. As shown in Figure A-3, CRC is used for both header and data. When an error is detected, a NAK message is sent to the transmitting node. The sequence number in the message block indicates the last "good" message received. Since DDCMP operates in a full-duplex mode, the line does not have to be turned around (compare this with BSC). The bad message will simply be added to the sequence of messages for the transmitter. Messages are retransmitted if no response is received from the receiving node before time-out or if the response number is received earlier than the last sequence number transmitted (see also Figure A-4).

Information coding. Three ASCII control characters are used: SOH (Start of Header), ENQ (Enquiry), and DLE (Data Link Escape) (see Figure A-3). The remainder of the message including the header is transparent.

Information transparency. The count field in the header (see Figure A-3) allows up to 16,383 bytes of transparent data in the information field. Any code can thus be used for header and text. The header CRC1 is validated before count is used to receive data.

Line utilization. DDCMP can use either half- or full-duplex circuits. In the full-duplex mode, the message acknowledgement is included in the response field of a following message for the opposite direction. Line utilization is optimized, as up to 255 multiple message acknowledgements may be handled by a single ACK.

Synchronization. Two ASCII SYN characters are used preceding the SOH, ENQ, or DLE. As long as no gaps exist between messages, synchronization is not necessary between them. Furthermore, character synchronization is unnecessary on serial asynchronous and parallel links.

Communications facility transparency. DDCMP is totally transparent since it can be used for both serial synchronous, asynchronous, and parallel facilities.

Bootstrapping. The DDCMP format allows for bootstrapping when the DLE ASCII control character is used. The text field, when DLE is used, will contain the down-line load programs.

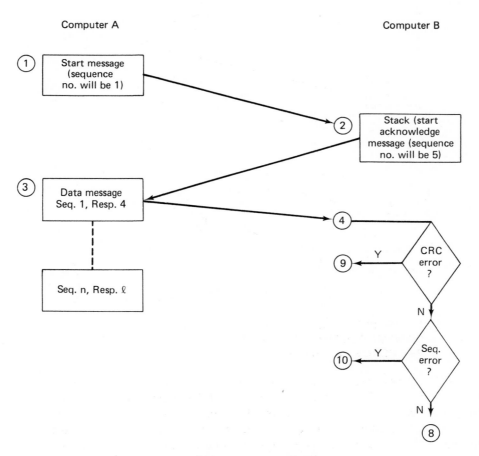

Figure A-4 Data Exchange rules for DDCMP.

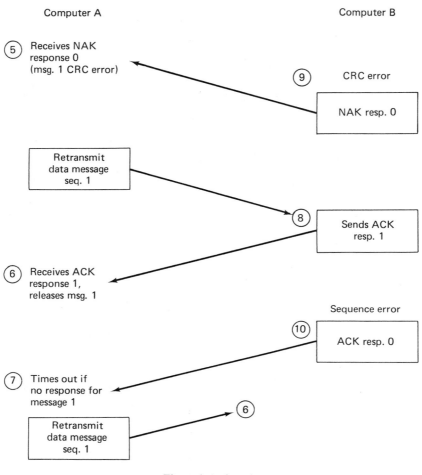

Figure A.4 **(cont.)**

A.4 ANSI'S ADVANCED DATA COMMUNICATION CONTROL PROCEDURES (ADCCP)

ADCCP was originated in 1973–1974 by the American National Standards Institute (ANSI) and initially defined in the X3.28–1976 Standard titled: "Procedures for the Use of the Communication Control Characters of American National Standard Code for Information Interchange in Specified Data Communication Links." It was proposed for use in computer-to-computer and computer-to-terminal interconnections over common carrier, satellite links, or dedicated lines. The characteristics of ADCCP are as follows:

Data transfer control. ADCCP message blocks are divided into three basic formats:

1. Basic Information Transfer Format
2. Supervisory Format
3. Unnumbered Format

The Basic Information Transfer Format is shown in Figure A-5, where Address Control and Block Check are positionally located between frame fields. The frame is a unique pattern based on the only occurrence of six 1's in the message block. The Address field is for a secondary station (the primary station is never identified). The Address may be a single, group, or global (all network nodes) address. The N(S) and N(R) field contains send and receive frame sequence numbers, respectively. The Extended Control Format shown in Figure A-5 allows up to 127 outstanding frames on a link. The P/F (bit position 5 in the Control Field) is a Poll/Final bit. P = 1 is sent by the primary node to authorize the secondary node to transmit. I = O is sent

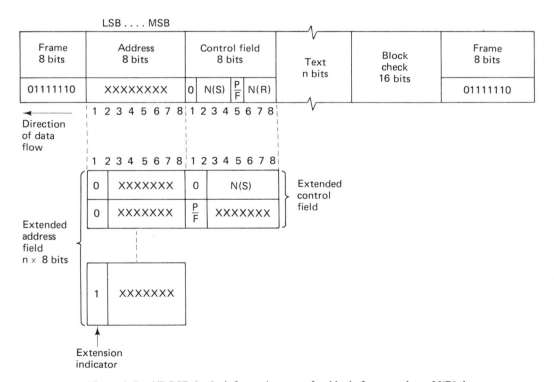

Figure A-5 ADCCP basic information transfer block format where N(R) is Receive Sequence Count and N(S) is Send Sequence Count and the first bit (bit 1) in the Control Field is the Information Transfer Format.

by the secondary node until final frame when F is set to one. Only one P-bit can be outstanding on a link at a time.

The ADCCP Supervisory format is shown in Figure A-6. S bits are for supervisory functions and X represents user-defined bit values for additional supervisory functions. The supervisory frame does not contain a text field. This frame is used primarily to acknowledge secondary node transmission and request additional transmissions. It is also used by a secondary node to acknowledge or reject primary transmissions or to request a wait before further transmission.

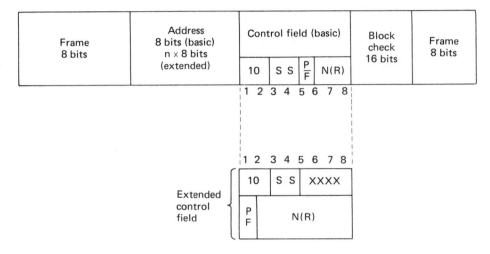

Figure A-6   ADCCP Supervisory Block Format where, in the Control Field, bits 1 and 2 are used for the Supervisory Format, bits 3 and 4 are used for the Supervisory Codes, and bits 6, 7, and 8 are used for the Receive Sequence Count (Module 8).

Finally, the ADCCP Unnumbered format, as shown in Figure A-7, is used primarily to initiate contention, switch channels, reset secondary nodes, perform hub polling, and reconfigure, test, or diagnose a link. It is also used by a secondary node to answer a poll or to initiate an asynchronous response. M bits, shown in Figure A-7, are modifier bits to define up to 32 additional supervisory functions. X represents user-defined bit values for additional supervisory functions. A text field is optional in the Unnumbered format that does not contain sequence numbers.

The codes for the ADCCP Control field, shown in Figure A-7, are summarized in Figure A-8 for bits 3 through 8. In the Normal Response Mode (NRM), when set, responses are initiated by secondary nodes only with permission of the primary node. The secondary node will then send one or more contiguous frames with continuous ARQ.

In the Asynchronous Response Mode (ARM), a secondary node has permission to initiate and asynchronous interrupt.

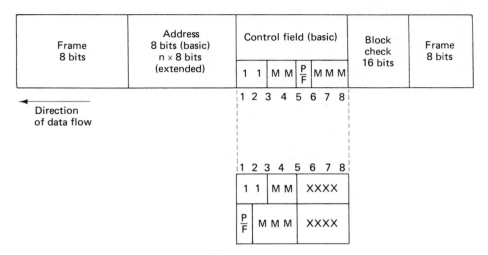

Figure A-7 ADCCP unnumbered block format.

Bits M3 M4 M6 M7 M8	Definition	D/F Used As Command (Poll)	Response (Final)
0 0 0 0 0	UI —Unnumbered Information Frame	×	×
0 0 0 0 1	SNRM —Set Normal Response Mode	×	
0 0 0 1 0	DISC —Disconnect	×	
0 0 1 0 0	UP —Unnumbered Poll (Optional Response Poll)	×	
0 0 1 1 0	UA —Unnumbered Acknowledge		×
1 0 0 0 0	SIM —Set Initialization Mode	×	
	RIM —Request Initialization Mode		×
1 0 0 0 1	RSPR —Response Reject	×	
	CMDR —Command Reject		×
1 1 0 0 0	SARM —Set Asynchronous Response Mode	×	
	DM —Disconnect Mode		×
1 1 0 1 0	SARME—Set ARM Extended	×	
1 1 0 1 1	SNRME—Set NRM Extended	×	
All Others	Reserved for Future Assignment		

Figure A-8 ADCCP control field coding for unnumbered blocks.

Similar to the Unnumbered Format, the Control Field coding for the Basic Information Transfer and Supervisory Blocks are summarized in Figure A-9.

An example of data exchange between two nodes (A and B), using ADCCP, is given in Figure A-10. Retransmission due to errors is based on continuous ARQ with pullback.

Format	Definition	P/F Used As	
		Command	Response
Basic information	I —Information	×	×
Supervisory	RR —Receive Ready	×	×
	RNR —Receive not Ready	×	×
	REJ —Reject	×	×
	SREJ—Selective Reject	×	×

Figure A-9 ADCCP control field coding for basic information and supervisory blocks.

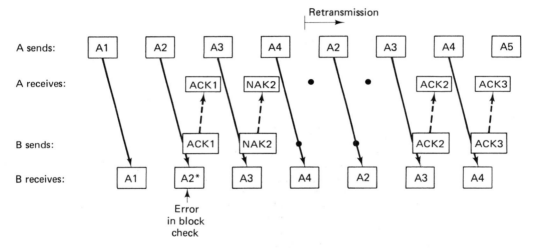

Figure A-10 Example of data exchange between nodes A and B using ADCCP. Transmission is full-duplex.

Error checking and recovery.   ADCCP uses a 16-bit frame-check sequence for CRC. The ACK/NAK is inserted in the control field of a normal message (see Figures A-5, A-6, and A-7) or in a separate message. Frame sequencing is provided for 7 outstanding frames on a link (127 frames with extended control field). As indicated in the previous section, retransmission is performed on the erroneous frame and all subsequent frames (see also Figure A-10).

Information coding.   A special character is used for the frame field (see Figure A-5). The leader is either 16 or 32 bits and the trailer consists of 16 bits. Any code can be used for the text since ADCCP provides code transparency.

Information transparency.   Header and text are transparent to any data. A zero bit is inserted after any occurrence of five consecutive 1's (bit stuffing), to prevent confusion with frame character (six consecutive 1's).

Line utilization.   ADCCP can be used with both half- and full-duplex lines for point-to-point, loop, or multipoint transmission. A single primary station or node (master) is designated for each line; all other stations or nodes on the line are secondaries (slaves).

Synchronization.   At least one frame character preceding the header must be used for synchronization. Where space exist between consecutive frames, frame characters may be transmitted.

Communications facility transparency.   Transparency exists only for serial synchronous transmission.

Bootstrapping.   ADCCP does not support bootstrapping but it can be implemented based on user agreement, as text is transparent to machine-language code.

A.5 IBM'S SYNCHRONOUS DATA LINK CONTROL (SDLC)

IBM's SDLC was originated in 1973 and, unlike BSC, is bit-oriented and is designed for both half- and full-duplex operation. It is employing the same basic format, special bit patterns, zero insertion and deletion, and error checking as ADCCP. The key characteristics of SDLC are as follows:

Data transfer control.   The SDLC message format is shown in Figure A-11. The only control character used in SDLC is the 8-bit flag character, which has the bit pattern 01111110. The address field is used to designate the particular secondary station or node to which the frame is addressed. (One address may designate more than one node.)

The 8-bit control field can be used to provide an information transfer format, a supervisory format, or a nonsequenced format. It contains frame sequence information for up to 7 outstanding frames (compared with 127 frames for ADCCP) and a poll/final bit that acts as a send/receive control signal, signifying whether a sending or receiving operation is taking place. A poll bit is sent to a secondary station to indicate that a transmission is requested and a final bit is sent from a secondary station in response to the poll bit-containing frame.

The supervisory format, shown in Figure A-11, can be used to designate ready or busy conditions such as the checking of a secondary station status although no data transmission will be taking place.

The third control field format, for nonsequenced message transmission, may be

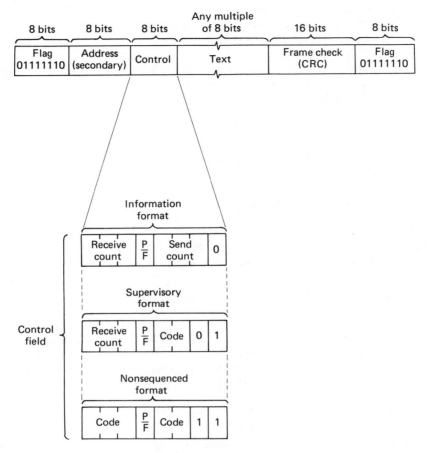

Figure A-11 SDLC message format.

used for data link management such as initialization of secondary stations or nodes. This is comparable to the ADCCP unnumbered block format shown in Figure A-7.

SDLC also allows for loop-type communications where each node on the loop derives its timing from the received data stream.

Communications on the loop rely on the fact that secondary nodes operate in a repeater mode where nodes retransmit incoming message blocks with a 1-bit time delay. This allows a secondary node to capture the loop and insert its message block.

The loop SDLC's frame structure is identical to the normal SDLC message format shown in Figure A-11; however, one character defined in the SDLC loop mode is not found in normal SDLC. This is the end-of-poll (EOP) character, which contains a binary zero followed by seven binary 1's. The EOP character controls loop activity.

Error checking and recovery. SDLC uses CRC to detect transmission errors. Like DDCMP, SDLC has a response field (3 bits in the control field, as shown in Figure A-11) and separate ACK/NAK messages. Unlike DDCMP, SDLC does not NAK transmission errors. Rather, when a bad message is received, a return message is sent to the original sending node that the message containing the error(s) has not been received. After a time-out period, the original sender will then retransmit the message.

Information coding. SDLC is not concerned with information exchange codes. Regardless of what exchange code is used, the only control character is the flag, as shown in Figure A-11. A higher level protocol must be used to define the information exchange code to be used to transfer data.

Information transparency. Header and text are transparent to any data as with ADCCP. Similar to ADCCP, bit stuffing is used to ensure that a flag character does not appear in the data portion of the message.

Line utilization. SDLC, similar to DDCMP and ADCCP, provides the ability to transmit on both half- and full-duplex lines.

The control character overhead is lower for SDLC (flag, header, and check bits for a total of 6 characters) rather than 8 characters for BSC and 10 characters for DDCMP.

Furthermore, no separate ACK messages are necessary.

Synchronization. SDLC synchronizes on the flag characters between messages. No SYN characters are needed.

Communications facility transparency. Since bit stuffing is used, SDLC cannot be utilized for bit-serial, asynchronous, or parallel transmission. (Asynchronous characters are fixed length.) Transparency exists, therefore, only for serial, synchronous transmission facilities.

Bootstrapping. SDLC does not provide for bootstrapping as part of its protocol.

A.6 HIGH-LEVEL DATA LINK CONTROL (HDLC) PROCEDURES

HDLC was formulated in 1974 by the International Standards Organization (ISO) and has, subsequently, been approved and published as Standard IS 3309. The HDLC message block format is shown in Figure A-12. The message is based on an 8-bit opening flag, followed by an 8-bit control field, an optional information field of *n*-bits, a 16-bit frame checking sequence, and an 8-bit flag. The format is, basically, the same as that of ADCCP (Figure A-5) with minor differences in definitions of some commands and responses.

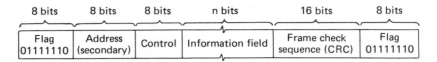

Figure A-12 HDLC message format.

A.7 CCITT'S X.25

The X.25 proposed by the CCITT and adopted by the ISO is a recognized standard for international data communications. The message format of the data link control level called Link Access Procedure (LAP) is the same as used by HDLC (see Figure A-12). X.25 permits two different modes of operation:

1. Primary-to-Primary Node
2. Primary-to-Secondary Node

In the first mode, each of two nodes connected can act either as the primary node (i.e., initiating command and control functions) or as the secondary node (i.e., executing the commands of another node).

In the second mode, one node is designated the primary node and the other the secondary node.

In fact, X.25 is more than a data link control standard. It also defines conventions whereby data terminal equipment establishes, maintains, and clears calls over access lines to a carrier data switching exchange.

Furthermore, X.25 defines formats for the packaging of data and control information into standard packets in a packet switching network and manages the flow of data over a single, real circuit to and from a packet network.*

A.8 CONTROL DATA COMMUNICATIONS CONTROL PROCEDURE (CDCCP)

CDC's CDCCP was originated in 1975 and is a bit-oriented protocol based on synchronous transmission for computer-to-computer or computer-to-terminal over common-carrier, satellite link, or dedicated lines. It is basically the same as ADCCP and includes ADCCP, SDLC, and HDLC as subsets.

A.9 BURROUGHS DATA LINK CONTROL (BDLC)

BDLC uses a frame format similar to HDLC's shown in Figure A-12. It differs from SDLC and X.25, however, in that, similar to ADCCP and HDLC, the address field may be extended in 8-bit increments to accommodate additional secondary sta-

---

*For additional information on X.25 see also P. E. Green, "An Introduction to Network Architectures and Protocols," IBM Systems Journal, Vol. 18, Nr. 2, 1979.

tions. The control field may also be expandable to 16 bits with the sequence number being expanded to 7 bits. The potential number of unacknowledged frames may thus be as high as 127.

A.10 COMPARISON OF DATA LINK PROTOCOLS

A comparison of the major protocols studied is shown in Figure A-13. It may be concluded that the newer bit-oriented protocols are generally superior in flexibility and simplicity compared with older character-oriented protocols. Bit-oriented protocols are applicable to half- and full-duplex operation on point-to-point, multipoint, and loop topologies with switched or nonswitched lines. Preliminary studies indicate high throughput efficiency and excellent response-time performance.*

Several caveats are in order concerning bit-oriented protocols. Although they are sufficiently similar in format to allow much commonality in hardware and software, they are not interchangeable. Control and response code differences exist. Also, the different bit-oriented protocols may not share the same classes of procedures. These classes establish procedural differences for different applications. Each class implements a subset of the elements of procedure; all classes use the standard frame structure. ANSI has defined six classes covering normal, asynchronous, and primary-to-primary modes. ISO has five classes covering basically the same applications.

While reviewing what line protocols are, it is equally important to consider what they are not. Line protocols are not the total solution to the communications problem. They are only a link-level control mechanism and thus are concerned solely with the transfer of data at that level. They are not a network protocol. They do not control the flow of information between users in a multinodal network. They can, however, be applied between nodes or between a node and a user. Any necessary end-to-end controls must be imbedded in the message text as information.

A.11 HARDWARE IMPLEMENTATION OF DATA LINK CONTROL PROTOCOLS

The software-supported data link control function is gradually being taken over by the data link control hardware chip. A comparison of data link control chip features is shown in Figure A-14.

The hardware chips listed in Figure A-14 are programmable and can thus support more than one data link control protocol.

Also, as shown in Figure A-14, some of these chips can support data rates up to 2 Mbps and several protocols such as Bisync and DDCMP.

In addition, features such as modern control for point-to-point communications, loop-back for self-test, secondary address comparison, and global address recognition have been incorporated into several of these chips.

---

*J. W. Conard, "Bit-Oriented Communication Control Protocols," VIM-23/FOCUS-14 Joint Conference, November 3–6, 1975.

Feature	IBM BISYNC	DEC DDCMP	ANSI ADCCP	IBM SDLC	ISO HDLC/X.25	CDC CDCCP	BURROUGHS BDLC
Half-Duplex	Yes	Yes	Yes	Yes	Yes	Yes	Yes
Full-Duplex	No	Yes	Yes	Yes	Yes	Yes	Yes
Message Formatted	Variable	Fixed	Fixed	Fixed	Fixed	Fixed	Fixed
Link Control	Control char. sequences optional header	Header (fixed)	Control field (8/16 bits)	Control field (8 bits)	Control field (8/16 bits)	Control field (8 bits)	Control field (8/16 bits)
Station Addressing	Header	Header	Address field	Address field	Address field	Address field	Address field
Error Checking	Information field only	Header information field	Entire frame	Entire frame	Entire frame	Entire frame	Entire frame
Error Detection	VRC/LRC-8 VRC/CRC-16 CRC-16 CRC-12	CRC-16	CRC-CCITT	CRC-CCITT	CRC-CCITT	CRC-CCITT	CRC-CCITT
Request for Retransmission	Stop and wait	Go back N	Go back N selected reject	Go back N	Go back N	Go back N	Go back N
Maximum Frames Outstanding	1	255	127	7	127	127	127
Framing—start	2 SYN's	2 SYN's	Flag	Flag	Flag	Flag	Flag
—end	Terminating characters	Count	Flag	Flag	Flag	Flag	Flag
Gaps between characters allowed	Yes	No	No	No	No	No	No
Information Transparency	Transparent mode	Inherent (count)	Inherent (zero insertion/deletion)	Inherent (zero insertion/deletion)	Inherent (zero insertion/deletion)	Inherent (zero insertion/deletion)	Inherent (zero insertion/deletion)
Character Codes	ASC11 EBCDIC transcode	ASC11 (control character only)	Any	Any	Any	Any	Any
Information Field Length	$n \times L$	$n \times 8$	Unrestricted	$n \times 8$	Unrestricted	Unrestricted	Unrestricted
Bootstrapping Capability	No	Yes	Yes	Yes	No	No	No
Bit-Parallel Capability	No	Yes	No	No	No	No	No
Asynchronous	No	Yes	No	No	No	No	No

Figure A-13 Comparison of data link protocol features.

Feature	Signetics 2652	SMC 5025	Zilog SIO	Fairchild 3846	Motorola 6854	Intel 8273	Western Digital 1933
Maximum date rate (b/s)	1M/2M	500K	550K/880K	1M	660K/1M	64K	1M
Package pins	40	40	40	40	28	40	40
Data bus pins	8 or 16	8 or 16	8	8 or 16	8	8	8
Modem control/general-purpose I/O pins	None	None	4 per channel	6	4	10	6
Character length (bits)	1–8	1–8	5–8*	5–8†	5–8	8	5–8
System clock required	No	No	Yes	No	Yes	No	No
Separate receiver and transmitter interrupts	Yes	Yes	No	Yes	No	Yes	No
Receiver First in/First out (FIFO) buffers	None	None	2	None	2	None	None
Transmitter FIFO buffers	None	None	None	None	2	None	None
Loop-back self-test mode	Yes	Yes	No	Yes	No	Yes	Yes
Multiprotocol (Bisync, DDCMP)	Yes	Yes	Yest	Yes	No	No	No
Bisync CRC handling	External	External	Start/stop CRC-16	Yes	N.A.	N.A.	N.A.
Secondary address comparison	Yes	Yes	Yes	Yes	No	Yes	Yes
Global address recognition	Yes	No	Yes	Yes	No	Yes	Yes

* 8-bit SYN character restricts character length to 8 bits in synchronous mode.

† Supports asynchronous ; 2 full-duplex channels.

N.A. = not applicable

Figure A-14 Off-the-shelf, data link control chip characteristics (from Alan J. Weissberger, "Data-Link Control Chips: Bringing Order to Data Protocols," June 8, 1978).

Reprinted from ELECTRONICS, June 8, 1978, Copyright © McGraw-Hill, Inc., 1978.

The use of these chips will reduce software requirements in a micro- and mini-computer, thereby allowing the designer to consider a smaller and less costly processor than he otherwise would have to use.

It is, however, expected that a large number of minicomputers will incorporate the hardware-implemented data link control chip into their overall design.

Sample Problem Solutions

Instr.	Mix (%)	Modcomp IV	DEC PDP-11/45	Data Gen. Eclipse	SEL-32	Interdata 7/32	Interdata 8/32
ADD S.P.	12.6	116	55	39	28	252	29
D.P.	1.4	21	11	4	4	28	5
MULT. S.P.	10.8	74	69	53	42	356	32
D.P.	1.2	16	12	10	8	40	5
DIV. S.P.	2.0	22	15	12	14	110	11
LOAD R-X	30.0	48	55	30	36	105	39
STORE R-X	20.0	32	37	19	24	68	40
BRANCH	10.0	15	9	60	6	25	4
COMP. R/M	2.0	5	8	4	2	12	4
SHIFT (16 bits)	7.0	24	22	27	25	47	9
AND/OR (M & R)	1.0	2	4	1	1	4	1
PGM I/O	2.0	3	4	5	1	9	8
Ave. Instr. Time:	100.0	3.78 μs	3.01 μs	2.10 μs	1.91 μs	10.56 μs	1.85 μs
KIPS:	—	265	332	476	523	95	541

S.P. = Single Precision (16 bits) except for the SEL and Interdata minis (32 bits).
D.P. = Double Precision (32 bits) except for the SEL and Interdata minis (64 bits).
Memory type used: Core, except for mix of MOS and core for PDP-11/45 and eight-way interleaved core for the Data General Eclipse.

Problem 1-3

The ratio of measured benchmark results to theoretical throughput or, rather, an arbitrary number of instructions performed based on an average instruction time derived from an assumed instruction mix is interpreted as follows: A low ratio indicates that, compared to a higher ratio, the particular computer, based on the assumed mix, performs relatively poorly.

This performance comparison must, however, also take into consideration the particular compiler having been used (it may be inefficient or tuned for minimizing the amount of memory being used rather than speed) and the relative cost of the minicomputers being compared. Benchmark results are generally timed with the internal clock in the CPU. If the benchmark run time is of the same order of magnitude as the period between clock pulses, significant errors can be introduced.

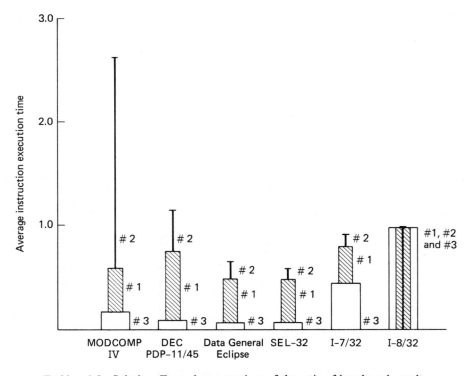

Problem 1-3 Solution. From the comparison of the ratio of benchmark results to the average instruction times for three mixes, it can be seen that mix No. 1 is closest to the assumed instruction mix.

Other elements the benchmark user is cautioned against is the method whereby

Computer	Ave. Instr. Time	Norm. A.I.T.*	Mix 1		Mix 2		Mix 3	
			(ms)	#1 A.I.T.	(ms)	#2 A.I.T.	(ms)	#3 A.I.T.
Modcomp IV	3.78	135	80	0.59	100	2.72	130	0.15
DEC PDP-11/45	3.01	107	78	0.73	33	1.13	50	0.07
D.G. Eclipse	2.10	75	40	0.53	13	0.64	20	0.04
SEL 32	1.91	68	36	0.53	11	0.59	14	0.03
Interdata 7/32	10.56	377	309	0.82	90	0.88	1060	0.44
Interdata 8/32	1.85	66	66	1.00	18	1.00	420	1.00

*"Average instruction time" normalized based on "fastest" mini: the Interdata 8/32 (541,000 instructions per second). Normalization performed for each of the three benchmark results, Mixes 1, 2, and 3 respectively. (Norm. A.I.T. = normalized average instruction time.)

benchmark results are printed out. Print or spooling times should obviously not be included in the results used.

The results of the comparisons also indicate that results from benchmark run No. 1 come closest to the theoretically derived average instruction times.

The benchmark results normalized to Modcomp IV results, based on Mix 2 are as follows:

	Mix 1	Mix 2	Mix 3
Modcomp IV	100	100	100
DEC PDP-11/45	97	33	38
D.G. Eclipse	50	13	15
SEL-32	45	11	11
Interdata 7/32	387	90	813
Interdata 8/32	82	18	322

The maximum throughputs for the minis above are ranked as follows:

	Mix 1	Mix 2	Mix 3
1	SEL-32	SEL-32	SEL-32
2	Eclipse	Eclipse	Eclipse
3	I-8/32	I-8/32	PDP-11/45
4	PDP-11/45	PDP-11/45	M-IV
5	M-IV	I-7/32	I-8/32
6	I-7/32	M-IV	I-7/32

Note that the computer performance ranking changes, depending on the particular mix used.

Chapter 2
Problem 2-6

The length of a data segment or packet on the LSM bus is primarily a function of processor compatibility and interface cost. A reasonable packet size would be 16 bits with loop-interconnected minis. The label size is principally a function of address or channel identification field length. For a 50% overhead, 6 bits can be selected for physical address (64 levels), leaving 2 bits for flags. For LSM, transmitting nodes obviously do not have an assigned slot or channel in which to write but must contend with other nodes for space on the loop.

Data collision can be avoided by each of the nodes if they were to check for a free line space, large enough to contain a full slot (16 bits) and then place their label and data byte on the loop. This would also minimize line buffering requirements for each node to one full slot, or 16 bits.

A data segment can be sent either from a transmitting node to a receiving node which would remove it or from a transmitting node, completely around the loop and back to the transmitting node, which would then have to remove it.

Addressing can be performed by either incorporating a destination field to each packet or using a virtual link approach. The incorporation of a destination field to each packet will create additional overhead and increase the cost of the line interface hardware. In a slotted loop, the sender's address contained in each slot may be thought of as a channel I.D., each processor or node having a unique channel. Once a receiver has decided to listen to a specific sender, it has but to "lock onto" that channel, trapping all segments with that I.D.

A link may be established by naming of the intended receiver only in the first packet transmitted. Nodes not currently in the process of receiving a message scan all "channels" looking for a first segment or packet with a destination matching their address. When one is found, the receiver acknowledges its detection and remembers the channel number of the originator, establishing the virtual link. To accomplish this, a flag bit may be used to distinguish the first byte in a message from the rest of the text. The second flag bit can be used to acknowledge each packet. Once a receiver "locks on" and responds, the originator may transmit the entire message without ever being aware of its physical destination.

The originator of a packet, recognizing it upon return, removes it from the loop and verifies that the acknowledgement flag bit was set. The latter verification will also provide error control. If the flag bit was not set, the packet was not seen by the intended receiver or the potential receiver was busy. The packet may then be retransmitted some finite number of times before the network operator is notified that an error has occurred.

Possible message protocol alternatives consist of using fixed-length messages, end-of-text characters, or a length count in the second packet or of defining an end-of-message pattern.

Problem 2-8

Line Nr.	Words/Mess.	Words/Job	Comm. Delay per Job*	Word Proc. Time*	Disc Access Time/Job†
1	10	100	$\frac{(1.2)(100)(16)}{(9600)} = 0.2$	2.5	45
2	10	100	$\frac{(1.2)(100)(16)}{(9600)} = 0.2$	2.5	45
3	30	300	$\frac{(1.2)(300)(16)}{(9600)} = 0.6$	7.5	45
4	10	100	$\frac{(1.2)(100)(16)}{(9600)} = 0.2$	2.5	45
5	60	600	$\frac{(1.2)(600)(16)}{(9600)} = 1.2$	15.0	45
6	20	200	$\frac{(1.2)(200)(16)}{(9600)} = 0.4$	5.0	45
			2.8	35.0	270

*Time in seconds.
†Time in milliseconds.

The following assumptions are made:

1. 20% overhead is incurred by headers and trailers.
2. The average processing time per word is 25 μsec.

The Steady-State Service is thus

$$S = \frac{35.0 + 270.0}{500.0} = 0.61$$

where the measured job turnaround time is 500 msec. It can be concluded that the Manufacturing Information System mini is I/O bound since only approximately 10% of the total time (270 msec + 35.0 msec out of 0.270 + 0.035 + 2.8 = 3.105 sec) is spent on processing messages and performing disc transfers. The measured job turn-around time indicates that the message traffic on incoming lines is bursty rather than continuous. For continuous traffic, the job turnaround time would exceed 5 sec using the Steady-State Service ratio above.

Chapter 3
Problem 3-3

The number of 16-bit words that can be handled by a 9600-bps line, assuming no retransmissions take place due to errors, and with no header/trailer overhead is

$$\frac{9600 \text{ bps}}{16 \text{ bits per word}} = 600 \text{ words per second}$$

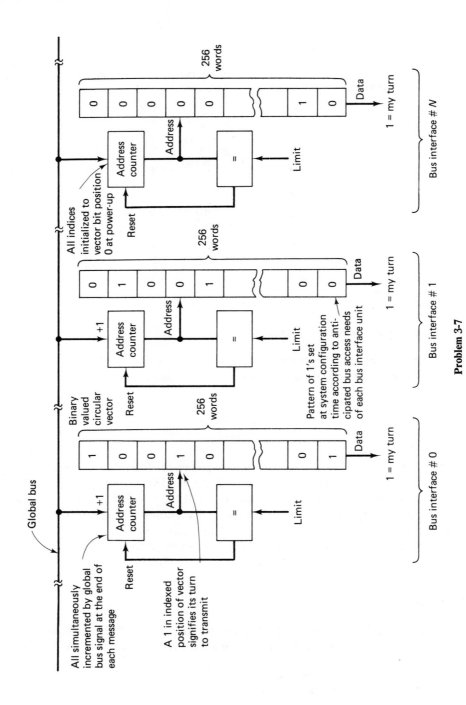

Problem 3-7

For a three-node configuration with full-duplex lines, the total network transfer rate is $3 \times 600 = 1800$ words per second.

For a five-node configuration the transfer rate is $5 \times 600 = 3000$ words per second. In reality the transfer rate for a three-node system is approximately 1300 words per second and for a five-node system, 2300 words per second.

The percentage overhead for a three-node system is $(500/1800)(100) = 28\%$.

The percentage overhead for a five-node system is $(700/3000)(100) = 23\%$.

The percentage change in overhead is thus an 18% decrease with the addition of two nodes to the system.

Chapter 4
Problem 4-4

As shown below, in order to reduce the total system cost, some of the NSC adapters are shared between two minis.

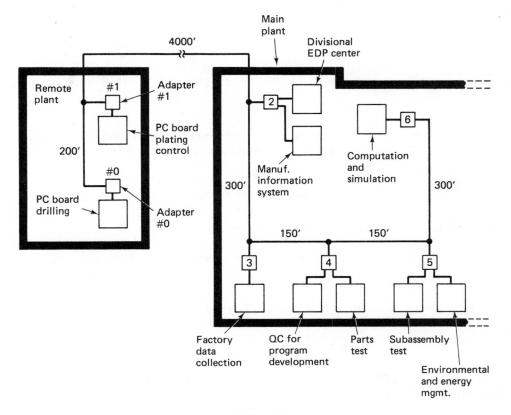

Problem 4-4

The delays between the various nodes are calculated as follows:

Node Nr.	Adapter	Delay Time (n-delay)
0	PC Board Drilling	0 μsec
1	PC Board Plating	0 + (4 nsec)(200 ft) = 0.8 μsec
2	Divisional EDP & Manuf. Inf.	0.8 μsec + (4 nsec)(4000 ft) = 16.8 μsec
3	Factory Data Collection	16.8 μsec + (4 nsec)(300 ft) = 18 μsec
4	QC-Pgm. Devel. & Parts Test	18 μsec + (4 nsec)(150 ft) = 18.6 μsec
5	Subass'y Test & Env. & Energy Management	18.6 μsec + (4 nsec)(150 ft) = 19.2 μsec
6	Comp. & Simulation	19.2 μsec + (4 nsec)(300 ft) = 20.4 μsec

The delays between transmitting and receiving nodes are determined as follows:

Job No.	From/To	Words to Message	Delay Time per Message (μsec)
1	0–2	10	16.8
2	3–2	10	18.0
3	5–2	30	19.2
4	5–2	10	19.2
5	6–2	60	20.4
6	2–2	20	0
		Total:	93.6 μsec

For 10 messages, the total delay time is thus 0.936 msec. For an unslotted bus the effective bandwidth, assuming 1.5-Mbps maximum rate for the NSC bus (see Table 4-2) is

$$\frac{1.5 \text{ Mbps}}{2e} = 186.5 \text{ Kbps}$$

The total number of bits transmitted for the six jobs are

(100 + 100 + 300 + 100 + 600 + 200) words per job $\times$ 16 bits per word

= 22,400 bits

The total transmission time, including bus delay, is, hence,

$$\frac{22,400 \text{ bits}}{186,500 \text{ bits/sec}} + 0.936 \text{ msec} = 121 \text{ msec}$$

This is less than the CPU time of 305 msec calculated in Problem 2-8. The Manufacturing Information System mini is therefore CPU bound.

Chapter 5
Problem 5-5

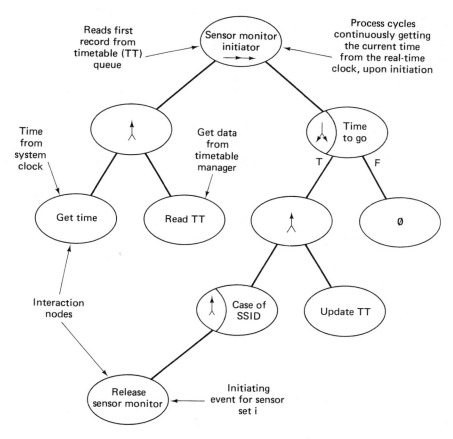

Problem 5-5 The Sensor Monitor Initiator tree.

A timetable (TT) queue record consists of

1. A Sensor Set Identifier (SSID) for the first record in TT.
2. A Time-to-Go value.
3. Cycle Rate.

The queue may be ordered by Time-to-Go values. If the current time exceeds the Time-to-Go for the first record in the queue, then the Sensor Monitor Initiator initiates the appropriate Sensor Monitor, updates the timetable queue computing a new Time-to-Go for the record, and reinserts it at an appropriate place in the queue.

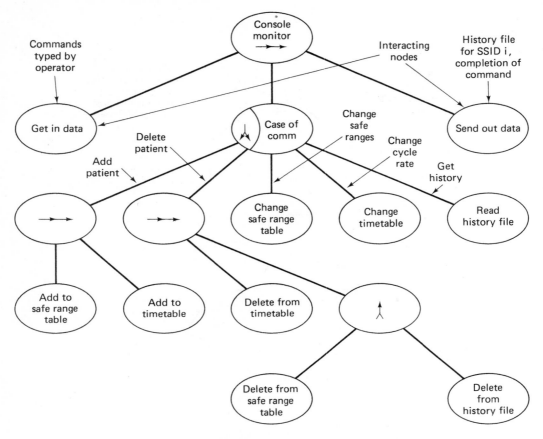

Problem 5-5 (cont.)   The Console Monitor tree.

The operator's input is assumed to consist of four values:

1. A Command Identifier (COMM).
2. A Sensor Set Identifier (SSID)—the same as in the Sensor Monitor Initiator.
3. A set of safe ranges for that sensor set (SR_i).
4. A cycle rate for that sensor set—the same as used by the Sensor Monitor Initiator.

The commands allowed may be as follows:

1. Add Patient.
2. Delete Patient.
3. Change Safe Range.
4. Change Cycle Rate.
5. Get History.

Upon receiving input data from the operator, the Console Monitor selects an appropriate routine on the basis of the command issued, implements the command, and returns to the operator any output data produced such as the sensor data history for a patient (if requested). Subsequently, appropriate modifications are made to the Safe Range Table, the timetable with cycle rate changes and the history file. The operator tree shows the process architecture associated with the environmental process. The operator decides whether or not to send an input command to the system and then becomes available to receive outputs.

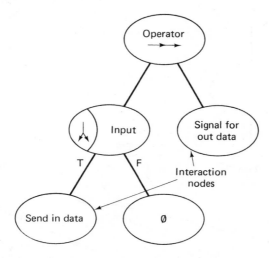

Problem 5-5 (cont.)   The Operator tree.

The nomenclature above is correlated with information provided in Figure 5-7. It shows the Sensor Monitor tree for the *i*th sensor set. As in Figure 5-7, the XA interaction is used since many sensors monitor processes, plus the console processes need to interact with a single, shared-variable manager process. The manager process would thus be composed of XC interactions, whereas the other processes interact using XA's.

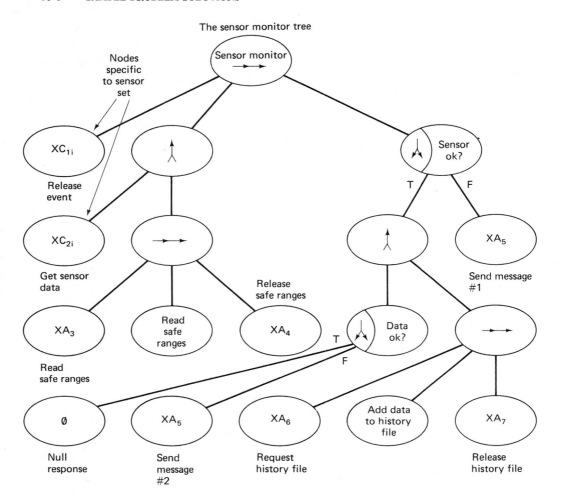

Problem 5-5 (cont.)   The Sensor Monitor tree.

Chapter 7
Problem 7-2

For a 10^{-5} error rate,

$$\frac{100,000 \text{ bits}}{1024 \text{ bits per packet}} = 97.656 \text{ packets}$$

can be transmitted over the links; i.e., an error will in the ninety-eighth packet. The transmission line efficiency of the terrestrial link is thus $98/99 = 0.9899$ (the ninety-eighth packet must be transmitted twice). For continuous ARQ with pullback satellite communications, the transmitter will be notified by the receiver

$$2 \times 270 \text{ msec} + \frac{1024 \text{ bits}}{9600 \text{ bps}} = 646.7 \text{ msec}$$

after a packet containing an error is received. At that instant in time

$$\frac{646.7 \text{ msec}}{1024 \text{ bits}/9600 \text{ bps}} = 6.06 \approx 7 \text{ packets}$$

plus the erroneous packet have been transmitted and must therefore be retransmitted. The satellite data link efficiency is thus $98/(98 + 8) = 0.9245$. The cost of the two links, adjusted to effective throughput is thus:

Terrestrial link $\quad \dfrac{\$600}{0.9899} = \$606 \text{ per month}$

Satellite link $\quad \dfrac{\$556}{0.9245} = \$601 \text{ per month}$

The satellite link is therefore marginally more cost effective.

The effective throughput can be improved upon using Selective Repeat ARQ; however, the error rates on satellite links are usually several orders of magnitude lower than 10^{-5}.

Index